Internet of Things
Principles and Paradigms

T0297739

Internet of Things
Principles and Paradigms

Edited by

Rajkumar Buyya

Cloud Computing and Distributed Systems (CLOUDS) Laboratory
Department of Computing and Information Systems
The University of Melbourne, Australia
Manjrasoft Pty Ltd, Australia

Amir Vahid Dastjerdi

Cloud Computing and Distributed Systems (CLOUDS) Laboratory
Department of Computing and Information Systems
The University of Melbourne, Australia

AMSTERDAM • BOSTON • HEIDELBERG • LONDON
NEW YORK • OXFORD • PARIS • SAN DIEGO
SAN FRANCISCO • SINGAPORE • SYDNEY • TOKYO

Morgan Kaufmann is an imprint of Elsevier

Morgan Kaufmann is an imprint of Elsevier
50 Hampshire Street, 5th Floor, Cambridge, MA 02139, USA

British Library Cataloguing-in-Publication Data
A catalogue record for this book is available from the British Library

Library of Congress Cataloging-in-Publication Data
A catalog record for this book is available from the Library of Congress

ISBN: 978-0-12-805395-9

For information on all Morgan Kaufmann publications
visit our website at https://www.elsevier.com/

Working together
to grow libraries in
developing countries

www.elsevier.com • www.bookaid.org

Publisher: Todd Green
Acquisition Editor: Brian Romer
Editorial Project Manager: Amy Invernizzi
Project Manager: Priya Kumaraguruparan
Designer: Maria Inês Cruz

Typeset by Thomson Digital

Contents

PART III IoT DATA AND KNOWLEDGE MANAGEMENT

List of Contributors

D. An
Keimyung University, Dalgubeol-daero, Dalseo-gu, Daegu, South Korea

M. Apetroaie-Cristea
Faculty of Engineering and the Environment, University of Southampton, Southampton, United Kingdom

D. Ban
Samsung Electronics, South Korea

B. Bardhi
Department of Information Engineering, Università Politecnica delle Marche, Ancona, Italy

R. Buyya
Cloud Computing and Distributed Systems (CLOUDS) Laboratory, Department of Computing and Information Systems, The University of Melbourne, Australia; Manjrasoft Pty Ltd, Australia

R.N. Calheiros
Cloud Computing and Distributed Systems (CLOUDS) Laboratory, Department of Computing and Information Systems, The University of Melbourne, Australia

V. Chellappan
Department of Computer Science and Engineering, Indian Institute of Technology Madras, Chennai, India

A. Claudi
ADB Broadband S.p.A., Viale Sarca, Milano, Italy

S.J. Cox
Faculty of Engineering and the Environment, University of Southampton, Southampton, United Kingdom

A.V. Dastjerdi
Cloud Computing and Distributed Systems (CLOUDS) Laboratory, Department of Computing and Information Systems, The University of Melbourne, Australia

C. Georgoulis
Athens Information Technology, Marousi, Greece

S.K. Ghosh
Department of Computer Science and Engineering, Indian Institute of Technology, Kharagpur, India

H. Gupta
Department of Computer Science and Engineering, Indian Institute of Technology, Kharagpur, India

S. Han
Samsung Electronics, South Korea

E. Heo
Samsung Electronics, South Korea

S. Hosseinzadeh
Department of Information Technology, University of Turku, Finland

S. Hyrynsalmi
Department of Information Technology, University of Turku, Finland

S.J. Johnston
Faculty of Engineering and the Environment, University of Southampton, Southampton, United Kingdom

S. Karunasekera
Department of Computing and Information Systems, The University of Melbourne, Australia

N. Kefalakis
Athens Information Technology, Marousi, Greece

F. Khodadadi
Cloud Computing and Distributed Systems (CLOUDS) Laboratory, Department of Computing and Information Systems, The University of Melbourne, Australia

J. Krishnamurthy
School of Computer Science, McGill University, Montreal, Quebec, Canada

C. Leckie
Department of Computing and Information Systems, The University of Melbourne, Australia

V. Leppänen
Department of Information Technology, University of Turku, Finland

K. Li
Department of Computer Science, State University of New York, NY, United States of America

X. Liu
Cloud Computing and Distributed Systems (CLOUDS) Laboratory, Department of Computing and Information Systems, The University of Melbourne, Australia

M. Maheswaran
School of Computer Science, McGill University, Montreal, Quebec, Canada

S. Majumdar
Department of Systems and Computer Engineering, Carleton University, Ottawa, Canada

S. Misra
Ericsson Canada, Montreal, Quebec, Canada

M. Moshtaghi
Department of Computing and Information Systems, The University of Melbourne, Australia

M. Noack
Communication Systems Group CSG, Department of Informatics IFI, University of Zurich, Zürich, Switzerland

C.E. Palau
Distributed Real-Time Systems Research Group, Escuela Tecnica Superior de Ingenieros de Telecomunicación at the Universitat Politecnica de Valencia, Spain

S. Petris
Athens Information Technology, Marousi, Greece

J.V. Pradilla
Escuela Técnica Superior de Ingenieros de Telecomunicación at the Universitat Politècnica de Valencia, Spain

S. Sarkar
Department of CSIS, Birla Institute of Technology and Science Pilani, K.K.Birla Goa Campus, Goa, India

C. Schmitt
Communication Systems Group CSG, Department of Informatics IFI, University of Zurich, Zürich, Switzerland

M. Scott
Faculty of Engineering and the Environment, University of Southampton, Southampton, United Kingdom

K.M. Sivalingam
Department of Computer Science and Engineering, Indian Institute of Technology Madras, Chennai, India

J. Soldatos
Athens Information Technology, Marousi, Greece

L. Spalazzi
Department of Information Engineering, Università Politecnica delle Marche, Ancona, Italy

B. Stiller
Communication Systems Group CSG, Department of Informatics IFI, University of Zurich, Zürich, Switzerland

G. Taccari
Par-Tec S.p.A., Milano, Italy

L. Taccari
Department of Information Engineering, Università Politecnica delle Marche, Ancona, Italy

W. Wu
Department of Computer Science, Sun Yat-sen University, Guangzhou, China

Z. Yang
Department of Computer Science, Sun Yat-sen University, Guangzhou, China

Y. Yoon
Hongik University, Wausan-ro, Mapo-gu, Seoul, South Korea

About the Editors

Rajkumar Buyya is a Fellow of IEEE, Professor of Computer Science and Software Engineering, and Director of the Cloud Computing and Distributed Systems (CLOUDS) laboratory at the University of Melbourne, Australia. He is also serving as the founding CEO of Manjrasoft, a spin-off company of the University, commercializing its innovations in Cloud Computing. He has authored over 500 publications and 6 textbooks including "Mastering Cloud Computing" published by McGraw Hill, China Machine Press, and Morgan Kaufmann for Indian, Chinese, and international markets respectively. He is currently serving as the Co-Editor-in-Chief of *Journal of Software: Practice and Experience*. For further information, please visit www.buyya.com

Amir Vahid Dastjerdi is a research fellow with the Cloud Computing and Distributed Systems (CLOUDS) laboratory at the University of Melbourne, Australia. He received his PhD in Computer Science from the University of Melbourne and his areas of interest include Internet of Things, Big Data, and Cloud Computing.

Preface

The Internet of Things (IoT) paradigm promises to make "things" including consumer electronic devices or home appliances, such as medical devices, fridge, cameras, and sensors, part of the Internet environment. This paradigm opens the doors to new innovations that will build novel type of interactions among things and humans, and enables the realization of smart cities, infrastructures, and services for enhancing the quality of life and utilization of resources.

IoT as an emerging paradigm supports integration, transfer, and analytics of data generated by smart devices (eg, sensors). IoT envisions a new world of connected devices and humans in which the quality of life is enhanced because management of city and its infrastructure is less cumbersome, health services are conveniently accessible, and disaster recovery is more efficient. Based on bottom-up analysis for IoT applications, McKinsey estimates that the IoT will have a potential economic impact of $11 trillion per year by 2025—which would be equivalent to about 11% of the world economy. They also expect that one trillion IoT devices will be deployed by 2025. In majority of the IoT domains such as infrastructure management and healthcare, the major role of IoT is the delivery of highly complex knowledge-based and action-oriented applications in real-time.

To realize the full potential of the IoT paradigm, it is necessary to address several challenges and develop suitable conceptual and technological solutions for tackling them. These include development of scalable architecture, moving from closed systems to open systems, dealing with privacy and ethical issues involved in data sensing; storage, processing, and actions; designing interaction protocols; autonomic management; communication protocol; smart objects and service discovery; programming framework; resource management; data and network management; power and energy management; and governance.

The primary purpose of this book is to capture the state-of-the-art in IoT, its applications, architectures, and technologies that address the abovementioned challenges. The book also aims to identify potential research directions and technologies that will facilitate insight generation in various domains from science, industry, business, and consumer applications. We expect the book to serve as a reference for systems architects, practitioners, developers, researchers, and graduate-level students.

ORGANIZATION OF THE BOOK

This book contains chapters authored by several leading experts in the field of IoT. The book is presented in a coordinated and integrated manner starting with the fundamentals, and followed by the technologies that implement them. The content of the book is organized into five parts:

1. IoT Ecosystem Concepts and Architectures
2. IoT Enablers and Solutions
3. IoT Data and Knowledge Management
4. IoT Reliability, Security, and Privacy
5. IoT Applications

Part I presents an overview of IoT and its related concepts and evolution through time. It throws light upon different IoT architectures and their components and discusses emerging paradigms such as

Fog computing. In addition, the essential element of a cloud computing infrastructure for IoT services is discussed and a novel framework for collaborative computing between IoT devices and cloud is presented.

Part II is dedicated to platforms and solutions supporting development and deployment of IoT applications. It covers embedded systems programming languages as they play an important role in the development of IoT. Moreover, this part provides an elaborate introduction to message passing mechanisms such as RPC, REST, and CoAP that are indispensable for distributed programming in IoT. Furthermore, techniques for resource sharing and partitioning to enable multitenancy are explored. Three basic virtualization techniques for embedded systems are considered: full virtualization, paravirtualization (as instances of hardware-level virtualization), and containers (as instances of operating-system-level virtualization). Besides, it introduces an architecture which utilizes both cloud and virtualization for effective deployment of Cyber Physical Systems.

Part III focuses on data and knowledge management which have always been an integral part of IoT applications. It explains how stream processing toolkits offer scalable and reliable solutions to handle a large volume of data in motion and how they can be utilized in IoT environments. Furthermore, this part introduces a framework for distributed data analysis (machine learning mechanism) based on the core idea of Fog computing to use local resources to reduce the overhead of centralized data collection and processing. It will explain how this can be achieved by learning local models of the data at the nodes, which are then aggregated to construct a global model at a central node.

Part IV presents an argument for developing a governance framework for tackling the data confidentiality, data integrity, and operation control issues faced by IoT. It outlines the organizational, structural, regulatory, and legal issues that are commonly encountered in the IoT environment. In addition, it provides a detailed overview of the security challenges related to the deployment of smart objects. Security protocols at the network, transport, and application layers are discussed, together with lightweight cryptographic algorithms to be used instead of conventional and demanding ones, in terms of computational resources. Many of IoT applications are business critical, and require the underlying technology to be dependable, that is, it must deliver its service even in the presence of failures. Therefore, this part discusses the notion of reliability and recovery oriented systems in general and then explains why this is important for an IoT-based system. A range of failure scenarios and reliability challenges are narrated and tackled by failure-prevention and fault-tolerance approaches to make an IoT-based system robust.

Part V introduces a number of applications that have been made feasible by the emergence of IoT. Best practices for architecting IoT applications are covered, describing how to harness the power of cutting-edge technologies for designing and building a weather station with over 10 sensors using a variety of electronic interfaces connected to an embedded system gateway running Linux. This part also introduces Internet of Vehicles (IoV) and its applications. It starts by presenting the background, concept, and network architecture of IoV, and then analyzes the characteristics of IoV and correspondingly new challenges in IoV research and development. Finally, this part discusses the role of IoT in enabling efficient management of smart facilities and presents architecture for a cloud-based platform for managing smart facilities and the underlying middleware services. Techniques for effective management of resources in sensor networks and in parallel systems performing data analytics on data collected on a facility are discussed.

Acknowledgments

First and foremost, we are grateful to all the contributing authors for their time, effort, and understanding during the preparation of the book.

Raj would like to thank his family members, especially his wife, Smrithi and daughters, Soumya and Radha Buyya, for their love, understanding, and support during the preparation of the book. Amir would like to thank his wife Elly and daughter Diana.

Finally, we would like to thank the staff at Morgan Kauffman, particularly, Amy Invernizzi, Priya Kumaraguruparan, Brian Romer, and Todd Green. They were wonderful to work with.

Rajkumar Buyya
The University of Melbourne and Manjrasoft Pty Ltd, Australia

Amir Vahid Dastjerdi
The University of Melbourne, Australia

IoT ECOSYSTEM CONCEPTS AND ARCHITECTURES

1

IoT ECOSYSTEM CONCEPTS AND ARCHITECTURES

INTERNET OF THINGS: AN OVERVIEW

1

F. Khodadadi*, A.V. Dastjerdi*, R. Buyya*,**

*Cloud Computing and Distributed Systems (CLOUDS) Laboratory, Department of Computing and Information Systems, The University of Melbourne, Australia;**Manjrasoft Pty Ltd, Australia

1.1 INTRODUCTION

After four decades from the advent of Internet by ARPANET [1], the term "Internet" refers to the vast category of applications and protocols built on top of sophisticated and interconnected computer networks, serving billions of users around the world in 24/7 fashion. Indeed, we are at the beginning of an emerging era where ubiquitous communication and connectivity is neither a dream nor a challenge anymore. Subsequently, the focus has shifted toward a seamless integration of people and devices to converge the physical realm with human-made virtual environments, creating the so-called Internet of Things (IoT) utopia.

A closer look at this phenomenon reveals two important pillars of IoT: "Internet" and "Things" that require more clarification. Although it seems that every object capable of connecting to the Internet will fall into the "Things" category, this notation is used to encompass a more generic set of entities, including smart devices, sensors, human beings, and any other object that is aware of its context and is able to communicate with other entities, making it accessible at any time, anywhere. This implies that objects are required to be accessible without any time or place restrictions.

Ubiquitous connectivity is a crucial requirement of IoT, and, to fulfill it, applications need to support a diverse set of devices and communication protocols, from tiny sensors capable of sensing and reporting a desired factor, to powerful back-end servers that are utilized for data analysis and knowledge extraction. This also requires integration of mobile devices, edge devices like routers and smart hubs, and humans in the loop as controllers.

Initially, Radio-Frequency Identification (RFID) used to be the dominant technology behind IoT development, but with further technological achievements, wireless sensor networks (WSN) and Bluetooth-enabled devices augmented the mainstream adoption of the IoT trend. These technologies and IoT applications have been extensively surveyed previously [2–5], however, less attention has been given to unique characteristics and requirements of IoT, such as scalability, heterogeneity support, total integration, and real-time query processing. To underscore these required advances, this chapter lists IoT challenges and promising approaches by considering recent research and advances made in the IoT ecosystem, as shown in Fig. 1.1. In addition, it discusses emerging solutions based on cloud-, fog-, and mobile-computing facilities. Furthermore, the applicability and integration of cutting-edge approaches like Software Defined Networking (SDN) and containers for embedded and constrained devices with IoT are investigated.

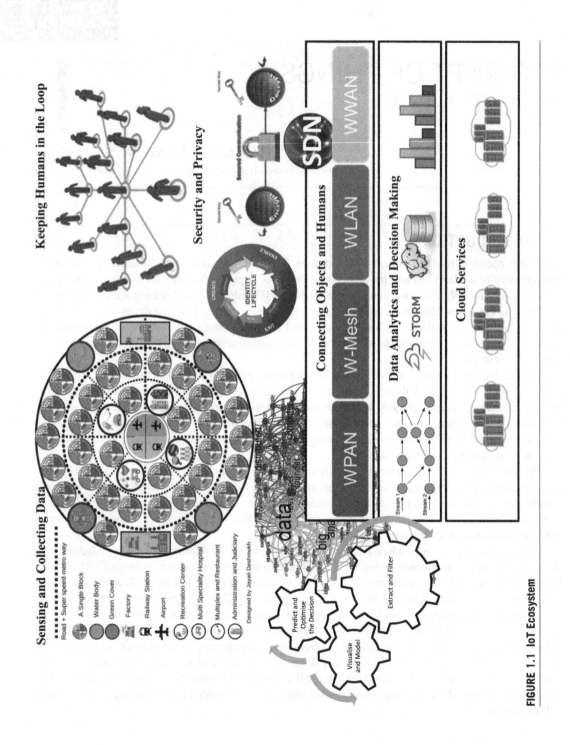

FIGURE 1.1 IoT Ecosystem

1.2 INTERNET OF THINGS DEFINITION EVOLUTION

1.2.1 IoT EMERGENCE

Kevin Ashton is accredited for using the term "Internet of Things" for the first time during a presentation in 1999 on supply-chain management [6]. He believes the "things" aspect of the way we interact and live within the physical world that surrounds us needs serious reconsideration, due to advances in computing, Internet, and data-generation rate by smart devices. At the time, he was an executive director at MIT's Auto-ID Center, where he contributed to the extension of RFID applications into broader domains, which built the foundation for the current IoT vision.

1.2.2 INTERNET OF EVERYTHING

Since then, many definitions for IoT have been presented, including the definition [7] that focuses mostly on connectivity and sensory requirements for entities involved in typical IoT environments. Whereas those definitions reflect IoT's basic requirements, new IoT definitions give more value to the need for ubiquitous and autonomous networks of objects where identification and service integration have an important and inevitable role. For example, Internet of Everything (IoE) is used by Cisco to refer to people, things, and places that can expose their services to other entities [8].

1.2.3 INDUSTRIAL IoT

Also referred to as Industrial Internet [9], Industrial IoT (IIoT) is another form of IoT applications favored by big high-tech companies. The fact that machines can perform specific tasks such as data acquisition and communication more accurately than humans has boosted IIoT's adoption. Machine to machine (M2M) communication, Big Data analysis, and machine learning techniques are major building blocks when it comes to the definition of IIoT. These data enable companies to detect and resolve problems faster, thus resulting in overall money and time savings. For instance, in a manufacturing company, IIoT can be used to efficiently track and manage the supply chain, perform quality control and assurance, and lower the total energy consumption.

1.2.4 SMARTNESS IN IoT

Another characteristic of IoT, which is highlighted in recent definitions, is "smartness." This distinguishes IoT from similar concepts such as sensor networks, and it can be further categorized into "object smartness" and "network smartness." A smart network is a communication infrastructure characterized by the following functionalities:

- standardization and openness of the communication standards used, from layers interfacing with the physical world (ie, tags and sensors), to the communication layers between nodes and with the Internet;
- object addressability (direct IP address) and multifunctionality (ie, the possibility that a network built for one application (eg, road-traffic monitoring) would be available for other purposes (eg, environmental-pollution monitoring or traffic safety) [10].

1.2.5 MARKET SHARE

In addition, definitions draw special attention to the potential market of IoT with a fast growing rate, by having a market value of $44.0 billion in 2011 [11]. According to a comprehensive market research conducted by RnRMarketResearch [12] that includes current market size and future predictions, the IoT and M2M market will be worth approximately $498.92 billion by 2019. Quoting from the same research, the value of the IoT market is expected to hit $1423.09 billion by 2020, with Internet of Nano Things (IoNT) playing a key role in the future market and holding a value of approximately $9.69 billion by 2020.

Besides all these fantastic and optimistic opportunities, for current IoT to reach the foreseen market, various innovations and progress in different areas are required. Furthermore, cooperation and information-sharing between leading companies in IoT, such as Microsoft, IBM, Google, Samsung, Cisco, Intel, ARM, Fujitsu, Ecobee Inc., in addition to smaller businesses and start-ups, will boost IoT adoption and market growth.

IoT growth rate with an estimated number of active devices until 2018 is depicted in Fig. 1.2 [13]. The increase of investment in IoT by developed and developing countries hints at the gradual change in strategy of governments by recognizing IoT's impacts and trying to keep themselves updated as IoT gains momentum. For example, the IoT European Research Cluster (IERC) (http://www.rfid-in-action.eu/cerp/) has conducted and supported several projects about fundamental IoT research by considering special requirements from end-users and applications. As an example, the project named Internet of Things Architecture (IoT-A) (http://www.iot-a.eu) aims at developing a reference architecture for specific types of applications in IoT, and is discussed in more detail in Section 1.3. The UK government has also initiated a 5 million project on innovations and recent technological advances in IoT [14]. Similarly, IBM in the USA [15] has plans to spend billions of dollars on IoT research and its industrial applications. Singapore has also announced its intention to be the first smart nation by investing in smart transport systems, developing the e-government structure, and using surveillance cameras and other sensory devices to obtain data and extract information from them [16].

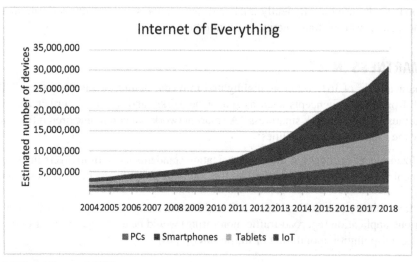

FIGURE 1.2 IoT Trend Forecast [13]

1.2.6 **HUMAN IN THE LOOP**

IoT is also identified as an enabler for machine-to-machine, human-to-machine, and human-with-environment interactions. With the increase in the number of smart devices and the adoption of new protocols such as IPv6, the trend of IoT is expected to shift toward the fusion of smart and autonomous networks of Internet-capable objects equipped with the ubiquitous computing paradigm. Involving human in the loop [17] of IoT offers numerous advantages to a wide range of applications, including emergency management, healthcare, etc. Therefore, another essential role of IoT is to build a collaborative system that is capable of effectively responding to an event captured via sensors, by effective discovery of crowds and also successful communication of information across discovered crowds of different domains.

1.2.7 **IMPROVING THE QUALITY OF LIFE**

IoT is also recognized by the impact on quality of life and businesses [8], which can revolutionize the way our medical systems and businesses operate by: (1) expanding the communication channel between objects by providing a more integrated communication environment in which different sensor data such as location, heartbeat, etc. can be measured and shared more easily. (2) Facilitating the automation and control process, whereby administrators can manage each object's status via remote consoles; and (3) saving in the overall cost of implementation, deployment, and maintenance, by providing detailed measurements and the ability to check the status of devices remotely.

According to Google Trends, the word "IoT" is used more often than "Internet of Things" since 2004, followed by "Web of Things" and "Internet of Everything" as the most frequently used words. Quoting the same reference, Singapore and India are the countries with the most regional interest in IoT. This is aligned with the fact that India is estimated to be the world's largest consumer of IoT devices by 2020 [18].

1.3 **IoT ARCHITECTURES**

The building blocks of IoT are sensory devices, remote service invocation, communication networks, and context-aware processing of events; these have been around for many years. However, what IoT tries to picture is a unified network of smart objects and human beings responsible for operating them (if needed), who are capable of universally and ubiquitously communicating with each other.

When talking about a distributed environment, interconnectivity among entities is a critical requirement, and IoT is a good example. A holistic system architecture for IoT needs to guarantee flawless operation of its components (reliability is considered as the most import design factor in IoT) and link the physical and virtual realms together. To achieve this, careful consideration is needed in designing failure recovery and scalability. Additionally, since mobility and dynamic change of location has become an integral part of IoT systems with the widespread use of smartphones, state-of-the-art architectures need to have a certain level of adaptability to properly handle dynamic interactions within the whole ecosystem.

Reference architectures and models give a bird's eye view of the whole underlying system, hence their advantage over other architectures relies on providing a better and greater level of abstraction, which consequently hides specific constraints and implementation details.

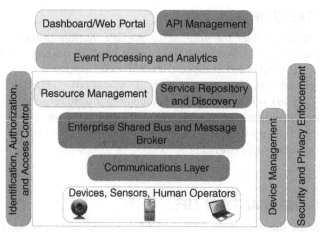

FIGURE 1.3 A Reference Architecture for IoT

Several research groups have proposed reference architectures for IoT [19,20]. The IoT-A [19] focuses on the development and validation of an integrated IoT network architecture and supporting building blocks, with the objective to be "the European Lighthouse Integrated Project addressing the Internet-of-Things Architecture." IoT-i project, related to the previously mentioned IoT-A project, focuses on the promotion of IoT solutions, catching requirements and interests. IoT-i aims to achieve strategic objectives, such as: creating a joint strategic and technical vision for the IoT in Europe that encompasses the currently fragmented sectors of the IoT domain holistically, and contributing to the creation of an economically sustainable and socially acceptable environment in Europe for IoT technologies and respective R&D activities.

Fig. 1.3 depicts an outline of our extended version of a reference architecture for IoT [20]. Different service and presentation layers are shown in this architecture. Service layers include event processing and analytics, resource management and service discovery, as well as message aggregation and Enterprise Service Bus (ESB) services built on top of communication and physical layers. API management, which is essential for defining and sharing system services and web-based dashboards (or equivalent smartphone applications) for managing and accessing these APIs, are also included in the architecture. Due to the importance of device management, security and privacy enforcement in different layers, and the ability to uniquely identify objects and control their access level, these components are prestressed independently in this architecture. These components and their related research projects are described in more detail throughout this chapter.

1.3.1 SOA-BASED ARCHITECTURE

In IoT, service-oriented architecture (SOA) might be imperative for the service providers and users [21,22]. SOA ensures the interoperability among the heterogeneous devices [23,24]. To clarify this, let us consider a generic SOA consisting of four layers, with distinguished functionalities as follows:

- Sensing layer is integrated with available hardware objects to sense the status of things
- Network layer is the infrastructure to support over wireless or wired connections among things

- Service layer is to create and manage services required by users or applications
- Interfaces layer consists of the interaction methods with users or applications

Generally, in such architecture a complex system is divided into subsystems that are loosely coupled and can be reused later (modular decomposability feature), hence providing an easy way to maintain the whole system by taking care of its individual components [25]. This can ensure that in the case of a component failure the rest of the system (components) can still operate normally. This is of immense value for effective design of an IoT application architecture, where reliability is the most significant parameter.

SOA has been intensively used in WSN, due to its appropriate level of abstraction and advantages pertaining to its modular design [26,27]. Bringing these benefits to IoT, SOA has the potential to augment the level of interoperability and scalability among the objects in IoT. Moreover, from the user's perspective, all services are abstracted into common sets, removing extra complexity for the user to deal with different layers and protocols [28]. Additionally, the ability to build diverse and complex services by composing different functions of the system (ie, modular composability) through service composition suits the heterogeneous nature of IoT, where accomplishing each task requires a series of service calls on all different entities spread across multiple locations [29].

1.3.2 API-ORIENTED ARCHITECTURE

Conventional approaches for developing service-oriented solutions use SOAP and Remote Method Invocation (RMI) as a means for describing, discovering, and calling services; however, due to overhead and complexity imposed by these techniques, Web APIs and Representational State Transfer (REST)-based methods were introduced as promising alternative solutions. The required resources range from network bandwidth to computational and storage capacity, and are triggered by request–response data conversions happening regularly during service calls. Lightweight data-exchange formats like JSON can reduce the aforementioned overhead, especially for smart devices and sensors with a limited amount of resources, by replacing large XML files used to describe services. This helps in using the communication channel and processing the power of devices more efficiently.

Likewise, building APIs for IoT applications helps the service provider attract more customers while focusing on the functionality of their products rather than on presentation. In addition, it is easier to enable multitenancy by the security features of modern Web APIs such as OAuth, APIs which indeed are capable of boosting an organization's service exposition and commercialization. It also provides more efficient service monitoring and pricing tools than previous service-oriented approaches [30].

To this end, in our previous research we have proposed Simurgh [31], which describes devices, sensors, humans, and their available services using web API notation and API definition languages. Furthermore, a two-phase discovery approach was proposed in the framework to find sensors that provide desirable services and match certain features, like being in a specific location. Similarly, Elmangoush et al. [32] proposed a service-broker layer (named FOKUS) that exposes a set of APIs for enabling shared access to the OpenMTC core. Novel approaches for defining and sharing services in distributed and multiagent environments like IoT can reduce the sophistication of service discovery in the application development cycle and diminish service-call overhead in runtime.

Shifting from service delivery platforms (SDPs) toward web-based platforms, and the benefits of doing so are discussed by Manzalini et al. [33]. Developers and business managers are advised to focus on developing and sharing APIs from the early stage of their application development lifecycle, so that eventually, by properly exposing data to other developers and end users, an open-data environment is created that facilitates collaborative information gathering, sharing, and updating.

1.4 RESOURCE MANAGEMENT

Picturing IoT as a big graph with numerous nodes with different resource capacity, selecting and provisioning the resources greatly impacts Quality of Service (QoS) of the IoT applications. Resource management is very important in distributed systems and has been a subject of research for years. What makes resource management more challenging for IoT relies on the heterogeneous and dynamic nature of resources in IoT. Considering large-scale deployment of sensors for a smart city use-case, it is obvious that an efficient resource management module needs considerable robustness, fault-tolerance, scalability, energy efficiency, QoS, and SLA.

Resource management involves discovering and identifying all available resources, partitioning them to maximize a utility function—which can be in terms of cost, energy, performance, etc., and, finally, scheduling the tasks on available physical resources. Fig. 1.4 depicts the taxonomy of resource management activities in IoT.

1.4.1 RESOURCE PARTITIONING

The first step for satisfying resource provisioning requirements in IoT is to efficiently partition the resources and gain a higher utilization rate. This idea is vastly used in cloud computing via virtualization techniques and commodity infrastructures, however, virtual machines are not the only method for achieving the aforementioned goal. Since the hypervisor, that is responsible for managing interactions between host and guest VMs, requires a considerable amount of memory and computational capacity, this configuration is not suitable for IoT, where devices often have constrained memory and processing power. To address these challenges, the concept of *Containers* has emerged as a new form of virtualization technology that can match the demand of devices with limited resources. Docker (https://www.docker.com/) and Rocket (https://github.com/coreos/rkt) are the two most famous container solutions.

Containers are able to provide portable and platform-independent environments for hosting the applications and all their dependencies, configurations, and input/output settings. This significantly reduces the burden of handling different platform-specific requirements when designing and developing applications, hence providing a convenient level of transparency for applications, architects, and developers. In addition, containers are lightweight virtualization solutions that enable infrastructure providers to efficiently utilize their hardware resources by eliminating the need for purchasing expensive hardware and virtualization software packages. Since containers, compared to VMs, require considerably less spin-up time, they are ideal for distributed applications in IoT that need to scale up within a short amount of time.

An extensive survey by Gu et al. [34] focuses on virtualization techniques proposed for embedded systems and their efficiency for satisfying real-time application demands. After explaining numerous Xen-based, KVM-based, and microkernel-based solutions that utilize processor architectures such as ARM, authors argue that operating system virtualization techniques, known as container-based virtualization, can bring advantages in terms of performance and security by sandboxing applications on top

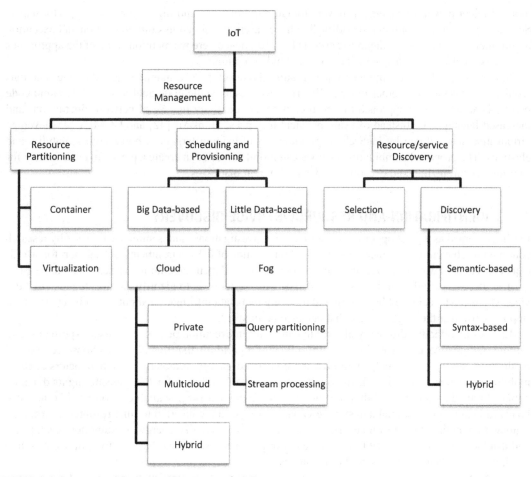

FIGURE 1.4 Taxonomy of Resource Management in IoT

of a shared OS layer. Linux VServer [35], Linux Containers LXC, and OpenVZ are examples of using OS virtualization in an embedded systems domain.

The concept of virtualized operating systems for constrained devices has been further extended to smartphones by providing the means to run multiple Android operating systems on a single physical smartphone [36]. With respect to heterogeneity of devices in IoT, and the fact that many of them can leverage virtualization to boost their utilization rate, task-grain scheduling, which considers individual tasks within different containers and virtualized environments, can potentially challenge current resource-management algorithms that view these layers as black box [34].

1.4.2 COMPUTATION OFFLOADING

Code offloading (computation offloading) [37] is another solution for addressing the limitation of available resources in mobile and smart devices. The advantages of using code offloading translate to more efficient power management, fewer storage requirements, and higher application performance. Several surveys about computation offloading have carefully studied its communication and execution requirements, as well as its adaptation criteria [38–40], hence here we mention some of the approaches that focus on efficient code segmentation and cloud computing.

Majority of code offloading techniques require the developers to manually annotate the functions required to execute on another device [39]. However, using static code analyzers and dynamic code parsers is an alternative approach that results in better adaptivity in case of network fluctuations and increased latency [41]. Instead of using physical instances, ThinkAir [42] and COMET [43] leverage virtual machines offered by IaaS cloud providers as offloading targets to boost both scalability and elasticity. The proposed combination of VMs and mobile clouds can create a powerful environment for sharing, synchronizing, and executing codes in different platforms.

1.4.3 IDENTIFICATION AND RESOURCE/SERVICE DISCOVERY

IoT has emerged as a great opportunity for industrial investigations, and is similarly pursued by research communities, but current architectures proposed for creation of IoT environments lack support for an efficient and standard way of service discovery, composition, and their integration in a scalable manner [44].

The discovery module in IoT is twofold. The first objective is to identify and locate the actual device, which can be achieved by storing and indexing metadata information about each object. The final step is to discover the target service that needs to be invoked.

Lack of an effective discovery algorithm can result in execution delays, poor user experience, and runtime failures. As discussed in Ref. [45], efficient algorithms that dynamically choose centralized or flooding strategies can help minimize the consumed energy, although other parameters such as mobility and latency should be factored in to offer a suitable solution for IoT, considering its dynamic nature. In another approach within the fog-computing context [46], available resources like network bandwidth and computational and storage-capacity metrics are converted to time resources, forming a framework that facilitates resource sharing. Different parameters like energy-consumption level, price, and availability of services need to be included in proposing solutions that aim to optimize resource sharing within a heterogeneous pool of resources.

The Semantic Web of Things (SWoT) envisions advanced resource management and service discovery for IoT by extending Semantic Web notation and blending it with IoT and Web of Things. To achieve this, resources and their metadata are defined and annotated using standard ontology-definition languages such as RDF and OWL. Additionally, search and manipulation of these metadata can be done through query languages like SPARQL. Ruta et al. [47] have adopted the SSN-XG W3C ontology to collect and annotate data from Semantic Sensor Networks (SSN); moreover, by extending the CoAP protocol (discussed in Section 1.6) and CoRE Link Format that is used for resource discovery, their proposed solution ranks resources based on partial or full request matching situations.

1.5 IoT DATA MANAGEMENT AND ANALYTICS

Although IoT is getting momentum to enable technology for creating a ubiquitous computing environment, special considerations are required to process huge amounts of data originating from, and circulating in, such a distributed and heterogeneous environment. To this extent, Big Data related procedures, such as data acquisition, filtering, transmission, and analysis have to be updated to match the requirements of the IoT data deluge.

Generally, Big Data is characterized by 3Vs, namely velocity, volume, and variety. Focusing on either an individual or a combination of these three Big Data dimensions has led to the introduction of different data-processing approaches. Batch Processing and Stream Processing are two major methods used for data analysis. Lambda Architecture [48] is an exemplary framework proposed by Nathan Marz to handle Big Data processing by focusing on multiapplication support, rather than on data-processing techniques. It has three main layers that enable the framework to support easy extensibility through extension points, scale-out capabilities, low-latency query processing, and the ability to tolerate human and system faults. From a top-down view, the first layer is called "Batch Layer" and hosts the master dataset and batch views where precomputed queries are stored. Next is the "Serving Layer," which adds dynamic query creation and execution to the batch views by indexing and storing them. Finally, the "Speed Layer" captures and processes recent data for delay-sensitive queries.

Collecting and analyzing the data circulating in the IoT environment is where the real power of IoT resides [49]. To this end, applications utilize pattern detection and data-mining techniques to extract knowledge and make smarter decisions. One of the key limitations in using currently developed data-mining algorithms lies in the inherent centralized nature of these algorithms, which drastically affects their performance and makes them unsuitable for IoT environments that are meant to be geographically distributed and heterogeneous. Distributed anomaly-detection techniques that concurrently process multiple streams of data to detect outliers have been well-studied in the literature [50]. A comprehensive survey of data-mining research in IoT has been conducted by Tsai et al. [51] and includes details about various classifications, clustering, knowledge discovery in databases (KDD), and pattern-mining techniques. Nevertheless, new approaches like ellipsoidal neighborhood factor outlier [52] that can be efficiently implemented on constrained devices are not fully benchmarked with respect to different configurations of their host devices.

1.5.1 IoT AND THE CLOUD

Cloud computing, due to its on-demand processing and storage capabilities, can be used to analyze data generated by IoT objects in batch or stream format. A pay-as-you-go model adopted by all cloud providers has reduced the price of computing, data storage, and data analysis, creating a streamlined process for building IoT applications. With cloud's elasticity, distributed Stream Processing Engines (SPEs) can implement important features such as fault-tolerance and autoscaling for bursty workloads.

IoT application development in clouds has been investigated in a body of research. Alam et al. [53] proposed a framework that supports sensor-data aggregation in cloud-based IoT context. The framework is SOA-based and event-driven, and defines benefits from a semantic layer that is responsible for event processing and reasoning. Similarly, Li et al. [54] proposed a Platform as a Service (PaaS) solution for deployment of IoT applications. The solution is multitenant, and users are provided with a virtually isolated service that can be customized to their IoT devices while they share the underlying cloud resources with other tenants.

Nastic et al. [55] proposed PatRICIA, a framework that provides a programming model for development of IoT applications in the cloud. PatRICIA proposes a new abstraction layer that is based on the concept of intent-based programming. Parwekar [56] discussed the importance of identity detection devices in IoT, and proposed a service layer to demonstrate how a sample tag-based acquisition service can be defined in the cloud. A simple architecture for integrating M2M platform, network, and data layers has also been proposed. Focusing on the data aspect of IoT, in our previous research we proposed an architecture based on Aneka, by adding support for data filtering, multiple simultaneous data-source selection, load balancing, and scheduling [57].

IoT applications can harness cloud services and use the available storage and computing resources to meet their scalability and compute-intensive processing demands. Most of the current design approaches for integrating cloud with IoT are based on a three-tier architecture, where the bottom layer consists of IoT devices, middle layer is the cloud provider, and top layer hosts different applications and high-level protocols. However, using this approach to design and integrate cloud computing with an IoT middleware limits the practicality and full utilization of cloud computing in scenarios where minimizing end-to-end delay is the goal. For example, in online game streaming, where perceived delay is an important factor for user satisfaction, a light and context-aware IoT middleware [58] that smartly selects the nearest Content Distribution Network (CDN) can significantly reduce the overall jitter.

1.5.2 REAL-TIME ANALYTICS IN IoT AND FOG COMPUTING

Current data-analytics approaches mainly focus on dealing with Big Data, however, processing data generated from millions of sensors and devices in real time is more challenging [59]. Proposed solutions that only utilize cloud computing as a processing or storage backbone are not scalable and cannot address the latency constraints of real-time applications. Real-time processing requirements and the increase in computational power of edge devices such as routers, switches, and access points lead to the emergence of the Edge Computing paradigm.

The Edge layer contains the devices that are in closer vicinity to the end user than the application servers, and can include smartphones, smart TVs, network routers, and so forth. Processing and storage capability of these devices can be utilized to extend the advantages of using cloud computing by creating another cloud, known as Edge Cloud, near application consumers, in order to: decrease networking delays, save processing or storage cost, perform data aggregation, and prevent sensitive data from leaving the local network [60].

Similarly, Fog Computing is a term coined by Salvatore Stolfo [61] and applies to an extension of cloud computing that aims to keep the same features of Cloud, such as networking, computation, virtualization, and storage, but also meets the requirements of applications that demand low latency, specific QoS requirements, Service Level Agreement (SLA) considerations, or any combination of these [62]. Moreover, these extensions can ease application development for mobile applications, Geo-distributed applications such as WSN, and large-scale systems used for monitoring and controlling other systems, such as surveillance camera networks [63,64]. A comparison of Cloud and Fog features is presented in Table 1.1 and Fig. 1.5 shows a general architecture for using cloud and fog computing together.

Stonebraker et al. [65] pointed out that the following requirements should be fulfilled in an efficient real-time stream processing engine (SPE):

- Data fluidity, which refers to processing data on-the-fly without the need for costly data storage
- Handling out-of-order, missing, and delayed streams
- Having a repeatable and deterministic outcome after processing a series or bag of streams
- Keeping streaming and stored data integrated by using embedded database systems
- Assuring high availability, using real-time failover and hot backup mechanisms
- Supporting autoscaling and application partitioning

Table 1.1 Cloud Versus Fog

	Fog	Cloud
Response time	Low	High
Availability	Low	High
Security level	Medium to hard	Easy to medium
Service focus	Edge devices	Network/enterprise core services
Cost for each device	Low	High
Dominant architecture	Distributed	Central/distributed
Main content generator—consumer	Smart devices—humans and devices	Humans—end devices

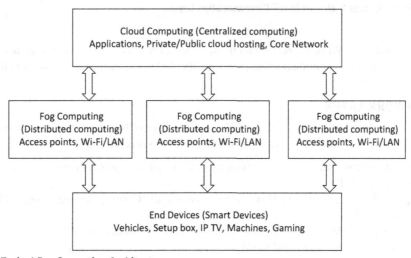

FIGURE 1.5 Typical Fog Computing Architecture

To harness the full potential of Fog computing for applications demanding real-time processing, researchers can look into necessary approaches and architectures to fulfill the aforementioned requirements.

1.6 COMMUNICATION PROTOCOLS

From the network and communication perspective, IoT can be viewed as an aggregation of different networks, including mobile networks (3G, 4G, CDMA, etc.), WLANs, WSN, and Mobile Adhoc Networks (MANET) [21].

Seamless connectivity is a key requirement for IoT. Network-communication speed, reliability, and connection durability will impact the overall IoT experience. With the emergence of high-speed mobile networks like 5G, and the higher availability of local and urban network communication protocols such

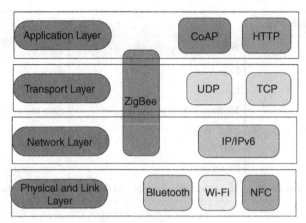

FIGURE 1.6 Use of Various Protocols in IoT Communication Layers

as Wi-Fi, Bluetooth, and WiMax, creating an interconnected network of objects seems feasible, however, dealing with different communication protocols that link these environments is still challenging.

1.6.1 NETWORK LAYER

Based on the device's specification (memory, CPU, storage, battery life), the communication means and protocols vary. However, the commonly used communication protocols and standards are listed below:

- RFID (eg, ISO 18000 series that comes with five classes and two generations, and covers both active and passive RFID tags)
- IEEE 802.11 (WLAN), IEEE 802.15.4 (ZigBee), Near Field Communication (NFC), IEEE 802.15.1 (Bluetooth)
- Low-power Wireless Personal Area Networks (6LoWPAN) standards by IEFT
- M2M protocols such as MQTT and CoAP
- IP layer technologies, such as IPv4, IPv6, etc.

More elaboration on the aforementioned network-layer communication protocols is available in Ref. [66], and a breakdown of layers in the IoT communication stack that these protocols will operate is shown in Fig. 1.6.

1.6.2 TRANSPORT AND APPLICATION LAYER

Segmentation and poor coherency level, which are results of pushes from individual companies to maximize their market share and revenue, has made developing IoT applications cumbersome. Universal applications that require one-time coding and can be executed on multiple devices are the most efficient.

Protocols in IoT can be classified into three categories:

1. general-purpose protocols like IP and SNMP that have been around for many years and are vastly used to manage, monitor, configure network devices, and establish communication links;

2. lightweight protocols such as CoAP that have been developed to meet the requirements of constrained devices with tiny hardware and limited resources;
3. device- or vendor-specific protocols and APIs that usually require a certain build environment and toolset.

Selecting the right protocols at the development phase can be challenging and complex, as factors such as future support, ease of implementation, and universal accessibility have to be considered. Additionally, thinking of other aspects that will affect the final deployment and execution, like required level of security and performance, will add to the sophistication of the protocol-selection stage. Lack of standardization for particular applications and protocols is another factor that increases the risk of poor protocol selection and strategic mistakes that are more expensive to fix in the future. In order to enhance their adoption, it is important to make sure that communication protocols are well documented; sensors and smart devices limit their usage in IoT.

Table 1.2 summarizes the characteristics of major communication protocols in IoT, while it also compares their deployment topology and environments.

M2M communication aims to enable seamless integration of physical and virtual objects into larger and geographically distributed enterprises by eliminating the need for human intervention. However, to achieve this, the enforcement of harmony and collaboration among different communication layers (physical, transport, presentation, application), as well as the approaches used by devices for message storage and passing, can be challenging [67].

The publish/subscribe model is a common way of exchanging messages in distributed environments, and, because of simplicity, it has been adopted by popular M2M communication protocols like MQTT. In dynamic scenarios, where nodes join or leave the network frequently and handoffs are required to keep the connections alive, the publish/subscribe model is efficient. This is because of using push-based notifications and maintaining queues for delayed delivery of messages.

Table 1.2 IoT Communication Protocols Comparison

Protocol Name	Transport Protocol	Messaging Model	Security	Best-Use Cases	Architecture
AMPQ	TCP	Publish/Subscribe	High-Optional	Enterprise integration	P2P
CoAP	UDP	Request/Response	Medium-Optional	Utility field	Tree
DDS	UDP	Publish/Subscribe and Request/Response	High-Optional	Military	Bus
MQTT	TCP	Publish/Subscribe and Request/Response	Medium-Optional	IoT messaging	Tree
UPnP	—	Publish/Subscribe and Request/Response	None	Consumer	P2P
XMPP	TCP	Publish/Subscribe and Request/Response	High-Compulsory	Remote management	Client server
ZeroMQ	UDP	Publish/Subscribe and Request/Response	High-Optional	CERN	P2P

On the other hand, protocols like HTTP/REST and CoAP only support the request/response model, in which a pulling mechanism is used to fetch new messages from the queue. CoAP also uses IPv6 and 6LoWPAN protocols in its network layer to handle node identification. Ongoing efforts are still being made to merge these protocols and standardize them, as to support both publish/subscribe and request/response models [68,69].

1.7 INTERNET OF THINGS APPLICATIONS

IoT promises an interconnected network of uniquely identifiable smart objects. This infrastructure creates the necessary backbone for many interesting applications that require seamless connectivity and addressability between their components. The range of IoT application domain is wide and encapsulates applications from home automation to more sophisticated environments, such as smart cities and e-government.

Industry-focused applications include logistics and transportation [70], supply-chain management [71], fleet management, aviation industry, and enterprise automation systems. Healthcare systems, smart cities and buildings, social IoT, and smart shopping are a few examples of applications that try to improve the daily life of individuals, as well as the whole society. Disaster management, environmental monitoring, smart watering, and optimizing energy consumption through smart grids and smart metering are examples of applications that focus on environment.

In a broader magnitude, Gascon and Asin [72] classified 54 different IoT applications under the following categories: smart environment, smart cities, smart metering, smart water, security and emergencies, retail, logistics, industrial control, smart agriculture, smart animal farming, domestic and home automation, and eHealth. For further reference, Kim et al. [73] have surveyed and classified research about IoT applications based on application domain and target user-groups.

In this section we present categorization of enterprise IoT applications based on their usage domain. These applications usually fall into the following three categories: (1) monitoring and actuating, (2) business process and data analysis, and (3) information gathering and collaborative consumption. The rest of this section is dedicated to characteristics and requirements of each category.

1.7.1 MONITORING AND ACTUATING

Monitoring devices via APIs can be helpful in multiple domains. The APIs can report power usage, equipment performance, and sensor status, and they can perform actions upon sending predefined commands. Real-time applications can utilize these features to report current system status, whereas managers and developers have the option to freely call these APIs without the need for physically accessing the devices. Smart metering, and in a more distributed form, smart grids, can help in identifying production or performance defects via application of anomaly detection on the collected data, and thus increase the productivity. Likewise, incorporating IoT into buildings, or even in the construction process [74], helps to move toward green solutions, save energy, and, consequently, minimize operation cost.

Another area that has been under focus by researchers is applications targeting smart homes that mainly target energy-saving and monitoring. Home monitoring and control frameworks like the ones developed by Verizon [75] and Boss support different communication protocols (Wi-Fi, Bluetooth, etc.) to create an interconnected network of objects that can control desired parameters and change configurations based on the user's settings.

1.7.2 BUSINESS PROCESS AND DATA ANALYSIS

Riggins et al. [76] categorized the level of IoT adoption through Big Data analytics usage to the following categories:

- *Society level*, where IoT mainly influences and improves government services by reducing cost and increasing government transparency and accountability
- *Industry level*, in which manufacturing, emergency services, retailing, and education have been studied as examples
- *Organizational level*, in which IoT can bring the same type of benefits as those mentioned in society level
- *Individual level*, where daily life improvements, individual efficiency, and productivity growth are marked as IoT benefits

The ability to capture and store vast amounts of individual data has brought opportunities to healthcare applications. Patients' data can be captured more frequently, using wearable technologies such as smart watches, and can be published over the Internet. Later, data mining and machine-learning algorithms are used to extract knowledge and patterns from the raw data and archive these records for future reference. Healthsense eNeighbor developed by Humana is an example of a remote controlling system that uses sensors deployed in houses to measure frequent daily activities and heath parameters of occupants. The collected data is then analyzed to forecast plausible risks and produce alerts to prevent incidents [77]. Privacy and security challenges are two main barriers that refrain people and industries from embracing IoT in the healthcare domain.

1.7.3 INFORMATION GATHERING AND COLLABORATIVE CONSUMPTION

Social Internet of Things (SIoT) is where IoT meets social networks, and, to be more precise, it promises to link objects around us with our social media and daily interaction with other people, making them look smarter and more intractable. SIoT concept, motivated by famous social media like Facebook and Twitter, has the potential to affect many people's lifestyles. For example, a social network is helpful for the evaluation of trust of crowds involved in an IoT process. Another advantage is using the humans and their relationships, communities, and interactions for effective discovery of IoT services and objects [78].

Table 1.3 contains a list of past and present open-source projects regarding IoT development and its applications.

1.8 SECURITY

As adoption of IoT continues to grow, attackers and malicious users are shifting their target from servers to end devices. There are several reasons for this. First, in terms of physical accessibility, smart devices and sensors are far less protected than servers, and having physical access to a device gives the attackers an advantage to penetrate with less hassle. Second, the number of devices that can be compromised are far more than the number of servers. Moreover, since devices are closer to the users, security leads to leaking of valuable information and has catastrophic consequences. Finally, due to heterogeneity and the distributed nature of IoT, the patching process is more consuming, thus opening the door for attackers [2,79].

Table 1.3 List of IoT-Related Projects

Name of Project/Product	Area of Focus
Tiny OS	Operating System
Contiki	Operating System
Mantis	Operating System
Nano-RK	Operating System
LiteOS	Operating System
FreeRTOS	Operating System
RIOT	Operating System
Wit.AI	Natural Language
Node-RED	Visual Programming Toolkit
NetLab	Visual Programming Toolkit
SensorML	Modeling and Encoding
Extended Environments Markup Language (EEML)	Modeling and Encoding
ProSyst	Middleware
MundoCore	Middleware
Gaia	Middleware
Ubiware	Middleware
SensorWare	Middleware
SensorBus	Middleware
OpenIoT	Middleware and development platform
Koneki	M2M Development Toolkit
MIHINI	M2M Development Toolkit

In an IoT environment, resource constraints are the key barrier for implementing standard security mechanisms in embedded devices. Furthermore, wireless communication used by the majority of sensor networks is more vulnerable to eavesdropping and man-in-the-middle (proxy) attacks.

Cryptographic algorithms need considerable bandwidth and energy to provide end-to-end protection against attacks on confidentiality and authenticity. Solutions have been proposed in RFID [80,81] and WSN [82] context to overcome aforementioned issues by considering light cryptographic techniques. With regard to constrained devices, symmetric cryptography is applied more often, as it requires fewer resources; however, public key cryptography in the RFID context has also been investigated [83].

WSN with RFID tags and their corresponding readers were the first infrastructure for building IoT environments, and, even now, many IoT applications in logistics, fleet management, controlled farming, and smart cities rely on these technologies. Nevertheless, these systems are not secure enough and are vulnerable to various attacks from different layers. A survey by Borgohain et al. [84] investigates these attacks, but less attention is given to solutions and counter-attack practices.

1.9 IDENTITY MANAGEMENT AND AUTHENTICATION

When talking about billions of connected devices, methods for identifying objects and setting their access level play an important role in the whole ecosystem. Consumers, data sources, and service providers are essential parts of IoT; identity management and authentication methods applied to securely connect these entities affect both the amount of time required to establish trust and the degree of confidence [4]. IoT's inherent features, such as dynamism and heterogeneity, require specific consideration when defining security mechanisms. For instance, in Vehicular Networks (VANETs), cars regularly enter and leave the network due to their movement speed; thus, not only do cars need to interact and exchange data with access points and sensors along the road, but they also need to communicate with each other and form a collaborative network.

Devices or objects in IoT have to be uniquely identified. There are various mechanisms, such as ucode, which generate 128-bit codes and can be used in active and passive RFID tags, and also Electric Product Code (EPC), which creates unique identifiers using Uniform Resource Identifier (URI) codes [85,86]. Being able to globally and uniquely identify and locate objects decreases the complexity of expanding the local environment and linking it with the global markets [84].

It is common for IoT sensors and smart devices to share the same geographical coordinates and even fall into same type or group, hence identity management can be delegated to local identity management systems. In such environments, local identity management systems can enforce and monitor access-control policies and establish trust negotiations with external partners. Zhou et al. [87] investigated security requirements for multimedia applications in IoT and proposed an architecture that supports traffic analysis and scheduling, key management, watermarking, and authentication. Context-aware pairing of devices and automatic authentication is another important requirement for dynamic environments like IoT. Solutions that implement a zero-interaction approach [88] to create simpler yet more secure procedures for creating a ubiquitous network of connected devices can considerably impact IoT and its adoption.

1.10 PRIVACY

According to the report published by IDC and EMC on Dec. 2012 [89], the size of the digital universe containing all created, replicated, and consumed digital data will be roughly doubled every 2 years, hence, forecasting its size to be 40,000 exabytes by 2020, compared to 2,837 exabytes for 2012. Additionally, sourced from statisticbrain.com, the average cost of storage for hard disks has dropped from $437,500 per gigabyte in 1980 to $0.05 per gigabyte in 2013. These statistics show the importance of data and the fact that it is easy and cheap to keep the user's data for a long time and follow the guidelines for harvesting as much data as possible and using it when required.

Data generation rate has drastically increased in recent years, and consequently concerns about secure data storage and access mechanisms has be taken more seriously. With sensors capable of sensing different parameters, such as users' location, heartbeat, and motion, data privacy will remain a hot topic to ensure users have control over the data they share and the people who have access to these data.

In distributed environments like IoT, preserving privacy can be achieved by either following a centralized approach or by having each entity manage its own inbound/outbound data, a technique known as privacy-by-design [84]. Considering the latter approach, since each entity can access only chunks

Table 1.4 IoT Standards

Organization Name	Outcome
Internet of Things Global Standards Initiative (IoT-GSI)	JCA-IoT
Open Source Internet of Things (OSIoT)	Open Horizontal Platform
IEEE	802.15.4 standards, developing a reference architecture
Internet Engineering Task Force (IETF)	Constrained RESTful Environments (CoRE), 6LOWPAN, Routing Over Low power and Lossy networks (ROLL), IPv6
The World Wide Web Consortium (W3C)	Semantic Sensor Net Ontology, Web Socket, Web of Things
XMPP Standards Foundation	XMPP
Eclipse Foundation	Paho project, Ponte project, Kura, Mihini/M3DA, Concierge
Organization for the Advancement of Structured Information Standards	MQTT, AMPQ

of data, distributed privacy- preserving algorithms have been developed to handle data scattering and their corresponding privacy tags [90]. Privacy-enhancing technologies [91,92] are good candidates for protecting collaborative protocols. In addition, to protect sensitive data, rapid deployable enterprise solutions that leverage containers on top of virtual machines can be used [93].

1.11 STANDARDIZATION AND REGULATORY LIMITATIONS

Standardization and the limitation caused by regulatory policies have challenged the growth and adoption rate of IoT and can be potential barriers in embracing the technology. Defining and broadcasting standards will ease the burden of joining IoT environments for new users and providers. Additionally, interoperability among different components, service providers, and even end users will be greatly influenced in a positive way, if pervasive standards are introduced and employed in IoT [94].

Even though more organizations and industries make themselves ready to embrace and incorporate IoT, increase in IoT growth rate will cause difficulties for standardization. Strict regulations about accessing radio frequency levels, creating a sufficient level of interoperability among different devices, authentication, identification, authorization, and communication protocols are all open challenges facing IoT standardization. Table 1.4 contains a list of organizations that have worked toward standardizing technologies either used within IoT context or those specifically created for IoT.

1.12 CONCLUSIONS

IoT has emerged as a new paradigm aimed at providing solutions for integration, communication, data consumption, and analysis of smart devices. To this end, connectivity, interoperability, and integration are inevitable parts of IoT communication systems. Whereas IoT, due to its highly distributed and heterogeneous nature, is comprised of many different components and aspects, providing solutions to integrate this environment and hide its complexity from the user side is inevitable. Novel approaches that utilize SOA architecture and API definition languages to service exposition, discovery, and composition will have a huge impact in adoption and proliferation of the future IoT vision.

In this chapter, different building blocks of IoT, such as sensors and smart devices, M2M communication, and the role of humans in future IoT scenarios are elaborated upon and investigated. Many challenges ranging from communication requirements to middleware development still remain open and need further investigation. We have highlighted these shortcomings, have provided typical solutions, and have drawn guidelines for future research in this area.

REFERENCES

[1] Hafner K, Lyon M. Where wizards stay up late: the origins of the Internet. New York: Simon and Schuster; 1998.
[2] Atzori L, Iera A, Morabito G. The internet of things: a survey. Comput Netw 2010;54(15):2787–805.
[3] Li S, Xu LD, Zhao S. The internet of things: a survey. Inform Syst Front 2014;17(2):243–59.
[4] Perera C, Zaslavsky A, Christen P, Georgakopoulos D. Context aware computing for the internet of things: a survey. Commun Surv Tutorials IEEE 2014;16(1):414–54.
[5] Miorandi D, Sicari S, De Pellegrini F, Chlamtac I. Internet of things: vision, applications and research challenges. Ad Hoc Netw 2012;10(7):1497–516.
[6] Ashton K. That 'internet of things' thing. RFiD J 2009;22(7):97–114.
[7] Gubbi J, Buyya R, Marusic S, Palaniswami M. Internet of Things (IoT): a vision, architectural elements, and future directions. Future Gener Comput Syst 2013;29(7):1645–60.
[8] L.R. LLC. An introduction to the Internet of Things (IoT). http://www.cisco.com/c/dam/en_us/solutions/trends/iot/introduction_to_IoT_november.pdf; 2013.
[9] Vilajosana X, et al. OpenMote: Open-source prototyping platform for the industrial IoT. In: Ad hoc networks. Springer International Publishing; 2015. p. 211–222.
[10] Da Xu L, He W, Li S. Internet of Things in industries: a survey. Ind Inform IEEE Trans 2014;10(4):2233–43.
[11] M.R. Group. Internet of Things (IoT) & M2M communication market—advanced technologies, future cities & adoption trends, roadmaps & worldwide forecasts 2012–2017. http://www.prnewswire.com/news-releases/internet-of-things-iot--machine-to-machine-m2m-communication-market---advanced-technologies-future-cities--adoption-trends-roadmaps--worldwide-forecasts-2012---2017-216448061.html; 2012.
[12] RnRMarketResearch. Internet of Things technology and application market by communication technology (ZigBee, Z-Wave, Bluetooth, Wi-Fi, NFC, RFID), application vertical (building automation, consumer, wearable electronics, industrial, automotive & transportation, agriculture) & geography—global trends & forecasts to 2014–2020. http://www.marketsandmarkets.com/Market-Reports/iot-application-technology-market-258239167.html; 2014.
[13] BI Intelligence. Research for the digital age. https://intelligence.businessinsider.com/; 2015.
[14] Wang F, Hu L, Zhou J, Zhao K. A survey from the perspective of evolutionary process in the Internet of Things. Int J Distrib Sens Netw 2015;2015:9.
[15] Ortutay B. IBM to invest $3-billion in new 'Internet of Things' unit. http://www.reuters.com/article/us-ibm-investment-idUSKBN0MR0BS20150331; 2015.
[16] Yu E. Singapore unveils plan in push to become smart nation. http://www.zdnet.com/article/singapore-unveils-plan-in-push-to-become-smart-nation/; 2014.
[17] Dastjerdi AV, Sharifi M, Buyya R. On application of ontology and consensus theory to human-centric IoT: an emergency management case study. In: Proceedings of the eighth IEEE international conference on Internet of Things (iThings 2015, IEEE CS Press, USA), Sydney, Australia, Dec. 11–13, 2015.

[18] Ryan A. India to be the largest Internet of Things market by 2020. http://www.metering.com/india-to-be-the-largest-internet-of-things-market-by-2020/; 2015.

[19] IoT-A, IoT-A Internet of Things—architecture. http://www.iot-a.eu/; 2012.

[20] WSO2, A reference architecture for the Internet of Things. http://wso2.com/wso2_resources/wso2_whitepaper_a-reference-architecture-for-the-internet-of-things.pdf; 2014.

[21] Castellani A, Bui N, Casari P, Rossi M, Shelby Z, Zorzi M. Architecture and protocols for the internet of things: a case study. In: Eighth IEEE international conference on pervasive computing and communications workshops (PERCOM workshops); 2010. p. 678–683.

[22] Ishaq I, Hoebeke J, Rossey J, De Poorter E, Moerman I, Demeester P. Enabling the web of things: facilitating deployment, discovery and resource access to IoT objects using embedded web services. Int J Web Grid Serv 2014;10(2):218–43.

[23] Guinard D, Trifa V, Karnouskos S, Spiess P, Savio D. Interacting with the SOA-based Internet of Things: discovery, query, selection, and on-demand provisioning of web services. IEEE Trans Serv Comput 2010;3(3):223–35.

[24] Stirbu V. Towards a restful plug and play experience in the web of things, In: IEEE international conference on semantic computing; 2008. p. 512–517.

[25] Guinard D, Trifa V, Mattern F, Wilde E. From the internet of things to the web of things: resource-oriented architecture and best practices. Architecting the Internet of Things. Berlin Heidelberg: Springer; 2011. pp. 97–129.

[26] Li B, Yu J. Research and application on the smart home based on component technologies and Internet of Things. Procedia Eng 2011;15:2087–92.

[27] Su K, Li J, Fu H. Smart city and the applications. In: International conference on electronics, communications and control (ICECC); 2011. p. 1028–1031.

[28] Dohr A, Modre-Opsrian R, Drobics M, Hayn D, Schreier G. The internet of things for ambient assisted living. In: Seventh international conference on information technology: new generations (ITNG); 2010. p. 804–809.

[29] Valipour MH, Amirzafari B, Maleki KN, Daneshpour N. A brief survey of software architecture concepts and service oriented architecture. In: Second IEEE international conference on computer science and information technology (ICCSIT 2009); 2009. p. 34–38.

[30] Datta SK, Bonnet C, Nikaein N. An iot gateway centric architecture to provide novel m2m services. In: IEEE world forum on Internet of Things (WF-IoT); 2014. p. 514–519.

[31] Khodadadi F, Dastjerdi AV, Buyya R. Simurgh: a framework for effective discovery, programming, and integration of services exposed in IoT. In: International conference on recent advances in Internet of Things (RIoT); 2015. p. 1–6.

[32] Elmangoush A, Magedanz T, Blotny A, Blum N. Design of RESTful APIs for M2M services. In: Sixteenth international conference on intelligence in next generation networks (ICIN); 2012. p. 50–56.

[33] Manzalini A, Minerva R, Moiso C. If the Web is the platform, then what is the SDP? In: Thirteenth international conference on intelligence in next generation networks (ICIN 2009); 2009. p. 1–6.

[34] Gu Z, Zhao Q. A state-of-the-art survey on real-time issues in embedded systems virtualization; 2012.

[35] Soltesz S, Pötzl H, Fiuczynski ME, Bavier A, Peterson L. Container-based operating system virtualization: a scalable, high-performance alternative to hypervisors. ACM SIGOPS Oper Syst Rev 2007;41(3):275–87.

[36] Andrus J, Dall C, Hof AV, Laadan O, Nieh J. Cells: a virtual mobile smartphone architecture. In: Proceedings of the twenty-third ACM symposium on operating systems principles; 2011. p. 173–187.

[37] Zhou B, Dastjerdi AV, Calheiros RN, Srirama SN, Buyya R. A context sensitive offloading scheme for mobile cloud computing service. In: Proceedings of the eighth IEEE international conference on cloud computing (Cloud 2015, IEEE CS Press, USA), New York, USA, June 27–July 2, 2015.

[38] Enzai M, Idawati N, Tang M, A taxonomy of computation offloading in mobile cloud computing. In: Second IEEE international conference on mobile cloud computing, services, and engineering (MobileCloud); 2014, p. 19–28.

[39] Cuervo E, Balasubramanian A, Cho D, Wolman A, Saroiu S, Chandra R, Bahl P. MAUI: making smartphones last longer with code offload. In: Proceedings of the eighth international conference on mobile systems, applications, and services; 2010. p. 49–62.

[40] Satyanarayanan M, Bahl P, Caceres R, Davies N. The case for vm-based cloudlets in mobile computing. Pervasive Comput IEEE 2009;8(4):14–23.

[41] Chun B-G, Ihm S, Maniatis P, Naik M, Patti A. Clonecloud: elastic execution between mobile device and cloud. In: Proceedings of the sixth conference on computer systems; 2011, p. 301–314.

[42] Kosta S, Aucinas A, Hui P, Mortier R, Zhang X. Thinkair: dynamic resource allocation and parallel execution in the cloud for mobile code offloading. In: INFOCOM, 2012 proceedings IEEE; 2012. p. 945–953.

[43] Gordon MS, Jamshidi DA, Mahlke SA, Mao ZM, and Chen X. COMET: code offload by migrating execution transparently. In: OSDI; 2012. p. 93–106.

[44] Wei Q, Jin Z. Service discovery for internet of things: a context-awareness perspective. In: Proceedings of the fourth Asia-Pacific symposium on Internetware; 2012. p. 25.

[45] Liu W, Nishio T, Shinkuma R, Takahashi T. Adaptive resource discovery in mobile cloud computing. Comput Commun 2014;50:119–29.

[46] Nishio T, Shinkuma R, Takahashi T, and Mandayam NB. Service-oriented heterogeneous resource sharing for optimizing service latency in mobile cloud. In: Proceedings of the first international workshop on mobile cloud computing & networking; 2013. p. 19–26.

[47] Ruta M, Scioscia F, Pinto A, Di Sciascio E, Gramegna F, Ieva S, Loseto G. Resource annotation, dissemination and discovery in the Semantic Web of Things: a CoAP-based framework. In: Green computing and communications (GreenCom), 2013 IEEE and Internet of Things (iThings/CPSCom), IEEE international conference on Cyber, Physical and Social Computing; 2013. p. 527–534.

[48] Nathan Marz JW. Big Data: principles and best practices of scalable realtime data systems. Greenwich, CT: Manning Publications; 2013.

[49] Misra P, Simmhan Y, Warrior J. Towards a practical architecture for the next generation Internet of Things, arXiv Prepr. arXiv1502.00797; 2015.

[50] Moshtaghi M, Bezdek JC, Havens TC, Leckie C, Karunasekera S, Rajasegarar S, Palaniswami M. Streaming analysis in wireless sensor networks. Wirel Commun Mob Comput 2014;14(9):905–21.

[51] Tsai C-W, Lai C-F, Chiang M-C, Yang LT. Data mining for internet of things: a survey. Commun Surv Tutorials IEEE 2014;16(1):77–97.

[52] Rajasegarar S, Gluhak A, Ali Imran M, Nati M, Moshtaghi M, Leckie C, Palaniswami M. Ellipsoidal neighbourhood outlier factor for distributed anomaly detection in resource constrained networks. Pattern Recognit 2014;47(9):2867–79.

[53] Alam S, Chowdhury MMR, Noll J. SenaaS: an event-driven sensor virtualization approach for Internet of Things cloud. In: Proceedings of the 2010 IEEE international conference on networked embedded systems for enterprise applications (NESEA); 2010.

[54] Li F, Vogler M, Claessens M, Dustdar S. Efficient and scalable IoT service delivery on cloud. In: Proceedings of the sixth international conference on cloud computing (CLOUD); 2013.

[55] Nastic S, Sehic S, Vogler M, Truong H-L, Dustdar S. PatRICIA— a novel programming model for IoT applications on cloud platforms. In: Proceedings of the sixth international conference on service-oriented computing and applications (SOCA); 2013.

[56] Parwekar P. From Internet of Things towards cloud of things. In: Second international conference on computer and communication technology (ICCCT); 2011, p. 329–333.

[57] Khodadadi F, Calheiros RN, Buyya R. A data-centric framework for development and deployment of Internet of Things applications in clouds. In: IEEE tenth international conference on intelligent sensors, sensor networks and information processing (ISSNIP); 2015. p. 1–6.

[58] Medvedev A, Zaslavsky A, Grudinin V, Khoruzhnikov S. Citywatcher: annotating and searching video data streams for smart cities applications. Internet of Things, smart spaces, and next generation networks and systems. Springer International Publishing; 2014. pp. 144–155.

[59] Belli L, Cirani S, Ferrari G, Melegari L, Picone M. A graph-based cloud architecture for big stream realtime applications in the internet of things. Advances in service-oriented and cloud computing. Springer International Publishing; 2014. pp. 91–105.

[60] Bonomi F, Milito R, Natarajan P, Zhu J. Fog computing: a platform for internet of things and analytics. Big Data and Internet of Things: a roadmap for smart environments. Springer International Publishing; 2014. pp. 169–186.

[61] Shachtman N. Feds look to fight leaks with fog of disinformation; 2012.

[62] Bonomi F, Milito R, Zhu J, Addepalli S. Fog computing and its role in the internet of things In: Proceedings of the first edition of the MCC workshop on mobile cloud computing; 2012. p. 13–16.

[63] Vaquero LM, Rodero-Merino L. Finding your way in the fog: towards a comprehensive definition of fog computing. ACM SIGCOMM Comput Commun Rev 2014;44(5):27–32.

[64] Aazam M, Khan I, Alsaffar AA, Huh E-N. Cloud of Things: integrating Internet of Things and cloud computing and the issues involved. In: Eleventh international Bhurban conference on applied sciences and technology (IBCAST); 2014. p. 414–419.

[65] Stonebraker M, Çetintemel U, Zdonik S. The 8 requirements of real-time stream processing. ACM SIGMOD Rec 2005;34(4):42–7.

[66] Rimal BP, Choi E, Lumb I. A taxonomy and survey of cloud computing systems. In: Fifth international joint conference on INC, IMS and IDC. NCM'09; 2009. p. 44–51.

[67] Elmangoush A, Steinke R, Magedanz T, Corici AA, Bourreau A, Al-Hezmi A. Application-derived communication protocol selection in M2M platforms for smart cities. In: Eighteenth international conference on intelligence in next generation networks (ICIN); 2015. p. 76–82.

[68] Teklemariam GK, Hoebeke J, Moerman I, Demeester P. Facilitating the creation of IoT applications through conditional observations in CoAP. EURASIP J Wirel Commun Netw 2013;2013(1):1–19.

[69] Kovatsch M, Lanter M, Shelby Z. Californium: scalable cloud services for the internet of things with CoAP. In: Proceedings of the fourth international conference on the Internet of Things (IoT 2014); 2014.

[70] Yuqiang C, Jianlan G, Xuanzi H. The research of Internet of Things supporting technologies which face the logistics industry. In: International conference on computational intelligence and security (CIS); 2010. p. 659–663.

[71] Chaves LWF, Decker C. A survey on organic smart labels for the internet-of-things. In: Seventh international conference on networked sensing systems (INSS); 2010. p. 161–164.

[72] Gascon D, Asin A. 50 sensor applications for a smarter world. http://www.libelium.com/top_50_iot_sensor_applications_ranking; 2015.

[73] Kim S, Kim S. A multi-criteria approach toward discovering killer IoT application in Korea. Technol Forecast Soc 2015;102:143–55.

[74] Moreno M, Úbeda B, Skarmeta AF, Zamora MA. How can we tackle energy efficiency in IoT based smart buildings? Sensors 2014;14(6):9582–614.

[75] Lee I, Lee K. The Internet of Things (IoT): applications, investments, and challenges for enterprises. Bus Horiz 2015;58(4):431–40.

[76] Riggins FJ, Wamba SF. Research directions on the adoption, usage, and impact of the Internet of Things through the use of Big Data analytics. In: Fourty-eighth Hawaii international conference on system sciences (HICSS); 2015. p. 1531–1540.

[77] Fox GC, Kamburugamuve S, Hartman RD. Architecture and measured characteristics of a cloud based internet of things. In: International conference on collaboration technologies and systems (CTS); 2012. p. 6–12.

[78] Atzori Luigi, et al. The social internet of things (SIoT)—when social networks meet the internet of things: concept, architecture and network characterization. Comput Netw 2012;56(16):3594–608.

[79] Babar S, Mahalle P, Stango A, Prasad N, Prasad R. Proposed security model and threat taxonomy for the internet of things (IoT). Recent trends in network security and applications. Springer Berlin Heidelberg; 2010. pp. 420–429.

[80] Poschmann A, Leander G, Schramm K, Paar C. New light-weight crypto algorithms for RFID. In: IEEE international symposium on circuits and systems (ISCAS 2007); 2007, p. 1843–1846.

[81] Fu L, Shen X, Zhu L, Wang J. A low-cost UHF RFID tag chip with AES cryptography engine. Secur Commun Netw 2014;7(2):365–75.

[82] Ebrahim M, Chong CW. Secure force: a low-complexity cryptographic algorithm for Wireless Sensor Network (WSN). In: IEEE international conference on control system, computing and engineering (ICCSCE); 2013. p. 557–562.

[83] Arbit A, Livne Y, Oren Y, Wool A. Implementing public-key cryptography on passive RFID tags is practical. Int J Inf Secur 2014;14(1):85–99.

[84] Borgohain T, Kumar U, Sanyal S. Survey of security and privacy issues of Internet of Things. arXiv Prepr. arXiv1501.02211; 2015.

[85] Mainetti L, Patrono L, Vilei A. Evolution of wireless sensor networks towards the internet of things: a survey. In: Nineteenth international conference on software, telecommunications and computer networks (SoftCOM); 2011. p. 1–6.

[86] Zorzi M, Gluhak A, Lange S, Bassi A. From today's intranet of things to a future internet of things: a wireless- and mobility-related view. Wirel Commun IEEE 2010;17(6):44–51.

[87] Zhou L, Chao H-C. Multimedia traffic security architecture for the internet of things. IEEE Netw 2011;25(3):35–40.

[88] Miettinen M, Asokan N, Nguyen TD, Sadeghi A-R, Sobhani M. Context-based zero-interaction pairing and key evolution for advanced personal devices. In: Proceedings of the 2014 ACM SIGSAC conference on computer and communications security; 2014. p. 880–891.

[89] McLellan C. Storage in 2014: an overview. http://www.zdnet.com/article/storage-in-2014-an-overview/; 2014.

[90] Aggarwal CC, Philip SY. A general survey of privacy-preserving data mining models and algorithms. USA: Springer; 2008.

[91] Argyrakis J, Gritzalis S, Kioulafas C. Privacy enhancing technologies: a review. Electronic government. Berlin Heidelberg: Springer; 2003. pp. 282–287.

[92] Oleshchuk V. Internet of things and privacy preserving technologies. In: First International Conference on Wireless Communication, Vehicular Technology, Information Theory and Aerospace & Electronic Systems Technology; 2009. p. 336–340.

[93] Roman R, Zhou J, Lopez J. On the features and challenges of security and privacy in distributed internet of things. Comput Netw 2013;57(10):2266–79.

[94] Jiang H, Zhao S, Zhang Y, Chen Y. The cooperative effect between technology standardization and industrial technology innovation based on Newtonian mechanics. Inf Technol Manag 2012;13(4):251–62.

OPEN SOURCE SEMANTIC WEB INFRASTRUCTURE FOR MANAGING IoT RESOURCES IN THE CLOUD

N. Kefalakis, S. Petris, C. Georgoulis, J. Soldatos
Athens Information Technology, Marousi, Greece

2.1 INTRODUCTION

Cloud computing and Internet of Things (IoT) are nowadays two of the most prominent and popular ICT paradigms that are expected to shape the next era of computing. The cloud computing paradigm [1] realizes and promotes the delivery of hardware and software resources over the Internet, according to an on-demand utility-based model. Depending on the type of computing resources delivered via the cloud, cloud services take different forms, such as Infrastructure as a service (IaaS), Platform as a service (PaaS), Software as a service (SaaS), Storage as a service (STaaS), and more. These services hold to promise to deliver increased reliability, security, high availability, and improved QoS at an overall lower total cost of ownership. At the same time, the IoT paradigm relies on the identification and use of a large number of heterogeneous physical and virtual objects (ie, both physical and virtual representations), which are connected to the Internet [2]. IoT enables the communication between different objects, as well as the in-context invocation of their capabilities (services) toward added-value applications. Early IoT applications are based on Radio Frequency Identification (RFID) and Wireless Sensor Network (WSN) technologies, and deliver tangible benefits in several areas, including manufacturing, logistics, trade, retail, and green/sustainable applications, as well as in other sectors.

Since the early instantiations and implementations of both technologies, it has become apparent that their convergence could lead to a range of multiplicative benefits. Most IoT applications entail a large number of heterogeneous geographically distributed sensors. As a result, they need to handle numerous sensor streams, and could therefore directly benefit from the immense distributed storage capacities of cloud computing infrastructures. Furthermore, cloud infrastructures could boost the computational capacities of IoT applications, given that several multisensor applications need to perform complex processing that is subject to timing and other QoS constraints. Also, a great deal of IoT services (eg, large-scale sensing experiments and smart-city applications) could benefit from a utility-based delivery paradigm, which emphasizes the on-demand establishment and delivery of IoT applications over a cloud-based infrastructure.

2.2 BACKGROUND/RELATED WORK

The proclaimed benefits of the IoT/cloud convergence have (early on) given rise to research efforts that attempted to integrate multisensory services into cloud computing infrastructures. Early efforts have focused on the development of pervasive (sensor-based) grid-computing infrastructures [3,4], which emphasized modeling sensors and their data as a resource, and, accordingly, enabling real-time access, sharing, and storage of sensor data [5]. Sensor Grids have been used for a number of pervasive computing applications, notably community-sensing applications such as meteorology [6]. With the advent of cloud computing, the convergence of the cloud computing with WSN infrastructures has been attempted, as an extension of the sensor grid concept in the scope of on-demand elastic cloud-based environments. The convergence of cloud computing with WSN aimed at compromising the radically different and conflicting properties of the two (ie, IoT and cloud) technologies [7]. In particular, sensor networks are location-specific, resource constrained, expensive (in terms of development/deployment cost), and generally inflexible in terms of resource access and availability. On the contrary, cloud-based infrastructures are location-independent and provide a wealth of inexpensive resources, as well as rapid elasticity [7]. Sensor clouds come to bridge these differences and endow WSN with some cloud properties. Other issues are associated with the energy efficiency and the proper handling of service-level agreements [8]. Most recent research initiatives are focusing on real-life implementation of sensor clouds, including open source implementations [9,10].

In addition to research efforts toward sensor-clouds, there are also a large number of commercial online cloud-like infrastructures, which enable end users to attach their devices on the cloud, while also enabling the development of applications that use those devices and the relevant sensor streams. Characteristic examples of such commercial systems include Xively (www.xively.com), ThingsSpeak (www.thingspeak.com), and Sensor-Cloud (www.sensor-cloud.com). These systems provide tools for application development, but offer very poor semantics and no readily available capabilities for utility-based delivery. There are also a number of other projects which have been using cloud infrastructures as a medium for machine-to-machine (M2M) interactions [11], however, without adapting the cloud infrastructure to the needs of the IoT delivery.

Although the previously mentioned projects explore the IoT/cloud integration, they address only a limited number of the issues that surround the IoT/cloud convergence. Specifically, their approach is mostly oriented toward interconnecting sensor streams and IoT services with existing cloud middleware, rather than building a converged cloud/IoT middleware infrastructure that could allow IoT services to fully leverage the capabilities of the cloud. Indeed, by streaming sensor data into the cloud, state-of-the-art projects take advantage of the elasticity and the storage capacity of the cloud in the scope of IoT applications. However, this streaming is not complemented by appropriate resource management mechanisms, which could optimize the usage of cloud resources by IoT applications. Note that efficient resource management is extremely important, given the vast amount of data that could be generated by IoT applications, which could result in high costs for cloud storage. Furthermore, the previously listed IoT cloud platforms feature very poor semantics in terms of the sensor/data streams that they manage, since they only manage minimal metadata that refer to the data streams. This lack of semantics is a serious setback for implementing effective resource management mechanisms, by identifying which sensors and/or data are required in the scope of specific IoT applications. At the same time, the lack of metadata prevents the dynamic selection of data streams and their data in the scope of IoT applications, thereby limiting the flexibility associated with the rapid reuse and repurposing of sensor/data streams across multiple applications. This rapid reuse and repurposing of data streams within the cloud could provide a sound basis for the cost-effective development and delivery of multiple IoT applications/services over the cloud infrastructure. Therefore, the ability to flexibly reuse and repurpose data streams stemming from the same sensors across multiple applications holds the promise to significantly reduce the Total Cost of Ownership (TCO) of the IoT services.

In order to alleviate the resource management issues, the cloud infrastructure needs to keep track of the resources that are consumed/used by the various IoT services. The tracking of these resources is a prerequisite for implementing resource optimization techniques at both the cloud (eg, caching mechanisms) and the sensors/IoT (eg, data streaming according to application needs) levels. This is because the various optimization strategies need to access information about the metadata of the sensors and their data (eg, location, orientation, timestamps, measurement units, reliability, accuracy, cost, data frequency). Furthermore, the richness of the metadata is a factor that could drive the sophistication and efficiency of the resource management schemes. A prominent way of keeping track of the IoT resources in the cloud is the scheduling of IoT services. Scheduling refers to the process of regulating how IoT services access the different resources of the IoT/cloud environment. It implies knowledge about how the various IoT services use the various cloud and sensor resources. The distinction between sensor and cloud resources is required, given that the various sensors are typically owned/managed by different administrative entities from the cloud provider. Although the scheduling concept is straightforward, its implementation is challenging, (mainly) given the volatility of the IoT environments, where sensors join and leave dynamically, at the same time as IoT services are being created and/or destroyed at fine time-scales.

In this chapter we introduce a novel architecture for IoT/cloud convergence, which alleviates several of the limitations of state-of-the-art infrastructures, notably the limitations that are associated with their poor semantics and their inability to support sophisticated resource management mechanisms. The novel characteristics of the introduced architecture are the integration of rich metadata (semantics) concerning the sensors and the data streams, as well as the provision of support for scheduling IoT services in the cloud. In terms of metadata integration, the architecture supports semantic web technologies and standards, including standardized ontologies for describing internet-connected objects and their data streams. In terms of scheduling mechanisms, the architecture provides the means for dynamically establishing IoT services in a way that reserves and keeps track of the resources that they require. Resource reservations are supported at both the (global) level of the cloud infrastructure and at the (local) level of individual sensor deployments. The introduced architecture aims at serving as a blueprint, for rapidly implementing and integrating IoT/cloud solutions. To this end, an open source implementation of its main components/modules is provided as part of the FP7 OpenIoT Project (www.openiot.eu), which is cofunded by the European Commission. In this blueprint direction we also present its use for instantiating and deploying sample IoT solutions. Furthermore, we illustrate how the scheduling process and the semantically rich metadata of the sensors can be used, in order to implement nontrivial resource management mechanisms. Note that the architecture and the modules that are presented in this chapter have been implemented as part of the OpenIoT Open Source Project (https://github.com/OpenIotOrg/openiot).

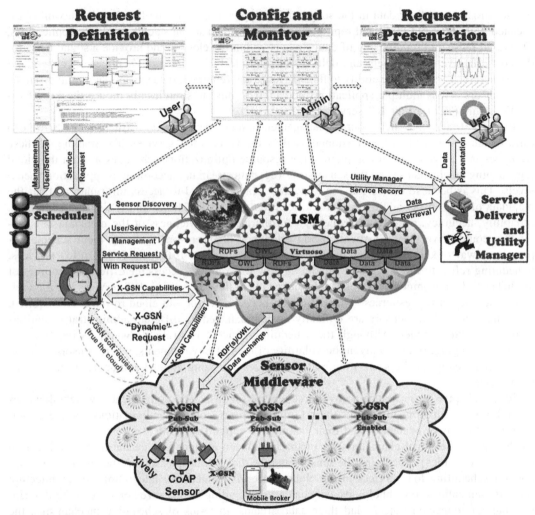

FIGURE 2.1 OpenIoT Architecture for IoT/Cloud Convergence

2.3 OPENIoT ARCHITECTURE FOR IoT/CLOUD CONVERGENCE

Our approach for converging IoT and cloud computing is reflected in the OpenIoT architecture, which is depicted in Fig. 2.1. The figure illustrates the main elements of the OpenIoT software architecture along with their interactions and functionalities, in particular:

- *The Sensor Middleware*, which collects, filters, and combines data streams stemming from virtual sensors (eg, signal-processing algorithms, information- fusion algorithms, and social-media data streams) or physical-sensing devices (such as temperature sensors, humidity sensors, and weather stations). This middleware acts as a hub between the OpenIoT platform and the physical world, as it enables the access to information stemming from the real world. Furthermore, it facilitates the interface to a variety of physical and virtual sensors, such as IETF-COAP-compliant sensors (ie, sensors providing RESTful interfaces), data streams from other IoT platforms (such as https://xively.com), and social networks (such as Twitter). Among the main characteristics of the sensor middleware is its ability to stream sensor data in the cloud, according to semantic format (ie, ontology). The Sensor Middleware is deployed on the basis of one or more distributed instances (nodes), which may belong to different administrative entities. The prototype implementation of the OpenIoT platform uses the GSN middleware [12]. However, other sensor middleware platforms (such as those reviewed in Ref. [13]) could also be used in alternative implementations and deployments of the introduced architecture.

- *The Cloud Computing Infrastructure*, which enables the storage of data streams stemming from the sensor middleware, thereby acting as a cloud database. The cloud infrastructure also stores metadata for the various services, as part of the scheduling process, which is outlined in the next section. In addition to data streams and metadata, computational (software) components of the platform could also be deployed in the cloud in order to benefit from its elasticity, scalability, and performance characteristics. Note that the cloud infrastructure could be either a public infrastructure [such as the Amazon Elastic Compute Cloud (EC2)] or a private infrastructure (such as a private cloud deployed, based on Open Stack). The cloud infrastructure can be characterized as a sensor cloud, given that it primarily supports storage and management of sensor data-streams (and of their metadata).

- *The Directory Service*, which stores information about all the sensors that are available in the OpenIoT platform. It also provides the means (ie, services) for registering sensors with the directory, as well as for the look-up (ie, discovery) of sensors. The IoT/cloud architecture specifies the use of semantically annotated descriptions of sensors as part of its directory service. The OpenIoT open source implementation is based on an enhanced version of the W3C SSN ontology [14]. As a result of this implementation technology, semantic Web techniques (eg, SPARQL and RDF) and ontology management systems (eg, Virtuoso) are used for querying the directory service. Furthermore, the exploitation of semantically annotated sensors enables the integration of data streams within the Linked Data Cloud, thereby empowering Linked Sensor Data. Note that other alternative implementations of the directory services (eg, based on publish/subscribe techniques) are also possible. The Directory Service is deployed within the cloud infrastructure, thereby providing the means for accessing sensor data and metadata residing in the cloud.

- *The Global Scheduler*, which processes all the requests for on-demand deployment of services, and ensures their proper access to the resources (eg, data streams) that they require. This component undertakes the task of parsing the service request, and, accordingly, discovering the sensors that can contribute to its fulfillment. It also selects the resources, that is, sensors that will support the service deployment, while also performing the relevant reservations of resources. This component enables the scheduling of all IoT services, as outlined in the following section.

- *The Local Scheduler component*, which is executed at the level of the Sensor Middleware, and ensures the optimized access to the resources managed by sensor middleware instances (ie, GSN nodes in the case of the OpenIoT implementation). Whereas the Global Scheduler regulates the access to the resources of the OpenIoT platform (notably the data streams residing in the cloud), its local counterpart regulates the access and use of the data streams at the lower level of the Sensor Middleware.

- *The Service Delivery and Utility Manager*, which performs a dual role. On the one hand, it combines the data streams as indicated by service workflows within the OpenIoT system, in order to deliver the requested service. To this end, this component makes use of the service description and the resources identified and reserved by the (Global) Scheduler component. On the other hand, this component acts as a service-metering facility, which keeps track of utility metrics for each individual service. This metering functionality is accordingly used to drive functionalities such as accounting, billing, and utility-driven resource optimization. Such functionalities are essential in the scope of a utility (pay-as-you-go) computing paradigm.
- *The Request Definition tool*, which enables the specification of service requests to the OpenIoT platform. It comprises a set of services for specifying and formulating such requests, while also submitting them to the Global Scheduler. This tool features a Graphical User Interface (GUI).
- *The Request Presentation component*, which is in charge of the visualization of the outputs of an IoT service. This component selects mashups from an appropriate library in order to facilitate service presentation. Service integrators and solution providers have the option to enhance or override the functionality of this component toward providing a presentation layer pertaining to their solution.
- *The Configuration and Monitoring component*, which enables management and configuration functionalities over the sensors, and the IoT services that are deployed within the platform. This component is also supported by a GUI.

Fig. 2.1 does not specify implementation technologies associated with the various components, thus providing an abstract presentation of the functional elements of the architecture. OpenIoT is, however, implemented on the basis of specific implementation technologies [such as GSN for the sensor middleware, W3C SSN for the directory service, and JSF (Java Server Faces) libraries (such as Primefaces)]. Alternative implementations based on alternate technologies are however possible. IoT solution providers and/or service integrators could adopt this architecture as a baseline for providing their own implementation, which may use only part of the open source components and technologies of the OpenIoT platform implementation, which is currently available at: https://github.com/OpenIotOrg/openiot.

The delivery of IoT services through the platform relies on data collected and streamed into the cloud through the (GSN) sensor middleware. Given the existence of multiple data streams within the cloud, a typical workflow associated with the use of the OpenIoT platform involves:

- The formulation of a request for an IoT service using the Request Definition tool, and its submission to the (Global) Scheduler component. The request specifies the needed sensors and the type of processing to be applied over the data, as well as the preferred visualization of the results.
- The parsing of the IoT service request by the scheduler, and the subsequent discovery of the sensors/ICOs to be used in order to deliver the IoT service. Toward discovering the required sensors, the Directory Service is queried and accessed.
- The formulation of the service (eg, in the form of a SPARQL query) and its persistence in the cloud, along with other metadata about the service. The metadata include a handle/identifier to the created IoT service.
- The execution of the service by end users (based on the handle of the target service) and the visualization of the results.

The platform caters to the optimization of the resources entailed in the delivery of IoT services. These optimizations leverage data formulated during the scheduling process, which is described in the following section, along with the functionalities of the Global Scheduler component.

2.4 SCHEDULING PROCESS AND IoT SERVICES LIFECYCLE

The Global Scheduler component is the main and first entry point for service requests submitted to the cloud platform. It parses each service request and accordingly performs two main functions toward the delivery of the service, namely the selection of the sensors/ICOs involved in the service, but also the reservation of the needed resources. The scheduler manages all the metadata of the IoT services, including: (1) The signature of the service (ie, its input and output parameters), (2) the sensors/ICOs used to deliver the service, and (3) execution parameters associated with the services, such as the intervals in which the service shall be repeated, the types of visualization (in the request presentation), and other resources used by the service. In principle, the Global Scheduler component keeps track of and controls the lifecycle of IoT services, which is depicted in Fig. 2.2. In particular, the following lifecycle management services are supported by the scheduler:

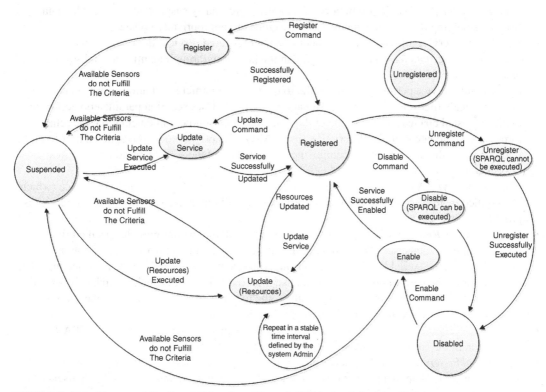

FIGURE 2.2 State Diagram of the OpenIoT Services Lifecycle Within the Scheduler Module

- *Resource Discovery*: This service discovers a virtual sensor's availability. It therefore provides the resources that match the requirements of a given request for an IoT service.
- *Register*: This service is responsible for establishing the requested service within the cloud database. To this end, it initially identifies and logs (within the cloud) all the sensors/ICOs, which are pertinent and/or needed for delivering the requested IoT service. The metadata of the IoT service (ie, signature, sensors/ICOs, and execution parameters) are persisted to the cloud, based on appropriate data structures. As part of the registration process, a unique identifier (ServiceID) is assigned to the requested IoT service. The current implementation of the "Register" service, as part of the OpenIoT Open Source Project, persists the service description as a SPARQL query (which covers a wide range of sensor queries/services against the W3C SSN directory service). Furthermore, the open source implementation maintains an appropriate set of data structures (within the cloud), which holds other metadata for each registered IoT service.
- *Unregister*: In the scope of the unregister functionality for given IoT service (identified through its ServiceID), the resources allocated for the service (eg, sensors used) are released (ie, disassociated from the service). In the case of an active service, a deactivation process is initially applied. The status of the service is appropriately updated in the data structures holding the metadata about the service.
- *Suspend*: As part of suspend functionality, the service is deactivated and therefore its operation is ceased. Note however, as part of the suspension the platform does not release the resources associated with the service.
- *Enable from Suspension*: This functionality enables a previously suspended service. The data structures holding the service's metadata in the cloud are appropriately updated.
- *Enable*: This service allows the enablement of an unregistered service. In practice, this functionality registers the service once again in the platform, through identifying and storing the required sensors/ICOs.
- *Update*: This service permits changes to the IoT service. In particular, it allows for the updating of the service's lifecycle metadata (ie, signature, sensors/ICOs, execution parameters) according to the requested changes. In the scope of the OpenIoT open source implementation, the scheduler formulates an updated service description (as SPARQL script), based on the updated user request. It also updates the data structures comprising the metadata of the service based on the updated information.
- *Registered Service Status*: This service provides the lifecycle status of a given IoT service (which is identified by its ServiceID). Detailed information (ie, all the metadata) about the IoT service is provided.
- *Service Update Resources*: This service checks periodically (at a configurable specified time-interval) all the enabled services, and identifies those using mobile sensors [eg, smartphones, UAVs (Unmanned Aerial Vehicles)]. Accordingly, it updates (if needed) the IoT service metadata on the basis of the newly defined sensors that support the IoT service. Such an update is needed in cases where a mobile sensor no longer fulfills the location-based criteria set by the service, or even in cases where additional (new) sensors fulfill these criteria.
- *Get Service*: This service retrieves the description of a registered service, that is, the SPARQL description in the case of the OpenIoT open source implementation.
- *Get Available Services*: This service returns a list of registered services that are associated with a particular user. Note that the various IoT services are registered and established by users of the platform.

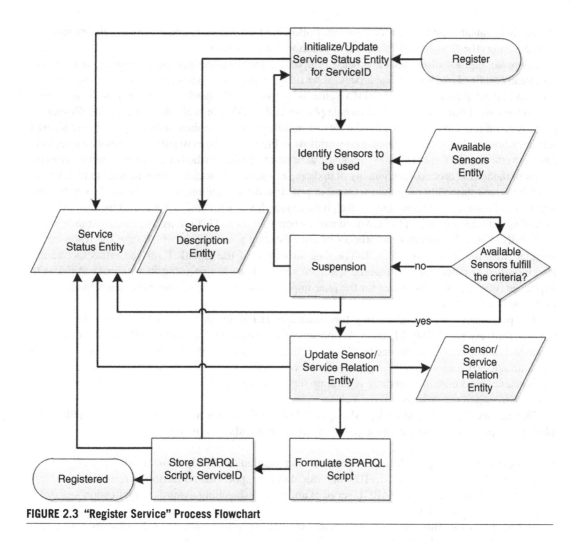

FIGURE 2.3 "Register Service" Process Flowchart

In order to support the lifecycle services outlined previously, the scheduler provides an appropriate API, which also enables the services' transition between the various lifecycle states. The platform also supports baseline authentication and access-control mechanisms, which allows specific users to access resources and services available within the platform. Note that only registered users are able to leverage these aforementioned lifecycle management functionalities.

The following figures illustrate the details of some lifecycle-management use cases within the Scheduler component. In particular, Fig. 2.3 illustrates the main workflow associated with the service registration process. In the scope of this process, the Scheduler attempts to discover the resources (sensors, ICO) that will be used for the service delivery. In case there are no sensors/ICOs that can fulfill the request, the service is suspended. In case a set of proper sensors/IOCs is defined, the relevant data entities are updated (eg, relationship of sensors to services) and a SPARQL script associated with the service is formulated and stored for later use. Following the successful conclusion of this process, the servicer enters the "Registered" state and is available for invocation.

Likewise, Fig. 2.4 illustrates the process of updating the resources associated with a given service. As already outlined, such an update process is particularly important when it comes to dealing with IoT services that entail mobile sensors and ICOs, that is, sensors and ICOs whose location is likely to change within very short timescales (such as mobile phones and UAVs). In such cases, the Update Resources process could regularly check the availability of mobile sensors and their suitability for the registered service whose resources are updated. The workflow in Fig. 2.4 assumes that the list of mobile sensors is known to the service (ie, the sensors' semantic annotations indicate whether a sensor is mobile or not).

Even though the process/functionality of updating resources is associated with the need to identify the availability and suitability of mobile sensors, in principle the Update process can be used to update the whole list of resources that contribute to the given service. Such functionality helps the OpenIoT platform in dealing with the volatility of IoT environments, where sensors and ICOs may dynamically join or leave.

Finally, Fig. 2.5 illustrates the process of unregistering a service, in which case the resource associated with the service is released. The data structures of the OpenIoT service infrastructure are also modified to reflect the fact that the specified service is no longer using its resources. As already explained, this update is important for the later implementation of the resource management and optimization functionalities.

The previously outlined scheduling functionalities enable the delivery of the service through the Service Delivery and Utility Manager component of the OpenIoT architecture. The latter component has a dual functionality: On the one hand (as a service manager) it is the module enabling data retrieval from the selected sensors comprising the IoT service. On the other hand, the utility manager maintains and retrieves information structures regarding service usage, and supports metering, charging, and resource management processes.

The Service Delivery and Utility Manager (SD&UM) provides an appropriate API, enabling the platform to provide the outcome of a given service. In particular, the module supports:

- *Subscription for a report*: This service enables invocation of already defined IoT services (identified based on their ServiceID). In particular, it supports the collection of results from a given IoT service (eg, a SPARQL service) and their dispatching toward an application's destination address (URI).
- *Callback service*: This service is instantiated in order to deliver a report to all subscribers to a given IoT service (identified based on its ServiceID). The report is delivered according to the schedule defined by the user at the service registration time.
- *Unsubscribe for a report*: This service is invoked by the user in order to cease its subscription to a given report.
- *Poll for a report*: This service enables the user to periodically invoke an already defined IoT service within specified time intervals.
- *Get the utility usage of a user*: This service enables the user to retrieve utility information associated with a specific user. It takes into account all the IoT services that have been used by the specific user.
- *Get the utility usage of a registered service*: This service enables the user to retrieve the utility information associated with a specific IoT service (identified based on its ServiceID). Note that this functionality enables the application of utility functions over utility metrics, in order to calculate prices/costs in accordance to the accounting policies of the IoT/cloud service provider.

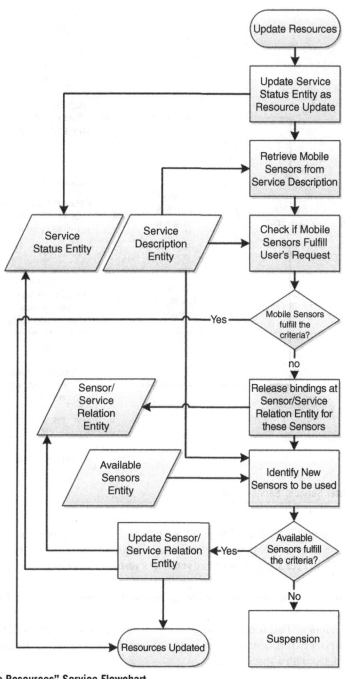

FIGURE 2.4 "Update Resources" Service Flowchart

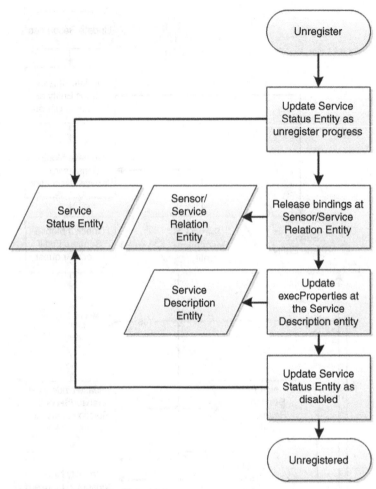

FIGURE 2.5 "Unregister Service" Service Flowchart

- *Record utility usage*: This functionality enables the recording/logging of usage information, associated with an IoT service, in terms of volume of requested data and the types of sensors/ resources used. Utility recording can be activated as a result of a polling request, as well as in the scope of a callback service.
- *Get service status*: This functionality provides access to the status of a specific IoT service by providing the ServiceID.
- *Get service description*: This functionality provides access to the description of the service.
- *Get available services*: This service functionality allows the user to access the list of IoT services, which are associated with a specific user.

As already outlined, the service delivery and utility management functionalities are based on the earlier scheduling of the requests for IoT services. In particular, the scheduling of requests ensures the logging of the appropriate information for managing service delivery to the various users, based on both push and pull functionalities (ie, supported by the "subscription" and "polling" models outlined previously). Furthermore, the management of scheduling information provides a basis for calculating utility metrics for metering, accounting, and billing purposes. With all of this information at hand, the introduced, converged IoT/cloud infrastructure provides the means for implementing resource management and optimization algorithms, which are outlined in the following section.

2.5 SCHEDULING AND RESOURCE MANAGEMENT

The OpenIoT scheduler enables the availability and provision of accurate information about the data requested by each service, as well as about the sensors and ICOs that will be used in order to deliver these data. Hence, a wide range of different resource management and optimization algorithms can be implemented at the scheduler component of the OpenIoT architecture. Furthermore, the envisaged scheduling at the local (ie, sensor middleware) level enables resource optimization at the sensor data-acquisition level (ie, at the edges of the OpenIoT infrastructure).

In terms of specific optimizations that can be implemented over the introduced IoT/cloud infrastructure are optimization techniques that have their roots in the WSN literature, where data management is commonly applied as a means to optimize the energy efficiency of the network [15]. In particular, the scheduler components (at both the global and the local levels) maintain information that could optimize the use of the network on the basis of aggregate operations [16], such as the aggregation of queries to the sensor cloud [17]. Furthermore, a variety of in-network processing and data management techniques can be implemented in order to optimize processing times and/or reduce the required access to the sensor network [18,19]. The criteria for aggregating queries and their results could be based on common spatial regions (ie, data aggregation based on sensors residing in geographical regions of high interest). In general, the in-network processing approaches previously outlined can be classified into three broad categories, namely push [20], pull [16,19], and hybrid approaches [18,21].

Another class of optimizations that are empowered by the introduced scheduling approach are caching techniques [22,23], which typically reduce network traffic, enhance the availability of data to the users (sink), and reduce the cost of expensive cloud-access operations (eg, I/O operations to public clouds). The caching concept involves maintaining sensor (data streams) data to a cache memory in order to facilitate fast and easy access to them. In the case of OpenIoT, caching techniques could obviate the need to execute the results of previously executed SPARQL queries.

As a proof-of-concept implementation, we have implemented two resource optimization schemes over the open source OpenIoT cloud platform. The first scheme concerns bandwidth and storage optimization through indirect control over the sensor, and falls in the broader class of in-network process approaches discussed previously. As part of this scheme, a pull approach is adopted in terms of accessing the sensor networks of the various nodes. In particular, a periodic timed (ie, polling) task is running on the X-GSN module, which is responsible for direct sensor management. This task queries the LSM/W3C SSN repository, in order to determine which sensors are needed and used by IoT services. The task compares the query results to the LSM (triplets), with the list of sensors that are currently active on the X-GSN sensor middleware module. Accordingly, X-GSN: (1) activates sensors that have needed/used an IoT service, which are not active on the module; and

(2) deactivates the sensors that are active on the module, but have not been used by any IoT service. This process is illustrated on the sequence diagram in Fig. 2.6. The implementation of this scheme ensures that no unnecessary data will be streamed from the sensors (and the X-GSN node that they are attached to) to the cloud, thereby saving in terms of bandwidth and costs associated with cloud access. Hence, the implemented pull approach can serve as a basis for optimizing both latency and monetary costs.

The resource optimization scheme was implemented on the basis of the caching of SPARQL queries/requests. Caching can alleviate one of the most significant drawbacks of the use of triple stores for the deployment of semantic technologies, which is their low performance compared to conventional relational databases. Besides the issue of performance, caching can also have monetary benefits, given that accessing remote data-stores like Amazon S3 or Google Cloud Data-Store incurs pay-as-you-go costs, depending on the provider's pricing scheme.

The caching solution that was implemented over the OpenIoT infrastructure is based on [24]. In particular, a small proxy layer is implemented and used to route all SPARQL queries. Whenever a query is entered into the system, the proxy layer checks whether the result has already been cached. In such a case, the result is returned to the client directly through the cache without accessing the SPARQL data store. In any other case the query is redirected to the SPARQL data store and the result is stored in the local cache before it is returned to the user (client).

As a validating example of the proxy layer implementation over the OpenIoT sensor cloud, we have a assumed a Pareto distribution for the probability density of the various SPARQL queries, as in [24], which is more practical compared to the assumption that all queries arrive with the same probability (as in the [25] benchmark). Note that the "a" parameter of the Pareto distribution $p(x) = \dfrac{ab^a}{x^{a=1}}$ allows the simulation of either a wider or narrower spectrum of repeated queries. As expected, the wider the variety of SPARQL queries (representing IoT services), the fewer unique queries that are serviced directly from the LSM implementation in the cloud, resulting ultimately in the majority of queries being serviced from the cache proxy. In order to simulate a practical scenario, we assume that the Amazon S3 public cloud data-store [which features a linear pricing-scheme (eg, $0.005/1000 requests)] is used in conjunction with the OpenIoT infrastructure. We also assume that the cache miss-rates are those depicted in [24] for a benchmark based on 10 million triples and 12,500 queries. Furthermore, yearly server operational costs that support a 20TB cache have been taken into account (Table 2.1). This cache capacity is considered sufficient to store all the query results obtained from the cloud data-store for this particular scenario.

Under these specific circumstances, Fig. 2.7 illustrates the total costs incurred for seven different scenarios of the SPARQL queries distribution that correspond to different varieties of queries. The different varieties correspond to different parameters of the Pareto distribution in [24], which result in different miss-rates [25].

As expected, for a low number of requests per hour, there is no benefit for using cache. At a medium-high number of hourly requests, such as the second category at 1450 Krph, the threshold where it becomes more efficient to use a caching solution is just hit. It is finally evident, in the last category at 2000 Krph, that at a high number of requests it is far more efficient to use cache. In order to achieve an efficient caching solution there must be a clear estimate, first of all, of the average requests per hour on the cloud data-store, as well as to what extent the cache storage capacity is sufficient. Finally, it is also evident by this simulation that the determining factor for cache performance

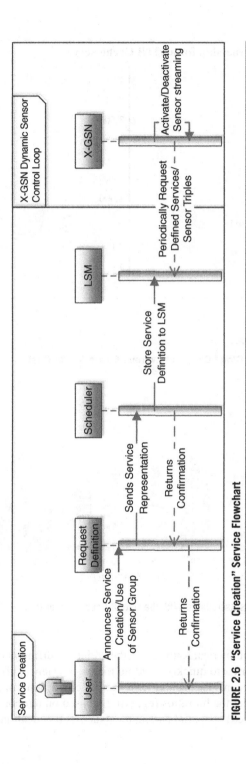

FIGURE 2.6 "Service Creation" Service Flowchart

Table 2.1 Total Cost of Ownership for a 20TB Cache Server

Caching Server Cost/Unit	
Server Disk Capacity (TB)	5
Unit Cost (€)	3,500
Lifespan (years)	3
PV Discount Rate (%)	5
Server Maintenance/Year (€)	1,500
Energy cost/year (€)	1,000
Server Cost/Year (Present Value)	
Cache Size Required (TB)	20
Servers Required	4
Cost/Year (PV)	22,635.00 €

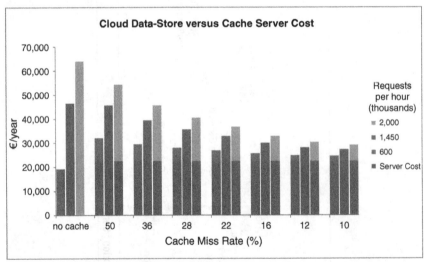

FIGURE 2.7 Comparison of Costs Associated With the Use of Cache Server to the Cost of the Use of a Public Cloud Data-Store

is not the absolute number of queries. Rather, it is the variety of different queries that are performed on the cloud data-store in order to quickly build up the cache. Hence, efficient implementations of the caching schemes could consider caching criteria that could minimize the spectrum of queries variance, thereby maximizing the hit ratios [eg, criteria based on temporal parameters (such as the time that the queries are asked) or spatial parameters (such as the location of the sensors entailed in the queries)].

2.6 VALIDATING APPLICATIONS AND USE CASES

The overall scheduling infrastructure has also been validated through the development of proof-of-concept IoT applications, which comprise multiple IoT services that have been integrated based on the OpenIoT infrastructure. One of the proof-of-concept applications falls in the wider realm of smart-city applications, aimed at providing a set of smart services within a student campus in Karlsruhe, Germany. In particular, this smart-campus application creates a semantic storage with an ontology-based description of real-world objects, which are identified by different labeling methods (QR-Codes, RFID-Tags). The objects are associated to their semantic description by unified resource identifiers and stored to the semantic storage. The semantic information about real-world objects is retrieved and updated via semantic queries (SPARQL), which are invoked through mobile devices. The information about the real-world objects (eg, rooms, books) is then displayed by dedicated views, and within existing views of standard smartphone applications, like a map application.

The second use-case concerns the implementation of IoT services for manufacturing, and, more specifically, for the printing and packing industry, with emphasis on the production of boxes. The IoT services support key production processes in this industry, such as printing on paper sheets and die-cutting (for perforation of the sheets), as well as gluing and folding the pieces of a box. A variety of sensors are employed to facilitate production-line automation and quality-control checks, including laser sensors, high-speed 1D/2D barcode verification cameras, weight sensors, contrast and color sensors (for marking code identification), as well as ultrasonic sensors (for measuring heights and material-reel diameters). In this environment, the OpenIoT infrastructure is used to enable the dynamic on-demand formulation, calculation, and visualization of KPIs (Key Performance Indicators) about the manufacturing processes. Interesting KPIs include, for example: (1) in the area of materials consumption, the rate of consumption and how much scrap is produced; (2) in the area of machine performance, how fast each machine is working, what is the rate of product/shipping container production, and the overall efficiency of the machines; (3) in the area of labor activity and performance, how much time is spent setting up/repairing the machine; and (4) in the area of machine operation, an interesting KPI relates to tracking the time that machines spend in their various modes (ie, setup/repair/idle/operation). To this end, high-level events captured, based on the processing of the aforementioned sensors, are announced as virtual sensors to the W3C SSN directory through the X-GSN middleware. In particular, KPI calculations are implemented as a set of X-GSN virtual sensors, and, accordingly, are published to the sensor cloud and made available for semantic querying. Requests to the OpenIoT system (via the scheduler) are able to define, select, filter, and visualize KPIs on the basis of various selection criteria, including location (plant, floor, type). At the same time, several other requests will be able to compose (eg, aggregate) KPIs on the basis of other, more elementary, KPIs. Note that composite KPIs could dynamically combine information from multiple machines and plants, as soon as these are published to the sensor cloud. Some examples of composite KPIs formulated and measured include: (1) find the rates of all machines in a company's factories (within location L1, L2, L3) and plot them together; (2) find the operation status of all machines of type X in a company's factories (within locations L1, L2, L3) and overlay them; and (3) find the rates of all machines in my factories (within locations L1, L2, L3) and the local temperatures at locations (L1, L2, L3), and plot them (eg, in order to understand how local temperature variations affect machine operation).

The third use-case (part of the "Phenonet" project) uses state-of-the-art sensor network technology, in order to gather environmental data for crop-variety trials, at a far higher resolution than conventional methods, and provides a high-performance real-time online data-analysis platform that allows scientists and farmers to visualize, process, and extract both real-time and long-term crop performance information. Phenonet uses a WSN in a wheat-variety trial at the Yanco Managed Environment Facility in New South Wales (NSW). This was a key part of an experiment to test the feasibility of using remote monitoring of crop performance in trials across Australia. The WSN consists of sensors measuring (1) local environmental data, including: solar radiation, air temperature, relative humidity, rainfall, and wind speed; and (2) crop performance data, including: soil moisture, soil temperature, and an infrared sensor that measures leaf (crop canopy) temperature. The sensors are linked by short-range digital radio to a base station that can return the results in real time to a server in Canberra via 3G wireless networking. The raw data are disseminated to the sensor cloud, and are made available for normalization, integration correlation, and real-time visualization.

2.7 FUTURE RESEARCH DIRECTIONS

An open source implementation of the introduced scheduling concepts is available as part of the OpenIoT Open Source Project. We expect this chapter to motivate the open-source community toward providing other implementations of scheduling concepts for IoT services, including their integration with cloud computing infrastructures. Such concepts could deal with caching of IoT service requests and response data, taking into account the spatiotemporal characteristics of the respective IoT queries. In terms of the OpenIoT middleware infrastructure, future research work includes the development of tools for visualizing IoT resources, as part of the Integrated Development Environment (IDE) of the OpenIoT project.

2.8 CONCLUSIONS

In this chapter we have introduced the OpenIoT architecture as a practical approach to the integration and convergence of IoT with cloud computing. As part of this architecture we have also illustrated the benefits of a scheduling approach for IoT services. Scheduling is one of the key merits and distinguishing characteristics of OpenIoT, when compared to state-of-the-art approaches for IoT/cloud integration. Indeed, the presented approach allows for the logging of a wide range of information associated with IoT services, which can enable the implementation of utility-based functionalities, as well as a wide range of resource optimizations, both of which are essential to both end-users and cloud-service providers. In most cases these optimizations are also very important in order to fully leverage the benefits of a cloud computing model for IoT services, such as cost efficiency and the adoption of utility-driven pay-as-you-go operational models.

The merits of the introduced scheduling architecture have been validated based on practical implementations of use cases, as well as of resource-optimization mechanisms. In terms of use cases, three distinct IoT applications have been developed, which utilize a variety of sensors and IoT services across three different application domains (smart cities, manufacturing, crop management). At the same time, the resource optimization capabilities have been validated on the basis of the implementation of two different schemes, one relating to in-network optimization of sensor information dissemination and another to caching of semantic-based requests (ie, queries) for IoT services.

ACKNOWLEDGMENTS

Part of this work has been carried out in the scope of the OpenIoT project (FP7-287305) (http://openiot.eu). The authors acknowledge help and contributions from all partners of the project. The smart campus, manufacturing, and crop-management use cases that have been briefly presented in Section 2.5 have been implemented by the OpenIoT consortium partners Fraunhofer-IOSB (http://www.iosb.fraunhofer.de/), SENSAP S.A (www.sensap.eu), and CSIRO (csiro.au), respectively.

REFERENCES

[1] McFedries P. The cloud is the computer. IEEE Spectr 2008;45(8):p. 20.

[2] Vermesan O, Friess P. Internet of Things—global, technological, and societal trends. River Pub Ser Commun 2011.

[3] Tham CK, Buyya R. SensorGrid: integrating sensor networks and grid computing. CSI Commun 2005;29:24–9.

[4] Gaynor M, Moulton SL, Welsh M, LaCombe E, Rowan A, Wynne J. Integrating wireless sensor networks with the grid. IEEE Internet Comput 2004;8:32–9.

[5] Lim HB, et al. Sensor grid, integration of wireless sensor networks and the grid. In: IEEE conference on local computer networks, 30th anniversary (LCN'05); 2005.

[6] Lim HB, Ling KV, Wang W, Yao Y, Iqbal M, Li B, et al. The national weather sensor grid. In: Proceedings of the fifth ACM conference on embedded networked sensor systems (SenSys 2007); 2007.

[7] Lee K. Extending sensor networks into the cloud using Amazon web services. In: IEEE 2010 international conference on networked embedded systems for enterprise applications; 2010.

[8] Mehedi Hassan M, Song B, Huh E-n. A framework of sensor-cloud integration opportunities and challenges. ICUIMC 2009;618–626.

[9] Fox GC, Kamburugamuve S, Hartman R. Architecture and measured characteristics of a cloud based Internet of Things, API workshop 13-IoT Internet of Things, machine to machine and smart services applications (IoT 2012). In: The 2012 international conference on collaboration technologies and systems (CTS 2012); 2012. p. 21–25.

[10] Soldatos J, Serrano M, Hauswirth M. Convergence of utility computing with the Internet of Things. In: International workshop on extending seamlessly to the Internet of Things (esIoT) 2012 IMIS international conference. Palermo, Italy, July 4–6, 2012.

[11] Kranz M, Roalter L, Michahelles F. Things that twitter: social networks and the Internet of Things, what can the Internet of Things do for the citizen (CIoT). In: Proceedings of the workshop at the eighth international conference on pervasive computing. Helsinki, Finland, 2010.

[12] Aberer K, Hauswirth M, Salehi A. Infrastructure for data processing in large-scale interconnected sensor networks. MDM 2007;198–205.

[13] Chatzigiannakis I, Mylonas G, Sotiris E. Nikoletseas, 50 ways to build your application: a survey of middleware and systems for wireless sensor networks. ETFA 2007;466–73.

[14] Taylor K. Semantic sensor networks: the W3C SSN-XG ontology and how to semantically enable real time sensor feeds. In: Proceedings of the semantic technology conference. San Francisco, CA, USA, June 5–9, 2011.

[15] Abadi DJ, Madden S, Linder W. REED: robust, efficient filtering and event detection in sensor networks. In: Proceedings of the thirty-first VLDB conference. Trondheim, Norway; 2005. p. 769–780.

[16] Yao Y, Gehrke J. The cougar approach to in-network query processing in sensor networks. SIGMOD Rec 2002;31(3):9–18.

[17] Meng M, Yang J, Xu H, Jeong B-S, Lee Y-K, Lee S. Query aggregation in wireless sensor networks. IJMUE 2008;3(1)19–26.

[18] Lee KCK, Lee WC, Zheng B, Winter J. Processing multiple aggregation queries in geo-sensor networks. In: Proceedings of the eleventh international conference on database systems for advanced applications (DASFAA); 2006. p. 20–34.

[19] Madden SR, Franklin MJ, Hellerstein JM, Hong W. Tinydb: an acquisitional query processing system for sensor networks. ACM Trans Data Base Syst (TODS) 2005;30(1):122–73.

[20] Ye F, Luo H, Cheng J, Lu S, Zhang L. In: A two-tier data dissemination model for large-scale wireless sensor network. In: MobiCom 2002: Proceedings of the eighth annual international conference on mobile computing and networking. Atlanta, GA: ACM; 2002. p. 148–159.

[21] Li X, Huang Q, Zhang Y., Combs, needles, haystacks: balancing push and pull for discovery in large-scale sensor networks, ACM sensys. Baltimore, MD; 2005.

[22] Li S, Zhu LJ. Data caching based queries in multi sink sensor networks. In: IEEE proceedings of the fifth international conference on mobile ad-hoc and sensor networks; 2009.

[23] Chow CY, Leong HV, Chan ATS. GroCoca: group-based peer-to-peer cooperative caching in mobile environment. IEEE J Sel Areas Commun 2007;25(1)179–191.

[24] Martin M, Unbehauen J, Auer S. Improving the performance of semantic web applications with SPARQL query caching. In: Proceedings of the extended semantic web conference (ESWC). Heraklion, Greece: Springer; 2010. p. 304–318.

[25] Bizer C, Schultz A. The berlin SPARQL benchmark. Int J Sem Web Inf Syst 2009;5(2):1–24.

DEVICE/CLOUD COLLABORATION FRAMEWORK FOR INTELLIGENCE APPLICATIONS

3

Y. Yoon*, D. Ban**, S. Han**, D. An†, E. Heo**

*Hongik University, Wausan-ro, Mapo-gu, Seoul, South Korea; **Samsung Electronics, South Korea;
†Keimyung University, Dalgubeol-daero, Dalseo-gu, Daegu, South Korea

3.1 INTRODUCTION

Cloud computing is now an established computing paradigm that offers on-demand computing and storage resources to the users who cannot afford the expenditure on computing equipment and management workforce. This computing paradigm first led to the notable commercial success of Amazon's EC2 [1] and Microsoft's Azure [2]. These companies have adopted the business model of renting out their virtualized resources to the public. More recently, Google and Facebook are now utilizing their data-center-based clouds to internally run machine-learning algorithms based on the large volume of data collected from their users. Google runs a popular proactive service, Google Now, which gives individualized recommendations based on the user's context inferred from the personal data [3]. Facebook leverages the user-uploaded images and social-network data to automatically recognize users and the relationship among them [4,5].

Despite the continuous growth, many organizations have raised the concerns about the cloud computing with respect to performance and privacy. In the following section, we elaborate on those issues.

3.2 BACKGROUND AND RELATED WORK

Public cloud-vendors have attracted institutions who have little incentive to pay the upfront cost of IT infrastructure, especially when the applications and services they host do not require high compute and storage capacity. However, once their applications and services become popular, the demand for higher compute and storage capacity may suddenly soar. This is the point when these institutions may not feel that public cloud is cost-effective anymore, and consider opting for a different cloud computing model.

For example, one may adopt a hybrid cloud computing model that utilizes both the public and the private cloud infrastructure [6]. A typical use case of this model is to do *workload bursting*, that is, offloading tasks from the public cloud to the self-managed private cloud for cost savings [7]. Some institutions may rather resort to embarking on an entirely private cloud infrastructure. For example, in

2015, Samsung Electronics migrated S Voice, its mobile voice-based personal-assistance service, from a proprietary public cloud to its home-grown cloud infrastructure. This migration has led to service performance improvement and reduced management cost. However, Samsung's own cloud infrastructure is small in scale and serves only a special purpose. Therefore, whether it can scale out to host various other services is questionable.

Some organizations have considered forming a community that shares cloud infrastructure and management resources. In this model, the community members can share their cloud resources with one another. In addition, the shared cloud resources can be offered to nonmembers to drive extra revenue. Recently, companies such as IBM and Samsung have teamed up to push for the community cloud-computing initiatives [8]. However, there are many hurdles ahead, such as crafting an optimal policy for sharing compute and management resources among the participants.

Whereas the aforementioned concerns are related to the cost and efficiency issues, many cloud users have also expressed their fears about the security and privacy breach. For example, a number of private photos of celebrities were leaked from Apple's iCloud in 2014 [9]. Since then, Samsung Electronics has had a hard time mobilizing on-device personal data to the cloud for analytics service because many device owners strongly demand privacy protection. These concerns hamper the effort of advancing personalized intelligence services because the collection of private data is critical for the quality of such services.

In the remainder of this chapter, we present a novel cloud-computing framework that improves both the scalability and the privacy-protection mechanism. At a high level, this framework leverages the compute and storage resources on the smart mobile devices. Also, this framework enables security solutions that protect privacy without degrading the quality of applications. Note that we focus on the applications that offer personalized intelligence service. Therefore, we demonstrate how the selected real-world intelligence applications take advantage of the new cloud-computing framework.

3.3 DEVICE/CLOUD COLLABORATION FRAMEWORK

In this section, we present a novel framework that enables collaboration between smart mobile devices and cloud for a more scalable and secure computing mechanism.

3.3.1 POWERFUL SMART MOBILE DEVICES

In 2014, more than 1 billion smartphones were sold worldwide, and more than 2 billion consumers are expected to get a smartphone by 2016 [10]. Smartphones[a] nowadays have enough computing capacity to process various computing tasks. However, the device usage can be constrained by limited battery life and network connectivity. Therefore, we can consider utilizing the highly available cloud resources in addition to the device.

In Fig. 3.1, we have illustrated a high-level layout of our device/cloud collaboration framework. In the following section, we will explain how the framework functions to address the aforementioned concerns on performance and privacy.

---

[a]We will focus on the smartphones as the representative smart mobile devices. In the remainder of this chapter, the term *device* will actually refer to smartphones.

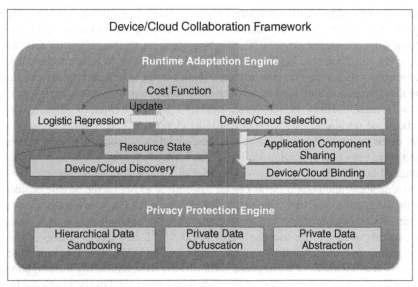

FIGURE 3.1 High-Level Layout of the Device/Cloud Collaboration Framework

3.3.2 RUNTIME ADAPTATION ENGINE

Given a computation task, our framework first faces a problem of choosing the entity to execute the task. Suppose we are given a task of processing a query issued over voice, and assume that we have a lightweight mobile version of a voice-query processing engine that is embedded in a smartphone. This mobile engine can answer the given query without the cost of transferring the voice data to the cloud over the network. However, it will consume the limited battery life of the device, and/or the accuracy of the result may not necessarily be as good as that of the cloud-based query processing engine, which runs on resources with higher compute capacity. If the lightweight voice-query engine returns a poor result, then the user may have to issue the query redundantly to the cloud-based query processing engine with the hope of getting a better result. This may hurt the overall quality of experience (QoE). This calls for a decision mechanism that automatically selects a better *agent* that can execute a given task. With the automatic selection process in place, users do not have to worry about going through extra interaction cycles for determining where to run a job.

Note that the *Runtime Adaptation Engine* (RAE) sits at the core of our framework, as shown in Fig. 3.1. The RAE maintains a list of available devices and cloud to utilize *Device/Cloud Discovery*, and monitors the state of their available resources. The RAE employs a *Logistic Regression* [11] algorithm to learn the most cost-effective policy for distributing tasks among devices and cloud, given the resource state. Here, the definition of the cost function is the weighted sum of the resource state (such as battery life), network, and CPU usage. The policy obtained by running the Logistic Regression is enforced by the *Device/Cloud Selection* module that chooses the most economical compute resources, based on the expected cost-value for a given task.

The mechanism of the RAE is actually an autonomous agent, which can be deployed on each device and cloud. RAEs communicate with each other to transparently share the resource state for determining the ways to distribute a given workload. The cloud-side RAE can also model its own cost function as a weighted sum of residual CPU cycles and storage space across the entire infrastructure. If the residual capacity falls below particular thresholds, the cloud may have to reject the resource-sharing request coming from the paired devices. This is because running the requested task would be too costly. Specifically, the cloud-side RAE advises the device-side RAE to either execute the task within the device or simply wait for the compute resource on the cloud to be freed up. As mentioned earlier, the RAEs on the devices and the cloud make decisions *autonomously*, without any supporting brokerage system in the middle. However, the device-side RAE has the burden of periodically monitoring the state of the cloud resources. On the other hand, the cloud-side RAE does not have to monitor the resource state of the millions of paired devices, as the cloud makes a relatively simple decision, that is, to either reject or accept a task-execution request. By default, our framework does not consider offloading cloud-initiated tasks to the devices. However, later in Section 3.4, we will show a case where the original cloud-side application components can be customized to run on the mobile devices.

We have focused on the case where the user's task is distributed between a *single* device and cloud. However, a recent study has revealed that more than 60% of the online-service users use at least two devices daily, and about 25% of the users use three devices [12]. This fact motivates us to consider the collaboration among devices, as well as through machine to machine (M2M) communication channels, such as Samsung's *AllShare* Convergence solution [13]. By considering the neighboring devices as well, the overall compute resource availability increases further, and the computation burden on the cloud can be reduced significantly. To support task distribution among the neighboring devices, the device/cloud collaboration framework implements discovery of devices (*Device/Cloud Discovery* in Fig. 3.1). Suppose a device (device-A) wants to collaborate with its neighboring device (device-B), which is not equipped with appropriate application components to process a given task. Then, device-A can transfer the necessary application components to device-B through the *Application Component Sharing* (shown in Fig. 3.1).

3.3.3 PRIVACY-PROTECTION SOLUTION

So far, we have focused on the aspects of the device/cloud collaboration framework that are concerned with performance and efficiency. Now, we turn our attention to the privacy-protection problem. Suppose we want to provide a location-based service to the users. To provide this service, location data such as the visited GPS coordinates, the point of interest (POI), and the time of visit have to be collected first. Based on these location data, the mobility pattern and the interest of individual users can be inferred. However, these data contain personal information. Hence, for these data, we can ask the user to decide whether to transfer them to cloud or not when accepting the location-based service. Based on the decision made by the user, our framework can assess the expected service-quality for the users. Suppose a user wants to transfer to the cloud a blurred location log with entries that are simply labeled either <at home> or <not at home>. Given this log with little detail, it is difficult to expect a service provider to offer a useful location-based recommendation. In such a case, our framework warns the user that disallowing the sharing of detailed private information would result in poor service quality.

Our framework employs the technology of protecting privacy by sandboxing hierarchically organized application-data [14]. This technology, implemented in the *Hierarchical Data Sandboxing* module (in Fig. 3.1), supports the user to explicitly specify a group of data in the hierarchy to be shared with the cloud or not. The group of data that is set to be kept only within a device will be protected by sandboxing. Although this approach supports a specification of fine-grained privacy-protection policies, such a declarative approach would be too cumbersome for many typical users. Thus, we can seek an alternative solution of obfuscating (encrypting) data to be transferred to the neighboring devices or to the cloud (*Data Obfuscation* in Fig. 3.1). A natural solution is to encrypt the data upon transferring to cloud [15]. However, the encrypted data can be revealed through decryption-key theft from the compromised servers on the cloud or by spoofing on the tapped network. For these security threats, the cost of countermeasures, such as secret (eg, decryption keys) sharing across replicated servers, is nonnegligible [16]. Instead, we can have a lighter approach of letting the cloud analyze the obfuscated data without deciphering it, and letting the device revert the obfuscated part of the analysis result generated at the cloud side. For instance, suppose a user wants to receive a location-based recommendation based on the personal log of visited POIs. Both the POI itself and the time of POI visits are first obfuscated on the device side. The mapping between the original data and the encrypted data is kept on the device side. The device sends over the encrypted data to the cloud that does not have a decryption key to decipher the encrypted data. On the cloud side, data analytics such as causal reasoning through sequence mining [17] are conducted, based on the encrypted information (eg, POIs and time of visits). For example, suppose a user has the following entries in the location log, as shown in Table 3.1. Each entry contains the mapping between the original data and the encrypted data.

Note that the cloud has to be aware of the data format, that is, the data contains POI and the time of visits. Assume that the sequence-mining engine on the cloud side infers the frequent mobility pattern that the user visits: `b731d61a5be2b9035a20ebef5aa9bfef` (actually Bryant Park) after the user visits: `24e3b66da54d1e21b177ea3351a0e4c2` (actually Starbucks). The cloud notifies this inference result to the device without knowing the actual private content. Once the device receives this result, it deciphers the content by checking the mapping between the encrypted data and the original data. Given the inferred mobility pattern, the device can invoke a third-party recommendation service to receive a list of recommended activities or events around Bryant Park whenever the user is about to leave Starbucks. Here, we assume a threat model that the third-party recommendation service independently enforces its own security measures to prevent the leakage of private queries, and the device itself is safe from being compromised.

Another approach is abstracting given data to hide the details, as shown in Table 3.2.

Table 3.1 A Mapping Between Original and Encrypted Location Data

Original Data	Encrypted Data
Starbucks on 575 5th Avenue, New York, NY, 11 am, Jan. 15th, 2015	`24e3b66da54d1e21b177ea3351a0e4c2,` `a44cdcecb384fd730553e59eed867e63`
Bryant Park in New York, NY, 1 pm, Jan. 15th, 2015	`b731d61a5be2b9035a20ebef5aa9bfef,` `84d9cfc2f395ce883a41d7ffc1bbcf4e`

Table 3.2 Mapping Between the Original and Abstracted Location Data

Original Data	Abstracted Data
Starbucks on 575 5th Avenue, New York, NY, 11 am, Jan. 15th, 2015	Café in the morning
Bryant Park in New York, NY, 1 pm, Jan. 15th, 2015	Public park in the afternoon

For example, a visit to *Starbucks on 575 5th Avenue, New York, NY at 11 am* can be abstracted as a visit to *a café in the morning*. The benefit of this approach is that it can generate recommendations directly on the cloud upon recognition of the frequent visiting patterns. However, the accuracy of the recommendation can be compromised due to the loss of detailed information.

3.4 APPLICATIONS OF DEVICE/CLOUD COLLABORATION

In this section, we show how our framework can be used by the real-world intelligence applications developed specifically at Samsung Electronics. The selected applications offer the following functionalities: *context-aware proactive suggestion, semantic QA caching, and automatic image/speech recognition*. We introduce the interesting practical engineering experiences of adapting the application in order to leverage the framework in the most effective manner.

3.4.1 CONTEXT-AWARE PROACTIVE SUGGESTION

Based on the personal data collected on each mobile device, we have devised Proactive Suggestion (PS), an application that makes context-aware recommendations. In Fig. 3.2, the individual components of the PS are laid out.

Analytics engines of PS produce hierarchical personal data that are interdependent to each other. Raw data such as GPS coordinates, call logs, application usage, and search queries are fed to a *Cooccurrence Analysis* engine, which is responsible for identifying activities that occurred at the same

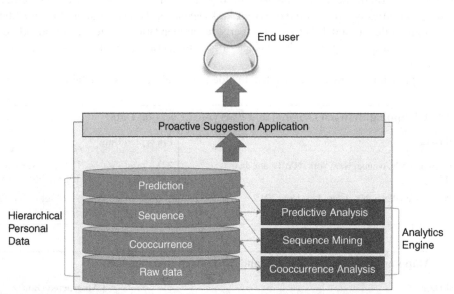

FIGURE 3.2 High-Level Layout of the Core Components for the Proactive Suggestion Application

Analytics engines process personal data to produce contextual data that are used for multilevel recommendations to the end user.

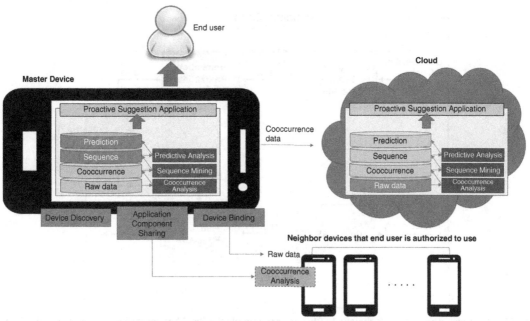

FIGURE 3.3 An Example of Utilizing the Device-Collaboration Framework for the Proactive Suggestion Application

time [18]. For example, the cooccurrence analysis engine may recognize that a user listens to live streaming music *while* walking in the park. Given such cooccurrence data, the *Sequence Mining* engine can infer causal relationships between personal activities that occurred over time [19]. The recognized sequential patterns can be fed into the *Predictive Analysis* engine to assess the probability of a particular activity taking place in a certain context [19].

Fig. 3.3 illustrates how PS implements the device/cloud collaboration framework. The master device can discover neighboring devices that the end user is authorized to use (*Device Discovery*). The master device can send over the data to one of the neighboring devices that has sufficient compute capacity (*Device Binding*). The neighboring device can retrieve an appropriate analytics engine for processing the data sent by the master device (*Application Component Sharing*). In this example, the highlighted pieces of data on the master device are shared between cloud and neighboring devices.

Note that the PS application initially opted for the *Hierarchical Data Sandboxing* for an explicit and declarative privacy-protection method. We could not afford to run an alternative privacy-protection method based on the data obfuscation, due to the limited resources on the device that was already bogged down by the analytics work. However, recall that our framework is flexible enough to allow user-defined cost functions. For example, if the cost of running an analytics operation (eg, the cost of consuming battery life) is excessive, then the *Device/Cloud Selection* module in the framework may decide to transfer the analytics task to the cloud or simply wait for the battery level to rise above the configured thresholds. It turned out that transferring the data over the network consumed as much energy as running the analytics operation within the device. Thus, the *Device/Cloud Selection* module opted for waiting until the battery got charged above the configured level.

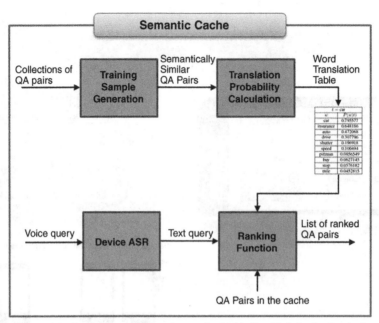

FIGURE 3.4 Illustrations of the Technique to Cluster Semantically Similar QA Pairs for Retrieving an Answer for a Newly Given Query Without Asking the QA Engine on the Cloud Side

3.4.2 SEMANTIC QA CACHE

Semantic QA cache is a mobile application that retrieves answers to a given query from the cache filled with answers to the semantically similar queries issued in the past. Semantic QA cache can be useful when there is no Internet connectivity or when the user is not in favor of transferring private queries to the cloud. Fig. 3.4 illustrates how the semantic QA cache is managed. Semantic QA cache returns a list of similar queries and the associated answers. Semantic QA cache constantly updates ranking function based on the word-translation table as explained in [20]. The ranking function measures the similarity between a newly issued query and the queries measured in the past.

In Fig. 3.5, we have demonstrated the implementation of the device/cloud collaboration framework by the semantic QA cache. Specifically, we have devised a custom ASR (Automatic Speech Recognition) engine for the mobile device and incorporated the cloud system for Samsung S Voice in the collaboration framework. The cloud system for S Voice consists of a Natural Language Understanding (NLU) module for query understanding, a DM (Dialog Manager) module for query answering, and a powerful ASR engine.

Note that we have adapted the framework to compute the probability of the on-device semantic QA cache to answer a given query correctly. If the probability is high enough, the *Device/Cloud Selection* module will take the risk of looking up the semantic QA cache for an answer. If the cache does not return the right answer and forces the user to ask the cloud again, then our framework will adjust the probability accordingly.

We evaluated the performance benefit of using the device/cloud collaboration framework for semantic QA cache. From the log of our voice-based QA application, we obtained the top-50 frequently issued queries about weather, restaurants, people, and device-specific commands. We selected a random query from the set according to uniformly random distribution (Method 1) and Zipf distribution

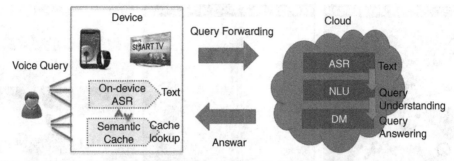

FIGURE 3.5 Semantic QA Cache Implementing the Device/Cloud Collaboration Framework

(Method 2). The latency of getting the response for a query was tested on the cloud-only mode and the device/cloud collaboration mode. In the cloud-only mode, server-version of Google Voice API was used for ASR, and DBpedia and Freebase were used for query answering. In the device/cloud collaboration mode, a custom-made ASR engine and semantic QA cache were used, along with a cloud-based QA service. Leveraging the device/cloud collaboration improved performance for both types of query workloads. The latency was reduced by 56.7 and 69.5% for Method 1 and Method 2, respectively.

3.4.3 IMAGE AND SPEECH RECOGNITION

Automatically recognizing images and speech can greatly enhance a user's experience in using applications. For example, with automatic image recognition, photos taken by a user can be automatically tagged with metadata and catalogued more easily. Similar to Amazon's Firefly [21], we have developed an application called Watch&Go, which lets users obtain detailed information about a product upon taking a photograph. Fig. 3.6 shows the snapshot of Watch&Go that guides users to properly focus on some electronics products, and automatically retrieve information such as type, vendor, model name, and the result of social sentiment about the product.

Practicality of these recognition applications has greatly improved, thanks to the recent advancement of Deep Learning (DL). The DL follows the approach of learning the correlation between the parameters across multiple layers of perceptron [22]. However, DL model training methods usually suffer a slow learning curve compared to the other conventional machine-learning methods. Although it is generally believed that the larger DL model improves the recognition accuracy through a set of well-refined training data, it has been challenging to acquire adequate parameters when we train multiple layers at the same time. The recent appearance of the Restricted Boltzmann Machine (RBM) method, which enables layer-wise and unsupervised training, can relax the aforementioned limitations to some degree. However, the overall computational overhead is still formidable, even for the cloud with abundant compute resources. This performance issue has motivated us to utilize our device/cloud collaboration framework as follows.

Through our framework, the compute-intensive part of DL (ie, the training) is assigned to cloud. Once the learning completes, our framework ports the recognition model to the device for the actual execution of the recognition task. Specifically, we used an *ImageNet-1000* model that was constructed based on a Convolutional Neural Networking (CNN) [23,24] method. With this model, classification of up to 1000 different objects is possible. However, an open-source image-classifier (OpenCV) on an Android device took more than 20 s to classify an object with ImageNet-1000. This was due to the

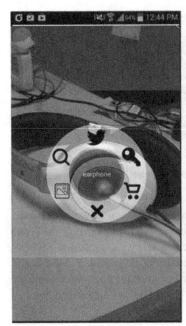

FIGURE 3.6 An Example of Automatically Tagging Recognized Images and Displaying Additional Information Such as Social Sentiment (eg, Positive or Negative Reviews)

inefficient matrix multiplication on the device. We have overcome this problem by parallelizing the matrix multiplication based on OpenCL [25], resulting in the classification latency dropping to an average of 400 ms per object. By utilizing the low-latency on-device image classifier on millions of pre-deployed mobile devices, we were able to reduce the computational burden on the cloud significantly.

We have achieved similar performance improvement for speech-recognition application with DL through our device/cloud collaboration framework. Specifically, we first extracted 400-h worth of speech data from Fisher Corpus. Contrary to the image-recognition problem, we have employed a Deep Neural Network (DNN) model, which is shown to be effective in constructing an accurate acoustic model [26]. Similar to image recognition, we have assigned the acoustic model-construction task and the classification task to cloud and mobile devices, respectively. Specifically, we ported Kaldi [27] to an Android device in order to process a speech-recognition request based on the constructed acoustic model. The task separation through our device/cloud collaboration framework and the additional acceleration through OpenCL helped us obtain the recognition result within 0.9 RT (Real Time),[b] which is a tolerable delay for the end users.

We could relieve the computational burden on the cloud side further by splitting the learning portion. Lightweight models can be constructed within a mobile device. However, the classification accuracy can be compromised when these models are used. We have observed that the tolerant accuracy level varies between different end-users. Hence, our framework can be adapted to learn the personal tolerance level and determine which model to construct accordingly.

---

[b]1RT is the criteria which decides the applicability of speech recognition (the lesser value is the better).

3.5 FUTURE WORK

Various ways of componentizing a given intelligence application come with different trade-offs. A more fine-grained componentization, as shown in the PS application, may yield more efficient task distribution among neighboring devices and cloud. Also, fine-grained privacy-protection policies can be applied to these components. However, computing more efficient task distribution incurs additional overhead. It may cost relatively lower overhead to determine execution entities for the coarse-grained. But it can be nontrivial to port a cloud-side coarse-grained component to a resource-limited device when it is deemed necessary. Even if the coarse-grained component is tailored to fit in the device, the quality of the component may degrade. As a future work, we plan to study the effect of different componentization strategies in various application scenarios and guide the developers to pick the best strategy that maximizes collaboration performance.

3.6 CONCLUSIONS

We have presented the benefits of using a collaborative computation framework between devices and cloud through the case studies of selected real-world intelligence applications devised at Samsung Electronics. Applications that implement the device/cloud collaboration framework can yield high performance, such as reduced latency in processing a user's request. In addition, the cost of managing the cloud can be reduced when the compute resources on the millions of smart mobile devices are utilized. Aside from the benefits in terms of cost and performance, the framework helps the application protect privacy of the end users by either processing personal data within a device or analyzing the obfuscated version of the personal data on cloud.

ACKNOWLEDGMENTS

This chapter is derived from the authors' work from The Grand Bleu Project that was conducted by Intelligence Solution Team (IST) at Samsung Electronics in 2014. We would like to thank Dr Kilsu Eo, who directed IST and initiated The Grand Bleu Project. We are also grateful for the guidance provided by the project leaders, Dr Honguk Woo and Dr Sangho Shin.

REFERENCES

[1] Amazon Elastic Compute Cloud (Amazon EC2). https://aws.amazon.com/ec2
[2] Microsoft Azure: Cloud Computing Platform & Services. https://azure.microsoft.com
[3] Google Now. https://www.google.com/landing/now
[4] Wang C, Raina R, Fong D, Zhou D, Han J, Badros G. Learning relevance from a heterogeneous social network and its application in online targeting. In: Proceedings of the thirty-fourth international ACM SIGIR conference on research and development in information retrieval. Beijing, China, July 24–28, 2011.
[5] Backstrom L, Sun E, Marlow C. In: Proceedings of the nineteenth international conference on World Wide Web, Raleigh, NC, USA, April 26–30, 2010.
[6] Sotomayor B, Montero R, Llorente I, Foster I. Virtual infrastructure management in private and hybrid clouds. IEEE Internet Comput 2009;13(5):14–22.

[7] Bossche R, Vanmechelen K, Broeckhove J. Cost-optimal scheduling in hybrid IaaS clouds for deadline constrained workloads. In: Proceedings of the 2010 IEEE third international conference on cloud computing, Miami, FL, USA, July 5–10, 2010.

[8] Briscoe G, Marinos A. Digital ecosystems in the clouds: towards community cloud computing. In: Proceedings of the third IEEE international conference on digital ecosystems and technologies. Istanbul, Turkey, June 1–3, 2009.

[9] 2014 Celebrity Photo Hack. https://en.wikipedia.org/wiki/2014_celebrity_photo_hack

[10] emarketer.com. http://www.emarketer.com/Article/2-Billion-Consumers-Worldwide-Smartphones-by-2016/1011694

[11] Cox DR. The regression analysis of binary sequences. J R Stat Soc Ser B Methodol 1958;20(2):215–42.

[12] Econsultancy.com. https://econsultancy.com/blog/64464-more-than-40-of-online-adults-are-multi-device-users-stats/

[13] Samsung AllShare Play. http://www.samsung.com/us/2012-allshare-play/

[14] Lee S, Wong E, Goel D, Dahlin M, Shmatikov V. PiBox: a platform for privacy preserving apps. In: Proceedings of the 2013 tenth USENIX conference on networked system design and implementation, Lambard, IL, USA, April 2–5, 2013.

[15] Pearson S, Shen Y, Mowbray M. A privacy manager for cloud computing. In: Proceedings of the first international conference on cloud computing. Bangalore, India, September 21–25, 2009.

[16] Itani W, Kayssi A, Chehab A. Privacy as a service: privacy-aware data storage and processing in cloud computing architectures. In: Proceedings of the eighth IEEE international conference on dependable, autonomic and secure computing. Chengdu, China, December 12–14, 2009.

[17] Agrawal R, Srikant R. Mining sequential patterns. In: Proceedings of the eleventh international conference on data engineering. Taipei, Taiwan, March 6–10, 1995.

[18] Srinivasan V, Moghaddam S, Mukherji A, Rachuri KK, Xu C, Tapia EM. MobileMiner: mining your frequent patterns on your phone. In: Proceedings of the 2014 ACM international joint conference on pervasive and ubiquitous computing. Seattle, USA, September 13–17, 2014.

[19] Mukherji A, Srinivasan V, Welbourne E. Adding intelligence to your mobile device via on-device sequential pattern mining. In: Proceedings of the 2014 ACM international joint conference on pervasive and ubiquitous computing: adjunct publication. Seattle, USA, September 13–17, 2014.

[20] Xue X, Jeon J, Croft W. Retrieval models for question and answer archives. In: Proceedings of the thirty-first annual international ACM SIGIR conference on research and development in information retrieval. Singapore, July 20–24, 2008.

[21] Amazon Firefly. https://developer.amazon.com/public/solutions/devices/fire-phone/docs/understanding-firefly

[22] Bengio Y, Goodfellow I, Courville A. Deep learning. USA: MIT Press; 2015.

[23] Hinton G. A practical guide to training restricted Boltzmann machine. Technical Report UTML TR 2010-003, Dept. of Computer Science, Univ. of Toronto; 2010.

[24] Krizhevsky A, Sutskever I, Hinton G. ImageNet classification with deep convolutional neural networks. In: Proceedings of the twenty-sixth annual conference on neural information processing systems (NIPS), Lake Tahoe, NV, USA, December 3–8, 2012.

[25] OpenCL (Open Computing Language). https://www.khronos.org/opencl/

[26] Graves A, Mohamed A, Hinton G. Speech recognition with deep recurrent neural networks. In: Proceedings of IEEE international conference on acoustics, speech and signal processing (ICASSP). Vancouver, BC, Canada, May 26–31, 2013.

[27] Kaldi Project. http://kaldi-asr.org/

FOG COMPUTING: PRINCIPLES, ARCHITECTURES, AND APPLICATIONS

4

A.V. Dastjerdi*, H. Gupta**, R.N. Calheiros*, S.K. Ghosh**, R. Buyya*,†

*Cloud Computing and Distributed Systems (CLOUDS) Laboratory, Department of Computing and Information Systems, The University of Melbourne, Australia; **Department of Computer Science and Engineering, Indian Institute of Technology, Kharagpur, India; †Manjrasoft Pty Ltd, Australia

4.1 INTRODUCTION

Internet of Things (IoT) environments consist of loosely connected devices that are connected through heterogeneous networks. In general, the purpose of building such environments is to collect and process data from IoT devices in order to mine and detect patterns, or perform predictive analysis or optimization, and finally make smarter decisions in a timely manner. Data in such environments can be classified into two categories [1]:

- *Little Data or Big Stream*: transient data that is captured constantly from IoT smart devices
- *Big Data*: persistent data and knowledge that is stored and archived in centralized cloud storage

IoT environments, including smart cities and infrastructures, need both Big Stream and Big Data for effective real-time analytics and decision making. This can enable real-time cities [2] that are capable of real-time analysis of city infrastructure and life, and provides new approaches for governance. At the moment, data is collected and aggregated from IoT networks that consist of smart devices, and is sent uplink to cloud servers, where it is stored and processed. Cloud computing offers a solution at the infrastructure level that supports Big Data Processing. It enables highly scalable computing platforms that can be configured on demand to meet constant changes of application requirements in a pay-per-use mode, reducing the investment necessary to build the desired analytics application. As mentioned previously, this perfectly matches requirements of Big Data processing when data is stored in centralized cloud storage. In such a case, processing of a large magnitude of data volume is enabled by on-demand scalability of Clouds. However, when data sources are distributed across multiple locations and low latency is indispensable, in-cloud data processing fails to meet the requirements.

4.2 **MOTIVATING SCENARIO**

A recent analysis [3] of Endomondo application, a popular sport-activity tracking application, has revealed a number of remarkable observations. The study shows that a single workout generates 170 GPS tuples, and the total number of GPS tuples can reach 6.3 million in a month's time. With 30 million users (as shown in Fig. 4.1), the study shows that generated data flows of Endomondo can reach up to 25,000 tuples per second. Therefore, one can expect that data flows in real-time cities with many times more data sources—GPS sensors in cars to air- and noise-pollution sensors—can easily reach millions of tuples per second. Centralized cloud servers cannot deal with flows with such velocity in real time. In addition, a considerable numbers of users, due to privacy concerns, are not comfortable to transfer and store activity-track-data into the cloud, even if they require a statistical report on their activities. This motivates the need for an alternative paradigm that is capable of bringing the computation to more computationally capable devices that are geographically closer to the sensors than to the clouds, and that have connectivity to the Internet. Such devices, which are at the *edge of the network* and therefore referred to as *edge devices,* can build local views of data flows and can aggregate data to be sent to the cloud for further offline analysis. To this end, Fog computing has emerged.

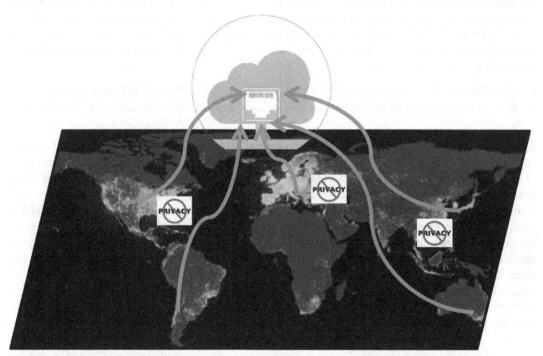

FIGURE 4.1 Endomondo has 30 Million Users Around the Globe, Generating 25,000 Records per Second

Centralized processing of the data flow of this magnitude neither satisfies latency constraints of users nor their privacy constraints.

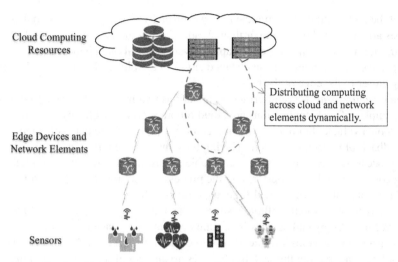

FIGURE 4.2 Fog Computing is a Distributed Computing Paradigm That Extends the Cloud Services to the Edge of the Network

4.3 DEFINITIONS AND CHARACTERISTICS

We define Fog computing as a distributed computing paradigm that fundamentally extends the services provided by the cloud to the edge of the network (as shown in Fig. 4.2). It facilitates management and programming of compute, networking, and storage services between data centers and end devices. Fog computing essentially involves components of an application running both in the cloud as well as in edge devices between sensors and the cloud, that is, in smart gateways, routers, or dedicated fog devices. Fog computing supports mobility, computing resources, communication protocols, interface heterogeneity, cloud integration, and distributed data analytics to address requirements of applications that need low latency with a wide and dense geographical distribution.

Advantages associated with Fog computing including the following:

- *Reduction of network traffic:* Cisco estimates that there are currently 25 billion connected devices worldwide, a number that could jump to 50 billion by 2020. The billions of mobile devices such as smart phones and tablets already being used to generate, receive, and send data make a case for putting the computing capabilities closer to where devices are located, rather than having all data sent over networks to central data centers. Depending on the configured frequency, sensors may collect data every few seconds. Therefore, it is neither efficient nor sensible to send all of this raw data to the cloud. Hence, fog computing benefits here by providing a platform for filter and analysis of the data generated by these devices close to the edge, and for generation of local data views. This drastically reduces the traffic being sent to the cloud.
- *Suitable for IoT tasks and queries:* With the increasing number of smart devices, most of the requests pertain to the surroundings of the device. Hence, such requests can be served without the help of the global information present at the cloud. For example, the aforementioned sports-tracker application Endomondo allows a user to locate people playing a similar sport nearby.

Because of the local nature of the typical requests made by this application, it makes sense that the requests are processed in fog rather than cloud infrastructure. Another example can be a smart-connected vehicle which needs to capture events only about a hundred meters from it. Fog computing makes the communication distance closer to the physical distance by bringing the processing closer to the edge of the network.

- *Low-latency requirement:* Mission-critical applications require real-time data processing. Some of the best examples of such applications are cloud robotics, control of fly-by-wire aircraft, or anti-lock brakes on a vehicle. For a robot, motion control depends on the data collected by the sensors and the feedback of the control system. Having the control system running on the cloud may make the sense-process-actuate loop slow or unavailable as a result of communication failures. This is where fog computing helps, by performing the processing required for the control system very close to the robots—thus making real-time response possible.
- *Scalability:* Even with virtually infinite resources, the cloud may become the bottleneck if all the raw data generated by end devices is continually sent to it. Since fog computing aims at processing incoming data closer to the data source itself, it reduces the burden of that processing on the cloud, thus addressing the scalability issues arising out of the increasing number of endpoints.

4.4 REFERENCE ARCHITECTURE

Fig. 4.3 presents a reference architecture for fog computing. In the bottommost layer lays the end devices (sensors), as well as edge devices and gateways. This layer also includes apps that can be installed in the end devices to enhance their functionality. Elements from this layer use the next layer, the network, for communicating among themselves, and between them and the cloud. The next layer contains the cloud services and resources that support resource management and processing of IoT tasks that reach the cloud. On top of the cloud layer lays the resource management software that manages the whole infrastructure and enables quality of Service to Fog Computing applications. Finally, the topmost layer contains the applications that leverage fog computing to deliver innovative and intelligent applications to end users.

Looking inside the Software-Defined Resource Management layer, it implements many middleware-like services to optimize the use of the cloud and Fog resources on behalf of the applications. The goal of these services is to reduce the cost of using the cloud at the same time that performance of applications reach acceptable levels of latency, by pushing task execution to Fog nodes. This is achieved with a number of services working together, as follows.

- *Flow and task placement:* This component keeps track of the state of available cloud, Fog, and network resources (information provided by the Monitoring service) to identify the best candidates to hold incoming tasks and flows for execution. This component communicates with the Resource-Provisioning service to indicate the current number of flows and tasks, which may trigger new rounds of allocations if deemed too high.
- *Knowledge Base:* This component stores historical information about application demands and resource demands that can be leveraged by other services to support their decision-making process.

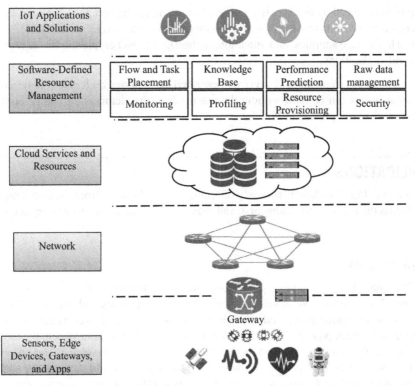

FIGURE 4.3 Fog Computing Reference Architecture

- *Performance Prediction:* This service utilizes information of the Knowledge- Base service to estimate the performance of available cloud resources. This information is used by the Resource-Provisioning service to decide the amount of resources to be provisioned, in times where there are a large number of tasks and flows in use or when performance is not satisfactory.
- *Raw-Data Management:* This service has direct access to the data sources and provides views from the data for other services. Sometimes, these views can be obtained by simple querying (eg, SQL or NOSQL REST APIs), whereas other times more complex processing may be required (eg, MapReduce). Nevertheless, the particular method for generation of the view is abstracted away from other services.
- *Monitoring:* This service keeps track of the performance and status of applications and services, and supplies this information to other services as required.
- *Profiling:* This service builds resource- and application-profiles based on information obtained from the Knowledge Base and Monitoring services.
- *Resource Provisioning:* This service is responsible for acquiring cloud, Fog, and network resources for hosting the applications. This allocation is dynamic, as the requirements of applications, as well as the number of hosted applications, changes over time. The decision on the number of resources is made with the use of information provided by other services (such as Profiling, Performance Prediction, and Monitoring), and user requirements on latency, as well

as credentials managed by the Security service. For example, the component pushes tasks with low-latency requirements to edge of network as soon as free resources are available.

- *Security:* This service supplies authentication, authorization, and cryptography, as required by services and applications.

Note that all of the elements and services described are reference elements only; complete fog stacks and applications can be built without the use of all of the elements, or can be built with other elements and services not present in Fig. 4.3.

4.5 APPLICATIONS

As demonstrated in Fig. 4.4, there is a variety of applications benefiting from the Fog-computing paradigm. We discuss the major applications first, and then we elaborate more on enablers and related work in the area.

4.5.1 HEALTHCARE

Cao et al. [4] propose FAST, a fog-computing assisted distributed analytics system, to monitor fall for stroke patients. The authors have developed a set of fall-detection algorithms, including algorithms based on acceleration measurements and time-series analysis methods, as well as filtering techniques to facilitate the fall-detection process. They designed a real-time fall-detection system based on fog computing that divides the fall-detection task between edge devices and the cloud. The proposed system achieves a high sensitivity and specificity when tested against real-world data. At the same time, the response time and energy consumption are close to the most efficient existing approaches.

Another use of fog computing in healthcare has been brought out by Stantchev et al. [5]. They proposed a three-tier architecture for a smart-healthcare infrastructure, comprised of a role model, layered-cloud architecture, and a fog-computing layer, in order to provide an efficient architecture for healthcare and elderly-care applications. The fog layer improves the architecture by providing low latency, mobility support, location awareness, and security measures. The process flow of the healthcare application is modeled using Business Process Model and Notation (BPMN) and is then mapped to devices via a service-oriented approach. The validity of the architectural model has been demonstrated by a use case as a template for a smart sensor-based healthcare infrastructure.

4.5.2 AUGMENTED REALITY

Augmented reality applications are highly latency-intolerant, as even very small delays in response can damage the user experience. Hence, fog computing has the potential to become a major player in the augmented reality domain. Zao et al. [6] built an Augmented Brain Computer Interaction Game based on Fog Computing and Linked Data. When a person plays the game, raw streams of data collected by EEG sensors are generated and classified to detect the brain state of the player. Brain-state classification is among the most computationally heavy signal-processing tasks, but this needs to be carried out in real time. The system employs both fog and cloud servers, a combination that enables the system to perform continuous real-time brain-state classification at the fog servers, while the classification models are tuned regularly in the cloud servers, based on the EEG readings collected by the sensors.

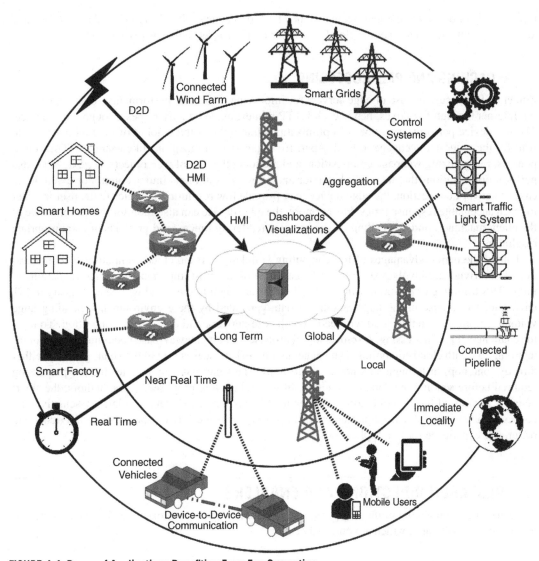

FIGURE 4.4 Range of Applications Benefiting From Fog Computing

Ha et al. [7] propose a Wearable Cognitive Assistance system based on Google Glass devices that assist people with reduced mental acuity. Because of the nature of cognitive devices with con-strained resources, the compute-intensive workloads of this application need to be offloaded to an ex-ternal server. However, this offloading must provide crisp, real-time responses; failing to do so would be detrimental to the user experience. Offloading the compute-intensive tasks to the cloud incurs a considerable latency, thus the authors make use of nearby devices. These devices may communicate with the cloud for delay-tolerant jobs like error reporting and logging. The aforementioned works are typical applications of fog computing, in that they perform latency-critical analysis at the very edge and latency-tolerant computation at the cloud—thus portraying fog as an extension of cloud.

4.5.3 CACHING AND PREPROCESSING

Zhu et al. [8] discuss the use of edge servers for improving web sites' performance. Users connect to the Internet through fog boxes, hence each HTTP request made by a user goes through a fog device. The fog device performs a number of optimizations that reduces the amount of time the user has to wait for the requested webpage to load. Apart from generic optimizations like caching HTML components, reorganizing webpage composition, and reducing the size of web objects, edge devices also perform optimizations that take user behavior and network conditions into account. For example, in case of network congestion, the edge device may provide low resolution graphics to the user in order to reach acceptable response times. Furthermore, the edge device can also monitor the performance of the client machines, and, depending on the browser rendering times, send graphics of an appropriate resolution.

One of the major advantages of fog computing is linking IoT and cloud computing. This integration is not trivial and involves several challenges. One of the most important challenges is data trimming. This trimming or pre-processing of data before sending it to the cloud will be a necessity in IoT environments because of the huge amount of data generated by these environments. Sending huge volumes of raw data to the cloud will lead to both core-network and data-center congestion. To meet the challenge of pre-processing, Aazam et al. [9] propose a smart gateway-based communication for integrating IoT with cloud computing. Data generated by IoT devices is sent to the smart gateway, either directly (one-hop) or through sink nodes (multi-hop). The smart gateway handles the pre-processing required before sending the data to the cloud. In the architecture proposed by the authors, the smart gateway is assisted by fog-computing services for operations on IoT data in a latency-sensitive and context-aware manner. Such a communication approach paves the way for the creation of a richer and better user experience for IoT applications.

4.6 RESEARCH DIRECTIONS AND ENABLERS

To realize the full potential of the Fog paradigm, researchers and practitioners need to address the following major challenges, which are outlined next.

4.6.1 PROGRAMMING MODELS

Computation offloading has been an active area of research in the mobile computing domain, with most of the proposals offloading workloads to the cloud [7,10,11]. Since offloading to the cloud may not always be possible or reasonable, Orsini et al. [12] propose an adaptive Mobile Edge Computing (MEC) programming framework named CloudAware [12], which offloads tasks to edge devices, thus facilitating the development of elastic and scalable edge-based mobile applications. The authors present the types of components that an MEC application should be broken into, so that the offloading decision is simplified. The framework offloads tasks, with objectives to: (1) speed up computation, (2) save energy, (3) save bandwidth, or (4) provide low latency.

The most fundamental development in the realm of Fog Computing has been made by Mobile Fog [13], an API for developing futuristic applications, which leverages the large-scale, geo-distribution, and low-latency guarantee provided by the fog-computing infrastructure. The proposed architecture is a hierarchy similar to the one demonstrated in Fig. 4.3. An application built using the proposed API has several components, each one running on a different level in the hierarchy of devices.

4.6.2 SECURITY AND RELIABILITY

Enforcing security protocols over a distributed system such as a fog is one of the most important challenges in its realization. Stojmenovic et al. [14] discuss the major security issues in fog computing. They point out that calling authentication at various levels of fog nodes is the main security challenge. Authentication solutions based on Public Key Infrastructure [1] may prove beneficial for this problem. Trusted execution environment (TEE) techniques [2,3] are potential solutions to this authentication problem in fog computing as well. Measurement-based methods may also be used to detect rogue devices and hence reduce authentication cost [3,15].

Dsouza et al. [16] describe the research challenges in policy management for fog computing, and propose a policy-driven security-management approach, including policy analysis and its integration with a fog-computing paradigm. Such an approach is critical for supporting secure sharing and data reuse in heterogeneous Fog environments. The authors also present a use case on Smart Transportation Systems to highlight the efficiency of the proposed approach.

Since fog computing is realized by the integration of a large number of geographically distributed devices and connections, reliability is one of the prime concerns when designing such a system. Madsen et al. [17] discuss the reliability issues associated with fog computing. They point out that for a reliable fog paradigm it is essential to plan for failure of individual sensors, network, service platform, and the application. To this end, the current reliability protocols for WSNs can be applied. They majorly deal with packet reliability and event reliability. The most basic facts about sensors, in general, are not that they are expensive, but that their readings can be affected by noise; in this case the information-accuracy problem can be resolved by redundancy.

4.6.3 RESOURCE MANAGEMENT

Fog devices are often network devices equipped with additional storage and compute power. However, it is difficult for such devices to match the resource capacity of traditional servers, let alone the cloud. Hence a judicious management of resources is essential for an efficient operation of a fog-computing environment. Aazam et al. [18] present a service-oriented resource management model for fog computing, which performs efficient and fair management of resources for IoT deployments. The proposed resource-management framework predicts the resource usage of customers and pre-allocates resources based on user behavior and the probability of using it in the future. This prediction allows greater fairness and efficiency when the resources are actually consumed. Lewis et al. [19] present resource-provisioning mechanisms for tactical cloudlets, a strategy for providing infrastructure to support computation offloading and data staging at the tactical edge. Cloudlets are discoverable, generic, stateless servers located in single-hop proximity of mobile devices, which can operate in disconnected mode, and are virtual-machine (VM) based to promote flexibility, mobility, scalability, and elasticity [20]. In other words, tactical cloudlet refers to the scenario when cloudlets serve as fog devices in order to provide infrastructure to offload computation, provide forward data-staging for a mission, perform data filtering to remove unnecessary data from streams intended for dismounted users, and serve as collection points for data heading for enterprise repositories. Tasks running on cloudlets are executed on Service VMs. The authors propose various policies for provisioning VMs on cloudlets, each policy having a unique implication on payload sent to cloudlet, application-ready time, and client energy spent. In addition, mechanisms for cloudlet discovery and application execution have also been laid out.

4.6.4 ENERGY MINIMIZATION

Since fog environments involve the deployment of a large number of fog nodes, the computation is essentially distributed and can be less energy-efficient than the centralized-cloud-model of computation. Hence the reduction of energy consumption in fog computing is an important challenge. Deng et al. [14] study the trade-off between power consumption and delay in a fog-computing system. They model the power consumption and delay functions for the fog system and formalize the problem of allocating workloads between the fog and cloud. Simulation results show that fog computing can significantly cut down the communication latency by incurring slightly greater energy consumption.

Do et al. [1] study a related problem, namely, joint resource allocation and reduction of energy consumption for video-streaming service in fog computing. Since the number of fog devices is enormous, a distributed solution for the problem has been proposed to eliminate performance and scalability issues. The algorithm is based on proximal algorithms, a powerful method for solving distributed convex-optimization problems. The proposed algorithm has a fast convergence rate with a reasonable solution quality.

4.7 COMMERCIAL PRODUCTS
4.7.1 CISCO IOx

Cisco is a pioneer in the field of fog computing, so much so, that the term "fog computing" was actually introduced by Cisco itself. Cisco's offering for fog computing, known as IOx, is a combination of an industry-leading networking operating system, IOS, and the most popular open-source Operating System, Linux. Ruggedized routers running Cisco IOx make compute and storage available to applications hosted in a Guest Operating System running on a hypervisor alongside the IOS virtual machine. Cisco provides an app store, which allows users to download applications to the IOx devices, and also an app-management console, which is meant for controlling and monitoring the performance of an application.

Using device abstractions provided by Cisco IOx APIs, applications running on the fog can communicate with IoT devices that use any protocol. The "bring your own interface" philosophy of IOx allows effortless integration of novel, specialized communications technology with a common IP architecture. Fog applications can also send IoT data to the cloud by translating nonstandard and proprietary protocols to IP.

Cisco IOx has been used by a number of players in the IoT industry to architect innovative solutions to problems. For example, Rockwell developed FactoryTalk AssetCentre, a centralized tool for secure tracking and management of automation- related asset information across the entire plant. OSIsystem's PI system, an industry standard in enterprise infrastructure for real-time event and data management, uses Cisco IOx to deploy its data-collection interfaces.

4.7.2 **DATA IN MOTION**

Cisco Data in Motion (DMo) is a technology providing data management and analysis at the edge of the network. Cisco DMo is built into solutions provided by Cisco and its partners. DMo provides a simple rule-based RESTful API for building applications. Rules can be added/deleted on the run without any downtime. DMo can be used to perform analysis on incoming data, such as finding specific data of interest, summarizing data, generating new results from data, and so forth. It is meant to be deployed on devices in a distributed fashion and control the flood of data originating from the IoT devices.

4.7.3 **LocalGrid**

LocalGrid's Fog Computing platform is an embedded software installed on network devices (switches, routers) and sensors. It standardizes and secures communications between all kinds of devices across all vendors, thus minimizing customization and service costs. LocalGrid's platform resides on devices between the edge and the cloud and provides reliable M2M communication between devices without having to go through the cloud. This allows applications to make real-time decisions right at the edge without having to deal with the high latency of communicating with the cloud. Moreover, all LocalGrid devices can communicate with the cloud through open- communication standards, realizing the concept of fog to be an extension of cloud. Applications running on LocalGrid's platform can utilize the interplay between the fog and cloud to solve more complex problems.

LocalGrid's Fog Computing platform is shipped with LocalGrid vRTU, a software-based virtual remote-terminal unit that transforms communications between edge devices into compatible open standards. vRTU can be installed on off-the-shelf as well as through custom solutions from OEMs, endowing devices with RTU capabilities and providing a single point for management of all the edge devices, thus cutting down on customization and maintenance costs.

4.7.4 **ParStream**

ParStream is a real-time IoT analytics platform. Cisco and ParStream are working together to build a fast, reliable, and highly scalable infrastructure for analysis on the fog. Cisco is planning to use this infrastructure to enhance its current offerings and provide new types of services.

ParStream's offering of a Big Data Analytics Platform for IoT is contingent on its patented database technology, ParStream DB. ParStream DB is a column-based in-memory database with a highly parallel and fault-tolerant architecture, which is built using patented indexing and compression algorithms. Being an in-memory database, it is ideal for fog devices—which typically limit disk space. ParStream can push down query execution to the edge where data is produced, and perform analytics in a highly distributed fashion. Furthermore, ParStream has a considerably small footprint, making it feasible to be deployed on embedded devices and fog-enabled devices such as Cisco IOx.

4.7.5 **PRISMTECH VORTEX**

VORTEX is a ubiquitous data-sharing platform made for IoT. It provides scalable end-to-end seamless, efficient, secure, and timely data-sharing across IoT-supporting devices, edges, gateways, and cloud.

VORTEX leverages the DDS 2.0 standard for interoperable data-sharing and extends it to support Internet Scale systems, mobility, and Web 2.0 applications. VORTEX also seamlessly integrates with common IoT message-passing protocols such as MQTT and CoAP. In addition, to address security and privacy requirements, VORTEX provides support for fine-grained access control and both symmetric and asymmetric authentication.

Each IoT device is connected to a Vortex edge device that executes all of Vortex's software. Each piece of software performs a function necessary for the realization of a globally shared DDS. A Vortex edge device with the IoT device connected to it forms a domain (a DDS entity), called fog-domain in this context. Equipped with such devices, VORTEX supports a number of deployment models.

- Fog + Cloud: IoT devices inside a fog-domain communicate with each other in a peer-to-peer fashion. Those across fog-domains need to communicate through the cloud.
- Fog + Cloud-Link + Cloud: Similar to the previous model, devices within the same fog-domain communicate peer-to-peer, whereas devices not in the same fog-domain exchange data through the cloud using a *Cloud Link* that handles the associated security issues and controls what information is exposed.
- Federated Fog: Each fog-domain has a Vortex Cloud-link running on the Vortex device. Federated Fog is a collection of fog domains, which are federated by Cloud-link instances. Information exchanged between fog-domains is controlled by Cloud-link instances.

4.8 CASE STUDY

A smart city is one of the key use-cases of IoT, which in itself is a combination of a variety of use cases, ranging from smart traffic management to energy management of buildings. In this section, we present a case study on smart traffic management and show that employing fog computing improves the performance of the application in terms of response time and bandwidth consumption. A smart traffic-management system can be realized by a set of stream queries executing on data generated by sensors deployed throughout the city. Typical examples of such queries are real-time calculation of congestion (for route planning), and detection of traffic incidents. In this case study, we compare the performance of a query DETECT_TRAFFIC_INCIDENT (as shown in Fig. 4.5) on fog infrastructure versus the typical cloud implementation.

In the query, the sensors deployed on the roads send the speed of each crossing vehicle to the query processing engine. The operator "Average Speed Calculation" calculates the average speed of vehicles from the sensor readings over a given timeframe and sends this information to the next operator. The operator "Congestion Calculation" calculates the level of congestion in each lane based on the average speed of vehicles in that lane. The operator "Incident Detection," based on the average level of congestion, detects whether or not an incident has occurred. This query was simulated on both a fog-based as well as a cloud-based stream query-processing engine. The comparison of both strategies is presented in the next sections.

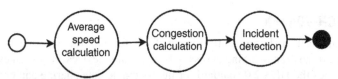

FIGURE 4.5 Dag of Query for Incident Detection

4.8.1 EXPERIMENT SETUP

4.8.1.1 Network Topology and Data Sources

The network topology used for the simulation was a hierarchical topology of fog devices, as described in [13]. The leaves of the treelike topology are the edge devices (gateways) and the cloud is located at the root. Intermediate nodes in the tree represent intermediate network devices between the cloud and the edge, which are able to host applications by utilizing their nascent compute, network, and storage capacity. Each fog device has both an associated CPU capacity and an associated uplink network bandwidth, which shall be utilized for running fog applications on them.

Traffic data fed to simulation was obtained from Sumo [15], a road-traffic simulator. Induction loops were inserted on the road that measured the speed of vehicles, and the information was sent to the query processing engine.

The simulation environment was implemented in CloudSim [16] by extending the basic entities in the original simulator. Fog devices were realized by extending the Datacenter class, whereas stream operators were modeled as a VM in CloudSim. Furthermore, tuples that were executed by the stream operators were realized by extending Cloudlets. Fog devices are entities with only one host, whose resources it can provide for running applications. Each tuple has an associated CPU and network cost for processing it.

4.8.2 PERFORMANCE EVALUATION

4.8.2.1 Average Tuple Delay

Average tuple delay, as the name suggests, is the amount of time (on average) that a tuple takes to be processed. Fig. 4.6 compares the average end-to-end tuple delay experienced when running the query on fog against the case when a traditional cluster-based stream processing-engine is used. The

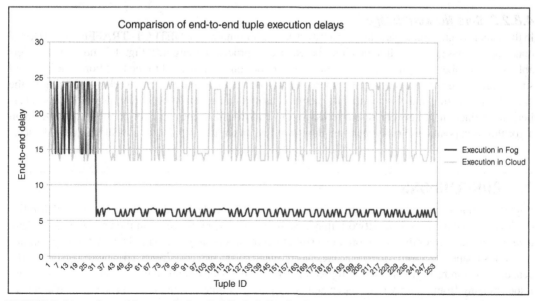

FIGURE 4.6 Comparison of Average End-to-End Tuple Execution Delays

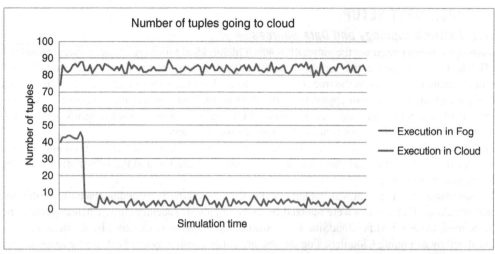

FIGURE 4.7 Comparison of Number of Tuples Reaching the Cloud for Processing: A Measure of Bandwidth Consumption

fog stream processing-engine dynamically places operators across fog devices when there is enough capacity to save bandwidth and minimize latency. As Fig. 4.6 shows, once operators are placed on fog devices the end-to-end tuple delay falls much below the delay of in-cloud processing, as data are processed closer to the sources. However, it is worth mentioning that if the operators are not placed optimally, resource contention in edge devices can cause more delay.

4.8.2.2 Core Network Usage

In this experiment, we compare the core network usage for running the DETECT_TRAFFIC_INCIDENT query on fog-based and traditional cloud-based stream processing-engines. Fig. 4.7 shows a considerably lower number of tuples traversing the core network once, compared to the traditional cloud-based stream processing. Thus, running the query on the edge devices reduces the workload coming to the cloud for processing and also reduces the network usages considerably. However, as we discussed earlier, this reduction in network resource usage and end-to-end latency is only possible if a placement algorithm is in position to push operators downward when enough capacity is available in edge devices.

4.9 CONCLUSIONS

Fog computing is emerging as an attractive solution to the problem of data processing in IoT. It relies on devices on the edge of the network that have more processing power than the end devices, and are nearer to these devices than the more powerful cloud resources, thus reducing latency for applications.

In this chapter, we introduced a reference architecture for IoT and discussed ongoing efforts in the academia and industry to enable the fog-computing vision. Many challenges still remain though, with issues ranging from security to resource and energy-usage minimization. Open protocols and architectures are also other topics for future research that will make fog computing more attractive for end users.

REFERENCES

[1] Misra P, Simmhan Y, Warrior J. Towards a practical architecture for the next generation Internet of Things. arXiv Prepr. arXiv1502.00797; 2015.

[2] Kitchin R. The real-time city? Big data and smart urbanism. GeoJournal 2014;79(1):1–14.

[3] Cortés R, Bonnaire X, Marin O, Sens P. Stream processing of healthcare sensor data: studying user traces to identify challenges from a Big Data perspective. Proc Comput Sci 2015;52:1004–1009.

[4] Cao Y, Songqing C, Hou P, Brown D. FAST: a fog computing assisted distributed analytics system to monitor fall for stroke mitigation. 2015 IEEE International Conference on Networking, Architecture and Storage (NAS), IEEE; 2015, p. 2–11.

[5] Stantchev V, Barnawi A, Ghulam S, Schubert Johannes, Tamm G. Smart items, fog and cloud computing as enablers of servitization in healthcare. Sensors Transducers 2015;185(2):121.

[6] Zao JK, et al. Augmented brain computer interaction based on fog computing and linked data. In: 2014 international conference on intelligent environments (IE); 2014.

[7] Kosta S, et al. Thinkair: dynamic resource allocation and parallel execution in the cloud for mobile code offloading. In: INFOCOM, 2012 proceedings IEEE; 2012.

[8] Jiang Z, Chan DS, Prabhu MS, Natarajan P, Hu H, Bonomi F. Improving web sites performance using edge servers in fog computing architecture. 2013 IEEE 7th International Symposium on Service Oriented System Engineering (SOSE), IEEE; 2013, p. 320–323.

[9] Mohammad A, Huh E-N. Fog computing and smart gateway based communication for cloud of things. 2014 International Conference on Future Internet of Things and Cloud (FiCloud), IEEE, 2014; p. 464–470.

[10] Chun BG, et al. Clonecloud: elastic execution between mobile device and cloud. In: Proceedings of the sixth conference on computer systems (ACM); 2011.

[11] Banerjee A, et al. MOCA: a lightweight mobile cloud offloading architecture. In: Proceedings of the eighth ACM international workshop on mobility in the evolving Internet architecture; 2013.

[12] Orsini G, Bade D, Lamersdorf W. Computing at the mobile edge: designing elastic Android applications for computation offloading; 2015.

[13] Hong K, et al. Mobile fog: a programming model for large-scale applications on the Internet of Things. In: Proceedings of the second ACM SIGCOMM workshop on mobile cloud computing; 2013.

[14] Dsouza C, Ahn GJ, Taguinod M. Policy-driven security management for fog computing: preliminary framework and a case study. 2014 IEEE 15th International Conference on Information Reuse and Integration (IRI), IEEE; 2014, p. 16–23.

[15] Behrisch M, et al. SUMO—simulation of urban mobility. In: The third international conference on advances in system simulation (SIMUL 2011). Barcelona, Spain; 2011.

[16] Calheiros RN, Ranjan R, Beloglazov A, De Rose CAF, Buyya R. CloudSim: a toolkit for modeling and simulation of cloud computing environments and evaluation of resource provisioning algorithms. Softw Pract Exp 2011;41(1):23–50.

[17] Madsen, H, et al. Reliability in the utility computing era: towards reliable fog computing. In: 2013 Twentieth international conference on systems, signals and image processing (IWSSIP); 2013.

[18] Mohammad A, Huh E-N. Dynamic resource provisioning through Fog micro datacenter. 2015 IEEE International Conference on Pervasive Computing and Communication Workshops (PerCom Workshops), IEEE; 2015, p. 105–110

[19] Lewis G, et al. Tactical cloudlets: moving cloud computing to the edge. In: 2014 IEEE military communications conference (MILCOM); 2014.

[20] Satyanarayanan M, Bahl P, Cáceres R, Davies N. The case for VM-based cloudlets in mobile computing. IEEE Pervasive Comput 2009;8(4):14–23.

IoT ENABLERS
AND SOLUTIONS

PART

IoT ENABLERS
AND SOLUTIONS

PROGRAMMING FRAMEWORKS FOR INTERNET OF THINGS

5

J. Krishnamurthy, M. Maheswaran

School of Computer Science, McGill University, Montreal, Quebec, Canada

5.1 INTRODUCTION

IoT devices are generally characterized as small things in the real world with limited storage and processing capacity, which may not be capable of processing a complete computing activity by themselves. They may need the computational capabilities of Cloud-based back-ends to complete the processing tasks and web-based front-ends to interact with the user. The Cloud infrastructure complements the things [1], by supporting device virtualization, availability, provisioning of resources, data storage, and data analytics. The IoT by its nature will extend the scope of Cloud computing to the real world in a more distributed and dynamic way [2]. IoT with Cloud will create new avenues for computing: huge storage capacity for IoT data in cloud; massive computing capabilities to collect, analyze, process, and archive those data; and new platforms such as SaaS (Sensing as a Service), SAaaS (Sensing and Actuation as a Service), and VSaaS (Video Surveillance as a Service) will open up to users.

With new opportunities, IoT also puts forth a major set of challenges for IoT application developers. Heterogeneity and the volume of data generated are two of the biggest concerns. Heterogeneity spans through hardware, software, and communication platforms. The data generated from these devices are generally in huge volume, are in various forms, and are generated at varying speeds. Since IoT applications will be distributed over a wide and varying geographical area, support for corrective and evolutionary maintenance of applications will determine the feasibility of application deployment. Further, some of the IoT applications such as traffic management will be latency-sensitive, and this warrants edge-processing support by the programming framework. Another difficulty to face when programming IoT is how to cope with frequent periods of nonavailability of devices, caused by mobilities and limited energy supplies from batteries. Developing a simplified programming model that can provide solutions for the above set of challenges will remain a continuous pursuit for the IoT community.

In this chapter, we explore the technologies that can aid and simplify IoT programming, summarize some of the key requirements of an IoT programming framework, and present a brief survey on various programming frameworks that have been recently developed for IoT. The organization of the chapter is as follows. In Section 5.2, we review the background technologies. In Section 5.3, we present some of the requirements for an IoT programming framework, along with a survey on general IoT programming frameworks. Section 5.4 we discuss future research direction, and in Section 5.5 we conclude the chapter.

5.2 BACKGROUND
5.2.1 OVERVIEW

During the lifecycle of IoT applications, the footprint of an application and the cost of its language runtime play a huge role in the sustainability of an application. C has been used predominantly in embedded applications development due to its performance; moreover, it can occupy the same position in IoT programming too. Further, the choice of communication protocols also has a huge implication in the cost of IoT applications on devices. Remote Procedure Calls (RPC), Representational state transfer (REST), and Constrained Application Protocol (CoAP) are some of the communication methods that are being currently incorporated into IoT communication stacks. A complete programming framework in a distributed environment requires not only a stable computing language such as C, but also a coordination language that can manage communications between various components of an IoT ecosystem. An explicit coordination language can tackle many of the challenges. It can manage communication between heterogeneous devices, coordinate interaction with the Cloud and devices, handle asynchronous data arrival, and can also provide support for fault tolerance. The method of using more than one language in a given application is known as polyglot programming. Polyglot programming is being widely used in web applications development, and it can provide the same advantages for IoT programming too.

In this section, we review some of the flavors of C language used in embedded programming, check adoptability of messaging approaches such as RPC, REST, and CoAP to IoT, explore some of the important features of various coordination languages, and, in the last part of this section, present the idea of polyglot programming.

5.2.2 EMBEDDED DEVICE PROGRAMMING LANGUAGES

Although there are various programming languages in the embedded programming domain, the vast majority of projects, about 80%, are either implemented in C and its flavors, or in a combination of C and other languages such as C++ [3]. Some of the striking features of C that aid in embedded development are performance, small memory foot-print, access to low-level hardware, availability of a large number of trained/experienced C programmers, short learning curve, and compiler support for the vast majority of devices [4]. The ANSI C standard provides customized support for embedded programming. Many embedded C-compilers based on ANSI C usually:

1. support low-level coding to exploit the underlying hardware,
2. support in-line assembly code,
3. flag dynamic memory-allocation and recursion,
4. provide exclusive access to I/O registers,

5. support accessing registers through memory pointers, and
6. allow bit-level access.

nesC, Keil C, Dynamic C, and B# are some of the flavors of C used in embedded programming.

5.2.2.1 nesC

nesC [5] is a dialect of C that has been used predominantly in sensor-nodes programming. It was designed to implement TinyOS [6], an operating system for sensor networks. It is also used to develop embedded applications and libraries. In nesC, an application is a combination of scheduler and components wired together by specialized mapping constructs. nesC extends C through a set of new keywords. To improve reliability and optimization, nesC programs are subject to whole-program analysis and optimization at compile time. nesC prohibits many features that hinder static analysis, such as function pointers and dynamic memory allocation. Since nesC programs will not have indirections, call-graph is known fully at compile time, aiding in optimized code generation.

5.2.2.2 Keil C

Keil C [7] is a widely used programming language for embedded devices. It has added some key features to ANSI C to make it more suitable for embedded device programming. To optimize storage requirements, three types of memory models are available for programmers: small, compact, and large. New keywords such as `alien`, `interrupt`, `bit`, `data`, `xdata`, `reentrant`, and so forth, are added to the traditional C keyword set. Keil C supports two types of pointers:

- *generic pointers*: can access any variable regardless of its location
- *memory-specific pointers*: can access variables stored in data memory

The memory-specific-pointers-based code execute faster than the equivalent code using generic pointers. This is due to the fact that the compilers can optimize the memory access, since the memory area accessed by pointers is known at compile time.

5.2.2.3 Dynamic C

Some key features in Dynamic C [8] are function chaining and cooperative multitasking. Segments of code can be distributed in one or more functions through function chaining. Whenever a function chain executes, all the segments belonging to that particular chain execute. Function chains can be used to perform data initialization, data recovery, and other kinds of special tasks as desired by the programmer. The language provides two directives `#makechain, #funcchain` and a keyword `segchain` to manage and define function chains.

`#makechain chain_name`: creates a function chain by the given name.

`#funcchain chain_name func_name[chain_name]`: Adds a function or another function chain to a function chain.

`segchain chain_name {statements}`: This is used for function-chain definitions. The program segment enclosed within curly brackets will be attached to the named function chain.

The language stipulates `segchain` definitions to appear immediately after data declarations and before executable statements, as shown in the following code snippet.

```
int foo(){
// data declarations
segchain recover{
// some statements which execute under function chain recover().
          }
segchain chain_x{
// some statements which execute under function chain chain_x().
          }
// function body of foo.

}

int foo1(){
// data declarations
segchain recover{
// some statements which execute under function chain recover().
          }
// function body of foo1.

}
```

Calling a function chain inside a program is similar to calling a void function that has no parameters.

```
int foo2(){
     .....
     .....
     recover()/* executes all the statements defined under
                 function chain recover */
     }
```

The order of execution of statements inside a function chain is not guaranteed. Dynamic C's costate statement provides support for cooperative multitasking. It provides multiple threads of control, through independent program counters that can be switched in between explicitly. The following code snippet is an example.

```
for(;;){
     costate{
          waitfor(tcp_packet_port_21());
          yield; // force context switch.
          ...
          }
     costate{
          waitfor(tcp_packet_port_23());
          }

     }
```

The yield statement immediately passes control to another costate segment. If the control returns to the first costate segment, then the execution resumes from the statement following the yield statement. Dynamic C also has keywords `shared` and `protected`, which support data that are shared between different contexts and are stored in battery-backed memory, respectively.

5.2.2.4 B#

B# [9] is a multithreaded programming language designed for constrained systems. Although C inspires it, its features are derived from a host of languages such as Java, C++, and C#. It supports object-oriented programming. The idea of boxing/unboxing conversions is from C#. For example, a float value can be converted to an object and back to float, as shown in the following code snippet.

```
class test{
static void Main(){
    float       i = 123;
    object      obj = i;            // boxing
    float       j = (float)obj;     // Unboxing
    }
}
```

The field property is also similar to C#. B# provides support for multithreading and synchronization through `lock` and `start` statements, which are similar to `when` and `cobegin`, from Edison. `lock` provides mutual exclusion and synchronization support, whereas `start` is used to initiate threads. Other important features are device-addressing registers and explicit support for interrupt handlers. These features are directly supported by the underlying Embedded Virtual Machine (EVM), which interprets and executes the binary code generated by the B# assembler on a stack-based machine. The B# EVM runs on a target architecture, thereby hiding the hardware nuances from the programmer. Presence of EVM promotes reusability of components. Also, since the EVM is based on the stack-machine model, the code size is much reduced. The EVM also has a small kernel for managing threads.

All of the previously described languages have been optimized for resource-constrained devices. While designing embedded programs, a measured choice on the flavor of C is quite an important decision from the viewpoint of an IoT programmer. An IoT programmer may not restrict himself or herself to a C-flavored language. Many other languages, such as C++, Java, and JavaScript have been stripped down to run on embedded devices.

5.2.3 MESSAGE PASSING IN DEVICES

In this section, we review some of the communication paradigms and technologies such as RPC, REST, and CoAP that can be used in resource-constrained environments.

5.2.3.1 RPC

RPC [10] is an abstraction for procedural calls across languages, platforms, and protection mechanisms. For IoT, RPC can support communication between devices as it implements the request/response communication pattern. Typical RPC calls exhibit synchronistic behavior. When RPC messages are transported over the network, all the parameters are serialized into a sequence of bytes. Since serialization of primitive data types is a simple concatenation of individual bytes, the serialization of complex data structures and objects is often tightly coupled to platforms and programming languages [11]. This strongly hinders the applicability of RPCs in IoT due to interoperability concerns.

Lightweight Remote Procedure Call (LRPC) [12] was designed for optimized communication between protection domains in the same machine, but not across machines. Embedded RPC (ERPC) in Marionette [13] uses a fat client such as a PC and thin servers such as nodes architecture. This allows resource-rich clients to directly call functions on applications in embedded devices. It provides poke and peek commands that can be used on any variables in a node's heap. S-RPC [11] is another lightweight remote procedure-call for heterogeneous WSN networks. S-RPC tries to minimize the resource requirements for encoding/decoding and data buffering. A trade-off is achieved based on the data types supported and their resource consumption. Also, a new data representation scheme is defined which minimizes the overhead on packets. A lightweight RPC has been incorporated into the TinyOS, nesC [14] environment. This approach promises ease of use, lightweight implementation, local call-semantics, and adaptability.

5.2.3.2 REST

Roy Fielding in his PhD thesis [15] proposed the idea of RESTful interaction for the Web. The main aim of the REST was to simplify the web-application development and interaction. It leverages on the tools available on the Internet and stipulates the following constraints on application development:

- Should be based on client-server architecture and the servers should be stateless
- Support should be provided for caching at the client side
- The interface to servers should be generic and standardized (URI)
- Layering in the application architecture should be supported and each of the layers shall be independent
- Optional code-on demand should be extended to clients having the capability

These constraints, combined with the following principles, define the RESTful approach to application development.

- Everything on the Internet is a resource
- Unique identifiers are available to identify the resources
- Generic and simple interfaces are available to work with those resources
- Communication between client and servers can be through representation of resources
- Resource representation through sequence of bytes is followed by some metadata explaining the organization of the data
- Since transactions are stateless, all interactions should be context-free
- Layering is supported, and hence intermediaries should be transparent

The authors in [16] have highlighted that the previous constraints and principles bring in many advantages to the distributed applications: scalability, loose coupling, better security, simple addressability, connectedness, and performance. Further, they compare RPC with REST for the same qualitative measures, and argue that RESTful approaches are always better for each of the previous measures. One more advantage of RESTful components is that they can be composed to produce mashups, giving rise to new components which are also RESTful. In [17] the author identifies essential characteristic features of a composing language that can compose RESTful components together:

- Support for dynamic and late binding
- Uniform interface support for composed resource manipulation
- Support for dynamic typing

- Support for content-type negotiation
- Support for state inspection of compositions by the client

Although the uniform interface constraint promotes scalability by shifting the variability from interface to resource representation, it also narrows the focus of RESTful approaches to data and its representation. Also, in the Internet, the exchanges need not be limited to data and its representation; there can be more than just the pure data. For these cases, the optional code-on demand constraint for clients has been found to be inadequate for exchanges other than content. Also, the RESTful approach poses a challenge for those applications that require stateful interactions.

CREST (Computational REST) [18] tries to address these problems. Here, the focus is on exchanges of computation rather than on data exchange. Instead of client-server nomenclature, everyone is addressed as peers; some may be strong and some may be weak, based upon the available computing power. Functional languages such as Scheme allow computations to be suspended at a point and encapsulated as a single entity to be resumed at a later point in time, through "continuation." CREST's focus is on these sorts of computation. It supports the model of "computations stopping at a point in a node, exchanged with another node, resumed from the suspended point at the new node." As said earlier, both the nodes are peers. CREST has some principles along the lines of REST [19]:

- All computations are resources and are uniquely identified
- Representation of resources through expressions and metadata
- All computations are context-free
- Support for layering and transparent intermediaries
- All the computations should be included inside HTTP
- Computations can produce different results at different times
- Between calls they can maintain states that may aid computations such as aggregation
- Between different calls, computations should support independence
- Parallel synchronous invocations should not corrupt data

Computations on a peer or on different peers can be composed to create mashups. Peers can share the load of computations to promote scaling and latency-sensitive applications.

5.2.3.3 CoAP

Since HTTP/TCP stack is known to be resource demanding on constrained devices, protocols such as Embedded Binary HTTP (EBHTTP) and Compressed HTTP Over PAN (CHoPAN) have been proposed. However, the issue of reliable communications still remains a concern. The IETF work group, Constrained RESTful Environments (CoRE), has developed a new web-transfer protocol called Constrained Application Protocol (CoAP), which is optimized for constrained power and processing capabilities of IoT. Although the protocol is still under standardization, various implementations are in use. CoAP in simpler terms is a two-layered protocol: a messages layer, interacting with the UDP, and another layer for request/response interactions using methods and response code, as done in HTTP. In contrast to HTTP, CoAP exchanges messages asynchronously and uses UDP.

The CoAP has four types of messages: *Acknowledgement, Reset, Confirmable (CON),* and *Non-Confirmable (NON)*. The non-confirmable messages are used to allow sending requests that may not require reliability. Reliability is provided by the message layer and will be activated when Confirmable messages are used. The Request methods are: GET, POST, PUT, and DELETE of HTTP. CoAP has been implemented on Contiki [20], which is an operating system for sensor networks and in TinyOS as Tiny-CoAP [21].

Many approaches have been used to evaluate the performance of CoAP. A Total Cost of Ownership (TCO) model for applications in a constrained environment has been used to compare HTTP versus CoAP [22]. The major observations from the comparison are as follows:

- CoAP is more efficient for applications on smart objects, engaged in frequent communication sessions
- CoAP is cost-effective whenever the battery/power-source replacements prove costly
- Whenever the charges for the data communication are volume-based, CoAP is found to be more cost-effective
- CoAP has been found to be more beneficial cost-wise in push mode than in pull mode

Fig. 5.1 illustrates the CoAP layers and the integration of constrained devices using CoAP with the Internet through a proxy.

For IoT/CoT, the advantages of CoAP can be summarized as follows.

- A compact binary header (10–20 bytes), along with UDP, reduces the communication overhead, thereby reducing the delay and minimizing the power consumption due to data transmission.
- Since asynchronous data push is supported, it enables things to send information only when there is a change of observed state. This allows the things to sleep most of the time and conserve power.
- The minimal subset of REST requests supported by CoAP allows the protocol implementations to be less complex when compared to HTTP. This lowers the hardware requirements for the smart-things on which it executes.

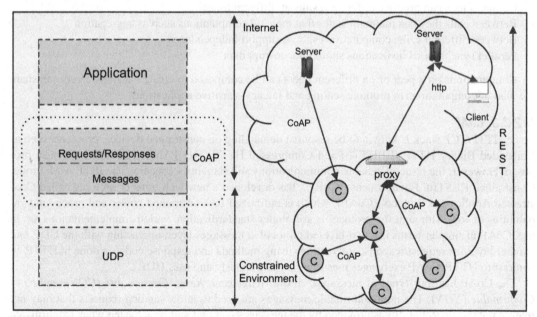

FIGURE 5.1 CoAP Layers and Integration of Constrained Devices With the Internet

- The M2M resource discovery is supported by CoAP to find a matching resource based on the CoRE link format.
- The draft CoAP proposal includes support for alternative non-IP messaging, such as Short Message Service (SMS) and transportation of CoAP messages over Bluetooth, ZigBee, Z-Wave, and so forth.

MQ Telemetry Transport (MQTT) protocol is another communication protocol designed for M2M communication, based on TCP/IP. Both CoAP and MQTT are expected to be widely used in IoT communication infrastructure in the future.

5.2.4 COORDINATION LANGUAGES

Carriero and Gelernter argue in [23] that a complete programming model can be built by combining two orthogonal models—a computation model and a coordination model. The computation model provides the computational infrastructure and programmers can build computational activity using them, whereas the coordination model provides the support for binding all those computational activities together. They argue that a computational model supported by languages such as C, by themselves cannot provide genuine coordination support among various computing activities. This observation is more relevant in IoT–Cloud programming, wherein there are numerous distributed activities which have to be coordinated in a reliable and fault-tolerant manner.

Coordination can be seen through two different perspectives: (1) based on centralized control, named as Orchestration and (2) based on distributed transparent control, named as Choreography. The W3C's Web services choreography working group defines Choreography as "the definition of the sequences and conditions under which multiple cooperating independent agents exchange messages in order to perform a task to achieve a goal state." Orchestration is seen as "the definition of sequence and conditions in which one single agent invokes other agents in order to realize some useful function." There are many languages that provide Choreography and Orchestration support. We briefly review some of the features in coordination languages such as Linda, eLinda, Orc, and Jolie.

5.2.4.1 Linda and eLinda

Linda is a coordination-programming model for writing parallel and distributed applications. It takes the responsibility of enforcing communication and coordination, while general-purpose languages such as C, C++, and Java are used for computational requirements of the application. The Linda model supports a shared-memory store called *tuple space* for communication between processes of the application. Tuple spaces can be accessed by simple operations such as "out" and "in." These operations can be either blocking or nonblocking. CppLINDA is a C++ implementation of the Linda coordination model.

The eLinda [24] model extends Linda. It adds a new output operation "wr" that can be used with the "rd" input operation to support broadcast communication. In Linda, if a minimum value of a dataset stored in a tuple space is required, all matching field values should be read, the reduction should be performed, and then the remaining data should be returned to the tuple space. While this procedure is accessing the tuple space to extract the minimum value, the tuple space is not accessible to other processes, which restricts the degree of parallelism by a large amount. eLinda proposes the "Programmable Matching Engine" (PME) to solve problems such as the previous one. The PME allows the programmer to specify a custom matcher that can be used internally to retrieve tuples from the shared store. The PME has been found to be advantageous for parsing graphical languages and video-on-demand systems.

5.2.4.2 Orc

Orc [25] is a coordination language for distributed and concurrent programming. It is based on process calculus. It provides uniform access to computational services, including distributed communication and data manipulation. A brief overview of the language features is as follows.

- The basic unit of computation in Orc is called a *site*, similar to a function or a procedure in other languages. The sites can be remote and unreliable.
- Sites can be called in the form of C(p); C is a site name and p is the list of parameters. The execution of a site-call invokes the service associated with the site. The call publishes the response if the site responds.
- Orc has the following combinator-operators to support various compositions and work-flow patterns [26]:
  - Parallel combinator "|" is used for parallel, independent invocation. For example, in $I \mid J$, expressions I and J are initiated at the same time independently. The sites called by I and J are the ones called by $I \mid J$, and any value published by either I or J is published by $I \mid J$. There is no direct interaction or communication between these two computations.
  - Sequential combinator "»" is used for invocations of sites in a sequential manner. In $I > y > J$, expression I is evaluated. Each value published by I initiates a separate and new execution of J. Now, the execution of I continues in parallel with the executions of J. If I does not publish even a single value, then there is no execution of J.
  - Pruning combinator "«" is a special type of combinator which can be seen as an asynchronous parallel combinator. For example, in $I < y < J$, both I and J execute in parallel. Execution of parts of I which do not depend on y can proceed, but site-calls in I for which y is a parameter are suspended until y has a value. If J publishes a value which can be assigned to y, then J's execution is terminated and the suspended parts of I can then proceed.

  The "»" combinator has the highest precedence, followed by "|" and "«."
- Orc provides several *fundamental sites*, such as Rwait(t), Prompt(), and so forth, to promote writing efficient programs.
- Orc allows users to define local *functions*. Function-calls act and look a lot like site-calls, with a few exceptions:
  - A site call will block if some of its arguments are not available, but a function call does not.
  - A site call can publish at most one value, but a function call can publish more than one value.

  Orc also supports functions and sites as arguments to a function call.
- The recent Orc implementation is allowing Java classes to be used as sites.

5.2.4.3 Jolie

Jolie (Java Orchestration Language Interpreter Engine) [27] is an orchestration language for services in Java-based environments. The statement composers and dynamic fault handling are two important features in this language. In dynamic fault handling [28], instead of fault handlers being statically programmed, they are installed dynamically at the execution time. This facilitates fine-tuning of fault handlers and termination handlers, depending upon which part of the code has already been executed.

In Jolie there are basically three statement composers: sequence, parallel, and input choice. Statements can be composed sequentially, using ";" operator. It means that the statement to the left of the sequence operator is executed first, and then the statement to the right of it. The syntax of the sequence statement is as follows.

```
statementx ; statementy
```

`statementx` gets executed first and then the `statementy`. The "|" operator is used to compose statements in parallel. The statements to the left and right of the parallel operator are executed concurrently. The syntax is as follows.

```
statementx | statementy
```

`statementx` and `statementy` are executed concurrently. The third composer is for guarded input. Here, message receiving is supported for any of the input statements that are listed. When a message for an input statement is received, all the other branches are deactivated and the corresponding branch behavior is executed. The syntax is as shown in the listing.

```
[IS_1]{branch_code_1}
[IS_2]{branch_code_2}
[IS_3]{branch_code_3}
```

If the message is received on the input statement `IS_2`, then `branch_code_1` and `branch_code_3` are disabled, and execution continues through `branch_code_2`. Since IoT is characterized by distributed execution, we believe explicit coordination- language support with at least minimal features for coordination and composition, for different work-flow patterns is a must for any IoT programming framework.

5.2.5 POLYGLOT PROGRAMMING

Polyglot programming is also called multilingual programming. It is an art of developing simpler solutions by combining the best possible solutions using different programming languages and paradigms. This is based on the observation that there is no single programming paradigm or a programming language which can suit all the facets of modern-day programming or software requirements. It is also called poly-paradigm programming (PPP), to appreciate the fact that many modern-day software combines a subset of imperative, functional, logical, object-oriented, concurrent, parallel, and reactive programming paradigms.

One of the oldest examples of polyglot programming is Emacs, which is a combination of parts written in both C and eLisp (dialect of Lisp). Web applications are generally based on three-tier architecture to promote loose coupling and modularity, and they are also a representation of polyglot software systems. Polyglot programming [29] has been observed to have increased programmer productivity and software maintainability in web development.

Although the word "Polyglot" has been used in software development since 2002, the definition of Polyglot programming is not standardized yet. Many different definitions by polyglot practitioners

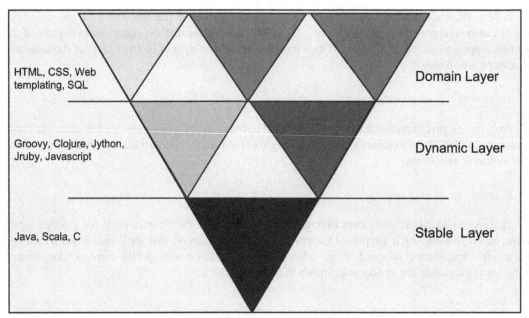

FIGURE 5.2 Inverse Pyramid for Polyglot Programming

have been documented in Harmanen [30] and Fjeldberg [29]. One of the definitions says "programming in more than one language within the same context." Another one says "using multiple programming languages on the same managed run-time." Fjeldberg extends the definition, taking into account the developers' perspective, as: "programming in more than one language within the same context, where the context is either within one team, or several teams where the integration between the resulting applications require knowledge of the languages involved."

In a Polyglot programming environment, the platform used for the integration, and the different programming languages supported by the given platform are the two essential aspects. An Inverse pyramid [29,30] can be used to categorize the programming languages in a polyglot software system. The Inverse pyramid has three layers: stable, dynamic, and domain, as shown in Fig. 5.2.

Statically typed programming-languages such as Java and C that provide well-tested and stable functionality settle toward the stable layer. The less powerful general-purpose technologies, such as HTML and CSS, which are tightly coupled to a specific part of the application, bubble up to the top layer, and the dynamic layer in the middle consists of a variety of programming languages such as Groovy and Clojure, which are more flexible and aid rapid functionality development. The inverse pyramid signifies the fact that it is the single stable language, which supports all of the previously described layers and various languages in a bedrock fashion.

Since IoT is characterized by heterogeneity in various forms, a single programming language or a single programming model may not be able to provide complete support for the application development in IoT. As we have already argued, at least a coordination language and a computational language is required in a unified programming model for IoT, which, in a way, is polyglot programming.

5.3 SURVEY OF IoT PROGRAMMING FRAMEWORKS
5.3.1 OVERVIEW

In this section, we present a summary of different programming frameworks for IoT and cloud that have been developed. These programming frameworks promote design reuse, implementation reuse, and validation reuse, thereby enhancing software extensibility, flexibility, and portability. The complexity of the domain and maturity of the problem are the biggest challenges in developing frameworks [31]. Since IoT domain itself is in its initial stages, many frameworks are also in the development and experimental stages. We propose the following set of minimal features to be fulfilled by the programming frameworks for IoT:

- *Coordination*: An IoT can have computing elements playing different roles: controllers, storage managers, and application processors. We need programming-language support for orchestrating their activities. The orchestration can be explicit (control driven) or implicit (data driven).
- *Heterogeneity*: The IoT brings disparate computing devices together for the purposes of running smart-computing applications. The programming framework should be capable of efficiently exploiting the system heterogeneity by allowing the developer to provide guidance on how the computations must be mapped to the computing elements.
- *Scalability*: For IoT to become a success, it is not sufficient to just interconnect massive numbers of devices. They should be programmed to run many creative applications, such that massive numbers of users would benefit from their deployment. Therefore, IoT needs programming frameworks that support a variety of programming patterns, and should also be able to perform load-balancing dynamically.
- *Fault tolerance*: In IoT, we can expect frequent system partitioning due to the mobility of computing elements. The programming framework should allow developers to create applications that can gracefully go between online and offline states as networks partition and heal their connections.
- *Lightweight footprint*: The programming framework should be lightweight both in terms of the runtime overhead and the programming effort needed by the developers.
- *Support for latency-sensitive applications*: IoT will have many applications which would be geographically distributed and hence may be latency-sensitive. Pushing all the computations to Cloud will not help these sorts of applications. The programming framework, including the runtime, has to support these sorts of requirements dynamically.

5.3.2 IoT PROGRAMMING APPROACHES

The following four approaches are used predominantly in IoT application development [32].

1. *Node-Centric Programming*: Here, every aspect of application development, communication between nodes, collection and analysis of sensor data, and issuing of commands to actuator nodes has to be programmed by the application developer. Although it has greater control over the way that programs work, it is too labor-intensive and does not promote portability.
2. *Database approach*: In this model, every node is considered to be a part of a virtual database. Queries as part of an application can be issued on sensor nodes by the developer. This model does not support application logic at this level, rendering it to be of little use in IoT application development.

3. *Macro Programming*: In this methodology, application logic can be specified and also abstractions are provided to specify high-level communication, thereby hiding low-level details from developers, which will aid in modular and rapid development of applications.
4. *Model-Driven Development*: This takes note of both vertical and horizontal separation of concerns. Vertical separation increases the level of abstraction, thereby reducing application-development complexity. Horizontal separation of concern reduces development complexity by describing the system, using different system views. Each perspective elaborates on a certain aspect of the system.

Many of the IoT development kits, which are available in the market, support one of the previously listed approaches. This categorization is not exhaustive, as new hybrid approaches may evolve as the IoT domain itself matures.

5.3.3 EXISTING IoT FRAMEWORKS

The IoT research communities from many academic and research organizations are constantly striving to simplify the efforts involved in IoT application development by developing new programming frameworks. We present a few of them and highlight their key features.

5.3.3.1 Mobile Fog

Cisco has proposed a new computing model called Fog computing [33]. Here, generic application logic is executed on resources throughout the network, including routers and dedicated computing nodes. In contrast to the pure Cloud paradigm, fog-computing resources perform low-latency processing near the edge, while latency-tolerant, large-scope aggregations are performed on powerful resources in the core of the network (Cloud).

Mobile fog [34] extends fog computing by providing a Platform as a Service (PaaS) programming model for IoT application development to simplify the task of application development that runs on heterogeneous devices distributed over a wide area, and also to provide support for dynamic scaling based on their workload.

Here, an application will contain processes distributed throughout the fog-computing infrastructure, on Cloud and on edge devices, based on geographical proximity and hierarchy. Each process can perform tasks with respect to its location and level in the network hierarchy, such as sensing, actuation, and aggregation. A process running on a device which is at the edge is a *leaf node*, whereas a process in the Cloud is the *root node* in a given hierarchy. Processes on nodes between devices and Cloud are intermediate nodes (routers, servers, etc.). Each process handles a workload from a certain geospatial region.

Mobile Fog provides API support through its runtime. Mobile Fog uses computing- instance requirements to provide dynamic scaling. It is based on user-provided policy, such as CPU utilization rate, bandwidth, and so forth.

5.3.3.2 ELIoT (Erlang Language for IoT)

Although the language Erlang was originally designed for embedded platforms, over a period of time it amassed a complex infrastructure, which is usually not required in devices and is a burden on resource-constrained things. ELIoT [35], Erlang language for IoT, tries to address this for IoT application development.

ELIoT provides a small library for developing decentralized sensing/actuation systems, an interpreter suited for resource-constrained IoT devices, and a simulator for testing the implementations in a fully or partially simulated environment. The ELIoT's virtual machine is a stripped-down, lightweight version of Erlang's virtual machine. Heavy libraries, which are not required for IoT, are removed (such as CORBA middleware systems). It includes a custom-networking stack for improving efficiency and for supporting new communication primitives. Instead of TCP, UDP is used for both reliable and non-reliable communication. A customized reliability layer is built on UDP.

Generally for IoT applications, strict layering of the networking stack may not be fully advantageous; some form of cross-layering is found to be helpful for IoT applications [19]. Erlang's network driver fills the incoming-message queue of the receiver with the payload of the message, hiding all of the other details, whereas the network driver of the ELIoT exposes additional information such as the IP address of the source node and the Received Signal Strength Indicator (RSSI) coming from the radio, which are treated as any other type of data.

The Erlang's uni-cast interprocess communication operator "!" is built on a complete TCP/IP stack, ensuring reliable communication for both local and remote communication. Since, TCP/IP stack comes with a cost and can be resource-draining on devices, in ELIoT, the ! operator is used only for communication between local processes. Remote communications in ELIoT are handled by a set of specific functions from the ELIoT library, whose semantics are its best effort, and is limited to SingleHop in wireless networks. Furthermore, the ELIoT library supports a rich set of communication patterns, including the broadcast mode.

ELIoT provides a simulator for supporting IoT application debugging and testing. The simulator can model a complete system through virtual nodes running unmodified ELIoT code. Also, it can run a mixed deployment where virtual nodes seamlessly interact with physical devices. The ELIoT simulator allows for debugging a system in a fully simulated deployment environment, which can seamlessly move into an actual deployment environment. The ELIoT framework provides wrappers on nodes, which are basically RESTful interfaces, through which nodes can be accessed by users through the normal HTTP operation.

ELIoT brings in the advantages of Erlang to IoT in a lightweight framework.

5.3.3.3 *Compose API*

Compose API [36] is an IoT service-provider platform through RESTful APIs, wherein things, users, and the Compose platform can interact with each other to provide services based on IoT, called Internet of Services (IoS). Compose platform is based on Web of Things (WoT): all of the physical objects connected to the platform are web-enabled and can interact among themselves using the web protocols. Along with the APIs, the compose platform consists of GUI, semantic registry, cloud runtime, and communication libraries.

Any object which implements the communication protocols of the Compose API is web- enabled and is called a Web Object (WO). Each WO holds a virtual identity inside the Compose platform, called the Service Object (SO). The SOs communicate with the external WOs through APIs. SOs can act as data endpoints or they can also act as intermediaries, feeding processed data to other SOs. Every time a sensor attached to WOs produces a new reading, it is forwarded as a Sensor Update (SU) on a stream to the Compose platform, to be collected by the corresponding SO for processing based on some processing logic. The processing logic is a combination of logical, string, and arithmetic operations implemented in the form of a processing pipeline. An SU goes through a number of stages in the pipeline in order to transform into a new output or a new SU. Connections between SOs are built through subscriptions, and communication between them is through events. A JSON document description deploys each SO in the platform.

Compose API simplifies node-centric programming and exposes nodes through RESTful APIs which can be further composed. Such a programming methodology is quite advantageous to IoT.

5.3.3.4 Distributed Dataflow Support for IoT

In this approach [37], existing IoT dataflow platforms such as WOTkit processor and Node-RED are extended to support distributed dataflow, which is one of the important characteristic features of IoT. Dataflow programs are generally called flows, which consist of nodes connected by "wires." The dataflows are generated using JSON documents. During execution, nodes get instantiated in the memory, and the code is executed as and when the node receives data on the incoming "wire."

The nodes do not share states with each other and are inherently independent and can execute code in parallel. This facilitates computation migration between heavy processors and devices seamlessly. Based on user choices and trade-offs, computations can be split and distributed, so that a part of them can execute in the cloud while the other parts can execute on edge devices. According to the authors, the present-day IoT dataflow platforms need to be extended to support distributed dataflow, for which three things are necessary: flow ownership, naming of nodes, and classification of connections (wires) as local or remote. This framework aims to incorporate these three attributes to WOTkit and Node-RED to aid in IoT application development from the dataflow perspective.

5.3.3.5 PyoT

PyoT [38] is a programming framework for WSNs, which have the capability to communicate with each other through the Internet, using 6LoWPAN and CoAP. PyoT abstracts WSNs as software objects, which can be manipulated and composed to perform complex tasks. PyoT uses CoAP's RESTful interface to interact with nodes. Applications can consider sensing and actuating capabilities of nodes, shared with the external world through URIs. The users can discover available resources, monitor sensors and actuators, store data, define events and actions, and program to interact with resources using Python. PyoT supports "in-network processing," in which a part of the application logic can be directly run on devices.

PyoT has five components: (1) Virtual Control Room, (2) Shell, (3) Storage Element, (4) Message Queue, and (5) one or more PyoT Worker Nodes. The Web user interface is the virtual control room that allows execution of basic operations, such as listing of resources, sensor monitoring, and data storage. The Shell allows macro programming for defining complex operations through a set of Python APIs for interacting with resources, which are abstracted as Python objects. The Storage Element maintains the system status. Each PyoT Worker Node generally manages an IoT-based WSN, by providing a set of processes that perform generic tasks and support communication activities with other nodes. The PyoT Worker Node also keeps track of nodes and their resources, provides updates to the Storage Element, performs sensor-data collection, and also supports event detection. The macro programming support by this framework will lessen the burden on IoT programmers.

5.3.3.6 Dripcast

Dripcast [39] is a Java-based application-development framework to integrate smart devices into the cloud-computing infrastructure. Further, it is a serverless framework for storing and processing Java objects in a cloud environment. These Java objects will be made available on smart things, and users can manipulate those objects as if they were local objects. It implements transparent Java remote procedure-calls and a mechanism to read, store, and process Java objects in a distributed, scalable data-store. Under Dripcast, all Java objects have a worldwide unique ID. The Dripcast framework consists of four components: Client, Relay, Engine, and Store.

1. *Client* is a Java library, which works on devices such as smartphones and tablets. It monitors the Java object on the client devices, and forwards remote procedure- calls, which are abstracted from the users to the Relay.
2. *Relay* is a stateless distribution-gateway. It forwards requests from clients to corresponding engine servers. A relay server knows the association of the object's unique ID and engine servers; a Distributed Hash Table (DHT) manages this association.
3. *Engine* is a set of engine servers. Each engine server runs JavaVM and executes Java methods of an object for a remote procedure-call request forwarded by the relay, and returns the result back to the relay. If there is a state change of the object, then the new state is stored back into the Store.
4. *Store* is a scalable distributed data-store for storing Java objects with the capability for replication and automatic recovery.

The Dripcast framework enables Java-based IoT application development.

5.3.3.7 Calvin

It is a framework [40] that merges IoT and cloud in a unified programming model. It combines the ideas of actor-model and flow-based computing. To simplify application development, it proposes four phases to be followed in a sequential fashion: Describe, Connect, Deploy, and Manage.

1. *Describe*: In this phase, the functional parts of the applications, which are reusable components, are described. In Calvin, everything is treated as an actor: devices, services, and even a piece of computation on cloud. These actors can communicate with each other through ports. To create an actor, a developer describes the actions, their input/output relations, the conditions for a particular action to be triggered, and also the priority between actions. Device manufacturers can supply actors that correspond to their devices as part of the support code shipped with their devices, thus enabling their devices to easily integrate with a Calvin application.
2. *Connect*: Once the actors have been described, the next step is to connect those actors by directed graphs between the ports of a number of actors.
3. *Deploy*: In this phase, an application is instantiated according to the graphs provided with its description. The description/connect phase does not specify where the various actors should execute, nor how the data should be transported between them. This is handled during deployment of the application. The distributed runtime present at the nodes where the application gets deployed shoulders this responsibility. By forming a mesh network of runtime on nodes, actors in a running application can migrate from one runtime to another. Once the runtime has been instantiated and connected to the actors locally, the distributed execution environment can move actors to any accessible runtime based on resources, locality, connectivity, and performance requirements.
4. *Manage*: In this phase, the distributed execution environment monitors the applications, handling migration of actors, updates, error recovery and scaling, along with book-keeping.

These phases are supported by the runtime, APIs, and communication protocols. The platform-dependent part of Calvin runtime manages communication between runtimes, transport layer support, the inter-runtime communication, and abstraction for I/O, sensing mechanisms to the upper levels of the runtime. The platform-independent runtime provides interface for the actors. The scheduler of the Calvin runtime resides in this layer. Calvin runtime supports multitenancy. Once an application is deployed, actors may share runtime with actors from other applications.

5.3.3.8 Simurgh

Simurgh [41] provides a high-level programming framework for IoT application development. The framework supports the exposing of IoT services as RESTful APIs, and also the composing of those IoT services to create various flow patterns in a simplified manner. The overall Simurgh architecture has two main layers: thing layer and Platform layer. In the thing layer there is a software component called *Network Discovery* and *Registration Broker*, which listens to the incoming connection requests from devices and handles them. There is a rich set of libraries providing device-specific interfaces. An API mediator assists programmers to expose their applications through RESTful APIs. Also, they provide RESTful wrappers for those low-level device interfaces which are not supported by native vendors, and, finally, an API manager which monitors API's access from the external world.

The platform layer has the following components:

1. *Thing Description Repository*: This stores information about things and services offered by them, periodically updated by the Network Discovery and Registration Broker and API Mediator component. Things are described using TDD (Thing Description Document). A TDD file consists of mainly two parts:
   a. *Entity Properties*: Usually a user-chosen name, last modification date and entity's location is stored.
   b. *Entity Services*: For each of the entities described earlier, entity services define APIs that are available on the entity. These API definition files can be in RESTful API Modeling Language (RAML) or in Swagger format.
2. *Two-Phase Discovery Engine*: This is used to discover an entity and its corresponding APIs in two phase. In the first phase, the engine will search in TDD repository to find entities based on given criteria. If the goal is finding an API of an entity capable of doing a certain task, then another search is performed on their respective API Description Documents.
3. *Flow Design*: This component assists in designing flows, which are chains of IoT services. Through this component, users can discover things, discover their APIs, and also can call the found APIs, thereby generating a flow.
4. *Flow Composition*: Two or more flows can be combined to build a new flow that can deliver a new functionality. This component performs those compositions.
5. *Flow Execution Engine*: This engine provides all the required resources during the execution of a flow. It configures them and executes all the necessary APIs to fulfill a request.
6. *Flow Template Management and Repository*: Flows are managed, and, also, to promote flow reusability, the used patterns are stored and are exposed to users when they are designing new flows.
7. *Request Management*: This component performs user-request matching to flow templates. If a match is not found, then the request will be forwarded to the Flow Composition module to match with composed flow patterns. Furthermore, if a flow is not found, then users can build the required flow using a flow-design interface.

The Simurgh framework provides detailed support for IoT development. Assistance to develop, manage, and reuse flow patterns as provided in this framework is crucial for IoT programmers.

5.3.3.9 High-Level Application Development for the Internet of Things

The authors [42] propose a detailed framework for developing IoT applications. They propose a new developmental methodology and a framework to support it. To simplify the process of IoT application development, this framework stresses identifying stakeholders and demarcating their responsibilities. They can be domain experts, software designers, application developers, device developers, and network managers.

In this framework, a conceptual model, which serves as a knowledge base for a problem, is built, taking into account four different areas of concern in IoT application development: domain-specific concepts, functional-specific concepts, deployment-specific concepts, and platform-specific concepts.

- *Domain-Specific Concepts*: The concepts in this category are unique to an application domain. For example, building automation is reasoned in terms of rooms and floors. There can be sensors, actuators, and storage devices too. These concepts are identified under: *Entity of Interest* (EoI), which can be any object (eg, room, book, plant); *Resources*, such as sensors, actuators, and storage devices; and the *Region* used to specify the location of a device.
- *Functionality-Specific Concepts*: These concepts describe computational elements of an application and interactions among them. These computational elements are software components that encapsulate and hide a subset of the system's functionality and data. Interactions among software components happen through request/response, publish/subscribe, and command mode.
- *Deployment-Specific Concepts*: These concepts describe information about devices. A device is an entity that provides resources the ability to interact with each other. Each device can host zero or more resources and is located in a region.
- *Platform-Specific Concepts*: These are computer programs that act as a translator between hardware devices and an application. They are categorized as *Sensor driver*, *Actuator driver*, *Storage Services*, and *End-user application*.

The developmental framework consists of modeling languages and automation techniques to support stakeholders to implement the conceptual model.

- *Support for Domain Concerns*: The developmental framework supports domain concerns in specifying the domain vocabulary using Srijan Vocabulary Language and compiling those vocabulary specifications. This compiled output supports the later phases.
- *Functional Concerns*: For this phase the developmental framework supports by specifying application architecture using Srijan Architecture Language, then compiling the architecture specification, and finally by implementing the application logic
- *Deployment Concerns*: The framework specifies the target deployment of devices using the Srijan Deployment Language, and maps a set of computational services to a set of devices.
- *Platform Concerns*: Here, the device drivers are implemented, and the linker generates packages that can be deployed on devices. It basically combines output of all the preceding phases, such as application logic and device drivers. Device-specific code is generated in this phase.

This framework takes the software-engineering approach to IoT development and supports model-driven development.

5.3.3.10 PatRICIA

PatRICIA [1] is a programming framework for IoT application development on Cloud platforms. The key feature of this framework is the "intent"-based programming model. The programmers can specify the intent and the scope of the intent. Intents can be either a monitoring task on devices or a controlling task of devices. The intent scope delimits the range of an intent. It is the responsibility of the framework to execute the intent on the devices demarcated by the scope of the intent. This programming model hides many of the underlying complexities of IoT programming from the end users. For example, if PatRICIA is being used in traffic management, then the end user can simply say "track all the vehicles exceeding the speed limit 90." Here, PatRICIA executes the intent: track the vehicles; and the scope of the intent: all those vehicles, which exceed the speed limit 90 kmph.

The architecture of the framework is four-tiered. The topmost layer is named *Development Support Layer*. It contains tools to aid in the application-development lifecycle. It has a module called *Application Manager*, whose responsibility is to configure, deploy, and license applications, along with providing a testing environment for IoT applications. The important part of this layer is that it exposes the programming model based upon "intent" to developers. The *Cloud System Runtime layer* provides support for intent-based programming by executing the intent on the "scope of the intent." The *Data and Device Integration layer* is responsible for data Management, IoT- device management, and virtualization. The *Device Communication layer* implements different connectors catering to heterogeneous devices. The physical layer has all the things, which can communicate through the Internet.

Intent-based programming model: This programming model provides tools to work with monitoring and control tasks. Control tasks help developers to operate, provision, and manage low-level components. They provide a high-level representation of underlying devices and their functionality. They are named "ControlIntent." Likewise, monitoring tasks, named "MonitorIntent," are used to subscribe to events from the physical environment, along with obtaining and provisioning devices' context. These tasks can be represented by application developers as "intents," which get automatically instantiated for the supplied intent scope.

Intent is a data structure representing a specific task, which can be performed in a physical environment. Based on the specified intent, a suitable task is selected (control or monitor), instantiated, and executed on the Cloud platform. The Intent thereby gets translated as a sequence of steps to process data or to perform some actuation on the underlying things. To subscribe to an event in the underlying physical environment or to perform some IoT control, developers can define and configure intents. This shields the developers from the inherent complexity of the IoT.

Intent scope is an abstraction of a group of physical entities which have some common properties. The demarcation of the physical layer for an intent scope is determined on the Cloud. By specifying the properties that have to be satisfied by physical entities to be in a scope, developers define Intent Scope. PatRICIA also provides operators such as *send*, *notify*, *poll*, and *delimit* to work with intents.

The support for intent-based programming in PatRICIA will hide many of the underlying heterogeneity, which is advantageous in IoT programming.

5.3.4 SUMMARY

Each of the programming frameworks discussed earlier have their own advantages in IoT development. We highlight some of their key features in Table 5.1.

Table 5.1 Highlights of Various IoT Programming Frameworks

Framework	Approach	Key Features	Program's Target	Coordination Support
Mobile Fog	Macroprogramming	Edge processing, dynamic scaling, cloud support, Runtime API support.	Devices	Coordination support through special APIs.
ELIoT	Macroprogramming	Extends Erlang for IoT, Support for broadcast communication, RESTful API support, simulator, virtual machine support.	Devices	Coordination support through Erlang language.
Compose API	Macroprogramming	RESTful APIs to access things, cloud support, composing of services through APIs.	Cloud and devices	Coordination support on Cloud.
Distributed Dataflow support for IoT	Macroprogramming, with dataflow support	Dataflow-based IoT application development, edge processing.	Devices	Coordination through choreography.
PyoT	Macroprogramming	Edge processing support for latency-sensitive applications, Python for macroprogramming, URIs for nodes, RESTful APIs.	Devices and web	Coordination support through macroprogramming.
Dripcast	Model-driven development (Java)	Services in terms of Java objects, remote management of objects, Cloud support.	Devices	No explicit coordination support.
Calvin	Model-driven development	Actor model and dataflow-based development, Cloud support, runtime multitenancy support for things.	Devices	Coordination through choreography.
Simurgh	Macroprogramming	RESTful API support, flow design and composition support with reusability.	Devices	Orchestration support for flow patterns.
High-level application development for IoT	Model-driven development (own languages)	Complete application development, lifecycle support, division of responsibilities between stakeholders, new languages for vocabulary, architecture, and deployment specification.	Devices	Coordination support specified during identification of functional concerns.
PatRICIA	Model-driven development	Intent-based programming, cloud support for control and monitoring of tasks.	Devices and Cloud	Coordination support on cloud, specified through scope of the intent.

5.4 FUTURE RESEARCH DIRECTIONS

It is estimated by Cisco that only 2% of the present devices are Internet-enabled. As more devices get connected, there arises a need for integrating the services provided by these devices into a bigger realm. Programming frameworks should support development of new applications by integrating these services in a simple manner. We believe this can revolutionize the field of future Internet application development. Also, these applications will be geographically distributed over a wide area spanning some hostile conditions, warranting fault tolerance and edge processing for latency-sensitive applications. New frameworks should lessen the impact of IoT application-development challenges on programmers. Also, due to the huge number of devices, the volume of data available will be astronomical, which can bring in Cloud computing as a back-end support for data management and analytics. Programming frameworks that can unify IoT and Cloud as a single programming model will be more advantageous from the developers' point of view.

In addition, we believe the IoT community should also be investigating the following problems:

1. Complete support for IoT application development lifecycle by programming frameworks.
2. Documentation of IoT programming patterns and antipatterns.
3. Standardization of the IoT application development process, something similar to Capability Mature Models in traditional software engineering.
4. Lighter versions of popular programming languages such as JavaScript, Python, and Java that will continue to evolve.
5. Standardization of communication protocols at the application layer for constrained environments.
6. Standardization of wrappers for integration of legacy programs in the embedded world to the IoT realm.
7. Polyglot programming, involving languages and standards such as C, C++, Java, Erlang, Go, Javascript, .NET, WS*, and so forth for IoT, can bring in a greater number of devices, applications, and users under a single programming platform.
8. Applications such as smart cities, smart roads, and smart classrooms that will trigger development of novel approaches for IoT application development.
9. Introducing intelligence into devices that can create novel applications that may warrant secure and reliable programming frameworks for application development on intelligent devices.
10. Lightweight GUI on devices to simplify IoT application usage and attract end users from nontechnical domains.

5.5 CONCLUSIONS

In this chapter we have reviewed the challenges and some of the essential features for IoT application development. Message-passing models and embedded language features that are necessary for IoT have been reviewed. The relevance of coordination languages and polyglot programming in IoT has been discussed. The section on programming frameworks highlights the programming approaches and key features in some of the frameworks that have been recently developed for IoT application development. There are so many challenges faced by IoT application developers, and, as the domain itself is new, the standardization of frameworks will require a continuous effort from the IoT community.

REFERENCES

[1] Nastic S, Sehic S, Vogler M, Truong HL, Dustdar S. PatRICIA—a novel programming model for IoT applications on cloud platforms. In: Proceedings of the IEEE sixth international conference on service-oriented computing and applications (SOCA). Kauai, Hawai, USA, December 16–18, 2013.

[2] Botta A, de Donato W, Persico V, Pescapé A. On the integration of cloud computing and Internet of Things. In: Proceedings of the international conference on future Internet of Things and cloud (FiCloud). Barcelona, Spain, August 27–29, 2014.

[3] The top programming languages. IEEE spectrum, http://spectrum.ieee.org/static/interactive-the-top-programming-languages; 2015.

[4] Barr M. Programming embedded systems in C and C++. O'Reilly Media, Inc., CA, U.S.A; 1999.

[5] Gay D, Levis P, Von Behren R, Welsh M, Brewer E, Culler D. The nesC language: a holistic approach to networked embedded systems. ACM Sigplan Notices 2003;38:1–11.

[6] Levis P, Madden S, Polastre J, Szewczyk R, Whitehouse K, Woo A, et al. In: Weber W, Rabaey JM, Aarts E, editors. Tinyos: an operating system for sensor networks, ambient intelligence. Berlin, Heidelberg: Springer; 2005.

[7] Cx51 user's guide: language extensions. http://www.keil.com/support/man/docs/c51/c51_extensions.htm; 2015.

[8] Jerraya AA, Yoo S, Verkest D, Wehn N. Embedded software for soc. USA: Kluwer Academic Publishers; 2003.

[9] Programming language for embedded systems. http://www.bsharplanguage.org/; 2015.

[10] Birrell AD, Nelson BJ. Implementing remote procedure calls. ACM Trans Comput Syst (TOCS) 1984;2(1):39–59.

[11] Reinhardt A, Mogre PS, Steinmetz R. Lightweight remote procedure calls for wireless sensor and actuator networks. In: IEEE international conference on pervasive computing and communications workshops (PERCOM workshops). Seattle, USA, March 21–25, 2011.

[12] Bershad BN, Anderson TE, Lazowska ED, Levy HM. Lightweight remote procedure call. ACM Trans Comput Syst (TOCS) 1990;8(1):37–55.

[13] Whitehouse K, Tolle G, Taneja J, Sharp C, Kim S, Jeong J, Hui J, Dutta P, Culler D. Marionette: using RPC for interactive development and debugging of wireless embedded networks. In: Proceedings of the fifth international conference on information processing in sensor networks. Nashville, USA, April 19–21, 2006.

[14] May TD, Dunning SH, Dowding GA, Hallstrom JO. An RPC design for wireless sensor networks. Int J Pervasive Comput Commun 2007;2(4):384–97.

[15] Fielding RT. Architectural styles and the design of network-based software architectures. PhD thesis, University of California, Irvine; 2000.

[16] Feng X, Shen J, Fan Y. REST: an alternative to RPC for web services architecture. In: Proceedings of the first international conference on future information networks. Beijing, China, October 14–17, 2009.

[17] Pautasso C. Composing restful services with Jopera. In: Proceedings of the eighth international conference on software composition. Zurich, Switzerland, July 2–3, 2009.

[18] Erenkrantz JR, Gorlick M, Suryanarayana G, Taylor RN. From representations to computations: the evolution of web architectures. In: Proceedings of the sixth joint meeting of the European software engineering conference and the ACM SIGSOFT symposium on the foundations of software engineering. Cavtat, Croatia, September 3–7, 2007.

[19] Sivieri A. ELIoT: a programming framework for the Internet of Things. PhD thesis, Politecnico De Milano, Italy; 2014.

[20] Kovatsch M, Duquennoy S, Dunkels A. A low-power CoAP for Contiki. In: Proceedings of the IEEE eighth international conference on mobile ad-hoc and sensor systems (MASS). Valencia, Spain, October 17–21, 2011.

[21] Ludovici A, Moreno P, Calveras A. TinyCoAP: a novel constrained application protocol (CoAP) implementation for embedding RESTful web services in wireless sensor networks based on TinyOS. J Sens Actu Netw 2013;2(2):288–315.

[22] Levä T, Mazhelis O, Suomi H. Comparing the cost-efficiency of CoAP and HTTP in Web of Things applications. Decis Support Syst 2014;63:23–38.

[23] Carriero N, Gelernter D. How to write parallel programs. MIT Press; 1990.

[24] Wells G. Coordination languages: back to the future with Linda. In: Proceedings of the second international workshop on coordination, adaption techniques for software entities (WCAT05). Glasgow, UK, July 25, 2005.

[25] Kitchin D, Quark A, Cook W, Misra J. The Orc programming language. In: Lee D, Lopes A, Poetzch-Heffter A, editors. Formal techniques for distributed systems. Berlin, Heidelberg: Springer-Verlag; 2009.

[26] Cook WR, Patwardhan S, Misra J. Workflow patterns in Orc. In: Ciancarini P, Wiklicky H, editors. Coordination models and languages. Berlin, Heidelberg: Springer; 2006.

[27] Montesi F, Guidi C, Lucchi R, Zavattaro G. Jolie: a Java orchestration language interpreter engine. Electron Notes Theor Comput Sci 2007;181:19–33.

[28] Montesi F, Guidi C, Lanese I, Zavattaro G. Dynamic fault handling mechanisms for service-oriented applications. In: Proceedings of the sixth European conference on web services. Dublin, Ireland, November 12–14, 2008.

[29] Fjeldberg, H-C. Polyglot programming: a business perspective. Master's thesis, Norwegian University of Science and Technology; 2008.

[30] Harmanen J. Polyglot programming in web development. Master's thesis, Tampere University of Technology; 2013.

[31] Schmidt DC, Gokhale A, Natarajan B. Frameworks: why they are important and how to apply them effectively. ACM Queue Mag 2004;2(5):66–75.

[32] Jardosh S, Patel P. Application development approaches for the Internet of Things: a survey. In: Proceedings of the IEEE conferentd: TENSYMP 2015. Ahmedabad, India, May 13–15, 2015.

[33] Bonomi F, Milito R, Zhu J, Addepalli S. Fog computing and its role in the Internet of Things. In: Proceedings of the first edition of the MCC workshop on mobile cloud computing. Helsinki, Finland, August 17, 2012.

[34] Hong K, Lillethun D, Ramachandran U, Ottenwälder B, Koldehofe B. Mobile fog: a programming model for large-scale applications on the Internet of Things. In: Proceedings of the second ACM SIGCOMM workshop on mobile cloud computing. Hong Kong, August 12, 2013.

[35] Sivieri A, Mottola L, Cugola G. Drop the phone and talk to the physical world: programming the Internet of Things with Erlang. In: Proceedings of the third international workshop on software engineering for sensor network applications. Zurich, Switzerland, June 2, 2012.

[36] Pérez JL, Villalba A, Carrera D, Larizgoitia I, Trifa V. The COMPOSE API for the Internet of Things. In: Proceedings of the companion publication of the twenty-third international conference on World Wide Web. Seoul, Korea, April 7–11, 2014.

[37] Blackstock M, Lea R. Towards a distributed data flow platform for the Web of Things. In: Proceedings of the fifth international workshop on Web of Things. Cambridge, USA, October 8, 2014.

[38] Azzara A, Alessandrelli D, Bocchino S, Petracca M, Pagano P. PyoT: a macroprogramming framework for the Internet of Things. In: Proceedings of the ninth IEEE international symposium on industrial embedded systems (SIES). Pisa, Italy, June 18–20, 2014.

[39] Nakagawa I, Hiji M, Esaki H. Dripcast-architecture and implementation of server-less Java programming framework for billions of IoT devices. J Infor Process 2014;23(4):458–64.

[40] Persson P, Angelsmark O. Calvin—merging cloud and IoT. Proc Comput Sci 2015;52:210–7.

[41] Khodadadi F, Dastjerdi AV, Buyya R. Simurgh: a framework for effective discovery, programming, and integration of services exposed in IoT. In: Proceedings of the international conference on recent advances in Internet of Things (RIoT). Singapore, April 7–9, 2015.

[42] Patel P, Cassou D. Enabling high-level application development for the Internet of Things. J Syst Softw 2015;103:62–84.

VIRTUALIZATION ON EMBEDDED BOARDS AS ENABLING TECHNOLOGY FOR THE CLOUD OF THINGS

6

B. Bardhi*, A. Claudi**, L. Spalazzi*, G. Taccari[†], L. Taccari*

*Department of Information Engineering, Università Politecnica delle Marche, Ancona, Italy;
**ADB Broadband S.p.A., Viale Sarca, Milano, Italy; [†]Par-Tec S.p.A., Milano, Italy

6.1 INTRODUCTION

Nowadays, the interlinked networks of sensors, actuators, and processing devices are creating a vast net of connected computing resources, things, and humans. NIST and NICT, in their joint report about cyber-physical cloud computing [1], refer to this scenario as Smart Networked Systems and Societies (SNSS) and propose several application domains; healthcare, disaster management, power-grid and energy saving, and automotive and transportation systems are some of them. In analyzing the requirements of such application domains, it turns out that an SNSS should be based on the following core technologies:

1. networking services,
2. real-time systems,
3. wireless sensor/actuator networks,
4. social networks, and
5. computing services.

Internet of Things (IoT) and cloud computing have seen an independent evolution, and each of them has been conceived to cover a part of the aforementioned technologies, namely: IoT covers points 1, 2, and 3, whereas cloud computing covers 1, 4, and 5 [2]. As a consequence, the integration of IoT and cloud computing, called Cloud of Things (CoT), can be considered as a first step toward the SNSS vision [1,3]. Indeed, the benefits that IoT and cloud computing receive from their integration are the following:

- *Pervasivity and ubiquity*: Pervasivity, that is, when things are placed everywhere, is typical of IoT; whereas ubiquity, that is, when resources are usable from everywhere, is typical of cloud computing.
- *Efficient use of resources*: CoT resources such as sensors and actuators can be shared among processes and systems. This implies a higher utilization, and, thus, a higher efficiency.
- *Modular composition*: CoT resources can be combined (orchestrated) in different ways to create a variety of smart-systems customized to individual stakeholders' needs.

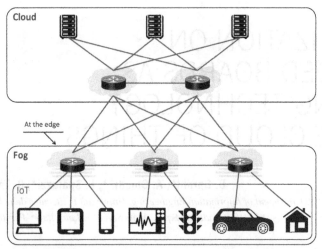

FIGURE 6.1 Cloud and Fog Computing

- *Rapid deployment and scalability*: The orchestration of CoT resources can be rapidly deployed when needed, scaled up or down when needs change, and released when no longer needed.
- *Reliability and resiliency*: The ability to dynamically change the resources used by the system helps the resulting systems to be reliable and resilient.

Very recently, a further extension of cloud computing, called fog computing [3,4], has been proposed, in order to reach "the very edge of the network" (Fig. 6.1).

This paradigm has been introduced to support some specific requirements of IoT applications:

- edge location and location awareness (instead of location ignorance, typical of cloud computing)
- geographical distribution of a very large number of nodes (instead of centralized clusters)
- mobility (through wireless access)
- real-time interaction (instead of batch processes)
- resource heterogeneity

As a consequence, this recent paradigm shift allows CoT to leave on the edge the part of the computation that involves sensing and actuating and, thus, to have low latency. Furthermore, this allows for shareable resources and multi-tenancy. Therefore, both CoT and fog computing can be delivered according to the three classical models of cloud computing (Fig. 6.2):

- *SaaS*: For each thing, a set of services are identified and then delivered (eg, see [5]).
- *PaaS*: Physical things are managed by the cloud provider; they may be used by means of programming languages, libraries, and tools supported by the provider (eg, see [6,7]). The consumer neither manages nor controls the underlying cloud infrastructure.
- *IaaS*: Physical things are virtualized in order to allow multi-tenancy and their sharing among different systems [8].

Each of these can be specialized to a specific delivery model, depending on the given specific problem to solve. Some examples [3] are Sensing and Actuation as a Service (SAaaS) that enables

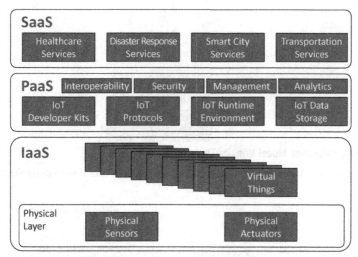

FIGURE 6.2 The Three Delivery Models of Fog and Cloud-of-Things Computing

ubiquitous management of sensors and actuators using typical control logics of cloud computing, Data as a Service (DaaS) that enables ubiquitous access to any kind of data, and Sensor Event as a Service (SEaaS) that enables services triggered by sensor events.

Put in a nutshell, IoT is moving toward cloud computing, and, then, toward fog computing. As a consequence of this trend, the virtualization inside embedded systems is required. At this point, two fundamental questions arise:

Q1. Are the current hardware technologies for embedded systems appropriate for virtualization?
Q2. Are the current virtualization techniques appropriate for embedded systems? If so, what is the most appropriate technique?

This chapter tries to provide answers to the aforementioned questions. In order to do that, Section 6.2 surveys three basic virtualization techniques [9–11] for embedded systems [12]: full virtualization and paravirtualization (as instances of hardware-level virtualization), and containers (as an instance of operating-system-level virtualization). Section 6.3 discusses which kinds of requirements are introduced by real-time needs. Section 6.4 faces the problem from a practical point of view, and reports some experimental results using as a testbed a Cubieboard2: a low-cost, low-energy, ARM Cortex-A7-based device with limited performance, but with hardware that supports virtualization. Such experiments first allow us to provide an answer to the aforementioned questions; however, some aspects, such as real time, should still be explored and be a part of future research. The latter is discussed in Section 6.5. Finally, some concluding remarks are reported in Section 6.6.

6.2 BACKGROUND

Since the origins of time-sharing operating systems, designers pointed to providing access to machine resources in a transparent manner, given to the applications the illusion that resources are owned by them even if they are shared among other applications [13]. In other words, each application runs on

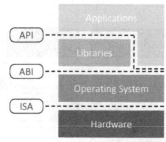

FIGURE 6.3 A Machine Reference Model With its Three Interface Levels

API, Application Programming Interface; *ABI*, Application Binary Interface; *ISA*, Instruction Set Architecture.

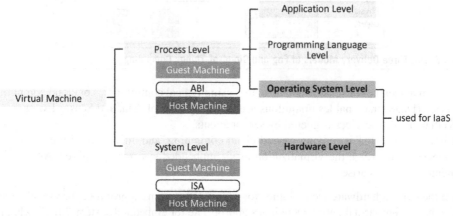

FIGURE 6.4 Virtualization Technique Taxonomy

a "virtual" machine. The resulting virtualization techniques to apply depend on the interface level at which they operate. According to a well-known machine reference model (Fig. 6.3), the virtualization techniques can operate at the Instruction Set Architecture (ISA) level or at the Application Binary Interface (ABI). As a consequence, the virtualization techniques can be classified in System Level virtualization (exposing an ISA) and Process Level virtualization (exposing an ABI), as depicted in Fig. 6.4.

Concerning hardware-level virtualization, basically two virtualization technologies are used: full virtualization and para-virtualization. In *full virtualization* the virtualized interface provided to the guest OSs is identical to the host machine, so the OSs do not have to be modified in order to run on guest VM. *Paravirtualization*, as the name suggests, provides an interface which differs from the host machine; in this case a modified OS is needed in order to run on virtual machines. Furthermore, it should be noted that hardware-level virtualization requires a hypervisor (also called Virtual Machine Manager or VMM) in order to manage VMs. As a consequence, hardware-level virtualization requires a hierarchical scheduling: an inter-VM scheduler to choose which VM will be executed, and an intra-VM scheduler for each VM to schedule VM tasks. Each scheduler is not aware of the existence of the others, due to the needing of isolation. There exists two kinds of hypervisors: Type-I hypervisors and Type-II hypervisors.

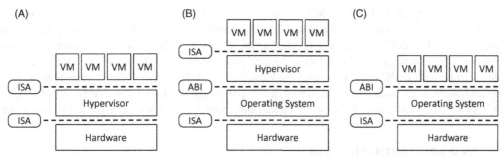

FIGURE 6.5 Hardware-Level and Process-Level Virtualization Taxonomy

(A) Hardware-level virtualization, Type I Hypervisor; (B) hardware-level virtualization, Type II Hypervisor; (C) operating system level virtualization, Container based.

Type-1 hypervisors, or bare-metal hypervisors (Fig. 6.5A), run directly on the physical hardware. They offer independent and isolated partitions that virtualize critical-hardware devices, and also provide services for interpartition communication and control. This type of hypervisor is particularly suited for real-time systems, because they are close to the hardware (thus having lower overhead than Type-2 hypervisors) and are able to use hardware resources directly. Examples of Type-1 hypervisors are VMWare, ESX, XtratuM [14], and Xen [9].

Type-2 hypervisors (Fig. 6.5B) run on top of operating systems, where they act like hosts. In this type of hypervisor, the host operating system runs on top of the hardware, and the hypervisor is a high-level software layer running different guest operating systems. Type-2 hypervisors are easier to use and manage, but they have a higher overhead than Type-1 hypervisors. Examples of Type-2 hypervisors are Virtualbox, Oracle VM Server, and KVM [15].

Concerning process-level virtualization, this chapter focuses on virtualization at operating-system-level, as this is the level that can be used for an IaaS delivery model. A popular technique for this kind of virtualization consists in the *container-based virtualization* [16] (Fig. 6.5C). It should be noted that such a solution, unlike hardware-level virtualization, does not need a hypervisor to run guest operating systems; rather, it is based on the virtualization of the OS system calls: thus, several software containers and physical resources can be shared to manage the system calls coming from each container. As a consequence, the guest operating system coincides with the host operating system that allows for multiple isolated user-space instances, and, thus, no hierarchical scheduling is required. Examples of container-based virtualization are LXC, FreeBSD Jails, and OpenVZ.

6.2.1 ARM VIRTUALIZATION EXTENSIONS

ARM processors gained virtualization extensions fairly recently, with the ARMv7 [17] and ARMv8 [18] architectures. This instruction set allows ARM processors to virtualize CPUs, memory, interrupts, and timers. In order to simplify the use of hypervisors on ARM architectures, ARM added a new processor mode, the Hyp mode, with higher privileges compared to conventional kernel and user modes. Hyp mode is used during the execution of a VM. When a VM requires servicing by the hypervisor, the hardware traps to the Hyp mode, giving control to the hypervisor. Once the hypervisor terminates its work, the CPU switches to kernel or user mode, and the control is returned to the VM. The virtualization of the physical memory is based on a translation mechanism. Indeed, VMs addresses are Intermediate Physical Addresses (IPAs) and they have to be translated into physical addresses (PAs), which refer to the physical memory. To that end, ARM provides Stage-2 page tables which allow the translation from guest addresses to host ones. In the ARM architecture, interrupts are virtualized, extending the Generic Interrupt Controller (GIC) architecture to Virtual GIC (VGIC). VGIC provides an interface for each CPU and a corresponding control interface to be used by the hypervisor. This way, each VCPU communicates with its own VGIC interface, using the kernel mode of the VM. Similar to interrupts, physical timers and counters are associated with virtual timers and virtual counters, respectively. Only the hypervisor in Hyp mode can manage the physical timers and counters, but VMs can control the virtual ones.

6.2.2 XEN ARM VIRTUALIZATION

Xen [9] is a lightweight, high-performance, open-source Type-1 hypervisor. Like KVM, it allows several instances of an operating system or different operating systems on the same physical host to run. As Type-1 hypervisors, in Xen, virtualization is based on a microkernel loaded during the boot process, which makes it possible to run several VMs. Such a microkernel has the advantage of having a small memory-footprint (around 1 MB) and a limited interface for guests that results in a more robust and secure virtualization as compared to other hypervisors. Upon such a microkernel, Xen runs two kinds of guest VMs, namely, domains. The Dom0 domain, one per physical host, is the privileged domain, and it is the only one that has direct access to the underlying hardware. This domain provides paravirtualized back-ends in order to give access to disks, NICs (Network Interface Cards), consoles, and other virtualized resources to the unprivileged domains (DomUs). Hence, DomUs are completely isolated from each other and can access physical resources by means of paravirtualized front-ends. In common configurations, Dom0 has the only role of a Xen controller, and DomUs are used to run guest VMs. On ARM architectures, Xen exploits, whenever possible, the ARM CPU hardware virtualization extensions. In particular, Xen completely runs in Hyp mode; the kernel uses the ARM hvc instruction to invoke hypercalls to Xen, and Xen uses second-stage translation to assign memory to VMs. This fosters Xen to be a mature virtualization solution for embedded boards, even if it requires a CPU which supports virtualization.

6.2.3 KVM ARM VIRTUALIZATION

KVM stands for Kernel-based Virtual Machine. KVM is a Type-2 hypervisor based on the Linux kernel, which supports a variety of processors with hardware virtualization extensions. KVM was merged in the Linux kernel in 2007, and over the years it was ported from x86 to a number of different architectures, including PowerPC and ARM. KVM consists of a loadable kernel module that provides the core virtualization infrastructure and different processor-specific modules. Using them, the Linux kernel acts as a host that can run multiple VMs, each with private virtualized hardware. On the ARM architecture porting, KVM introduces split-mode virtualization, allowing a hypervisor to split its execution across CPU modes [19]. This means that KVM can use the Hyp mode provided by ARM processors with hardware virtualization capabilities. The hypervisor is split into low-visor and high-visor components. The low-visor runs in Hyp mode, deals directly with the hardware, and manages interrupts and the isolation of execution contexts. The high-visor, instead, runs in kernel mode and uses the Linux kernel to execute operations that do not directly need access to the Hyp mode. As a Type-2 hypervisor, KVM allows the VMs to use the real-host processor (thus being transparent to them), using context switches to alternate the host and the VMs on the processor. As such, the role of the hypervisor is to save and restore the state of the host and/or VMs during the context switches. On the ARM architecture, during these operations the Hyp stack is used to store register content, and the Stage-2 page table base-register-content is modified accordingly to the VM or host that has to be executed. On every architecture, interrupts may be trapped, depending on which kernel is going to be executed. KVM uses the Stage-2 translation page-table in order to access the memory allocated to each VM, thus simplifying memory virtualization architecture. I/O virtualization, instead, is based on load and store operations to MMIO device regions. The Stage-2 translation makes it impossible for a VM to use the physical devices directly. Finally, KVM virtualizes the interrupts, using the kernel to trap physical-device interrupts to the Hyp mode, and forwarding them to the VMs by means of virtual interrupts. Timer virtualization, instead, is based directly on ARM hardware virtualization features, allowing VMs to directly read timers and counters.

6.2.4 CONTAINER-BASED VIRTUALIZATION

Aside from hypervisors, in recent years a new virtualization technology has reached the proper maturity level to be adopted as a virtualization solution in enterprise environments. Such technology is based on containers [11,16,20,21], a software solution which provides hardware resource-sharing and enables the isolation of processes confined to a container from others that run on other containers. The basic principle of containers is to guarantee resource sharing and isolation without needing hardware virtualization or hardware requirements. Container technology is based on kernel ABI virtualization, and does not use hypervisors. In this way, groups of processes may use the same operating system without needing hardware-level virtualization; they only need access to the function provided by the underlying kernel. Originally, this idea was introduced in container-based operating systems, such as Solaris 10 [22], Virtuozzo [23], and Linux-VServer [24]. It is worth mentioning the BSD chroot() [25], introduced in 1982, which proposes a first method to obtain isolation by creating different containers where processes may run without access to others running in other containers. Because virtualization acts at the OS system call-level and it does not need hypervisors or other mechanisms to virtualize an entire physical machine, container-based virtualization provides near-native performance in terms of overhead, while maintaining a good level of isolation [26]. In recent years, container technology has become popular in GNU/Linux operating systems with the Linux Containers (LXC) [27]. Similar to other container-based virtualization solutions, Linux Containers takes advantage of OS system calls to enable virtualization. With respect to other solutions, Linux Containers became a de-facto standard for container-based virtualization, and became a part of the official Linux kernel. Modern Linux containers take advantage of cgroup [28] and namespaces, which guarantee isolation among the containers. cgroups can be thought of as resource controllers that work on groups of processes. In the Linux kernel there are cgroups for controlling block devices, CPU resources, CPU affinity for a group of processes, devices, suspending and resuming processes, memory allocation, packet classification and prioritization, and access to performance events. These controllers manage resources assigned to groups of processes (processes that run inside a container). Forked processes inside a container inherit permission from their parent processes. Namespaces can be thought of as extensions of chroot(), which remap host resources (network interfaces, process IDs, hosts, mount points, users) to resources shown in the containers. By means of namespaces, processes may access the real resources of the host, maintaining a point of view on virtualized ones. Hence, container-based virtualization solutions give the illusion of working on a real system, but abstract only the system-calls' access. For this reason, this kind of virtualization does not need any particular requirement when it is used on embedded hardware. However, by design, each container is tightened to the host-kernel version.

6.3 VIRTUALIZATION AND REAL-TIME

As stated in Section 6.1, cloud- and fog-computing architectures and methodologies are increasingly applied in IoT scenarios, thus generating the need for virtualization solutions for embedded systems. Indeed, in recent years a wide range of virtualization technologies has been deployed in the embedded-systems domain, including avionic systems, industrial automation, telecommunication systems, etc. Computing applications in these domains often have strict timing and performance constraints, thus making virtualization in embedded systems very different from conventional virtualization. Virtualization on embedded systems typically places a stronger emphasis on issues like real-time performance, security, and dependability in open and shared computing environments. [29]. This means that to meet real-time requirements, virtualized real-time systems not only have to guarantee service-level agreements, such as in typical cloud applications, but must also enforce temporal and spatial isolation between different VMs. The increasing need to control the temporal behavior of the virtualized applications and enhance their predictability led to several real-time virtualization techniques [30]. Following the terminology adopted in [31], VMs using these techniques are named in the following as real-time virtual machines (RT-VMs).

A number of commercial real-time hypervisors are available on the market, such as the ones produced by WindRiver, Acontis Technology, SysGO, OpenSynergy, LynuxWorks, or Real Time Systems GmbH. However, these hypervisors are usually strongly tied to particular application domains, and their use in different domains frequently highlights suboptimal performance and raises low-level compatibility problems [31]. At the same time, open-source general-purpose hypervisors like Xen and KVM are the focus of strong research and development efforts to make them compliant with real-time requirements outlined previously. This makes it possible to compare Type-1 and Type-2 hypervisors with respect to real-time requirements through two different widely deployed and well-documented solutions. A different approach to real-time virtualization is to base it on OS-level virtualization and a real-time operating system (RTOS) at the host level. This simplifies some of the challenges to integrate real-time computing with virtualization, in general at the cost of diminished flexibility, compared to that of Type-1 and Type-2 hypervisors. An example of this approach is LXC [32].

The main technical and research challenges to integrate real-time computing in virtualization are:

- Design of a hypervisor compliant with real-time requirement
- Real-time scheduling, both inter- and intra-RT-VMs
- Network communication between RT-VMs

Regarding the design of a real-time hypervisor compliant with the requirements previously outlined, we can further identify three different areas of intervention: interrupts translation, timer access, and SMP (symmetric multiprocessing) support.

Interrupts translation consists of transforming hardware interrupts to software interrupts, and forwarding them to the host operating system. It is an operation typically done by the hypervisor. For a real-time hypervisor, interrupt translation is of great importance, because it can be a source of unexpected latencies. Indeed, each VM is typically associated with a queue of interrupts to be serviced, but will serve them only when the hypervisor scheduler designs them for execution. This means that if more virtual CPUs are ready to execute, then interrupts can be serviced with latencies of up to tens of milliseconds.

Timer access is also of great importance in the design of a real-time hypervisor. Time measurements must be immediately available to applications requiring access to them. RT-VMs need time measurements to perform critical tasks such as scheduling, resource management and accounting.

To avoid unpredictable behaviors, the real-time hypervisor scheduler must be designed to influence RT-VM time measures as little as possible.

A good real-time hypervisor must also ensure a uniform progress rate among the virtual CPUs, especially in the presence of multicore RT-VMs. A typical problem that can arise when virtual CPUs are not guaranteed a uniform progress rate is the lock-holder preemption problem [29], which happens when the kernel of an RT-VM attempts a spin-lock operation, waiting for a different RT-VM which was preempted before. This can result in latencies in the order of tens of milliseconds, whereas a typical spin-lock operation concludes in tens of microseconds.

Scheduling is of paramount importance for real-time virtualization. In general, both Type-1 and Type-2 hypervisors have no knowledge about tasks within each VM, and schedules them like black-boxes, trying to minimize VM response time; this enhances modularity and is in general an approach good enough for general-purpose virtualization. However, in a real-time virtualization architecture the hypervisor must ensure that all tasks—including tasks within each VM—meet their deadlines. Therefore, for a real-time hypervisor it is essential to access to task details within each VM. This is called task-grain scheduling [33]. There are three different approach to task-grain scheduling.

- In Type-1 virtualization, the guest OS is modified to disclose information about its internal tasks to the real-time hypervisor via hypercalls
- In Type-2 virtualization, information about internal VM tasks are inferred by the real-time hypervisor, without modification to the guest OS
- OS-level virtualization architecture can be modified to use the host OS scheduler, thus letting the real-time kernel handle the scheduling of all tasks [34].

The solutions outlined previously for Type-1 and Type-2 hypervisors make use of hierarchical scheduling techniques. Hierarchical scheduling enables resource partitioning and allocation among a set of virtualized real-time applications, enhancing temporal isolation and yielding a reduction of complexity in applications [35]. In real-time hypervisors, hierarchical scheduling is usually deployed on two hierarchical levels: a real-time inter-VM scheduler and a real-time intra-VM scheduler. This architecture is used both in Xen and in KVM approaches to real-time virtualization on ARM embedded architectures.

An example of a Type-1 real-time hypervisor is RT-Xen [15,36]. RT-Xen is a fork of the Xen project, including a fixed-priority scheduler based on the real-time scheduling theory, and used to schedule VMs. The schedulability of the system can be formally examined because the real-time hypervisor scheduler (inter-VM scheduler) and the real-time scheduler (intra-VM scheduler) in the RT-VMs are placed in a hierarchical scheduling architecture. RT-Xen exhibits only a moderate scheduling overhead and can provide real-time scheduling services to RT-VMs with a quantum of 1 ms [15]. RT-Xen recently evolved into RT-Xen 2.0, providing a new multicore real-time scheduler, which can be used for global and partitioned scheduling. Several server algorithms are also provided to schedule low-critical tasks in combination with high-critical ones [37].

Type-2 real-time hypervisors have received far less attention from the real-time community. In recent years, the bulk of the efforts focused on KVM. Technical challenges and possible solutions to make KVM a real-time hypervisor are presented in [38]. It is possible to devise a real-time scheduling architecture to enhance KVM real-time capabilities, using SCHED_DEADLINE [39] for host OS scheduling, and coupling it with proper real-time scheduling policies to schedule RT-VM tasks. In this way it is possible to use real-time theoretical techniques to analyze system schedulability, as it happens for RT-Xen. To the best of our knowledge, there is no paper published that details progress in this respect.

OS-level real-time virtualization ensures temporal and spatial isolation between real-time applications through the use of multiple domains with different namespaces; this also allows achievement of a certain degree of security and protection between different applications. As stated previously, it is impossible to run different kernels on the same host OS using OS-level virtualization; however, this is hardly a limitation on embedded architectures, which are often conceived to run a set of pre-determined applications. Thus, being more lightweight of system-level virtualization solutions, OS real-time virtualization can be a good candidate for virtualization on embedded systems. Among the different OS-level virtualization mechanisms, LXC seems to be the most promising with respect to real-time requirements. Currently, LXC does not enforce a real-time scheduling policy and does not manage resources according to real-time requirements by default; instead it uses the standard Linux kernel policies, that is, CFS to schedule containers for execution and CFQ to manage resource access. However, it is possible to modify these policies, and use instead real-time scheduling policies, like SCHED_DEADLINE [39] to schedule containers, and the deadline scheduler for I/O activities.

6.4 EXPERIMENTAL RESULTS

This section details experimental results on three different virtualization setups that we have created in our lab. Experiments were carried on the same testbed, a System-on-a-chip (SoC) offering virtualization features. We compared three different virtualization approaches using three different software configurations: Xen was chosen as an instance of a Type-1 hypervisor, KVM as an instance of a Type-2 hypervisor, and LXC was tested as an OS-level virtualization solution. Each experiment was repeated for the three- software configuration.

The first part of this section describes the reference architecture of the SoC used in the experiments and the software configurations used. Test benchmark suites that we used in the experiments are also described. Finally, experimental results are presented and discussed.

6.4.1 REFERENCE ARCHITECTURE

We chose a CubieTech Cubieboard2 SoC for our experiments. The Cubieboard2 is a low-cost, low-energy, Allwinner A20 SoC. This SoC has the following components:

- CPU: Dual-core ARM Cortex-A7 MPCore
- GPU: Mali-400 MP2
- Memory: 1 GB DDR3 RAM
- Storage: 4 GB NAND, microSD slot, SATA port
- Network: 100 Mbit/s ethernet
- USB: 2 USB 2.0 port, 1 USB 2.0 OTG

The ARM Cortex-A7 MPCore (and other processors of the ARMv7-A and ARMv8-A families) provides the ARM Hardware Virtualization Extensions [40]. These hardware extensions are required both by Xen and KVM hypervisors. An 8GB microSD Class 10 was used as a storage device for all of the described configurations. Please note that the GPU, SATA port, and USB 2.0 ports were not used for any of the benchmark tests described later.

All three software configurations were based on Debian [41] GNU/Linux armhf. Unfortunately, different packages needed for Xen and KVM were not available in the major GNU/Linux distributions, and so they had to be cross-compiled. In particular, we needed to cross-compile Linux-3.18.18, Xen-4.5.1, and Qemu-2.3.0.

For each virtualization solution, an ad-hoc kernel configuration was used in order to enable just the needed drivers for the SoC and drivers for the particular virtualization solution. Only those services that were strictly needed were installed and enabled, both in host systems and guest systems, in order to avoid potential performance degradations.

6.4.2 BENCHMARKING TOOLS

The benchmark tool used for evaluating CPU-bound operations, memory allocation, and transfer speed was called "sysbench." "sysbench" is modular, cross-platform, multi-threaded, and allows for the evaluation of OS parameters that are important for a system running a database under intensive load [42]. The evaluation of I/O-bound operations was done by means of "dd" and "iPerf3." "dd" first appeared in Unix version 6 and it simply copies an input file to an output file. It was used to analyze the microSD performances in writing sequential data. "iPerf3" is a tool for active measurements of the maximum achievable bandwidth on IP networks. It supports tuning of various parameters related to timing, protocols, and buffers. For each test it reports bandwidth, packet loss, and other parameters [43]. "iPerf" was originally developed by NLANR/DAST (National Laboratory for Applied Network Research, Distributed Application Support Team); it was rewritten and is now currently maintained and developed by ESnet, part of Lawrence Berkeley National Laboratory. "iPerf" was used to measure TCP/IP bandwidth for the integrated 100 Mbit/s ethernet port.

6.4.3 DISCUSSION

6.4.3.1 CPU Performance Analysis

To analyze CPU performance, sysbench provides a CPU benchmark that consists of the calculation of prime numbers up to an arbitrary value provided as an option. All the calculations are done with 64-bit integers, using Euclid's algorithm.

In order to analyze the latencies introduced by the virtualization solutions, the test was performed first without any DomUs, KVM guests, or LXC containers, and then by increasing the number of DomUs, KVM guests, and LXC containers up to four simultaneously:

- 0 DomUs/guests/containers
- 1 DomUs/guests/containers, two virtual CPUs each DomUs/guests/containers, memory: 512 MB each DomUs/guests/containers
- 2 DomUs/guests/containers, two virtual CPUs each DomUs/guests/containers, memory: 256 MB each DomUs/guests/containers
- 4 DomUs/guests/containers, two virtual CPUs each DomUs/guests/containers, memory: 128 MB each DomUs/guests/containers

As sysbench's CPU test allows spawning several threads, for all of the previous configurations, 1, 2, and 4 threads were used to do the calculation. All of the CPU tests calculated the first 10,000 prime numbers. The results are reported in Table 6.1 for the host machines and Table 6.2 for the guest machines.

Table 6.1 Benchmark Completion Time (Hosts)

Host	1 Thread								2 Threads								4 Threads							
	KVM		XEN		LXC				KVM		XEN		LXC				KVM		XEN		LXC			
#VM	Avg.	Std. dev.	Avg.	Std. dev.	Avg.	Std. dev.			Avg.	Std. dev.	Avg.	Std. dev.	Avg.	Std. dev.			Avg.	Std. dev.	Avg.	Std. dev.	Avg.	Std. dev.		
0	290.31	0.00	291.36	0.00	290.47	0.00			145.51	0.00	145.87	0.00	145.32	0.01			145.70	0.01	145.97	0.01	146.30	0.01		
1	290.28	0.00	293.79	0.00	290.85	0.00			292.94	0.00	292.27	0.01	290.92	0.01			218.44	0.02	292.58	0.02	291.23	0.01		
2	439.77	0.00	443.31	0.00	435.13	0.00			439.28	0.05	439.36	0.01	436.63	0.02			291.70	0.03	439.89	0.13	436.54	0.02		
4	746.82	0.00	752.09	0.00	728.66	0.00			732.71	0.03	734.38	0.01	727.61	0.04			439.75	0.03	735.58	0.04	728.04	0.06		

Table 6.2 Benchmark Completion Time (Guests)

GUEST	1 Thread								2 Threads								4 Threads							
	KVM		XEN		LXC				KVM		XEN		LXC				KVM		XEN		LXC			
# VM	Avg.	Std. dev.	Avg.	Std. dev.	Avg.	Std. dev.			Avg.	Std. dev.	Avg.	Std. dev.	Avg.	Std. dev.			Avg.	Std. dev.	Avg.	Std. dev.	Avg.	Std. dev.		
1	295.37	0.00	293.71	0.00	290.82	0.00			290.28	0.00	291.73	0.02	290.90	0.00			292.43	0.02	291.99	0.03	291.21	0.02		
2	442.80	0.00	443.14	0.00	436.24	0.00			440.65	0.00	438.51	0.05	436.74	0.03			442.89	0.02	438.97	0.05	436.38	0.05		
4	753.89	0.00	751.19	0.00	727.59	0.00			739.60	0.03	732.83	0.02	727.19	0.02			742.71	0.09	733.77	0.16	727.61	0.07		

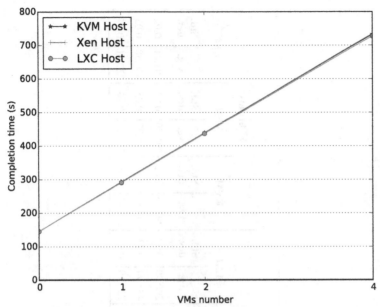

FIGURE 6.6 Benchmark Completion Time (Hosts) for the Configuration With 2 Threads

In Table 6.1, we can see the benchmark's completion time for Xen, KVM, and LXC hosts, depending on the number of VMs. Performances are very similar, with LXC performing slightly better when four VMs are used. Fig. 6.6 represents the hosts' performance for the configuration, with 2 threads for each host and VM. It should also be noted that in the 4-thread experiment, the KVM host shows better performance with respect to Xen and LXC. This result is a consequence of the fact that KVM uses the Linux kernel scheduler as the inter-VM scheduler. This means that from the scheduler point of view each VM is a task to be scheduled on the host, just like the benchmark's tasks; thus tasks running on VMs suffer from an overhead.

In Table 6.2, the benchmark's completion time for guests is depicted. In this case, too, as the number of VMs increases, LXC performs slightly better than virtualization solutions based on hypervisors. Fig. 6.7 represents the guests' performance for the configuration, with 2 threads for each host and VM.

6.4.3.2 Memory Performance Analysis
To analyze write memory (RAM) allocation and write speed, sysbench provides a memory benchmark that by default sequentially writes blocks of memory. In order to analyze the memory-write performance, 2 GB data were sequentially written in the memory in blocks of 1024 bytes—one at a time—on the host and on the guest. Finally, two virtual CPUs and 512 MB of memory were assigned to the guest systems.

Fig. 6.8 illustrates experimental results. Performances are similar, with hypervisor solutions slightly suffering indirect access to memory, with the notable exception of the KVM host. LXC performs better than Xen and KVM.

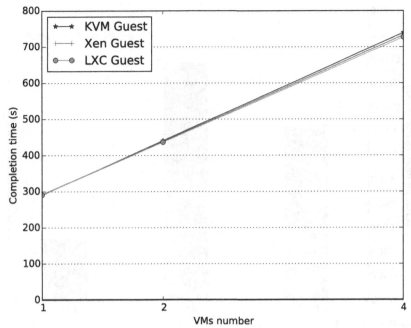

FIGURE 6.7 Benchmark Completion Time (Guests) for the Configuration With 2 Threads

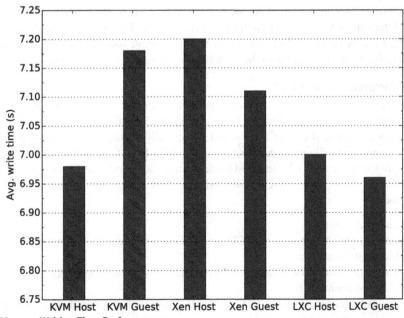

FIGURE 6.8 Memory-Writing Time Performances

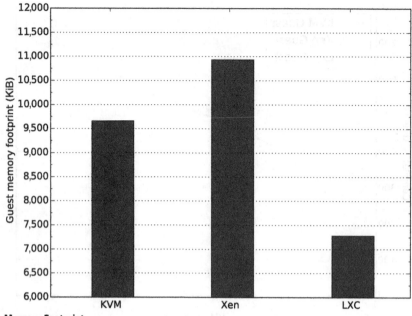

FIGURE 6.9 Memory Footprint

6.4.3.3 Memory Footprint Analysis

The memory footprint for the three virtualization solutions taken into consideration are analyzed. The analysis is performed booting a single VM, waiting for the boot process to settle, and then using standard tools to determine VM's memory footprint on the system. Fig. 6.9 shows experimental results. Unsurprisingly, LXC is relatively light on its memory footprint; indeed, the gap between LXC and hypervisor virtualizers' data is similar to the Linux kernel image size, as expected.

6.4.3.4 I/O Performance Analysis

Unix "dd" utility was used to analyze microSD performance. "dd" allows reading and writing data from arbitrary files. The tests were done by reading from the zero device (/dev/zero)— that on Unix systems generates an infinite stream of zeros—and sequentially writing to a file stored in the microSD. 100 blocks was written in a file selecting a block size of 1024 KiB (for small block sizes the microSD performances are mediocre). In order to avoid kernel-buffer cache and wait for I/O completion respectively, the dd "direct" and "dsync" flags were used. The tests were done with a configuration similar to the CPU tests:

- 0 DomUs/guests/containers
- 1 DomUs/guests/containers, two virtual CPUs each DomUs/guests/containers, memory: 512 MB each DomUs/guests/containers
- 2 DomUs/guests/containers, two virtual CPUs each DomUs/guests/containers, memory: 256 MB each DomUs/guests/containers
- 4 DomUs/guests/containers, two virtual CPUs each DomUs/guests/containers, memory: 128 MB each DomUs/guests/containers

Table 6.3 Disk I/O Performances (Host)

| HOST | 100 MiB | | | | | |
| | KVM | | XEN | | LXC | |
# VM	s	KiB/s	s	KiB/s	s	KiB/s
0	11.09	9,457.96	11. 15	9,407.81	10.34	10,142.54
1	52.93	1,980.95	20.00	5,242.38	92.17	1,137.67
2	176.00	595.77	30.81	3,403.72	177.18	591.81
4	440.07	238.28	162.81	644.06	291.64	359.54

Table 6.4 Disk I/O Performances (Guest)

| GUEST | 100 MiB | | | | | |
| | KVM | | XEN | | LXC | |
# VM	s	KiB/s	s	KiB/s	s	KiB/s
1	126.68	827.76	26.57	3946.82	105.74	991.65
2	263.29	398.25	44.86	2337.19	286.67	365.77
4	595.08	176.21	248.56	421.86	496.38	211.24

For the tests, we used a "dd" process running on each host and guest system simultaneously. Execution time and bandwidth for hosts and guests are reported in Tables 6.3 and 6.4, respectively. The bandwidths are also plotted in Figs. 6.10 and 6.11.

It is possible to see that in both cases Xen outperforms KVM and LXC, scaling better than them with the number of VMs used in the experiment.

6.4.3.5 Network Performance Analysis

Network performance analysis has been conducted by means of "iPerf3." "iPerf3" allows the evaluation of both TCP and UDP throughput. It can act either as a server or as a client. A second machine was directly connected to the Cubieboard2 via an ethernet crossover cable, and used as a server, with the Cubieboard2 acting as a client. The DomU, KVM guest, or LXC container was connected to the network interface of the respective host system via a virtual network bridge.

In that way, the VM was transparently accessible from the machine that acted as a server. In order to measure latencies introduced by the virtualization solutions, two tests were performed: one for the host and another one for the guest, for the three virtualization solutions taken in exam. The results are depicted in Fig. 6.12. Fig. 6.12 shows how all of the different virtualization solutions have similar performances, both hosts and guests. KVM guests that achieve slightly poorer results represent the only exception.

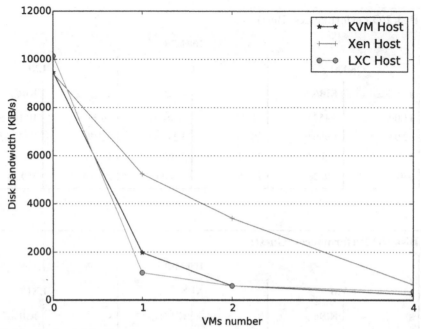

FIGURE 6.10 Disc I/O Bandwidth (Hosts)

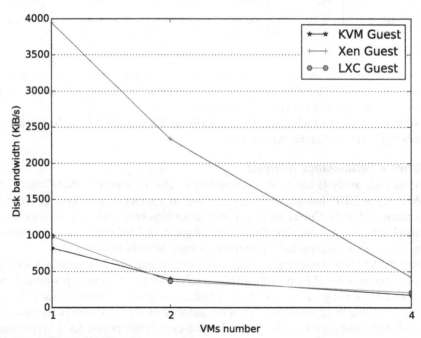

FIGURE 6.11 Disc I/O Bandwidth (Guests)

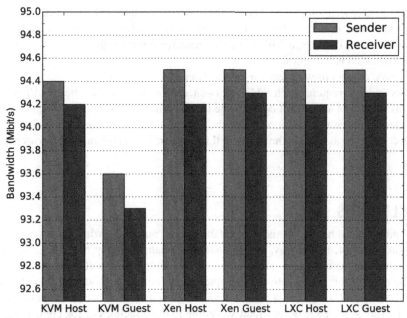

FIGURE 6.12 Network Bandwidth Performance

6.5 FUTURE RESEARCH DIRECTIONS

The experiments reported in the previous section provided a satisfactory answer to the two questions stated at the beginning of this chapter. As discussed in the next section, virtualization on embedded systems provides a support to most of the IoT requirements. Nevertheless, some more questions worth being answered arise, and some of them are reported here. The first one is the following:

Q3. *Are virtualization techniques appropriate for systems with real-time constraints?*
Virtualization introduces a latency in CPU performance that seems to grow with a linear law, according to Tables 6.1 and 6.2 and Figs. 6.6 and 6.7. Is it possible for a real-time scheduler to take into account such a latency in a precise way so as not to violate deadlines? The integration of real time and virtualization is still unstable, and therefore has not been possible yet to test. From a theoretical point of view, if the performance-decaying law is known, it is possible to define an appropriate real-time scheduling algorithm. From a practical point of view, this should still be proved; as a consequence, a future research-direction consists of studying real-time aspects in a virtualized environment.
Another question is the following:

Q4. *Are embedded devices appropriate for storage?*
According to the experimental results reported in the previous section, microSD are cheap storage devices with limited performances, and, thus, are not appropriate for virtualization. This is in line with the current trend of storing sensor data in suitable datacenters. Nevertheless, the world of storage technologies is moving fast, and it is reasonable to assume that, in a few years,

faster and cheaper technologies will be available. In the meantime, it would be interesting to test embedded devices with different present-day storage technologies, for example, devices equipped with a SATA storage. This is another research direction to explore.

One more question is the following:

Q5. *Are embedded devices appropriate for internal network virtualization?*

The SNSS scenario requires each VM to be connected with the rest of the cloud/fog. Usually this means that a VM should not be connected to the other VMs running on the same device. Nevertheless, a different scenario may require an internal network connection. This scenario has not been considered as outside the scope of this chapter, but is still another research direction to explore.

6.6 CONCLUSIONS

The principal aim of this chapter consisted of establishing if and under what assumptions, can embedded systems (ie, low-cost, low-energy, and limited-performance computing architectures) be virtualized. The experimental results seem encouraging: a very simple architecture such as a Cubieboard2 turns out to be enough for virtualization of computing and network resources. This allows the board to be used to host virtual things (ie, a virtual device with sensors and actuators), and, thus, push the computational effort on the edge of the cloud according to the principles of fog computing. Looking at the two questions stated at the beginning of this chapter, it is now possible to provide a positive answer for both of them. Regarding what would be the appropriate virtualization technology for embedded devices, it seems there is no silver bullet. All of the three technologies have the same performance for what concerns CPU virtualization and network controller virtualization (KVM has just a slightly lower performance). Regarding the storage, Xen performs better than KVM and LXC, but it should be noted that they all have poor performance in general. This seems to suggest that, at the current state-of-the-art, such devices seem to be inappropriate for storage. Nevertheless, it should be pointed out that this result mainly depends on the kind of storage that has been adopted and its low performance. A different kind of storage, as, for example, one with a SATA interface, would have better performance. On the other hand, that type of device is still too expensive or energy consuming. As a consequence, devices with limited storage performance should still be taken into account in the SNSS scenario. This justifies and explains the recent trend of moving sensor data into cloud datacenters instead of leaving them on "things."

REFERENCES

[1] Simmon E, Kim KS, Subrahmanian E, Lee R, de Vaulx F, Murakami Y, Zettsu K, Sriram RD. A vision of cyber-physical cloud computing for smart networked systems. NISTIR 7951. NIST; 2013.
[2] Gubbi J, Buyya R, Marusic S, Palaniswami M. Internet of Things (IoT): a vision, architectural elements, and future directions. Future Gen Comput Syst 2013;29(7):1645–60.
[3] Botta A, de Donato W, Persico V, Pescapé A. On the integration of cloud computing and Internet of Things. In: Future Internet of Things and cloud (FiCloud) international conference, EEEI; 2014. p. 23–30.
[4] Bonomi F, Milito R, Zhu J, Addepalli S. Fog computing and its role in the Internet of Things. In: Proceedings of the first edition of the MCC workshop on mobile cloud computing (ACM); 2012. p. 13–16.

[5] Botts M, Percivall G, Reed C, Davidson J. OGC® sensor web enablement: overview and high level architecture. GeoSensor networks. Berlin, Heidelberg: Springer; 2008. p. 175–90.

[6] OpenIoT Consortium. Open source solution for the Internet of Things into the cloud. http://www.openiot.eu/; 2012.

[7] Alam S, Chowdhury MM, Noll J. Senaas: an event-driven sensor virtualization approach for Internet of Things cloud. In: Networked embedded systems for enterprise applications (NESEA). 2010 IEEE international conference; 2010. p. 1–6.

[8] Yuriyama M, Kushida T. Sensor-cloud infrastructure-physical sensor management with virtualized sensors on cloud computing. In: Network-based information systems (NBiS). 2010 thirteenth international conference on IEEE; 2010. p. 1–8.

[9] Barham P, Dragovic B, Fraser K, Hand S, Harris T, Ho A, Warfield A. Xen and the art of virtualization. ACM SIGOPS Operat Syst Rev 2003;37(5):164–77.

[10] Kivity A, Kamay Y, Laor D, Lublin U, Liguori A. Kvm: the linux virtual machine monitor. In: Proceedings of the linux symposium; 2007. p. 225–230.

[11] Soltesz S, Pötzl H, Fiuczynski ME, Bavier A, Peterson L. Container-based operating system virtualization: a scalable, high-performance alternative to hypervisors. ACM SIGOPS Operat Syst Rev 2007;41(3):275–87.

[12] Heiser G. The role of virtualization in embedded systems. In: Proceedings of the first workshop on isolation and integration in embedded systems (ACM); 2008. p. 11–16.

[13] Soltesz S, Pötzl H, Fiuczynski ME, Bavier A, Peterson L. Container-based operating system virtualization: a scalable, high-performance alternative to hypervisors. ACM SIGOPS Operat Syst Rev 2007;41(3):275–87.

[14] Popek GJ, Goldberg RP. Formal requirements for virtualizable third generation architectures. Commun ACM 1974;17(7):412–21.

[15] Xi S, Wilson J, Lu C, Gill C. Rt-xen: towards real-time hypervisor scheduling in xen. In: Proceedings of the international conference on embedded software (EMSOFT), IEEE; 2011. p. 39–48.

[16] Scheepers MJ. Virtualization and containerization of application infrastructure: a comparison. In: 2014 Twenty-first twente student conference on IT; 2014, vol. 21. June 23. University of Twente.

[17] ARM Architecture Reference Manual. ARMv7-A and ARMv7-R Edition (Issue C). Cambridge, UK: ARM Ltd.; 2014.

[18] ARMv8-A Reference Manual (Issue A.c). Cambridge, UK: ARM Ltd.; 2014.

[19] Dall C, Nieh J. KVM/ARM: The design and implementation of the linux ARM hypervisor. In: Proceedings of the nineteenth international conference on architectural support for programming languages and operating systems; 2014.

[20] Xavier MG, Neves MV, Rossi F, Ferreto TC, Lange T, De Rose CAF. Performance evaluation of container-based virtualization for high performance computing environments. In: 2013 Twenty-first euromicro international conference on parallel, distributed and network-based processing (PDP), IEEE; 2013. p. 233–240.

[21] Biederman EW. Linux networx. Multiple instances of the global Linux namespaces. In: Proceedings of the Linux symposium; 2006.

[22] Oracle Solaris 10. http://www.oracle.com/us/products/servers-storage/solaris /solaris10/overview/index. html; 2015.

[23] Virtuozzo. http://openvz.org/Virtuozzo; 2015.

[24] Linux-VServer. http://linuxvserver.org/; 2015.

[25] Chroot(2). https://www.freebsd.org/cgi/man.cgi?query=chroot&sektion=2; 2015.

[26] Felter W, Ferreira A, Rajamony R, Rubio J. An updated performance comparison of virtual machines and Linux containers. IBM Research Division; 2014.

[27] Linux Containers. https://linuxcontainers.org/; 2015.

[28] Cgroups. https://www.kernel.org/doc/Documentation/cgroups/cgroups.txt; 2015.

[29] Gu Z, Zhao Q. A state-of-the-art survey on real-time issues in embedded systems virtualization. J Softw Engin Applic 2012;5:277–90.

[30] Taccari G, Taccari L, Fioravanti A, Spalazzi L, Claudi A. Embedded real-time virtualization: state of the art and research challenges. Real-time Linux workshop; 2014.

[31] García-Valls M, Cucinotta T, Lu C. Challenges in real-time virtualization and predictable cloud computing. J Syst Archit 2014;60(9):726–40.

[32] Xavier MG, Neves MV, Rossi FD, Ferreto TC, Lange T, De Rose CAF. Performance evaluation of container-based virtualization for high performance computing environments. In: Twenty-first euromicro international conference on parallel. Distributed and network-based processing; 2013.

[33] Kinebuchi Y, Sugaya M, Oikawa S, Nakajima T. Task grain scheduling for hypervisor-based embedded system. In: Proceedings of the tenth IEEE international conference on high performance computing and communications; 2008.

[34] Augier C. Real-time scheduling in a virtual machine environment. In: Proceedings of junior researcher workshop on real-time computing (JRWRTC), Nancy, March 29–30, 2007.

[35] Carnevali L, Pinzuti A, Vicario E. Compositional verification for hierarchical scheduling of real-time systems. IEEE Trans Softw Engin 2013;39(5):638–57.

[36] Lee J, Xi S, Chen S, Phan LT, Gill C, Lee I, Lu C, Sokolsky O. Realizing compositional scheduling through virtualization. In: 2012 IEEE 18th real-time and embedded technology and applications symposium (RTAS); 2012. p. 13–22.

[37] Xi S, Xu M, Lu C, Phan LTX, Gill CD, Sokolsky O, Lee I. Real-time multi-core virtual machine scheduling in Xen. In: ACM international conference on embedded software (EMSOFT'14); 2014.

[38] Kiszka J. Towards Linux as a real-time hypervisor. In: Proceedings of the eleventh real-time Linux workshop; 2009. p. 215–224.

[39] Faggioli D, Trimarchi M, Checconi F, Bertogna M, Mancina A. An implementation of the earliest deadline first algorithm in Linux. In: Proceedings of the 2009 ACM symposium on applied computing (ACM); 2009. p. 1984–1989.

[40] Varanasi P, Heiser G. Hardware-supported virtualization on ARM. In: Proceeding APSys'11 proceedings of the second Asia-Pacific workshop on systems, ACM. 2011. p. 1–5.

[41] Debian—The Universal Operating System. http://www.debian.org/; 2015.

[42] SysBench, a modular, cross-platform and multi-threaded benchmark tool. https://github.com/akopytov/sysbench; 2015.

[43] iPerf3, TCP and UDP bandwidth performance measurement tool. http://software.es.net/iperf/; 2015.

MICRO VIRTUAL MACHINES (MicroVMs) FOR CLOUD-ASSISTED CYBER-PHYSICAL SYSTEMS (CPS)

J.V. Pradilla*, C.E. Palau**

*Escuela Técnica Superior de Ingenieros de Telecomunicación at the Universitat Politècnica de Valencia, Spain;
**Distributed Real-Time Systems Research Group, Escuela Tecnica Superior de Ingenieros de Telecomunicación at the Universitat Politecnica de Valencia, Spain

7.1 INTRODUCTION

At present, there is growth in the areas of application of information and communication technologies (ICT). This expansion has managed to cover many human activities in an almost transparent way to the own actors of the activity, making the man/machine relationship much closer.

Several reasons can be found supporting this phenomenon, including some directly linked to ICT and its current development, such as: increased capacity, miniaturization, lower prices, and the acceptance of people in everyday use.

Moore's Law (PhD Gordon Moore, 1965) describes the increased capacity in ICT, which becomes clear by watching trends like these over time: operations per second of a processor, available volatile memory for processing, non-volatile storage space, and interconnection speed in networks [1].

Similarly, miniaturization of ICT components also fits Moore's Law, particularly the number of transistors in an integrated circuit. As transistors and integrated circuits are the basic building blocks of current hardware, evidence can be found of miniaturization in the size of sensors, actuators, robots, computers, and smartphones [1].

For its part, the lowering prices of the components of ICT can be modeled by Robert's Law (PhD Lawrence Roberts, 1969), and can be evidenced by reviewing the computer performance per dollar or the price of magnetic storage units over time [2].

In addition, other prominent factors linked to ICT growth are the availability of various devices that fit applications or complex environments in time, environmental characteristics, prices, security, and personal preferences. A widely known case is that of smartphones, which adapt to complex, diverse markets and environments around the world.

Moreover, this trend of growth and scope of ICT glimpses a hyper-connected future in which devices are ubiquitous and our interaction with them becomes more natural and close, creating a synergy between humans and machines for the development of information that allows for the effective use of natural resources.

Part of the man/machine relationship is based on the generation of data and information. Assuming that man is a creative and social being who can take advantage of making his knowledge lasting and accessible, and that, broadly, a machine is an instrument that processes data to generate actions or information, a meeting point between man and machine can be found through the capture, storage, and processing of data and information.

Thus, in reviewing the history of humanity, it is found that, information has been transmitted among humans in oral or written form for centuries, having its first major revolution with the advent of printing, and its second great revolution with the birth of the Internet. These two revolutions have enabled global accessibility to information, reducing transfer costs, and making everyone who wanted it to be a producer and consumer of knowledge.

However, under this paradigm, machines are far removed from that role of information producer/consumer; they are relegated to be appropriate tools for the transmission and storage of that information.

For example, with the advent of Internet, information flow focused on human-oriented services, such as the World Wide Web, email, file transfer, on-line conversations, telephony, and television. Moreover, communication between machines focused on support services: routing, error handling, security, and quality of service.

However, the big leap in the machines' role came with the search engines, which began using the services intended for humans and generating information relevant to us. Meanwhile, news aggregators did their thing, by using a service destined to share content and to create condensed and classified information according to user preferences. Spam generators were other great pioneers in the role of consumer/producer of information, because they looked for email addresses on the web and adapted message templates to the recipients.

However, these examples are just some of the machines' incursions to create information. At industry level, they began to automate the supply and distribution chains; in addition, many factories gave way to robots that auto-adjusted their production routines, depending on the quality of inputs or external production conditions. Similarly, at home, machines that made decisions on specific conditions at the time of execution started to appear; artificial intelligence and fuzzy logic were two tools that allowed the exploitation of this information for the efficient use of resources.

Moreover, man and machine have begun to share information to generate synergies that allow better decision-making or improving processes. Recent examples of this interaction are found with sports-measuring devices, which measure vital signs of the person, and generate reports in real time, which can be used to tailor a sports routine or improve sleep patterns. Another outstanding example is found in the software that supports management decision-making, which simulates possible scenarios for the future of the company, based on the record of the current processes and on some business rules that humans have inserted. These possible scenarios are useful for the management to define a set of actions to take in order to obtain the simulated result.

However, there was still one missing step to complete the current situation: provide a way for machines to share information so that there would be a collective knowledge usable for the same machines. This form of generating, sharing, and using information by machines without human intervention was called the Internet of Things (IoT).

Likewise, machine to machine (M2M) communication has become more common today; vending machines that report income and request inventory, virtual stores that send orders to automated transport centrals and packages, and cars that publish their location and status to a command and control center are examples that are becoming more common every day, of a network of machines working together.

This is how the current state of information and communications technologies is reached: machines that communicate with each other in automated and collaborative processes, of which data is stored and analyzed by computer systems, which, in turn, generate consolidated information useful for humans and machines, who, in turn, make decisions or perform actions that affect the behavior of the entire system—thus creating a closed information cycle. These information/communication systems in a closed cycle that influence and are influenced by the physical reality are known as cyber-physical systems (CPS).

CPS are born from a precise intersection between computing, networking, and physical processes [3]. They perceive the world through sensor networks and affect it by making use of actuators, robots, and drones [4], while operations are monitored, coordinated, controlled, and integrated by a core of computations and networks [5]. Thus, a feedback loop is created where physical processes affect calculations and vice versa.

This intrinsic coupling of a CPS is manifested from the millimeter scale (micro-robots) to the kilometric scale (SmartGrid), and independently (pacemaker), or as part of a larger CPS (robotic arm on an assembly line). At the same time, the CPSs are linked to embedded systems and control theory [3].

Communication networks that enable the interconnection between components of a CPS are essential, either in small, independent systems, or in large systems composed of other CPSs. They must adjust to the environment in which the sensors/actuators are deployed, and to the system requirements so that they can provide specific services, such as response time, bandwidth, or noise resistance.

For its part, the core that allows for coordination, monitorization, and control of operations must deploy informatic systems that store and process data to generate information that can be used in an automated way or with human intervention.

There are several examples of CPS today; the highlights include: aerospace systems, medical devices, intelligent vehicles and roads, defense systems, robots, processes control, factory automation, building control, environment control, and smart spaces [5]. IoT [3] is one of the CPS of more interest.

The IoT has been defined in many ways, and can be considered a concept still in development that often goes beyond the limits set by a specific definition. This chapter will consider the IoT as a special case of CPS.

Thus, according to IERC, the IoT is "A dynamic global network infrastructure with self-configuring capabilities based on standard and interoperable communication protocols where physical and virtual 'things' have identities, physical attributes, and virtual personalities, use intelligent interfaces, and are seamlessly integrated into the information network" [6]. This definition contains important concepts, such as that IoT is a global network and IoT integrates virtual and physical "stuff" through an information network.

Another interesting definition of IoT for this chapter has been described by Gartner, which defines the IoT as a "Network of physical objects that contain embedded technology to communicate and sense or interact with their internal states or the external environment" [7].

Finally, to gain a more specific understanding about the concept of IoT, the original article by Kevin Ashton can be referred to, where he describes the need to "empower computers with their own means of gathering information, so they can see, hear and smell the world for themselves, in all its random glory. RFID and sensor technology enable computers to observe, Identify and understand the world—without the limitations of human-entered data" [8]; this highlights the machine's role of producer/consumer.

After one is clear on what CPS and the IoT are, it is interesting to deepen one's understanding on how these two concepts are related. In general, and as previously mentioned, the IoT is a specific case of a CPS [3] of a large scale, and it can be composed, in turn, of other CPSs.

Unlike CPS, the concept of IoT proposes two restrictions: the first is that each object must be identifiable, and the second is that there must be a global interconnection [3]. In contrast, there are CPSs that differ from the IoT by not including these two constraints. Examples of these are smart grids, warplanes, and robot swarms.

CPSs differ in shape, size, and complexity [4]. However, once established, they are limited in their processing, storage, bandwidth, mobility capacity, or algorithms available, which may make them less flexible to adapt to a changing physical world.

For example, take a body-area network that is composed of sensors of blood pressure, heart rate, and blood-oxygen level that continuously measures these parameters every 3 min, and that in case of any abnormal level in these parameters, it activates an alarm to the user through a bracelet that vibrates and shines, and sends a message to a determined personal contact and to the family doctor, so that together (the user and the doctor) they can make a decision on the course of action to follow. If this CPS is faced with a serious event in which blood-oxygen levels begin to fall dangerously, it may be useful to increase the frequency of blood-oxygen samples from 3 min to 30 s. However, although memory and processing capacities available in the described CPS and in regular scenarios is normally sufficient, it may be exceeded, and, if so, a dynamic scaling would be needed to addresses these new requirements.

Another example of CPS that can be exceeded under certain circumstances is found in a domotic system, which is adapted to meet a specific housing requirement, and the habits of the inhabitants of the same requirement. When the inhabitants decide to move to a new home, the CPS remains anchored to the previous home. However, it would be desirable that when arriving at the new house (which also has a domotic system), their preferences and settings would be transferred with little human intervention and would not require a manual configuration of the system or a period of adaptation to the new inhabitants.

For cases like these in which CPS needs to adapt to the changing physical world and expand its capabilities dynamically, this chapter offers an architecture and some use-cases for it.

7.2 RELATED WORK

7.2.1 VIRTUAL MACHINES AND MICRO VIRTUAL MACHINES

Virtual machines (VM) are an important tool that has been used along with cloud computing and has allowed great adaptability and security to the systems deployed in them. Similarly, for a cloud-assisted CPS they are critical because they enable scaling within the infrastructures that contain them, allowing the CPS to increase its capabilities and services.

A virtual machine simulates the hardware resources of a device, defining in this way the real hardware resources to which the VM will have access. This is important because it allows multiple VMs to share the same real device and enables that their established resource limitation can be dynamically modified, provided that they do not exceed the actual capabilities of the hardware on which they are deployed [9].

Therefore, by simulating hardware resources, a VM can be treated like a real machine; the VM hardware may differ from the real hardware, but what really counts is the place where it is being deployed. This brings the advantage that the virtual machine can be transported and deployed in different devices, while still maintaining its integrity and functionality.

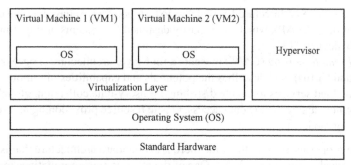

FIGURE 7.1 Virtual Machine Architecture

Similarly, a virtual machine defines a security domain, which is isolated from other virtual machines running on a single device, as if it were a completely separate machine. This fact, coupled with the hardware independence, makes virtual machines ideal for cases requiring backup, mobility, rapid deployment of infrastructure, and high fault-tolerance.

Within the VMs, an operating system that interacts with the simulated hardware is installed, allowing its use by applications and services. It is necessary to specify that the virtual machines be deployed on an ecosystem that includes the VM manager or hypervisor, the actual hardware, and the operating system of the actual device (Fig. 7.1) [10].

For their part, micro virtual machines (microVM) are a subset of the VM in which simulated hardware resources are limited and the operating system installed on them is very light. In this case, a microVM is considered a synonym for the micro instances of performance with bursts of the Amazon EC2 service (t2.micro), which have about 1 GB of RAM and a vCPU with two different CPU allocation levels: background level and max level. Background level allocation provides a consistent baseline CPU resource allocation. Max level allocation is allowed for short periods of time to accommodate short spikes in CPU requirements. This means that the micro instance may be feasible for low-throughput applications with occasional workload spikes [11].

These microVM allow for simulating limited devices such as RaspberryPi B+ (512 MB of RAM and ARM processor at 700 MHz), which are ideal for the deployment of small computing devices, near the user, that take care of storing and processing information interactively while maintaining a low cost.

Finally, it is important to know that a microVM must have an operating system installed that is quite contained and that operates efficiently under these restrictions. One of the most important in the last year is Snappy Ubuntu Core, which is a GNU/Linux distribution with transactional updates based on Ubuntu Core.

7.2.2 OTHER ARCHITECTURES

There are proposals of architectures that are related to the one discussed in this chapter, either because they are complementary, specific use-cases, or alternative options. Within these architectures three stand out:

- *Cloud4Sens* is a cloud-oriented solution to integrate heterogeneous monitoring infrastructures (MI) into the cloud, offering services based on the datacentric and device-centric models [12]

- *Californium* is a system architecture for scalable IoT cloud services based on the Constrained Application Protocol (CoAP), which is primarily designed for systems of tiny, low-cost, resource-constrained IoT devices [13].
- *Cloud-assisted remote sensing (CARS)* presents a four-layer architecture (Fog, Stratus, Altocumulus, and Cirrus), and describes the potentials and capabilities of remote sensing when empowered via cloud services to enable distributed sensory-data collection, global resource and data sharing, remote and real-time data access, elastic resource provisioning and scaling, and pay-as-you-go pricing models [14].

Although these proposals exist, at this time there is no standard architecture that is accepted within the global technological-development frame. One of the most promising initiatives to achieve a shared architecture for the IoT is currently under development by The Alliance for Internet of Things Innovation (www.aioti.eu). An adaptation of the proposal that is part of this chapter has been taken to this institution as a contribution to the debate that seeks consensus in this emerging area of knowledge.

7.3 ARCHITECTURE FOR DEPLOYING CPS IN THE CLOUD AND THE EXPANSION OF THE IoT

Architectures set the pace at the time of designing a system; they are a starting point that allows adaptations to use cases and they present a common language in which to debate the advantages and disadvantages of a development. Therefore, proposing an architecture is often the first step in consolidating knowledge in information and communications technologies.

In this way, taking as a reference the actual development in sensors/actuators networks and joining it with new cloud-computation trends, an architectural proposal is made for CPS that it is considered will respond to the cases in which the CPS must dynamically widen its capacities (Fig. 7.2).

Sensors/actuators networks, whose goal is to capture events and interfere in a physical way with reality, compose the closest level to the physical world. In this first level, physical phenomena are monitored and described by a standard language, and are shared by employing well-defined interfaces. Likewise, action signals over the real environment are transmitted following the same scheme.

It has to be taken into account that this level may contain in itself other CPSs. This is the case in which robots, drones, or smartphones employ their sensors/actuators, along with their processing and storage capacity, to interact with the physical world.

The second level of the proposed architecture is composed of information processing and storage units that have the possibility of scaling, on demand, the resources that a specific CPS deployed in it has. These units contain the CPS's virtual instances and provide a basic set of services to resize these instances according to specific needs.

These processing and storage units are called "fog sites," and constitute a simile of "cloud sites" in cloud computation, but to a lower scale, thus conforming to an implementation of what is actually known as a fog computational level.

Additionally, to complete this level's function, apart from the services linked to the resource administration, it must count with services such as performance monitoring, event-driven alerts, account use, backup, and security. These additional services allow for an adequate administration of this fog computational layer.

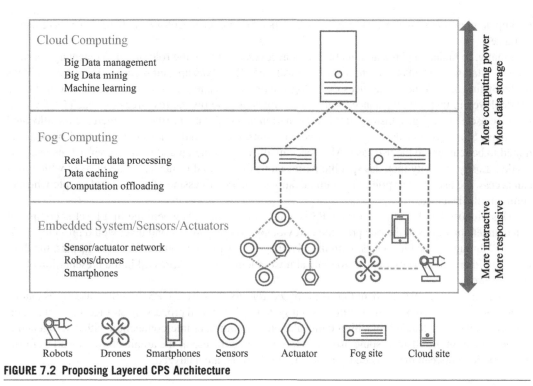

FIGURE 7.2 Proposing Layered CPS Architecture

Therefore, for this level to be effective, it must be linked with the first level through wideband connections, and with good-quality service; this second level is generally located physically close to the first-level devices, and offers great interactivity and fast response.

In the second level, the concept of CPS virtual instance has to be explored. A CPS virtual instance contains all information storage and processing logic, along with the necessary procedures to interact with the physical world; it must be self-contained, that is, it must count with all necessary dependencies to function independently of the deployment location and other virtual instances.

In this way, a CPS virtual instance, along with the sensors/actuators networks and other first-level CPSs of the architecture associated with it, conform to a traditional CPS, with the advantage of being able to attend to the changing reality in which it operates.

For its part, the third level of the proposed architecture augments almost indefinitely the second-level capacities, bringing the resource administration services along with the complementary services to all CPS virtual instances where the fog site is insufficient.

This accommodates three forms of interaction between the second and third level. The first one occurs in the case where horizontal scaling in the fog site reaches its limit, and therefore the CPS virtual instance should scale up to a cloud site to prevent the interruption of the work in progress. The second form of interaction occurs in the form of distributed computing, in which certain processing or storage activities that require large resources are performed in the third level, while the daily activities take place on the second level. Finally, the third form of interaction between the second and third level is when the cloud site serves as a gateway for CPS virtual instances, for example, as a restoration of a backup, a migration of the virtual instance to another fog site, or redeployment based on a pre-existing instance.

Finally, to understand the architecture, it is necessary to know the role of complementary services such as catalog, performance monitoring, event-driven alerts, backup, and security. The catalog allows for the listing of the types of services that a fog site or a cloud site provides, and what virtual instances are deployed in them. Performance monitoring allows us to know the resources that each CPS virtual instance uses, to manage a history of this information and to define thresholds to increase the allocated resources. Similarly, the alerts service, based on events, records and sends alerts that have been determined to be relevant to the use case. Also, backup allows backing up and restoring virtual instances as needed. Lastly, security includes specific permissions on a virtual instance, the services to which they can access, the use of encryption in communications, and the accessing of accounts of people who can configure the instance.

This proposed architecture for the CPS is applicable to the IoT, where the first level is composed in a manner analogous to the one presented previously, whereas the second level would provide "intelligence" through virtual instances, with the advantages of using fog computation. For its part, the third level would provide that extra layer to scale almost indefinitely, as expressed in the presentation of the architecture.

Applying the architecture here that is proposed for cloud-assisted CPS, complex use-cases can be faced that require interconnection with external systems, distributed processing/storage, context awareness, big/small data, data mining, high fault-tolerance, mobility, or interconnection with heterogeneous systems. Later in the chapter, some use-cases that illustrate the use of the architecture, as well as forms of interaction between the proposed second and third levels, are analyzed.

7.4 EXTENDING THE POSSIBILITIES OF THE IoT BY CLOUD COMPUTING

The proposed architecture applied to the IoT provides the ability to adapt to a constantly changing world so that it can accommodate a large number of scenarios, including those in which it would be necessary to have computing capabilities on demand, information backup, mobility, distribution of information, and context awareness.

Thus, the adaptive computing capacity on demand covers the adjustment in the amount of processing memory (RAM), as in the long-term storage memory (hard drive), in addition to the adjustment in the number of processors to use, the usage time of each processor, and the available bandwidth.

Likewise, it can be considered that the computing capacity on demand includes using algorithms that are highly demanding of resources, those that are useful only in very specific moments in the lifecycle of the system, or those that require increasing the number of routines to run only at specific times.

Also in this category, it can consider access to massive information present within the system or in external databases, and the processing of this information to either analyze or to generate consolidated or dynamic reports in which people can interact. Finally, adaptation on demand of the computing capabilities includes the possibility to interconnect systems without degrading performance or compromising the security of the same.

Meanwhile, data backup includes backup and restore processes, in addition to the possibility of a rapid deployment from other stored instances.

In the same way, mobility refers to the ability to migrate a virtual instance of a fog/cloud site-provider to another, without losing the information and the processes related to the deployment of IoT. Another possibility is to migrate the instance between "fog sites" in order to ensure the best connection performance.

Furthermore, the distribution of information is vital within the IoT. In this, data can be shared between CPS virtual instances that are part of the IoT, or between client/server relations between CPSs belonging to the IoT.

Finally, context awareness allows for the adaptation of the number of sensors/actuators that are used simultaneously according to an activity, for modifying the accuracy or the format in which data is collected from sensors and stored, or for employing artificial intelligence to make decisions without involving people, thus creating intelligent and adaptable environments.

7.5 MICRO VIRTUAL MACHINES WITH THE SENSOR OBSERVATION SERVICE, THE PATH BETWEEN SMART OBJECTS AND CPS

7.5.1 VIRTUAL MACHINES AND SENSOR OBSERVATION SERVICE

A virtual machine is an abstraction of a computer in which, through software, specific hardware resources are simulated so that it can be used as if it were a real device, allowing for the installation of an operating system and programs within it.

Usually, virtual machines are used to provide Infrastructure as a Service (IaaS), allowing for several simulated device configurations to be accommodated in a server's farm. They are also widely used to test software without being influenced by other processes. There are many other uses that are given to virtual machines, and the one proposed in this chapter is one of them, which is based on the use of microVMs.

A microVM is a program that simulates a device with limited resources, which provides an isolated domain between the microVM and the host operating system, and between the microVM and other microVMs from the same host. It differs from a conventional virtual machine because of the few resources that it needs to operate, and therefore in the initial limitations with which it is executed.

Although a microVM demands more resources than a process within a conventional operating system, this approach offers some advantages that would be difficult to attain by running a process.

These advantages include a self-contained microVM that can be copied and transferred without losing the integrity of processes or information. This also provides complete isolation so that it does not affect other instances. It is more fault tolerant and improves security. It is also very versatile by allowing different processes to deploy within it, giving greater freedom to implement diverse technologies.

Within the proposed architecture, microVMs fit perfectly within the concept of virtual instance and its use within the cloud/fog sites, with microVMs being a versatile and immediate solution to implement the concepts and benefits of the presented architecture.

One of the benefits of employing a microVM as a virtual instance is the possibility of using low-resource equipment as a "fog site" in the proposed second level, and that an instance of a microVM inhabits it. Using low-cost equipment enables that this second level is very close to where it interacts with the physical world, thus improving response time and overall system performance.

In addition, by using the microVM in this way, it is possible to make fast migrations and deployments of virtual instances within a CPS because they are lightweight enough for transmission over the network while maintaining their integrity.

Similarly, when virtual instances are microVMs, the classic mechanisms of virtual machines can be used for vertical and horizontal scaling.

For its part, the Sensor Observation Service (SOS) is the intermediary between the client and present and past data generated by a sensor, in addition to the metadata associated with these [15]. It is a standard created by the Open Geospatial Consortium (OGC) and released in order to be exploited by the large consortium of companies that make up the OGC. SOS has taken several years to develop, and its development has been based on Web standards such as SOAP, WSDL, and XML.

The SOS forms part of the Sensor Web Enablement (SWE) framework. The SWE is a set of standards that allow exploitation of sensors and sets of sensors connected to a communications network. The group of SWE specifications covers sensors, related data models, and services that offer accessibility and control over the Web. The SWE architecture is composed of two main models: the information model and the service model (Fig. 7.3) [16]. The conceptual models refer to transducers, processes, systems, and observations.

The information model describes the conceptual models and encodings, whereas the service model specifies related services, grouped into three information models and four service implementation specifications. The three information models are: Observations & Measurements Schema (O&M) [17,18], Sensor Model Language (SensorML) [19], and Transducer Markup Language (TransducerML or TML) [20]. The four service-implementation specifications are: SOS [21], Sensor Planning Service (SPS) [22], Sensor Alert Service (SAS) [23], and Web Notification Services (WNS) [24].

As can be seen, SOS standard specification is complex and requires robust equipment for deployment. However, in many cases it can exceed the needs of the deployed system. Thus, in some cases it is necessary to have a lighter SOS that provides the basic capabilities according to the standard, but that

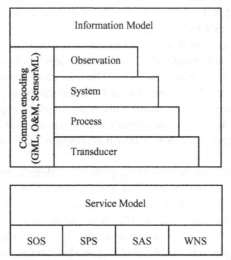

FIGURE 7.3 Sensor Web Enablement Components

can be deployed in low-resource equipment and facilitates the deployment near the sensor networks, due to the low cost that it can carry.

An SOS designed like this serves as a distributed database with which interaction can be made through well-defined interfaces, and it can transmit messages with standard structures while consuming little computational resources.

Using a light SOS (SOSLite) or a set of these, aggregations of data can be made to generate consolidated analysis for use in decision-making, whether automated or mediated by humans.

If the proposed architecture is taken into account and we want to make a real deployment of this for a CPS, the microVM and SOSLite can be taken as key technological components to carry it out. Being in the first instance the right combination for sensor networks that rely on fog computing, which is composed of several virtual instances on microVMs, and that are deployed in low-resource "fog sites," each microVM offers a SOSLite service for the interaction of data from sensors and between instances.

Using microVM and SOSLite allows us to take advantage of the proposed architecture by defining an autonomous and self-contained unit, with a security domain and with well-defined interfaces, to communicate with. This combination presents an excellent example of how a virtual instance can be made in these systems.

7.5.2 IMPLEMENTATION

In order to implement the selected use cases, a complete implementation of a SOSLite has been conducted, and Snappy Ubuntu Core was used as the operating system (a GNU/Linux distribution for the IoT). For the "fog sites" Raspberry Pi B+ was used, and for the "cloud sites" Amazon's Elastic Compute Cloud (EC2) service was used.

The SOSLite implementation was made in PHP, as database mongoDB is used, a NoSQL database, and NGINX is used as a server. The choice of PHP as development language is based on the proximity of the SOS specification with Web standards and the good implementation that PHP makes of them. For its part, using MongoDB facilitates data storage because its nature is minimally relational, but it has high rates of queries and storage operations. Finally, the use of NGINX is based on the nature of the data transmitted on these systems and that it is event-driven.

Thus, in each Raspberry Pi, Snappy Ubuntu Core is installed as the operating system, and on it the NGINX and MongoDB services are deployed. Additionally, the PHP scripts are published, in which the SOSLite functionalities are coded.

Meanwhile in Amazon's Elastic Compute Cloud (EC2), virtual machines limited to the specifications close to a Raspberry Pi are configured, and a similar configuration of the hardware is installed in each.

With a deployment of these characteristics, significant use cases can be modeled, with which the usefulness and scope of the proposed architecture is validated, along with its importance to define the path between smart objects and CPS.

7.6 IoT ARCHITECTURE FOR SELECTED USE CASES

To determine the usefulness of the proposed architecture and the use of microVMs for CPSs on the cloud, three use-cases are illustrated. The first one is linked to eHealth, the second one to precision agriculture, and the last one to domotics.

7.6.1 eHEALTH

One of the greatest concerns of health entities is elderly care, so that they may have a healthy and fulfilling life that eliminates any limitation and/or dependency. With this objective, prevention is one of the paths that have been shown to be most efficient, and within this, automatic monitoring is the area where technology can make a difference.

Therefore, a CPS that responds to the automatic monitoring needs of the elderly is a proposal in accord with the actual technological advances, where it can be counted on for connectivity almost anywhere, and at a time where physical scanning devices are more affordable each day.

In this way, a system is proposed that integrates body-area sensors that evaluate the person's vital constants, and both home-comfort and city ambient-monitoring sensors, along with programs for food and medicine intake, physical activity and virtual interaction in social networks, in addition to giving support to the interconnection with emergency services and providing sanitary feedback with health specialists.

The architecture for this cloud-assisted CPS (Fig. 7.4) presents three levels (as in the proposed reference architecture). The first one is composed of the body-sensors network that evaluates parameters relative to the functioning of the human body (cardiac rhythm, blood oxygen, amount of steps taken during the day, etc.). Also included in this level are the home sensors that measure air quality, ambient temperature and movement, and also the city sensors that measure air quality, weather, noise, and traffic. For its part, the second level presents equipment that is economical and resource-limited, deployed in the person's home network, and whose function is to store and analyze the information provided by both the personal-area and home sensors, at the same time that it queries the public information given to it by the city sensors. Finally, the third level provides additional intelligence by making analyses and

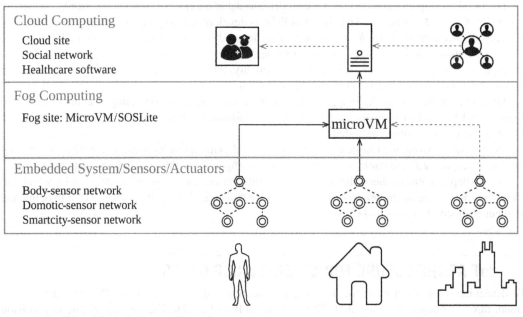

FIGURE 7.4 Layered eHealth CPS Architecture

predictions, and it is linked to the emergency services and sanitary feedback that the elderly person is affiliated with.

In this way, the first level handles the recording and transmission of interest-data, the second level stores, shares, and analyzes collected data, while the third level provides interconnection with the other systems and facilitates the generation of statistics and personal and group predictions. All levels are independent of the hardware used, and allow the interconnection of heterogeneous systems by using the combination of MicroVM/SOSLite.

Entering in details, personal sensors can be grouped in two categories: continuous-use sensors and occasional-use sensors. Included in continuous-use sensors are wrist bracelets/clocks that register activity, and skin-tattooed sensors that automatically register the measurements made. For their part, occasional-use sensors may require the manual input of data through a mobile or a web app. All data registered by these sensors is stored in the user's personal network, in a resource-limited device that plays the part of a "fog site" and holds a microVM.

In the same way, home sensors measure air quality, ambient temperature, and movement within the enclosure, with the objective of analyzing this data along with the personal-sensor data, to identify whether any of the ambient factors have directly influenced the person's health. With this same objective, the city sensors are queried and its data is analyzed (air quality, weather, noise, and traffic). So, the data registered by the sensors in the microVM and deployed in the user's "fog site" are analyzed to determine hazardous conditions for the person, and/or to relate personal or ambient conditions to any specific ailment.

One of the most interesting factors to determine the health-risk agents in older people is their virtual activity in social networks, to detect personal interactions and the amount of activities in which the person has been involved. The analysis of this data is one of the factors of interconnection with other systems where the third level is widely used. This analysis does not determine immediate risk, and therefore does not require a real-time communication. However, it is an operation that can consume significant resources, and, therefore, the ideal is not to occupy the limited resources of the user's hardware.

Finally, using the cloud for the interconnection with other systems enables sending alarms and consolidated data to the health provider to which the person is affiliated. So that when he or she makes routine visits to his or her medical doctor, the doctor can evaluate the patient's behavior. Alternatively, in case of an emergency, a notification can be sent to the medical team that will attend to this emergency.

7.6.2 PRECISION AGRICULTURE

Precision Agriculture (PA) has been more relevant in the agrarian sector because technology enables the optimization of resource use in the productive parcels. It is in an advanced development phase, and some producers have started to implement PA in their terrains, and have obtained promising results, managing to return the investment necessary for its implementation.

PA systems are an excellent case study of the implementation of CPS, and, in this case, of how cloud computation can help enhance its reach.

Thus, the activities linked to PA include: identification and localization of crops, weeds, and machinery; performance monitoring; variable dozing of fertilizers, herbicides, insecticides, and fungicides; planting monitoring; and ground classification and mapping.

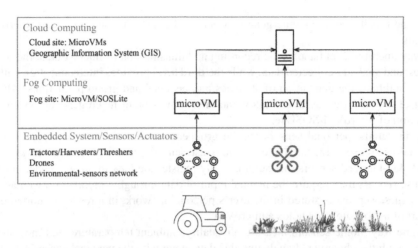

FIGURE 7.5 Layered PA CPS Architecture

To achieve the fulfillment of these activities, usually information is gathered through satellites, drones, or sensors/actuators, either mounted on agricultural machinery (fertilizer, combiner, cutter, fumigator, seeder) or on saddle (cropper, ripper, subsoiler, etc.).

For this case, the proposed architecture is adopted (Fig. 7.5) so that in the first-level environmental sensors network, drones and sensors/actuators either mounted on agricultural machinery or on saddles are found. The second level is composed of several microVMs associated with the environmental sensors network, with each drone, and with every machine used in the parcel. Finally, the third level groups the diversity of data coming from the second level, and provides a unified vision through the Geographic Information System (GIS).

Entering in details, environmental sensors measure: temperature, rainfall, wind velocity, air humidity, ground humidity, and ground PH, among other factors. They are distributed in the property as small meteorological stations and sensors. All sensors report their data to a centralized microVM.

For their part, drones are equipped with wide-spectrum cameras, which allow the monitoring of crop-development parameters and high-resolution cameras to build topographic information. They are also accompanied by positioning sensors to determine the location of the data gathered. Each drone includes its own microVM, where it stores data and shares it with the third level.

In the same way, the network of sensors/actuators mounted on saddles or agricultural machinery is responsible for the measuring of parameters such as the production in a determined area, and for operations such as determining the optimal amount of fertilizer to apply in an area. Each of these machines carries equipment where the microVM is deployed, and where parameters such as performance rates or weed presence can be calculated. Later, this information is centralized in the third level.

The cloud level, in this use case, centralizes the information from diverse microVMs deployed in the whole parcel, and allows its visualization through the GIS. In addition to this, through computational analysis, it gives support to the decision-making process and it integrates external systems to make projections and estimations. Therefore, this third level brings in the integration, interconnection, and visualization of data in real time, whether it be historical or projected for a property.

Finally, as it has been mentioned, in the third level, interconnections can be made with external systems such as the local weather system, where historical and predicted information about the weather in the area can be found, or with satellite systems such as those provided by ESA/NASA, where ground data at a global level can be found.

7.6.3 DOMOTIC

A cyber-physical domotic system is responsible for the automation of a home to achieve greater security and electrical efficiency, at the same time that it enhances comfort and is able to respond to emergency conditions. It is composed of sensors/actuators and a local system that centralizes and coordinates all actions in the home. By being supported in a cloud system, the interconnection possibilities with other systems are extended, and the capacities of the system to provide greater computational resources are enhanced.

In this case, a system arises (Fig. 7.6) in which the first level contains all home sensors/actuators, and the second level contains a virtual instance in which all data is registered and decisions are made about which actions to take. In addition, the second level utilizes small data to achieve optimization of energy costs and automatic alarm activation. The third level, in turn, provides the interconnection with the systems in the building where the home is located, and with the systems in the city, such as fireman alerts in case of fire.

In depth, it can be noted that the security subsystem is composed of movement sensors, door- and window-opening sensors, alarms, cameras, and automatic locks. Sensors register data and send it to the microVM, where it is decided whether alarms should be activated or alerts should be sent; in addition, historical data is analyzed and it is established whether automatic locks should be activated.

Another subsystem involved is the one responsible for people's comfort, in which it is very common to monitor humidity and temperature, thus regulating air conditioning or the home's cross-ventilation

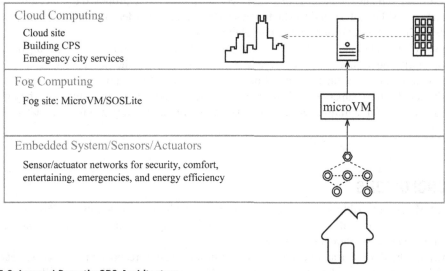

FIGURE 7.6 Layered Domotic CPS Architecture

system; also air-quality measuring systems can be included. Just like in the security subsystem, data and actions are centralized in the second-level microVM.

For its part, the entertainment subsystem controls lights and ambient sound, and personalizes music playlists and videos according to user preference. In this case, users can be identified through their smartphones, and profiles can be created for everyone so that preferences are recorded, resulting in more accurate recommendations. This "intelligence" job is made in the local device.

Similarly, the emergency system, which is responsible for sensing a water leak, a gas leak, or a fire, could automatically close gas valves and/or activate water sprinklers. In addition, once the information is centralized in the microVM, it can generate alarms or alerts to the home's residents and emergency services. An interesting point in this subsystem is that, through the cloud level, it can connect with the emergency systems and automatically generate alerts to the authorities. For example, in case of a fire, it can alert the area firemen and send additional information about the fire's origin if it had been detected according to the sensor's sequence of activation. Another interesting aspect is that in this third level it interconnects with the building's emergency system, and, in case of an incident, it can give information to the authorities regarding both the number of people and their location inside the home.

Additionally, the energy-efficiency subsystem is considered, which registers movement in a room to activate or inactivate lights. It can automatically activate some home appliances, such as the washing machine and dryer, when the electricity is more affordable (as in a variable-rate energy model).

Finally, the subsystems should be seen as part of a greater CPS, and that, among them, there is a constant interaction based on the analysis of the data registered by the sensors, including the interconnection with external systems through cloud computation.

7.7 FUTURE RESEARCH DIRECTIONS

Once the architecture has been proposed and the implementation is done, tests are performed in different use-cases that validate the benefits that have been attributed to the proposed architecture. Based on the given use-cases, laboratory and production tests are initiated in order to consolidate the system and thoroughly evaluate the performance of the implementation.

The research area of cloud-assisted CPS is in its early stages of development. Proposing an architecture is a first step, and various proposals should be tested to evaluate their performance, and the cases where one is more effective than another. Subsequently, applications should be discovered in which cloud-assisted CPSs have superior performance over other CPS developments. Initially, they would be considered in cases of integration between Big Data and artificial intelligence for automated decision-making.

7.8 CONCLUSIONS

The microVMs are a flexible and efficient approach to enable the cloud-assisted CPS, because they allow horizontal and vertical scaling of these, thus maintaining optimum performance and enabling interoperability between heterogeneous systems.

Meanwhile, the three-tier architecture presented in this chapter responds to a wide variety of use cases, in which sensor networks/actuators or other CPSs can be integrated successfully with storage, processing, and analysis systems that equip these use cases with a level of artificial intelligence and human interaction necessary to effectively affect physical processes.

Similarly, the use cases that have been presented illustrate the wide variety of applications of technologies standardized and guided by an adaptive architecture. Future work should find new use-cases and exhaustively test each of these, giving the architecture more substance that would consolidate it as a reference in the deployment of cloud-assisted CPS.

Finally, technological developments corresponding to the writing of this chapter, along with the content exposed in it, are the beginning of a wide area of research on CPSs and their application in the real world. The steps currently taking place in this area will largely demarcate the future development of information and communication technologies.

REFERENCES

[1] Mack C. Fifty years of Moore's law. IEEE Trans Semicond Manufac 2011;24(2):202–7.

[2] Roberts LG. Beyond Moore's law: internet growth trends. Computer 2000;33(1):117–9.

[3] Stojmenovic I. Machine-to-machine communications with in-network data aggregation, processing, and actuation for large-scale CPS. IEEE IoT J 2014;1(2):122–8.

[4] Soulier P, Li D, Williams JR. A survey of language-based approaches to cyber-physical and embedded system development. Tsinghua Sci Technol 2015;20(2):130–41.

[5] Rajkumar R. A cyber-physical future. Proc IEEE 2012;100(Special Centennial Issue):1309–12.

[6] Research Cluster on the Internet of Things. http://www.internet-of-things-research.eu/about_iot.htm; 2015.

[7] Gartner. http://www.gartner.com/it-glossary/internet-of-things/; 2015.

[8] Ashton K. RFID Journal/That 'Internet of Things' Thing. http://www.rfidjournal.com/articles/view?4986; 2015.

[9] Smith JE, Nair R. The architecture of virtual machines. Computer 2005;38(5):32–8.

[10] Manzalini A, Minerva R, Callegati F, Cerroni W, Campi A. Clouds of virtual machines in edge networks. IEEE Commun Mag 2013;51(7):63–70.

[11] Iqbal W, Dailey MN, Carrera D. Low cost quality aware multi-tier application hosting on the amazon cloud. In: International conference on future Internet of Things and cloud (FiCloud). Barcelona, Spain, August 27–29, 2014.

[12] Fazio M, Puliafito A. Cloud4sens: a cloud-based architecture for sensor controlling and monitoring. IEEE Commun Mag 2015;53(3):41–7.

[13] Kovatsch M, Lanter M, Shelby Z. Californium: scalable cloud services for the Internet of Things with CoAP. In: 2014 international conference on the Internet of Things (IoT). Cambridge, UK, 2014.

[14] Abdelwahab S, Hamdaoui B, Guizani M, Rayes A. Enabling smart cloud services through remote sensing: an Internet of Everything enabler. IEEE IoT J 2014;1(3):276–88.

[15] Botts M, Percivall G, Reed C, Davidson J. OGC® sensor web enablement: overview and high-level architecture. Open Geospatial Consortium (OGC); 2007.

[16] Gimenez P, Molina B, Palau CE, Esteve M. Systems, man, and cybernetics (SMC). In: 2013 IEEE international conference on SWE simulation and testing for the IoT. Manchester, UK, October 13–16, 2013.

[17] Cox S. Observations and measurements—Part 1—observation schema. Open Geospatial Consortium (OGC); 2007.

[18] Cox S. Observations and measurements—Part 2—sampling features. Open Geospatial Consortium (OGC); 2007.

[19] Na A, Priest M. Sensor observation service implementation specification. Open Geospatial Consortium (OGC); 2006.

[20] Havens S. Transducer markup language implementation specification. Open Geospatial Consortium (OGC); 2006.

[21] Botts M, Robin A. Sensor model language (SensorML) implementation specification. Open Geospatial Consortium (OGC); 2007.

[22] Simonis I, Dibner P. Sensor planning service implementation specification. Open Geospatial Consortium (OGC); 2007.

[23] Simonis I, Echterhoff J. Sensor alert service implementation specification. Open Geospatial Consortium (OGC); 2006.

[24] Simonis I, Wytzisk A. Web notification service. Open Geospatial Consortium (OGC); 2003.

IoT DATA AND KNOWLEDGE MANAGEMENT

PART

III

STREAM PROCESSING IN IoT: FOUNDATIONS, STATE-OF-THE-ART, AND FUTURE DIRECTIONS

8

X. Liu*, A.V. Dastjerdi*, R. Buyya*,**

*Cloud Computing and Distributed Systems (CLOUDS) Laboratory, Department of Computing and Information Systems, The University of Melbourne, Australia; **Manjrasoft Pty Ltd, Australia

8.1 INTRODUCTION

The emergence of stream processing is driven by the incompetence of the traditional batch-processing paradigm, when it comes to processing fast data. Nowadays, building a modern information-technology system demands the ability of (1) processing an unprecedented volume of data using possibly distributed resources, and (2) exploring the concealed value of data within a tight time-constraint. Having gained extensive attention from the research and industrial community, the batch-processing model derives a series of techniques to accomplish the first goal. MapReduce, for example, is a highly scalable and widely adopted programing model that is specialized in processing parallelization [1]. It moves the computing power to the vicinity of data so that the enormous processing target can be divided and conquered. Analogously, various NoSQL databases are developed alongside traditional relational databases, which allows for an extent of flexibility in data representation to handle the increasing variety of data formats and to obtain finer control over scalability and availability [2]. By taking the horizontal scaling ability as a principle of design, these batch-based techniques are relatively competent in terms of handling the ever-growing data volume and increasingly complex data format. However, they are all struggling to meet the second goal, in which the strict time-constraint has eliminated the luxury of storing the data somewhere before executing relevant operations against it.

In this context, stream processing is proposed as the antithesis of the batch paradigm that caters to the need of processing continuous data-volume in real-time. Both data aggregation and analysis in the streaming model normally have a strict deadline specified, which means completing the job beyond the deadline is not only considered as degradation of performance, but as a failure to deliver the immediate insights that merit the effort in the first place. Guaranteeing the timeliness of aggregation and analysis is a nontrivial task, the streaming paradigm has to continuously aggregate the target-data elements right after its generation to form possible endless streams over the network. When it comes to the data-processing phase, these streams flow through a computation topology where continuous queries (ie, long-standing queries that usually operate over time and buffer windows) are installed to be processed in a record-by-record manner. In contrast to the batch model where data are persisted for future analysis, the streaming model essentially deals with the dynamic

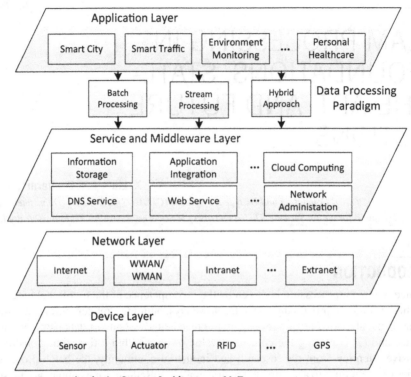

FIGURE 8.1 Stream Processing in the System Architecture of IoT

data-streams that had recently come in, and it incrementally updates the query results. Those data that have passed the processing system cannot be easily retrieved, resulting in an implicit trade-off between the processing accuracy and the real-time promise.

Stream processing has always been an integral part of Internet of Things (IoT) applications, as it offers a scalable, highly available, and fault-tolerant solution to handle a high volume of data in motion. As shown in Fig. 8.1, the architecture of IoT outlines the importance of stream processing and how it is connected with the rest of the system. From the perspective of an application developer, stream processing mainly works as a connecting bridge between the application layer and the service and middleware layer, which allows the upper logic to make appropriate use of the underlying general-purpose services and infrastructures. For example, the streaming paradigm may decide that only the synopsis of incoming data needs to be preserved in the storage system so that no external database is required, or the runtime framework that conducts the data analytics needs be placed in a cloud environment to take advantage of its elasticity feature. In addition to that, the stream-processing paradigm also has a significant impact on the organization of the network layer and the device layer to keep that real-time promise. As a matter of fact, the major part of latency between the data generation and result delivery lies in the data-collection phase rather the processing phase. Therefore, it is essential for an IoT application to properly select the substructures that suit its particular time-sensitivity requirement.

On the other hand, the applications from the IoT domain have always been the driving force that motivates the development and adoption of the stream-processing paradigm. The primary cause is that the way of data generation has become increasingly active in the emerging IoT applications. Previously, data in the conventional scenarios resulted from passive reactions to real-world events or user queries, but nowadays IoT data are mostly automatically generated by large-scale sensor networks for monitoring and decision-making purposes. As a consequence, not only has the amount of data being generated soared, but also the places of data production have become much more geographically dispersed than before. In some cases, leveraging the stream-processing model to handle data in motion is the only viable option.

Besides, the value of IoT data has also become increasingly sparse and deeper hidden, which results in a significant change in the relevant processing techniques. Prior to the IoT era, we had intended to collect comparatively a small fraction of data with high precision to quickly perform analysis and get results in time. However, today the data format used by IoT application is known to be heterogeneous, unstructured, and fine-grained. This is a result of numerous factors, including the advancement of mobile and internet technologies, popularity of social media, and widespread deployment of sensors and actuators in a mutable environment. For example, to make the city more desirable and liveable, the smart-city program installed in Rio de Janeiro, Brazil in 2010 has set up an operations center to analyze real-time data 24/7 from 30 municipal institutions. In this program, raw information is collected from various data sources to support the central surveillance and analytics at a single hub, including live video from traffic and public transport, position information from Google Maps, and real-time alarms from the sensor networks on utility and emergency-service readouts [3]. Such an explosion on data dimensionality has made it impossible to meaningfully correlate the small datasets from these sources, regardless of how precise they are. Revealing the true value of IoT data therefore largely depends on the processing of a massive amount of heterogeneous data, where stream processing comes up as a handy tool, as it provides the required availability, high throughput, and real-time support.

This chapter aims to provide a discussion on the concept and general architecture of a stream-processing system in the context of IoT, with a focus on comparing various platforms that are available to process continuous logic according to specific application needs. To this end, we first analyze the characteristics of stream data, and then we present a general stream-processing architecture, which is determined by the associated processing demands of each characteristic. Finally, this chapter concludes with an outlook that explores the future directions and trending topics regarding the development of stream processing in the IoT domain.

8.2 THE FOUNDATIONS OF STREAM PROCESSING IN IoT

There is a considerable ambiguity related to the terms "stream processing" and "stream analytics," as they have been simultaneously used by a diverse range of research communities. For example, stream processing in the context of parallel processing refers to a computer programming paradigm that allows applications to better exploit computation parallelism using a combination of heterogeneous resources, such as CPU, GPU, or field-programmable gate arrays (FPGAs) [4]. On the other hand, stream processing in the field of connection-oriented communications means to transmit and interpret digitally encoded coherent signals in order to convey data packets for the higher-level network abstraction [5]. In the jargon of the database community, "processing stream" refers to a particular ability owned by active DBMS to handle external updates with reactive behaviors, according to the predefined Event Condition Action (ECA) rules [6]. Nevertheless, these definitions of stream are either overly limited or not directly related to our topic, which is the processing of either distributed events or data items for real-time IoT applications. In order to clarify the scope of this chapter, we first define the terms "stream" and "stream processing" in the IoT context.

8.2.1 **STREAM**

A stream is a sequence of data elements ordered by time. The structure of a stream could consist of discrete signals, event logs, or any combination of time-series data, but the way of recovering data from one to another must be append-only, resembling a conveyor belt that continuously carries data elements through a processing pipeline. In terms of representation, a data stream has an explicit timestamp associated with each element, which serves as a measurement of data order. Based on this, we formally define the denotation of *stream* in the context of IoT, as a Data Element–Time pair (s, Δ), where

1. s is a sequence of data elements that are made available to the processing system over time. A data element may consist of several attributes, but it is normally atomic, as these attributes are tightly coupled with one another for logical consistency.

   Typical element types include immutable data tuples of the same or similar category, as well as heterogeneous events that come from a variety of sources. Depending on the specific application scenario, data elements can be either regularly generated by sensor networks that have monitoring intervals, or randomly produced by real-world events such as user clicks on a website, updates to a particular database table, and system logs produced by Internet services.

2. Δ is a sequence of a timestamp that denotes the sequence of data elements. Since heterogeneous elements could be aggregated into a single stream out-of-order due to the uncertainty of distributed data-collection and transmission procedures, the use of a timestamp is necessary to reconstruct the logic sequence for the following analytics. In addition, timestamps can be also used to evaluate the real-time property of a stream-processing system, by checking on whether the results have been presented on time.

   Normally, timestamps can be implemented in two forms: (1) as a string of absolute time-values, which consumes more resources to be processed, but makes it easier for developers to devise joint algorithms on separate streams; or (2) as a sequence of positive real-time intervals that only record the relative order of data elements in the same stream. The latter form alleviates the stress of the network by reducing the size of the timestamp, but it is harder to reorder the sequence of events across different streams with only in-stream intervals.

8.2.2 **STREAM PROCESSING**

Stream processing is a one-pass data-processing paradigm that always keeps the data in motion to achieve low processing-latency. As a higher abstraction of messaging systems, stream processing supports not only the message aggregation and delivery, but also is capable of performing real-time asynchronous computation while passing along the information. The most important feature of the streaming paradigm is that it does not have access to all data. By contrast, it normally adopts the one-at-a-time processing model, which applies standing queries or established rules to data streams in order to get immediate results upon their arrival.

All of the computation in this paradigm is handled by the continuously dedicated logic-processing system, which is a scalable, highly available, and fault-tolerant architecture that provides system-level integration of a continuous data stream. As a consequence of the timeliness requirement, computations for analytics and pattern recognition should be relatively simple and generally independent, and it is common to utilize distributed-commodity machines to achieve high throughput with only sub-second latency.

Table 8.1 Comparison of the Stream Model and the Batch Model		
Aspects	**Stream Model**	**Batch Model**
Management target	Transient streams	Persistent data batch and relations
Amount of data	Possibly infinite	Finite
Processing model	In-memory processing	Store-then-process and in-memory processing
Query model	Continuous and standing-by query	One-time query
Access model	Sequential access	Random access
Result repeatability	Nearly impossible	Easy
Pattern of result update	Incremental update	Global update
Focus of processing	Low latency and high throughput	High accuracy and comprehensiveness

However, there is another subclass of stream-processing systems that follows the microbatch model. Compared to the aforementioned one-at-a-time model, in which it is difficult to maintain the processing state and guarantee the high-level fault-tolerance efficiently, the microbatch model excels in controllability as a hybrid approach, combining a one-pass streaming pipeline with the data batches of very small size. It greatly eases the implementation of windowing and stateful computation, but at the cost of higher processing-latency. Although such a model is called *microbatch*, we still consider it to be a derived form of stream processing, as long as the target data remains constantly on the move while it is being processed. In order to better illustrate the basic idea of stream processing, we compare it to the well-known batch paradigm in Table 8.1. Although these two paradigms share some similarities in terms of the objective and functionality of processing, they differ significantly in the way that data is organized and processed.

When it comes to the application of stream processing, we have identified two utterly different types of use cases. The first one is *Data Stream Management*. The system falling in this category is normally called *Data Stream Management System (DSMS),* analogous to the traditional DBMS, whose goal is also to manipulate a huge amount of available data to constitute data synopsis, schema, or some other mathematical or statistical model that is easy to understand and interpret. Specifically, data streams within the DSMS are joined, filtered, and transformed according to specific application logic with the use of continuous and long-standing queries. In the early days of DSMS, an application developer could easily set up those queries using SQL-like declarative language, whereas the real implementation was left to be transparently handled by the DSMS. However, since the throughput requirement of stream processing has soared during the recent decade, and the corresponding DSMS has become increasingly distributed, sticking to such a declarative model makes it painful to horizontally scale, and even harder to maintain the required availability and fault-tolerance ability. Therefore, the state-of-art DSMS mostly adopts the imperative way to implement long-time queries, by using the provided programming API, where a segment of code is performed upon the arrival of each incoming data element to compose the whole-analysis logic. Additionally, the responsibility of managing the processing state now rests on the shoulders of the application developers, resulting in a nontrivial effort to debug the application, as well as tune the performance on a specific platform. A typical use-case of DSMS includes face recognition from a continuous video stream, and the calculation of user preference according to his or her click history.

The other use case is called *Complex Event Processing (CEP)*, which is essentially tracking and processing streams of raw events in order to derive significant events and identify meaningful insights from them. There are several techniques being used to achieve that goal. The most notable one is to implement and configure the processing logic as a set of inferring rules in the knowledgebase so that they could be used in the decision-making process of identifying complex patterns. To define and preserve the mutual relationship of events, various types of event-processing languages have been proposed to correlate the seemingly independent events with the relationships such as causality, membership, and timing. Besides, CEP systems normally require that the maintenance of state and the preservation of event relationship be provided at the system level rather than the application level, which makes the microbatch model a preferable option compared to the one-at-a-time model.

In contrast to the primary goal of DSMS, which performs stream analytics at a geographically concentrated place, the major concern of CEP is to infer the needed insight from the vast volume of raw events to stream as fast as possible. Therefore, the computation complexity of CEP logic is usually lower than that of DSMS, and it is preferable to make the rule-matching process take place somewhere near the data generation.

For the sake of clarity, we summarize the major differences between DSMS and CEP in Table 8.2.

However, the boundary of CEP and DSMS is not clearly demarcated in terms of the implementation. A CEP system can be built on top of DSMS by implementing event rules with query languages, whereas the functionality of DSMS can be provided by certain CEP systems that have analytic logic integrated into the rule-based knowledgebase. Actually, there is an ongoing trend that a single stream-processing platform is able to serve both the use cases without requiring too much modification. For example, Apache Storm, a prevalent real-time computation framework that receives a lot of attention recently, has the one-at-a-time model at its core, which makes it an ideal platform for data-stream

Table 8.2 Differences Between Two Use-Cases of Stream Processing: DSMS and CEP		
Aspects	**DSMS**	**CEP**
Processing target	Continuous streams of data	Discrete events
Typical data sources	Video or audio stream, user clicks, social media context.	Sensory information System and service logs
Data variety	Structured, semi/unstructured	Normally structured
Logic implementation	Continuously queries	Event-matching rules or state automaton
Amount of applied logic	Small	Large
Typical application scenario	Quantitative analytics	Qualitative inference
Scalability	Horizontal scale-out	Vertical scale-up
Preferred venue of processing	Collect and aggregate information to a single location to achieve centralized processing	Amortize the processing task throughout the data chain and bring the computation near the data source to relieve the network overhead
Notification of decision	Usually provide analytics result for another system to make a decision	Make decision based on detected insight and inform the outside world as fast as possible

management. But with the built-in Trident abstraction, Apache Storm can easily fulfill the requirement of CEP by using the microbatch paradigm to become a typical event-processing platform that is capable of identifying meaningful patterns from incoming raw events. Such increasing unity has made it possible to propose an abstract architecture of a stream-processing system which generally satisfies the processing needs coming from both the DSMS and CEP domains.

To this end, we first present a detailed analysis on the characteristics of stream data, as well as their relevant processing requirements. Then we investigate the general architecture of a stream-processing system to cater to these particular requirements and shed some light on how an integral data-processing chain is constituted by the independent streaming components.

8.2.3 THE CHARACTERISTICS OF STREAM DATA IN IoT

As suggested by its name, stream data in IoT constitutes inherently dynamic, continuous, and unidirectional data flows that are normally processed in a one-pass manner. Such a dynamic paradigm has endowed it with several common properties, such as timeliness, randomness, endlessness, and volatility.

8.2.3.1 Timeliness and Instantaneity

Ensuring the timeliness of processing requires the ability to collect, transfer, process, and present the stream data in real-time. As the value of data may vanish over time rather rapidly, the streaming architecture needs to perform all the calculation and communication on the fly with the data that has newly arrived.

On the other hand, the data generation in IoT environments mainly depends on the status of data sources. The amount of data that is generated at low-activity periods can be dramatically less than the number observed at peak times. Usually the stream-processing platform has no control over the volume and complexity of the incoming data stream. Therefore, it is necessary to build an adaptive platform that can elastically scale with respect to fluctuating processing demands, and still remain portable and configurable in order to stay agile in response to the continuously shifting processing needs.

8.2.3.2 Randomness and Imperfection

Randomness and data imperfection are two direct consequences of the dynamic nature of stream data. There could be several unforeseeable factors that affect the processing chain. For example, the data generation process may induce randomness because the data sources are normally independently installed in different environments, which makes it nearly impossible to guarantee the sequence of data arrival across different streams. Besides, the data transmission process can also result in disorder and other defections in the same data stream, as some tuples may be lost, damaged, or delayed due to the constantly changing network conditions. Stonebraker et al. have elaborated on the possible types of data imperfection found in stream data, and list the capability of handling imperfections on the fly as one of the eight requirements of real-time stream processing [7].

8.2.3.3 Endlessness and Continuousness

As long as the data sources are alive and the stream-processing system is properly functioning, newly generated data will be continuously appended to the data channel until the whole application is explicitly turned off. Therefore, processing stream data needs the support of high-level availability to avoid any possible interruption of data flow, which may lead to the accumulation of backlogs, and, finally, the breach of the real-time promise.

Table 8.3 Characteristics of Stream Data and the Corresponding Processing Requirements

Characteristics	Corresponding Requirement
Timeliness and instantaneity	1. Data cannot be detained in any phase of the processing chain, so there should be a comprehensive data-collection subsystem working as a driving force that powers the data in motion once they are generated. 2. For compute-intensive applications, a data aggregation subsystem is needed to gather the collected data for centralized processing. 3. Each phase of the processing chain is preferable to be horizontal scalable in order to keep pace with the fluctuated workload.
Randomness and imperfection	1. For cleansing and coordination purposes, data should be first buffered in a message subsystem before being processed. 2. A declarative or imperative CLPS is responsible for implementing the application logic and handling possible data-stream imperfections.
Endlessness and continuousness	1. The storage subsystem can only be used as an assistance component that preserves the data synopsis or the query results. 2. Ensuring the availability is one of the core design principles due to the continuousness of workload.
Volatility and unrepeatability	1. The data value and insights discovered from the streams should be immediately submitted to other services or presented to users through a presentation subsystem. 2. The fault-tolerance ability is another system design principle, as it is costly or even impossible to replay the incoming stream during the recovery of system failures.

8.2.3.4 Volatility and Unrepeatability

Most of the stream data will be discarded once they have finished traversing through the stream-processing system, which makes the existence of data quite volatile. Even if the data sources are able to replay the data stream upon the retransmit request, the new stream is unlikely to be exactly the same as the previous one. Also, the timeliness of result presentation would be impaired because of the reprocessing.

Table 8.3 summarizes the processing requirements with regard to the corresponding characteristics, where the phrases in italic denote the streaming components that need to be implemented in the different stages of the data-processing chain.

Apart from these common properties, stream data in IoT is known to be highly dynamic and heterogeneous. The dynamism not only refers to the varying data volumes, but also it denotes the constantly changing data quality, credibility, and presentation model that are caused by the dynamicity of the environment. Since there could be a series of resource constraints that confine the ability of data sources and even alter the structure of the data transmission network, the stream-processing system is required to be workload-adaptive and context-aware so it can keep on finding meaningful insights from the ever-changing raw data.

Heterogeneity is another notable characteristic brought on by the IoT context. As an example, smart-city application, a mobile app that automatically searches for empty parking spaces for the car, the driver needs to collect various formats of data from different places to make a comprehensive decision. For instance, the app uses the GPS signal from the driver's personal device to determine the current position, inquires a vacancy pool to show the possible alternatives, including the location and permitted parking hours, and makes a recommendation among these alternatives, using the traffic conditions from a road- monitoring system. As most of the raw data are extracted from the sensory information through distributed smart-devices and embedded sensors in real time, it is a great challenge for the data collection system to achieve data federation and provide a unified view from the upcoming heterogeneous sets of data and the prior knowledge extracted from the history information.

8.2.4 THE GENERAL ARCHITECTURE OF A STREAM-PROCESSING SYSTEM IN IoT

First of all, we argue that a *stream-processing architecture* should include an integral data-processing chain that covers the whole lifespan of data (from its generation up to its consumption). However, most of the previous research had used this term in a narrower sense, only referring to the organization of a logic-processing system where the relevant analytics are performed.

For example, a widespread survey written by Gugola et al. broke down the general architecture of an information-processing system into five major components: the *receiver, decider, producer,* and *forwarder* that manipulate data streams according to the designated logic, and a *knowledgebase* that assists the *decider* during the decision-making process [8]. This usage implicitly assumes that the incoming data has already been shaped as continuous streams and can be readily obtained by the receiver, so that the counting of processing latency should start from the time at which the data streams enter the system, rather than the time when data is generated. However, this assumption regarding the triviality of data collection and aggregation is tenable only when the research purpose is to evaluate the correctness and competence of a particular logic-processing subsystem. When it comes to building stream applications for real-world scenarios, such an assumption is poorly suited because collecting and aggregating data from geo-distributed data sources are inherently costly procedures. There are a series of development and deployment hurdles to be overcome by the use of dedicated streaming components.

Fig. 8.2 presents a general architecture of a stream-processing system that is tailored to the IoT peculiarities. This architecture breaks down the whole data-processing chain into several stages according

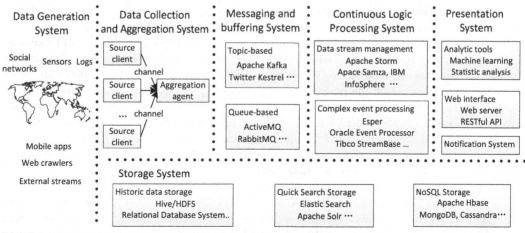

FIGURE 8.2 General Architecture of a Stream Processing System in IoT

to the functionality and target; we have identified six separate streaming components which are responsible for data generation, collection, buffering, logic processing, storage, and presentation, respectively.

The data-generation system denotes the spectrum of data sources that continuously produce raw information for the data-processing chain. There are a lot of entities that can fulfill this definition, which makes a full enumeration nearly impossible. However, we can still categorize the generated data into three types, in accordance with their modalities.

The first type, *static data*, refers to the long-term information that has already been stored in on-premise infrastructures or remote locations. As these data are mostly derived from the validated knowledge and are not frequently updated, they are usually fetched by the stream-processing system on a regular basis, serving as reference information during the analytic procedure. The second type, *centralized stream data*, is a special type of stream that only comes from a single centralized data source. Data of this type sometimes even demands to be processed right in the same place where it is generated, so there would be no need for aggregating data to achieve a unified data-view. However, this type of data is also not the mainstream input for IoT stream applications, for the reason that it is rather rare that one data source can generate all the information that is required for the analytic process. Apart from these two, *Distributed stream data* is the most common data type used in IoT applications. Data of this type dynamically come from various distributed places in heterogeneous formats, such as sensory information from sensor networks, personal preferences from mobile devices, and social-media streams from Internet services. The volume of distributed stream data and the time sensitivity of its application actually determine the performance requirement for a particular stream-processing system.

However, no matter which form of data is being produced, the data sources have to generate a unique timestamp associated with it to denote the time of generation. These timestamps are used to build the continuous processing logic and further evaluate the timeliness of execution.

The *Data Collection and Aggregation System* combining with the *Messaging and Buffering System* plays the role of a message broker in the whole data-processing chain. To collect and aggregate different types of data, various forms of source clients are independently installed to drive the newly generated data in motion, while several aggregation channels are provided to gather these stream data into a centralized buffer, using hierarchical aggregation agents. There are two types of message buffers in terms of implementation: some are topic-based, which support a higher-level programmability, whereas the others are queue-based, and thus mainly optimized for performance concerns.

The *storage system* and *presentation system* are two supportive components for a stream-processing architecture. Keeping all the historical data in the storage system is neither feasible in implementation nor necessary in terms of the processing requirement. Therefore, data that need to be stored are either established knowledge, which can guide the future processing, or meaningful data synopsis, which might arouse the future interest of users. On the other hand, the presentation system serves as an interface of the stream-processing system, wherein it immediately hands over the data value to the higher-level analytic tools, or directly delivers the results or notifications to the end users. It is also responsible for receiving search-command or query updates from the external environment so that it can make the stream-processing system more adaptive and responsive.

As the core of the data-processing chain, the *Continuous Logic Processing System* (CLPS) deserves to be separately reviewed in the next section. As suggested by the name, it is responsible for processing aggregated data according to the designated continuous logic, which could either come from the Data Stream Management or Complex Event Processing background.

8.3 **CONTINUOUS LOGIC PROCESSING SYSTEM**

In particular, we thoroughly discuss the history of the CLPS from an evolutionary perspective, and then outline the differences among some state-of-the-art CLPS implementations.

The origin of the CLPS dates back to the beginning of this century. As shown in Fig. 8.3, the first generation of CLPS, pioneered by NiagaraCQ [9] and STREAM [10], is merely several prototypes from the research community and only suited for certain processing scenarios in which only a small amount of data are generated. In addition to that, the types of operations supported by these prototypes are also limited, which means that they are usually used as functional extensions of the existing Data Base Management Systems (DBMS).

On the other hand, these prototypes are ground-breaking explorations in the new area of stream processing. NiagaraCQ [9], for example, defines a simple command-language to create and drop continuous queries over XML files on the fly. It also supports grouping continuous queries based on their structures, and performs incremental evaluations of each group by considering only the changed portion of the targeted XML file. Besides, this command language adopts a declarative syntax to make it developer-friendly, which can help the existing queries written in transitional SQL to be transplanted into the new stream-processing platform.

In contrast to NiagaraCQ, the focus of STREAM [10] developed by Stanford is to transfer from persistent relations to transient data streams with window-based data processing and approximate query answering. STREAM directly supports SQL-like query language so that it can be regarded as a functional extension of traditional DBMS. With the lessons learned from STREAM, the authors also discuss models and issues in managing data-stream systems [11].

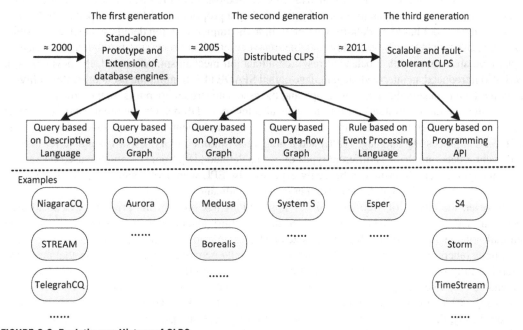

FIGURE 8.3 Evolutionary History of CLPS

There are also some CLPSs that are directly built on top of existing databases. TelegraphCQ [12] is an example of a system falling into this category. It is developed on PostgreSQL to cope with the high-value and diverse data streams, and enables the possibility of adaptive querying.

Aurora [13] is the last breakthrough founded in the first generation of CLPS. Within the help of the "boxes and arrows" paradigm, the continuous queries are implemented by explicit operator graphs rather than declarative query languages such as SQL. As a result, the performance of stream processing is significantly improved at the cost that the query implementations and internal processing mechanisms are no longer transparent to the developer.

Around 2005, the research front advanced to distributed stream processing, where the CLPS is able to take advantage of a set of distributed hosts to achieve better scalability and fault-tolerance. The project Medusa [14] is an extension to Aurora, which leads to a scalable and QoS-oriented architecture. As a result of distribution, the logical entities of Medusa are no longer tightly coupled and they have to communicate with each other through a naming, discovering, and message-passing process. In addition to that, the problem of load balancing and resource management also emerged as a great challenge in distributed CLPSs, for example, as an operator node could be split into several atomic units and re-mapped to participating machines, it is important to design a dynamically partitioned operator network to improve the resource utilization.

Borealis [15] engine was developed on top of Medusa in order to integrate some advanced capabilities, including dynamic query modification, result revision, and flexible monitoring. Apart from that, Borealis also introduces the concept of a replicated processing node, and defines several new tuple types, such as punctuation tuples and priority tuples, to gain finer control over the fault-tolerance and manageability of the distributed platform.

In contrast to the academic projects such as Aurora, Medusa, and Borealis, whose queries are mostly implemented based on an operator graph, System S [16], a proprietary CLPS developed by IBM, proposed a query model based on data-flow graph to hide the implementation details as much as possible. The core objective is to achieve highly scalable, resource-efficient processing through a user-oriented declarative abstraction with a balanced resource-allocation mechanism. Afterward, the developers in IBM also introduced an intermediate language called SPADE [17] to grant the users more flexibility by allowing them to design the data-flow graph and the associate stream operators on their own.

The aforementioned systems all fall into the subcategory of DSMS. On the other hand, the project Esper chooses a different evolutionary path in terms of the implementation of continuous logic. By using the event processing language (EPL) and a pluggable runtime library, Esper is suitable for distributed event processing that has different types of events defined [18]. Some commonly used operations like joint splitting and filtering can be easily expressed by EPL with a very similar syntax to SQL, so that the programming burden of the developer is also significantly relieved.

However, the advent of Web 2.0 and IoT applications has brought the previous CLPSs to their knees. Around the year of 2011, CLPS evolved into the third generation, which is inherently scalable and fault-tolerant, and designed for a large-size cluster composed of commodity machines.

Among others, S4 [19] developed by Yahoo! is generally perceived as the first CLPS that meets the criteria of fully scalable and fault-tolerant. It offers intuitive programming API similar to MapReduce that can be used to develop streaming applications. However, S4 does not guarantee the correctness of processing, so streaming data could be either lost or repeatedly executed during the processing process.

Fortunately, the emergence of the Storm project [20] gracefully handles this requirement by introducing the anchor mechanism. With anchor, Storm is able to process a tuple with either an exactly once, at least once, or at most once, guarantee. Besides, it supports almost arbitrary programming languages such as Clojure, Java, Ruby, and Python to implement the spouts and bolts, which are the logical operations in Storm. It also greatly enhances its fault-tolerant ability with finely grained task-level parallelization, as when a host fails, all of the running tasks on it could be transferred to other healthy hosts.

TimeStream [21] is another scalable CLPS written in C# by Microsoft. According to the authors' evaluation, it is able to handle an advertising aggregation data-source with a data generation speed of 700,000 URLs per s, 1 per a 6-node commodity cluster, all within 2 s. Similar to Storm and S4, TimeStream adopts a task DAG to denote the sequence of logical operators. To make the system adaptive and autonomous, there is a resilient substitution mechanism to dynamically adjust and reconfigure task DAG in accordance with the changes to incoming streams or in the presence of any failed nodes.

There are also some other state-of-the-art CLPSs that are available to be inserted into the data-processing chain. As shown in Table 8.4, we compare these alternatives in terms of:

- *System architecture*: it outlines internally how a CLPS is organized and coordinated
- *Data transmission*: the way that streaming data feeds the processing system. *Pull-based* means that CLPS is responsible for actively fetching data, whereas *push-based* means passive message- reception
- *Development language*: which languages are being used to develop the CLPS
- *Programming*: which components need to be programmed to apply the continuous logic
- *Partitioning and parallelism*: how data is partitioned to achieve processing parallelization
- *Accurate recovery*: whether the CLPS is able to accurately reproduce the same processing result when failures occur to the system
- *State consistency*: whether the system is able to ensure the consistency state for all of the participating components during the processing procedure

8.4 CHALLENGES AND FUTURE DIRECTIONS

The current stream-processing systems have been greatly improved to cater to the emerging needs of IoT applications. A state-of-the-art stream-processing system now should satisfy the following criteria: (1) horizontal scalability to accommodate different sizes of processing needs, (2) easy to program and manage while concealing the tedious low-level implantation from its users, and (3) capable of dealing with possible hardware faults with graceful performance degradation rather than sudden termination.

However, there is still a long way to go before the stream-processing systems achieve their full maturity. The following aspects summarize the challenges that still need to be further addressed, and also point toward the possible research directions that should attract more attention from the research community.

8.4.1 SCALABILITY

Scalability does not just refer to the ability to expand the system to catch up to the ever-increasing data streams, so that the promise of the Quality of Service (QoS) or Service Level Agreement (SLA) could be honored. Elasticity, the ability to dynamically scale to the right size on demand, is the future and advanced form of scalability. An efficient resource-allocation strategy should be adopted, by which the stream-processing system can start running with only limited resource usages, especially when the data sources are temporarily idle during the application-deployment phase. Afterward, as the workload of IoT may fluctuate and the user requirement may change over time, the system should dynamically

Table 8.4 Comparison Between State-of-the-Art CLPS Implementations

Aspects	Apache Storm	S4	Spark Streaming	Apache Samza	Apache Flink	Esper
System architecture	Master–slave	Symmetric	Master–slave	Master–slave	Master–slave	Master–slave
Data transmission	Pull-based	Push-based	1. Push-based with flume 2. Pull-based with a custom sink	Pull-based	Push-based	Pull-based
Develop language programming	Clojure	Java	Scala, Java	Java	Java, Scala	Java, C# EPL
Partitioning and parallelism	Spouts and Bolts	Processing elements	Distributed datasets	Samza job	Data stream and transformations	
	Sending to different tasks	Based on key-value pairs	Sending to different tasks	Sending to different tasks	Sending to different tasks	Partition based on context
Accurate recovery	Yes, with trident	No	Yes	Yes	Yes	No
State consistency	No	No	Yes, with state DStream	Yes, with embedded key-value store	Yes, with asynchronous distributed snapshots	No

provision new resources by taking into account the characteristics of the available hardware infrastructure, and free up some of them when they are no longer needed. Such an awareness of underlying infrastructure can help the system to perform more reasonable elastic operations, and is also useful for scheduling task loads in case of hardware failures.

8.4.2 ROBUSTNESS

Fault-tolerance is a commonplace topic when it comes to the design and implantation of stream-processing systems, especially when considering that its availability is one of the most crucial prerequisites to guarantee the correctness and significance of real-time processing. The previous research and practice on fault-tolerance mostly rely on either system replication or state checkpointing, which are both not flexible enough to tailor to the robustness for operations in accordance with the trending fault-types. Designing a hybrid and configurable fault-tolerance mechanism that is capable of recovering the system from unforeseeable failures is an open research-question left to be answered.

8.4.3 SLA-COMPLIANCE

How to negotiate the SLA for stream-processing systems has been rarely discussed in the previous research. It also depends on which platform the system is running on, and how stakeholders are involved. But an inherent requirement is to achieve cost-efficiency, which translates to minimizing the monetary cost for the users, as well as reducing the operational cost for the provider (possibly data centers). Achieving SLA-compliance requires the stream-processing system to be equipped with the ability to trade-off between the justifiable metrics, such as performance and robustness, with the running cost, the balance of which should be left for the user to decide when signing up for SLA.

As the stream data from the IoT background tends to be more dynamic and bursty, it would also be interesting to investigate the possibility of providing probabilistic SLA guarantees rather than traditional rule-based promises.

8.4.4 LOAD BALANCING

Currently, the applied load-balance schemes are very simplistic, the major target of which is to normally improve the performance of the system, especially by maximizing the throughput. However, the importance of load balance goes far beyond performance optimization. A wrong balancing decision may lead to unnecessary load-shedding, dropping arrived messages when the system is deemed to be overloaded, which ultimately impairs the veracity of the processing result. It is challenging to take the low-level metrics such as task capacity or lengths of thread-message-queues into consideration during the load-balancing process, but the perspective is very promising, as currently the system utilization rate is still moderate; even the stream-processing system is already saturated, where the inefficient load-balance mechanism is the culprit to blame.

8.5 CONCLUSIONS

To summarize, we have presented the emergence of stream processing as a complement to the batch paradigm, which is especially suited to the IoT context. We discussed the relationship between IoT and stream processing in the introduction, and then outlined the formal definition of stream data as well as the associate stream-processing concept in the following section. We have also identified the unique characteristics of stream data in IoT and investigated how the processing requirements of them would affect the organization of a stream-processing system. Based on the aforementioned analysis, we presented a general architecture for such a system, and explained in detail about the history and comparison of different continuous logic-processing subsystems. The challenges and open questions for stream processing in IoT are also discussed in this chapter.

It can be concluded that the research on utilizing the stream-processing paradigm to build real-time IoT applications is gradually arousing a storm of hype. Ultimately, the prevalence of such applications requires the development of adaptive and autonomous stream-processing systems to better uncover the connotative value that is hidden within the huge volume of volatile streams.

REFERENCES

[1] Dean J, Ghemawat S. MapReduce: simplified data processing on large clusters. Commun ACM 2008;51(1):107–13.
[2] Cattell R. Scalable SQL and NoSQL data stores. SIGMOD Rec 2011;39(4):12–27.
[3] Kitchin R. The real-time city? Big data and smart urbanism. GeoJournal 2013;79(1):1–14.
[4] Humphreys G, Houston M, Ng R, Frank R, Ahern S, Kirchner PD, Klosowski JT. Chromium: a stream-processing framework for interactive rendering on clusters. In: Proceedings of the twenty-ninth annual conference on computer graphics and interactive techniques. New York, NY, USA; 2002. p. 693–702.
[5] Taylor MG. Phase estimation methods for optical coherent detection using digital signal processing. J Light Technol 2009;27(7):901–14.
[6] McCarthy D, Dayal U. The architecture of an active database management system. In: Proceedings of the 1989 ACM SIGMOD international conference on management of data. New York, NY, USA; 1989. p. 215–224.
[7] Stonebraker M, Çetintemel U, Zdonik S. The 8 requirements of real-time stream processing. SIGMOD Rec 2005;34(4):42–7.
[8] Cugola G, Margara A. Processing flows of information: from data stream to complex event processing. ACM Comput Surv 2012;44(3):15:1–15.
[9] Chen J, DeWitt DJ, Tian F, Wang Y. NiagaraCQ: a scalable continuous query system for Internet databases. In: Proceedings of the 2000 ACM SIGMOD international conference on management of data. New York, NY, USA; 2000. p. 379–390.
[10] Arasu A, Babcock B, Babu S, Cieslewicz J, Ito K, Motwani R, Srivastava U, Widom J. Stream: the Stanford data stream management system; 2004.
[11] Babcock B, Babu S, Datar M, Motwani R, Widom J. Models and issues in data stream systems. In: Proceedings of the twenty-first ACM SIGMOD-SIGACT-SIGART symposium on principles of database systems, New York, NY, USA; 2002. p. 1–16.
[12] Chandrasekaran S, Cooper O, Deshpande A, Franklin MJ, Hellerstein JM, Hong W, Krishnamurthy S, Madden SR, Reiss F, Shah MA. TelegraphCQ: continuous dataflow processing. In: Proceedings of the 2003 ACM SIGMOD international conference on management of data. New York, NY, USA; 2003. p. 668–668.
[13] Abadi DJ, Carney D, Çetintemel U, Cherniack M, Convey C, Lee S, Stonebraker M, Tatbul N, Zdonik S. Aurora: a new model and architecture for data stream management. VLDB J 2003;12(2):120–39.
[14] Cherniack M, Balakrishnan H, Balazinska M, Carney D, Cetintemel U, Xing SY, Xing Y, Zdonik SB. Scalable distributed stream processing. CIDR 2003;3:257–68.
[15] Abadi DJ, Ahmad Y, Balazinska M, Cetintemel U, Cherniack M, Hwang JH, et al. The design of the borealis stream processing engine. CIDR 2005;5:277–89.

[16] Wu KL, Hildrum KW, Fan W, Yu PS, Aggarwal CC, George DA, Gedik B, Bouillet E, Gu X, Luo G, Wang H. Challenges and experience in prototyping a multi-modal stream analytic and monitoring application on system S. In: Proceedings of the thirty-third international conference on very large data bases. Vienna, Austria; 2007. p. 1185–1196.

[17] Gedik B, Andrade H, Wu HL, Yu PS, Doo M. SPADE: the system S declarative stream processing engine. In: Proceedings of the 2008 ACM SIGMOD international conference on management of data. New York, NY, USA; 2008. p. 1123–1134.

[18] Anicic D, Fodor P, Rudolph S, Stojanovic N. EP-SPARQL: a unified language for event processing and stream reasoning. In: Proceedings of the twentieth international conference on World Wide Web. New York, NY, USA; 2011. p. 635–644.

[19] Neumeyer L, Robbins B, Nair A, Kesari A. S4: distributed stream computing platform. In: 2010 IEEE international conference on data mining workshops (ICDMW); 2010. p. 170–177.

[20] Toshniwal A, Taneja S, Shukla A, Ramasamy K, Patel JM, Kulkarni S, Jackson J, Gade K, Fu M, Donham J, Bhagat N, Mittal S, Ryaboy D. Storm@Twitter. In: Proceedings of the 2014 ACM SIGMOD international conference on management of data. New York, NY, USA; 2014. p. 147–156.

[21] Qian Z, He Y, Su C, Wu Z, Zhu H, , Zhang T, Zhou L, Yu Y, Zhang Z. TimeStream: reliable stream computation in the cloud. In: EuroSys; 2013.

A FRAMEWORK FOR DISTRIBUTED DATA ANALYSIS FOR IoT

9

M. Moshtaghi, C. Leckie, S. Karunasekera

Department of Computing and Information Systems, The University of Melbourne, Australia

9.1 INTRODUCTION

In this chapter, we discuss a framework for data analysis as part of a monitoring system where the data are distributed in the network and edge devices have limited capacity in terms of memory and computational power. The main idea of this framework is to support efficient local processing and summarization of the data at the nodes, followed by global processing of the local summaries. We introduce this framework within the context of distributed anomaly detection but it can be easily extended to a wider range of tasks. Our framework follows a similar idea to Fog computing [1] in the sense that it reduces the amount of data routed over the network backbone using the computational capabilities of the devices collecting the data.

The proposed framework covers three aspects: local data modeling, communication, and global data modeling. The local data modeling requires an efficient algorithm with low computational cost. The algorithm calculates local summaries of the data and identifies anomalies in the local data. Only the summaries of the data are communicated to a central location which we refer to as *sink*. Limiting the communication to only data summaries alleviates the overhead of communicating all the data over the network. The global data modeling component, which is located in a central location, is responsible for finding global summaries and anomalies.

We start this chapter by providing an introduction on the anomaly detection task in IoT followed by more detailed description of what constitutes an anomaly and a formal problem statement. In Section 9.5, the distributed anomaly detection framework is described. We show the performance of the approach with three examples from real-life and synthetic datasets. In Section 9.6, we introduce an efficient incremental approach to estimate summaries of the data to increase the flexibility and accuracy of the framework. We summarize the findings discussed in this chapter in Section 9.7.

9.2 PRELIMINARIES

Recent advancements in sensing technologies provide a cost-effective platform for monitoring applications to gather detailed observations from different environments including factories, mines, agriculture, and urban areas. An important aspect of a monitoring system is the ability to detect significant events or unusual behavior in the environment. These unusual patterns are also called outliers, surprises, novelties, or events in different applications. Anomaly detection methods play an important role in modeling and detecting these anomalous events in IoT applications and have been applied in a variety of applications [2], including intrusion detection [3,4], event detection [5], and quality assurance [6]. Numerous factors affect the use of anomaly detection in these applications, such as mobility in sensors, the condition of the environment (benign or adverse [7]), the dynamics of the environment, and energy constraints. However, the most common approach in anomaly detection is to build a model of the normal data and then identify deviations from this model as anomalies.

Therefore, the challenge is to build a model of the multidimensional data distributed in the network in a robust and efficient manner—robust in the sense that the model accurately captures the characteristics of the data, and efficient in the sense that the model satisfies the resource constraints of the network. There is a wide range of anomaly detection techniques applied to monitoring applications [8–14]. However, only few techniques consider both communication and computational constraints of the nodes in such network. In this chapter we describe a set of techniques based on the basic distributed anomaly detection technique proposed by Rajasegarar et al. in Ref. [8]. These techniques focus on reducing the communication and computational cost of detecting anomalies in the data.

There are two components in the distributed framework by Rajasegarar et al. [8]: a local hyperellipsoidal model of the data and a distributed anomaly detection model. This framework relies on hyperellipsoidal models for anomaly detection, which are extensions of the 3σ *rule* for outlier detection to multivariate data. The 3σ rule is based on the fact that 99% of a univariate Gaussian distribution with mean μ and standard deviation of σ lies in $\mu \pm 3\sigma$. For example, if the height distribution of Australian adult males has a mean of 175 cm and a standard deviation of 8, there is only 1% chance of encountering a person from this population whose height is outside this interval [151 199]. The 3σ rule treats these rare observations as outliers. This interval has a hyperellipsoidal shape in higher dimensions and it is defined based on the mean and the covariance matrix of the data. A formal definition of this hyperellipsoidal interval (boundary) and its calculation are given in Section 9.4.1.

In the distributed framework of the Rajasegarar et al. [8] (shown in Fig. 9.1), each node constructs a hyperellipsoidal decision boundary for its local data (local model) and sends the parameters of this decision boundary (step 1) to a sink node where all the local models are merged to find a global decision boundary for the network (step 2). The parameters of the global decision boundary are then sent back to the nodes (step 3).

The main advantage of this framework is that it can reduce in-network communication by limiting communication overhead to the parameters of the decision boundaries, which can be orders of magnitude smaller than sending all the raw data to a single location in the network. The applied hyperellipsoidal model provides a robust decision boundary for a variety of different types of data distribution and can be calculated efficiently.

Other advantages of this framework are as follows:

- The hyperellipsoidal model has linear computational complexity at each node.
- The hyperellipsoidal model can tolerate some degree of noise in the training data.
- The framework can detect both local (within node) and global (within network) anomalies.

A key assumption in this framework is that the environment is *homogeneous*, that is, there is no difference between the distribution of the data observed at each node. Another limitation of this approach is that it uses a batch calculation of the hyperellipsoidal decision boundaries, which requires each node to have enough memory to buffer some window of the data. Batch calculation also incurs

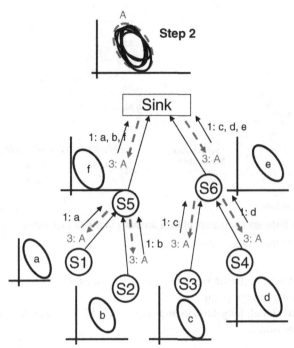

FIGURE 9.1 A Diagram of the Distributed Anomaly Detection Technique

Nodes in the network are shown with a circle, and each ellipse, marked with a letter, is a local model calculated at each node.

delays in the network during model recalculation. In this chapter, we discuss approaches to generalize this framework to suit *non-homogeneous* environments where the underlying distribution of normal measurements varies from node to node. Later, we show how local hyperellipsoidal boundaries (step 1, Fig. 9.1) can be calculated online to improve the efficiency and practicality of the framework. In the next section, we start by a giving a brief introduction of anomaly detection task.

9.3 ANOMALY DETECTION

Anomaly detection is an important unsupervised data processing task which enables us to detect abnormal behavior without having a priori knowledge of possible abnormalities. An anomaly can be defined as a pattern in the data that does not conform to a well-defined notion of normal behavior [2]. This definition is very general and is based on how patterns deviate from normal behavior. On this basis we can categorize anomalies in the data into three categories:

- Outliers—Short anomalous patterns that appear in a nonsystematic way in the collected data, usually arising due to noise or faults, for example, due to communication errors.
- Events/Change—These patterns appear with a systematic and sudden change from previously known normal behavior. The duration of these patterns is usually longer than outliers. In

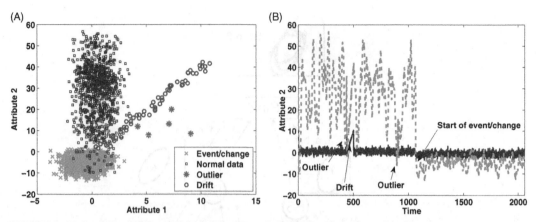

FIGURE 9.2 An Example of Different Categories of Data Anomaly in a Two-Dimensional Dataset

(A) Scatter plot overview. (B) Time series overview.

environmental monitoring, extreme weather conditions are examples of events. The start of an event is usually called a change point.
- Drifts—Slow, unidirectional, long-term changes in data [15]. This usually happens due to the onset of a fault in a sensor.

Fig. 9.2 shows an example of each of these categories using a synthetically generated dataset. Notice that long-term characteristics of the data are usually reflected in the scatter plot of the data whereas the time series of the data represent the dynamics of each attribute in the dataset.

Another categorization of anomalies is given in Ref. [8] considering the topology of a network. Three categories of anomalies identified in this study are as follows:

- First order—Anomalies can occur in an individual node, that is, some observations at a node are anomalous with respect to the rest of the data.
- Second order—All of the observed data at a node can be anomalous with respect to the neighboring nodes. In this case, such a node is considered as an anomalous node in the network.
- Third order—A cluster of nodes are anomalous with respect to other nodes in the network.

Fig. 9.3 demonstrates this categorization in a network topology.

There is a large body of research on anomaly detection techniques for different applications [2,4,14,16,17]. Many different techniques have been applied for anomaly detection in these applications. Here, we briefly introduce some of the main types of techniques used in anomaly detection. Detailed descriptions of these techniques can be found in surveys on anomaly detection techniques such as those by Chandola et al. [2,7] and Rajasegarar et al. [4].

The first type of anomaly detection techniques uses rule-based methods. Owing to their simplicity and low computational overhead, these techniques have been successfully implemented in many applications such as intrusion detection. In these approaches, if an observed data sample does not match a predefined set of rules, it is considered as an anomaly [18,19]. The next type of anomaly detection approaches use dynamic system modeling to model the normal behavior of the data, and anomalous behavior is then identified by the extent of deviation from the normal model of the data [20]. Dynamic

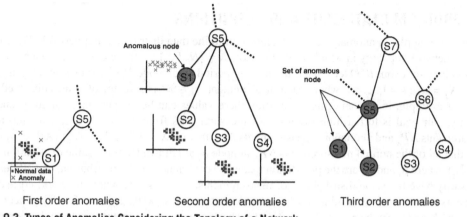

First order anomalies   Second order anomalies   Third order anomalies

FIGURE 9.3 Types of Anomalies Considering the Topology of a Network

In the scatter plot, crosses represent anomalous measurements and dots represent normal measurements.

Bayesian networks are a common pattern recognition technique used in this area [21]. In statistical approaches for anomaly detection, anomalies are considered as those data points that have low likelihood given the expected distribution of the data. The main assumption in these approaches is that the distribution of the data is known and the parameters of the distribution need to be estimated using the normal data [12]. Density-based and nearest neighborhood approaches identify data points that reside in areas of the input space with low density as anomalous [5,13]. One-class classifiers such as one-class support vector machines have also been used to identify anomalies in a set of data [11] by finding a discriminant between the main body of the data and potential outliers. Clustering techniques as a basic knowledge discovery process can also be used for anomaly detection on unlabeled data [22].

In traditional techniques for anomaly detection the data are assumed to be in one location. However, collecting all the data from the nodes in one location is not always possible. If we expect to run anomaly detection locally, the processing unit at each node may not be powerful enough to support sophisticated anomaly detection algorithms. Therefore, there is a need for distributed and efficient anomaly detection algorithms suitable for IoT applications. A distributed approach to anomaly detection exploits the limited computational resources of the nodes for anomaly detection. Nodes can perform the detection locally by collaborating with each other. This can save a considerable amount of energy at the nodes by avoiding raw data transmission. Therefore, in this case the benefits of using anomaly detection techniques are twofold: (1) the ability to detect interesting samples and (2) the ability to conserve energy resources at the nodes.

As mentioned in the introduction, a practical approach for distributed anomaly detection is proposed by Rajasegarar et al. in Ref. [8]. The authors present a hyperellipsoidal model for distributed anomaly detection, where a single hyperellipsoid is used to determine the distribution of all measurements in the network. However, if the monitored environment is nonhomogeneous, comprising a mixture of different distributions, then this distributed anomaly detection approach will result in low detection accuracy. This situation can arise in environments, for example, where some sensors are exposed to direct sunlight, while others lie in shadow. In this situation, the measurements from each sensor node are drawn from one of the two different underlying distributions, and the anomaly detection algorithm needs to accommodate this type of normal behavior.

9.4 PROBLEM STATEMENT AND DEFINITIONS

Our aim is to apply an anomaly detection algorithm to the data distributed in a network. We consider a sensor network topology in which a set of sensors $N = \{N_j : J = 1,...,l\}$ are connected in a hierarchical tree topology to a sink B. Over a fixed monitoring period, each node N_j observes a set of n_j measurements $X_j = \{x_k^j : k = 1,...,n_j\}$ where each measurement $x_k^j \in \Re^d$ is a vector of values observed at the node, for example, in a monitoring application these values can be temperature, humidity, and light intensity. Our goal is to partition the set X of measurements from all nodes $\bigcup_{j=1,...,l} X_j$ into normal measurements NP_X and anomalous measurements AP_X, that is, $X = NP_X \bigcup AP_X, NP_X \bigcap AP_X = \varnothing$. We assume that all of the normal measurements NP_{Xj} at node N_j are drawn from the same distribution $NP_{xj} \approx X(\mu_r, \Sigma_r)$, where μ_r and Σ_r are the population mean and covariance of the distribution. Not all the nodes necessarily have the same distributions of measurements, so across the whole network, normal measurements are drawn from a mixture of c possible distributions $\{X(\mu_r, \Sigma_r): r = 1,...,c\}$, where $c \ll l$. Hence the N nodes can be grouped according to whether their measurements are from the same distribution. In Ref. [8], the authors have addressed this problem for the case where $c = 1$.

9.4.1 HYPERELLIPSOIDAL ANOMALY DETECTION

Hyperellipsoids are remarkably flexible and can capture the central tendencies of a wide range of datasets. We introduce the formulas for calculating a hyperellipsoidal decision boundary to detect anomalies.

Let $\mathbf{x}$ be an observation of the random vector $\mathbf{X} = (X_1,...,X_d)^T \sim \mathbf{X}(\mu, \Sigma)$ with *population mean* $\mu = (\mu_1,...,\mu_d)^T$ and (positive definite) *population covariance matrix* $\Sigma = [\text{cov}(\mathbf{X})]$. For fixed $\mu \in \Re^d$, the level set of $Q(\mathbf{x} - \mu) = (\mathbf{x} - \mu)^T \Sigma^{-1}(\mathbf{x} - \mu) = \| (\mathbf{x} - \mu) \|_{\Sigma^{-1}}^2$ for scalar $t^2 > 0$ is

$$\text{surf}(\Sigma^{-1}, \mu; t) = \{\mathbf{x} \in \Re^d \mid \|\mathbf{x} - \mu\|_{\Sigma^{-1}}^2 = t^2\} \tag{9.1}$$

where Σ^{-1} is sometimes called the *characteristic matrix* of Q, and $\|\mathbf{x} - \mu\|_{\Sigma^{-1}} = \sqrt{(\mathbf{x} - \mu)^T \Sigma^{-1}(\mathbf{x} - \mu)}$ is the statistical (Mahalanobis) distance between $\mathbf{x}$ and μ. Geometrically, $\text{surf}(\Sigma^{-1}, \mu; t)$ is the surface of the *hyperellipsoid* (more simply, ellipsoid) in d-space induced by Σ^{-1}, all of whose points are at a constant Mahalanobis distance (t) from its center μ. The parameters of this ellipsoid are μ, Σ, and t. We can estimate μ and Σ using the sample mean and sample covariance matrix at each node N_j,

$$\mathbf{m}_j = \sum_{k=1}^{n_j} \mathbf{x}_k^j / n_j = (m_1,...,m_d)^T \tag{9.2}$$

$$S_j = \sum_{k=1}^{n_j} (\mathbf{x}_k^j - \mathbf{m}_j)(\mathbf{x}_k^j - \mathbf{m}_j)^T / (n_j - 1) \tag{9.3}$$

Now, we can define normal and anomalous measurement relative to the ellipsoidal parameters $(S_j^{-1}, \mathbf{m}_j)$, as

$$NP_{X_j} \equiv NP_{X_j}(S_j^{-1}, \mathbf{m}_j; t) = \{\mathbf{x}_{j,k} \in X_j \mid \|\mathbf{x_k} - \mathbf{m}_j\|_{S_j^{-1}}^2 \le t^2\} \sim (\text{normal points in } X_j) \text{ and} \tag{9.4}$$

$$AP_{X_j} \equiv NP_{X_j}(S_j^{-1}, \mathbf{m}_j; t) = \{\mathbf{x}_{j,k} \in X_j \mid \|\mathbf{x_k} - \mathbf{m}_j\|_{S_j^{-1}}^2 > t^2\} \sim (\text{anomalous points in } X_j) \tag{9.5}$$

We choose $t^2 = (\chi^2_d)^{-1}_\gamma$ (ie, the inverse of the χ^2 statistic with d-degrees of freedom at $\gamma \in [0,1]$). This results in a hyperellipsoidal boundary that covers at least $100\gamma\%$ of the data under the assumption that the data have a Gaussian distribution [23]. For example, the choice of $\gamma = 0.99$ results in a hyperellipsoidal boundary that is the equivalent of the 3σ rule in one dimension. The Gaussian assumption is rarely true in real life; however this threshold is a close approximation for any unimodal distribution. We recommend choosing $\gamma \in [0.95, 0.99]$ for anomaly detection. We now have all the three parameters of the ellipsoid that partitions the data into anomalous and normal points. In the next section, we describe a framework to apply this anomaly detection technique over a network.

9.5 DISTRIBUTED ANOMALY DETECTION

In this section, we generalize the distributed anomaly detection approach proposed in Ref. [8] to the case of learning a multimodal global model of normal behavior in the network. We first model the normal data of each node using the ellipsoidal boundary described in Section 9.4.1. We then communicate the parameters of the hyperellipsoid from each node to the sink, where we cluster these l hyperellipsoids to c clusters that reflect the global distribution of measurements in the network.

The c merged hyperellipsoids corresponding to these clusters are then reported back to the nodes where anomaly detection can be performed. The final step is based on the idea that at some point in time all the nodes will observe all the modes in the environment. In some applications, the network may have multiple subsections which are expected to have different characteristics. In these cases, this algorithm should be run independently within each subsection. The steps of the algorithm are shown in Box 9.1.

9.5.1 CLUSTERING ELLIPSOIDS

In this section, we introduce a clustering approach to group similar ellipsoids together instead of simply merging all the ellipsoids into one ellipsoid. The main purpose of clustering ellipsoids is to remove redundancy between the ellipsoids reported by the nodes that have the same underlying distributions.

ALGORITHM 9.1 DISTRIBUTED ANOMALY DETECTION BY CLUSTERING ELLIPSOIDS

Step 1—At each node $N_j \in N$
- Calculate the local ellipsoid e_j from X_j
- Transmit parameters of e_j to the sink B

Step 2—At base station B
- Receive ellipsoid parameters e_j from each node
- Calculate similarity $s(e_j, e_i)$ between all pairs of ellipsoids
- Estimate the number of clusters c among the ellipsoids $E = \{e_j | j = 1,\dots,l\}$
- Cluster ellipsoids E into c merged ellipsoids $E' = \{e'_r | r = 1,\dots,c\}$
- Transmit parameters of merged ellipsoids E' to each sensor $N_j \in N$

Step 3—At each sensor
- Use merged ellipsoids E' to detect global anomalies by marking any observation that falls outside all the merged ellipsoids.

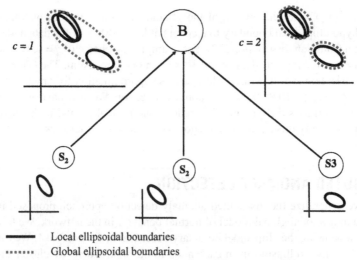

FIGURE 9.4 Global Ellipsoidal Boundaries for the Cases of a Single Global Ellipsoid ($c = 1$) and Multiple Global Ellipsoids ($c = 2$) After Clustering

This clustering generalizes the approach in Ref. [8] to the case where we have a set of global ellipsoids E'. Note that the method in Ref. [8] is a special case of the clustering approach where $c = 1$. Fig. 9.4 illustrates the two approaches for $c = 1$ and $c = 2$.

To illustrate the importance of detecting anomalies using multiple ellipses at the global level in nonhomogeneous environments, consider the example shown in Fig. 9.5, which shows measurements from two

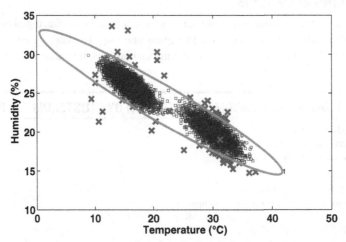

FIGURE 9.5 Example of Global Measurements in a Nonhomogeneous Environment (Normal Measurements are Represented by Squares, Whereas Anomalies Introduced Into the Data are Represented by Crosses)

Note that trying to fit a single ellipsoid to these measurements results in a poor approximation of the underlying distribution.

groups that have distinct and separate distributions. Trying to fit a single ellipse ($c = 1$) to these data results in underfitting, whereas two global ellipses ($c = 2$) can provide an accurate fit for normal measurements.

To determine global anomalies in nonhomogeneous environments, each node N_j sends the parameters ($S_j^{-1}, \mathbf{m}_j, n_j$) of its local ellipsoid e_j to the sink B. As shown in Box 9.1, the sink gathers these parameters from each node, and clusters the ellipsoids. If needed, the sink can report the parameters of the clustered ellipsoids back to the nodes to provide them with a set of global decision boundaries. We now describe the main steps in more detail.

Calculating similarities between ellipsoids—To compare and cluster ellipsoids, we first need a similarity or distance measure between a pair of ellipsoids. We use a simple similarity measure based on the distance between the centers of the ellipsoids. Let m_1 and m_2 be the centers of ellipsoids e_1 and e_2, respectively. The similarity function $s(e_1, e_2)$ that we use was first suggested in Ref. [24] as follows:

$$s(e_1, e_2) = e^{-\|m_1 - m_2\|} \tag{9.6}$$

Estimating the number of clusters—Before clustering the ellipsoids $E = \{e_j | j = 1, \ldots, l\}$, we need to estimate the number of clusters c. Juhász proved in Ref. [25] that a nonsymmetric $n \times n$ matrix consisting of c blocks (clusters) has c large eigenvalues of order c while the other characteristic values remain of order $\sqrt{n}$ as n tends to infinity. A similarity matrix that can be perfectly divided into c clusters would have a c-block diagonal shape. Fallah et al. [26] used this theorem as a preclustering assessment method to help when choosing the best number of clusters, by looking for a "big jump" in a plot of the square roots of the ordered eigenvalues (called a PRE plot) of a similarity matrix S (square roots just improve the visual interpretation of where the big jump occurs). Note that the theory underlying this strategy is not tied to any clustering algorithm.

To detect the number of clusters automatically from a PRE plot, we adapt an approach given in Ref. [26]. A PRE plot diagram of a similarity matrix can be characterized by an initially high negative gradient followed by a horizontal gradient. The point on the x-axis where these two gradients intersect yields the number of clusters c. To detect this change in the PRE plot, the gradient between each pair of consecutive points on the plot is calculated, and a large difference between consecutive gradient values is used to choose the value of c where there is a change in the order of magnitude of the eigenvalues. Note that the calculation of eigenvalues is performed at the sink, and not at the nodes. The sink is not considered to be constrained in computational power.

Clustering ellipsoids—Having defined a similarity measure between ellipsoids, the given set of ellipsoids E can be clustered using bottom-up hierarchical clustering with single linkage. For this algorithm, the parameter for the number of clusters c in the hierarchical clustering is based on the value derived from the PRE plot as described earlier.

The clustering partitions E into c sets of ellipsoids, where each set of ellipsoids in a partition needs to be merged into a single ellipsoid, that is, $E \rightarrow E' = \{e'_k | k = 1, \ldots, c\}$. Ellipsoids can be merged in a pairwise manner as follows. Let ($S_i^{-1}, \mathbf{m}_i, n_i$) and ($S_j^{-1}, \mathbf{m}_j, n_j$) be the parameters of ellipsoids e_i and e_j, then the parameters ($S^{-1}, \mathbf{m}, n$) of the ellipsoid $é$ derived from merging e_i and e_j are [27]

$$n = n_i + n_j \tag{9.7}$$

$$m = \frac{n_i}{n} m_i + \frac{n_j}{n} m_j \tag{9.8}$$

$$S = \frac{n_i - 1}{n - 1} S_i + \frac{n_j - 1}{n - 1} S_j + \frac{n_i n_j}{n(n-1)} \left[(m_i - m_j)(m_i - m_j)^T \right] \tag{9.9}$$

Note that the Eq. (9.9) is given to merge two sample covariance matrices and not the inverse of the sample covariance matrices, which are transmitted by the nodes. The sink should perform the necessary inverse operations to calculate S^{-1}. After merging, the merged ellipsoids E' can be transmitted back to the sensor nodes to detect global anomalies.

9.5.2 EXPERIMENTAL RESULTS

We now provide three examples (one real-life data set and two synthetic datasets where the modes or partitions in the data can be controlled) to illustrate how the distributed anomaly detection approach described earlier works. We compare the single global ellipsoid approach in Ref. [8] and the ellipsoidal clustering approach discussed here. We also use a centralized approach where all the data are transferred to the sink as a baseline. In the baseline approach, we first cluster all the data at the sink using the k-means clustering algorithm. Then, ellipsoidal decision boundaries are calculated using the data in each cluster and anomalies are flagged using all decision boundaries. Note that in the baseline, the cost of transferring all the data to the sink can be large compared to the first two methods.

The synthetic datasets—To investigate the effect of a nonhomogeneous environment, data from each node were generated randomly according to the distribution (cluster) assigned to that node. We used multiple bivariate Gaussian distributions with different parameters, and assigned a distribution from the available distributions to each node. Data in each node are randomly generated using the assigned distribution to the node. In the first dataset two distributions, and in the second dataset three distributions were considered across the network. The data are generated in the network so that 30 nodes observe data from the first cluster, 18 nodes from the second, and 6 nodes (in the second dataset) from the third cluster. To account for anomalies, 20 points in four nodes are perturbed by uniform noise from the interval of $[-6, 6]$. The scatter plot of the data is shown in Fig. 9.6.

The IBRL dataset—The IBRL Wireless Sensor project [28] consists 54 nodes installed in a large office environment in March 2004. Each node is equipped with temperature and humidity sensors and collects measurements at 30 s intervals. Temperature and humidity data of 12 h periods from 8:00 am to 8:00 pm from the first 18 days of March has been extracted from this dataset. In this period, node (#18)

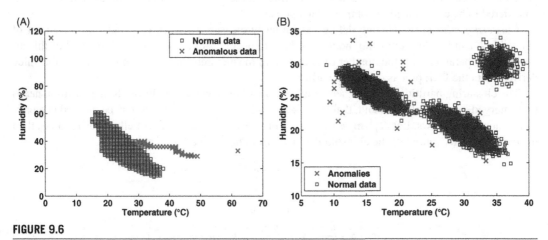

FIGURE 9.6

Scatter plots the IBRL (A) and synthetic (B) datasets.

started to report erroneous data as a result of a systematic problem causing the readings of the nodes to drift in one direction. Scatter plots for the IBRL and second synthetic dataset are depicted in Fig. 9.6.

Results—The effectiveness of an anomaly detection algorithm can be measured by the number of false alarms and true alarms. Since in the IBRL dataset there are no predefined labels for anomalous data, we visually assessed the data and labeled the drift portion and two other data points that fall outside of the expected value range, that is, temperature > 50 or humidity > 100, as anomalous. The rest of the data was treated as normal. For the elliptical clustering we first needed to determine the number of clusters. As mentioned before, the PRE plot was used to determine the number of clusters. The PRE plots for the first and second synthetic datasets are plotted in Fig. 9.7. The PRE plot showed two and three clusters for the first and second synthetic datasets, respectively. Global elliptical boundary(s) for each algorithm are shown below each PRE plot in Fig. 9.7. As shown in this figure, with the increase in the number of disjoint distributions in the dataset, the single elliptical boundary lost its capabilities and covered a large portion of the input space, while the clustering methods were suitable for modeling such environments. The ellipsoidal clustering algorithm produced comparable results to that of the centralized data collection using the k-means algorithm, while significantly reducing the amount of the data communicated over the network. To quantify this reduction, we count the number of floating points that each approach needs to communicate over the network to obtain the decision boundaries at the sink over the second synthetic dataset with 6944 data points spread in the network. In the centralized approach all the data have to be communicated to the sink and since each data point has two dimensions, 13,888 floating point numbers should be transmitted over the network. In the distributed model discussed here, each node sends only the parameters of the local ellipsoid $(S_i^{-1}, \mathbf{m}_i, n_i)$. In two dimensions, each ellipsoid can be represented with seven floating points. With 54 nodes in the network, only 378 floating points have to be sent to the sink. This is approximately a 36-fold reduction in the amount of data communicated over the network, while maintaining the accuracy in the detection of anomalies.

In the IBRL dataset the PRE plot suggests four clusters as shown in the last column of Fig. 9.7. This plot works best when the data can be well separated into clusters. In this case the data, which is our ellipsoids, are not well separated in the feature space, so the number of suggested clusters was higher than expected. However, as shown in Fig. 9.7, the ellipsoidal clustering method had a five times lower false alarm rate than the other two methods. As for the other two methods, they generated almost the same number of false alarms. This is because in the clustering approach the modeling is initially done at each node; thus the tails of the overall distribution have been better accounted for in the global model. When the data are accumulated in one place the density of the data in the tail becomes so small that many learning algorithm, in this case K-means clustering, sacrifices the tail to get better coverage in the main body of the distribution. So the discussed distributed framework not only reduces the communication overload but also can potentially increase the accuracy of the global model.

9.6 EFFICIENT INCREMENTAL LOCAL MODELING

One of the drawbacks of the proposed approach is that its local modeling is performed in batch mode. Each node has to buffer *a window* of measurements, then calculates the local ellipsoidal boundary, and sends it to the sink. The anomaly detection can be done according to both local and global ellipsoids at the node. However, selecting an appropriate window is known to be a difficult task, as a small window

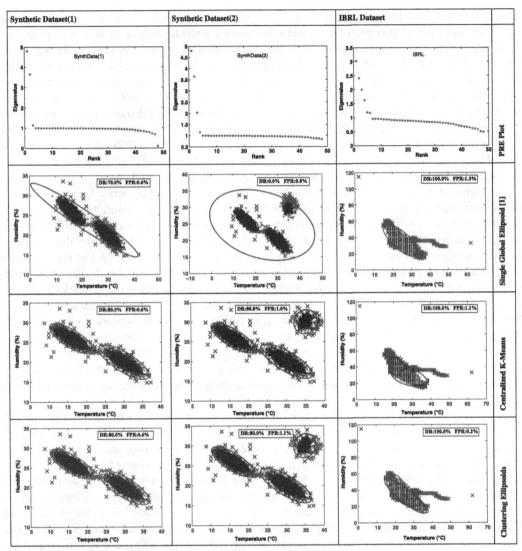

FIGURE 9.7 Evaluation Results for Different Algorithms and Datasets

DR (detection rate) is the percentage of anomalies that have been found, and FPR (false positive rate) is the percentage of the whole data which is falsely reported as anomalous.

may result in an inaccurate estimate of the local ellipsoid, and the data in a larger window size might not come from a unimodal distribution, which contradicts the assumption of the model. Another consideration about the batch calculation of the parameters of the local model is the limited computational and memory capacity of each node. The computational complexity of calculating the parameters of the ellipsoidal model (especially in low dimensions) is considered to be low, but when done in batch mode can restrict the function of the node for an extended time. Many current nodes in IoT networks have very limited memory, which limit the practicality of the batch approach for the computation of the local model. In this section, we describe an incremental approximation of the batch local ellipsoids that can address the aforementioned shortcomings of the local batch calculation of the ellipsoidal model. This approach:

1. does not require a window size;
2. enables the node to have an updated local ellipsoidal boundary at any point in time to potentially remove anomalies before incorporating them into the model;
3. Breaks down the batch calculation of the ellipsoids to smaller updates after each sample using an efficient incremental update formula.

9.6.1 INCREMENTAL UPDATES

The parameters of the local ellipsoid at each node N_j at time n $(S_{j,n}^{-1}, \mathbf{m}_{j,n})$ can be estimated incrementally (sometimes called "recursively"). Incremental updates for the mean and covariance matrix at Eqs. (9.2) and (9.3) are (for clarity of exposition we dispense with the index j)

$$\widehat{\mathbf{m}}_n = \widehat{\mathbf{m}}_{n-1} + \frac{(\mathbf{x}_n - \widehat{\mathbf{m}}_{n-1})}{n} \tag{9.10}$$

$$\widehat{S}_n = \left(\frac{n-1}{n}\right)\widehat{S}_{n-1} + \frac{(\mathbf{x}_n - \widehat{\mathbf{m}}_{n-1})(\mathbf{x}_n - \widehat{\mathbf{m}}_{n-1})^{\mathrm{T}}}{n} \tag{9.11}$$

It is fairly simple to prove that (9.2) and (9.10) yield the same mean (ie, $\widehat{\mathbf{m}}_n = \mathbf{m}_n$), but (9.11) does *not* produce the same matrix as (9.3); rather, it provides an estimate $\widehat{S}_n \approx S_n$. Applying the matrix identity $(A + \mathbf{xy}^{\mathrm{T}})^{-1} = A^{-1} - (A^{-1}\mathbf{xy}^{\mathrm{T}}A^{-1}/1 + \mathbf{y}^{\mathrm{T}}A^{-1}\mathbf{x})$ to (9.11) yields

$$\widehat{S}_n^{-1} = \left(\frac{n-1}{n-2}\right)\left[\widehat{S}_{n-1}^{-1} - \frac{\widehat{S}_{n-1}^{-1}(\mathbf{x}_n - \widehat{\mathbf{m}}_{n-1})(\mathbf{x}_n - \widehat{\mathbf{m}}_{n-1})^{\mathrm{T}}\widehat{S}_{n-1}^{-1}}{\frac{(n)(n-2)}{n-1} + (\mathbf{x}_n - \widehat{\mathbf{m}}_{n-1})^{\mathrm{T}}\widehat{S}_{n-1}^{-1}(\mathbf{x}_n - \widehat{\mathbf{m}}_{n-1})}\right] \tag{9.12}$$

Equation (9.12) is the exact inverse of (9.11) and an approximate inverse for the sample covariance matrix at (9.3), which provides a way to make iterative updates to ellipsoids used to detect anomalies. The difference between the batch ellipsoids and this approximation is negligible after a small number of iterations [29]. However, since it is a close approximation of the batch, it is still sensitive to observing a series of data coming from a multimodal distribution (a mixture model).

One solution to this problem is based on the assumption that the multimodal data stream is fairly stationary and does not switch between the modes constantly. This is a realistic assumption in many applications such as monitoring urban air quality where the air quality indicators change with certain events like rush hour traffic and weather related events. These changes are persistent for an extended period of time. This assumption allows us to build a more sophisticated incremental model that incorporates a forgetting factor to allow a graceful degradation of the influence of inputs collected in the (distant) past. In this way, the incremental model only becomes inaccurate for a short period of time after a change while allowing for the effects of the data from the last distribution before the change to fade from the model.

Introducing a forgetting factor in the incremental update formulas discussed earlier begins by replacing the incremental update for the sample mean at (9.10) with the exponential moving average of the samples:

$$\widehat{\mathbf{m}}_{n,\lambda} = \lambda \widehat{\mathbf{m}}_{n-1,\lambda} + (1-\lambda)\mathbf{x}_n, 0 < \lambda < 1; n \geq 3 \tag{9.13}$$

This update weights the sample x_{n-j} observed j times ago by the exponential factor λ^j. The value of λ determines how rapidly this sample is effectively "forgotten." Since λ is less than 1, λ^j will rapidly decrease to zero as j increases, so the influence of x_{n-j} will decrease as it becomes further from the current input in time. For algorithms with exponential forgetting a value of λ less than 1 and very close to 1 is chosen, typically in the range [0.98, 0.995).

A formula for the update of the inverse of the covariance matrix is introduced in Ref. [30] as shown in Eqs. (9.14).

$$\widehat{S}_{n,\lambda}^{-1} = \left(\frac{(n_\lambda - 1)\widehat{S}_{n-1,\lambda}^{-1}}{\lambda(n_\lambda - 2)} \right) \left(I - \frac{(\mathbf{x}_n - \widehat{\mathbf{m}}_{n-1,\lambda})(\mathbf{x}_n - \widehat{\mathbf{m}}_{n-1,\lambda})^\mathrm{T} \widehat{S}_{n,\lambda}^{-1}}{\frac{(n_\lambda - 2)}{\lambda} + (\mathbf{x}_n - \widehat{\mathbf{m}}_{n-1,\lambda})^\mathrm{T} \widehat{S}_{n-1,\lambda}^{-1}(\mathbf{x}_n - \widehat{\mathbf{m}}_{n-1,\lambda})} \right) \tag{9.14}$$

In this formula $n_\lambda = \max\{n, 3/(1-\lambda)\}$ is called the effective size of the stream.

9.6.2 IMPLEMENTATION OF INCREMENTAL UPDATES

We now discuss some of the implementation details of the incremental algorithm. Similar to any incremental algorithm the values $(S_{n,\lambda}^{-1}, \mathbf{m}_{n,\lambda})$ have to be initialized for the first step. We can initialize these values after the first observation x_1 by setting $\mathbf{m}_{n,\lambda} = x_1$ and initialize $S_{n,\lambda}^{-1}$ with the identity matrix (diagonal matrix with all diagonal values equal to 1). This will result in a hypersphere with x_1 as the center. The incremental formula in Eqs. (9.13) and (9.14) can take over the updates for upcoming samples. However, initially for the first few samples, the ellipsoidal boundary can potentially change significantly and are expected to be inaccurate. Therefore, a *stabilization period* for the incremental algorithm has to be considered before using the resultant model for anomaly detection. A stabilization period between 30 and 50 samples has been suggested in the literature [29,30].

There are different ways of incorporating the incremental approach into our distributed framework. One approach would be for the sink to poll each node for the latest local ellipsoidal boundary at certain intervals. Then the sink can propagate the global decision boundaries back to the nodes so that each node in the network has a picture of the whole network. Another approach would require nodes to send their stabilized local models to the sink at certain intervals or when the nodes deemed it necessary, for example, when the local decision boundary becomes significantly different than the global models.

Compared to the batch approach, incremental approach allows the nodes to filter anomalies (local or global) when building a model of the data, thus obtaining a better model of the normal behavior in the network.

9.6.3 EXPERIMENTAL RESULTS

To demonstrate how the incremental algorithm works at each node, we test the algorithm on two synthetic datasets for detecting local anomalies. These datasets are generated by considering two modes,

Table 9.1 Parameters of the Two Normal Distributions Used to Generate Synthetic Datasets

	S1	S2
M_1	$\Sigma_1 = \begin{pmatrix} 0.6797 & 0.1669 \\ 0.1669 & 0.7891 \end{pmatrix}$	$\Sigma_1 = \begin{pmatrix} 10.0246 & 1.2790 \\ 1.2790 & 2.1630 \end{pmatrix}$
	$\mu_1 = (20, 20)$	$\mu_1 = (45, 42)$
M_2	$\Sigma_2 = \begin{pmatrix} 0.7089 & 0.1575 \\ 0.1575 & 0.8472 \end{pmatrix}$	$\Sigma_2 = \begin{pmatrix} 7.6909 & 0.6646 \\ 0.6646 & 2.1624 \end{pmatrix}$
	$\mu_2 = (5, 5)$	$\mu_2 = (5, 5)$

M_1 and M_2, with different normal distributions $N(\Sigma_1, \mu_1)$ and $N(\Sigma_2, \mu_2)$, and nine intermediate modes. The parameter values of the modes M_1 and M_2 are shown in Table 9.1. M_1 is the initial mode and M_2 is the final mode. M_1 is transformed as follows.

First, 500 samples $\{k = 1,\ldots,500\}$ are drawn from M_1. Sampling continues as each individual value in the covariance matrix and the mean is changed in 10 equal steps. After the first step, 200 samples $\{k = 501,\ldots,700\}$ are taken from the new normal distribution. After each new step 200 more samples are added to the dataset. The final step ends at mode M_2. In the first dataset, S1, the steps are much smaller than the second dataset, S2. In this way, we can examine how the size of the steps affects the tracking methods. In Fig. 9.8, ellipses with $t^2 = (\chi_d^2)_{0.98}^{-1}$ are shown at M_1 and M_2 and intermediate steps. The dots are the data samples. The stars show 1% of the samples at each normal distribution which are perturbed by a uniform noise from $[-10, 10]$. These samples are labeled real anomalies, whereas the rest of the samples are labeled normal. This labeling is used to calculate the detection and false alarm rates for these data sets.

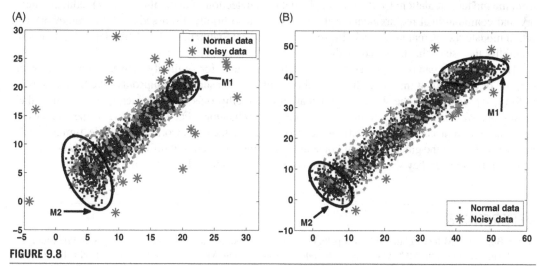

FIGURE 9.8

Scatter plots of synthetic datasets used for evaluation. (A) S1 and (B) S2.

Table 9.2 Comparison of the Anomaly Detection Capability of Incremental vs. Batch Approach over Two Synthetic Datasets

Dataset	Batch		Incremental	
	Detection (%)	False Alert (%)	Detection (%)	False Alert (%)
S1	55	2.1	96	3.1
S2	29	1	85	3.3

We compare the incremental approach with the batch approach in Ref. [8] using the two synthetic datasets. The detection rate and false alarm rates are shown in Table 9.2. The incremental approach achieves much better accuracy than the batch method in these datasets which represent nonstationary environments. This is because the data used for batch learning do not come from a single distribution, so the assumption of normality is a weak one that results in the inability of the model to detect anomalies.

9.7 SUMMARY

In this chapter, we have presented a framework for distributed anomaly detection in IoT networks, where the ellipsoidal summaries of the data are sent to a sink where they are clustered to calculate a set of global ellipsoidal decision boundaries. This approach achieved higher accuracy and significantly lower complexity than a centralized approach based on clustering the raw data. We further introduced an incremental learning method to calculate the local ellipsoidal summaries. Four main advantages of this method over batch calculations are: (1) increasing the independence of the local ellipsoidal model to the selection of window size; (2) increasing the accuracy of the approach by removing anomalies from the model calculation; (3) decreasing the delay in detection of anomalies; and (4) reducing memory and computational requirements at the nodes. We also briefly discussed how the framework can accommodate the incremental local ellipsoids calculations. Synthetic and real-life datasets are used to exemplify the use of the discussed methods.

The framework can be improved by using better measures for similarity between ellipsoids for the purpose of clustering at the sink. Three possible similarity measures for ellipsoids have been discussed in Ref. [31], which take the shape and orientation of the ellipsoids into consideration, as well as their separation. We aim to test the framework in specific applications. For specific use of the framework, application-specific considerations have to be incorporated in the framework, for example, timing and the number updates to the global decision boundaries and how anomalies at different levels should be dealt with, that is, whether they should be discarded or reported and how they affect the incremental updates.

REFERENCES

[1] F Bonomi, R Milito, J Zhu, and S Addepalli, Fog computing and its role in the internet of things, In Proceedings of the first edition of the MCC workshop on Mobile cloud computing (MCC '12). ACM, New York, NY, 13–16. 2012.
[2] Chandola V, Banerjee A, Kumar V. Anomaly detection: a survey. ACM Comput Surv July 2009;41:1–58.

[3] Djenouri D, Khelladi L, Badache A. A survey of security issues in mobile adhoc and sensor networks. IEEE Commun Surv Tutor 2005;7(4):2–28.

[4] Rajasegarar S, Leckie C, Palaniswami M. Anomaly detection in wireless sensor networks. IEEE Wireless Commun 2008;15(4):34–40.

[5] S Subramaniam, T Palpanas, D Papadopoulos, V Kalogeraki, and D Gunopulos, Online outlier detection in sensor data using nonparametric models, in Proceedings of the Thirty Second International Conference on Very Large Data Bases, September 2006, pp. 187–198.

[6] Rajasegarar S, Leckie C, Palaniswami M. Detecting data anomalies in wireless sensor networks. Security in Ad-hoc and Sensor Networks. World Scientific Publishing Inc; July 2009. pp. 231–260.

[7] C. Chong and S Kumar, Sensor networks: evolution, opportunities, and challenges, in Proc IEEE, 91, 2003, 1247–1256.

[8] Rajasegarar S, Bezdek JC, Leckie C, Palaniswami M. Elliptical anomalies in wireless sensor networks. ACM Trans Sensor Netw (ACM TOSN) 2009;6(1).

[9] S Rajasegarar, C Leckie, and M Palaniswami, CESVM: Centered hyperellipsoidal support vector machine based anomaly detection, in Proceedings of the IEEE International Conference on Communication, 2008, pp. 1610–1614.

[10] Rajasegarar S, Leckie C, Palaniswami M, Bezdek J. Distributed anomaly detection in wireless sensor networks. In: Proceedings of the IEEE International Conference on Communication Systems; October 2006Singapore. pp. 1–5.

[11] S Rajasegarar, C Leckie, M Palaniswami, and J Bezdek, Quarter sphere based distributed anomaly detection in wireless sensor networks, in Proceedings of the IEEE International Conference on Communication Systems, June 2007, pp. 3864–3869.

[12] Ribeiro A, Giannakis GB. Bandwidth-constrained distributed estimation for wireless sensor networks—Part I: Gaussian case. IEEE Trans Sig Process 2006;54:1131–43.

[13] B Sheng, Q Li, W Mao, and W Jin, Outlier detection in sensor networks, in Proceedings of the Eighth ACM International Symposium on Mobile Ad Hoc Networking and Computing (MobiHoc), 2007, pp. 219–228.

[14] Xiao Z, Chen Z, Deng X. Anomaly detection based on a multi-class CUSUM algorithm for WSN. J Comput 2010;5(2).

[15] M Takruri, S Rajasegarar, S Challa, C Leckie, and M Palaniswami, Online drift correction in wireless sensor networks using spatio-temporal modeling, in Proceedings of the Eleventh International Conference on Information Fusion, July 2008, pp. 1–8.

[16] Chandola V, Banerjee A, Kumar V. Anomaly detection for discrete sequences: a survey. IEEE Trans Knowl Data Eng May 2012;24(5):823–39.

[17] C Panos, C Xenakis, and I Stavrakakis, An evaluation of anomaly-based intrusion detection engines for mobile ad hoc networks, in Proceedings of the Eighth International Conference on Trust, Privacy and Security in Digital Business (TrustBus), 2011, pp. 150–160.

[18] Akyildiz I, Su W, Sankarasubramaniam Y, Cayirci E. Wireless sensor networks: a survey. Comput Netw 2002;38(4):393–422.

[19] Bhuse V, Gupta A. Anomaly intrusion detection in wireless sensor networks. J High Speed Netw 2006;15:33–51.

[20] A Meka and AK Singh, Distributed spatial clustering in sensor networks, in Proceedings of the Tenth International Conference on Extending Database Technology, March 2006, pp. 980–1000.

[21] I Paschalidis and Y Chen, Anomaly detection in sensor networks based on large deviations of Markov chain models in Proceedings of the IEEE Conference on Decision and Control, 2008, pp. 2338–2343.

[22] L Portnoy, E Eskin, and S Stolfo, Intrusion detection with unlabeled data using clustering, in Proceedings of ACM CSS Workshop on Data Mining Applied to Security (DMSA), 2001, pp. 5–8.

[23] DM Tax and RP Duin. Data description in subspaces. International Conference on Pattern Recognition, 2:672–675, 2000.

[24] Shepard RN. Toward a universal law of generalization for psychological science. Science 1987;237:1317–23.

[25] Juhasz F. On the characteristic values of non-symmetric block random matrices. J Theor Probab 1990;3(2).

[26] Fallah S, Tritchler D, Beyene J. Estimating number of clusters based on a general similarity matrix with application to microarray data. Stat Appl Gen Mol Biol 2008;7.

[27] P Kelly, An algorithm for merging hyperellipsoidal clusters, Los Alamos National Laboratory, Los Alamos National Laboratory, Tech. Rep. LA-UR-94-3306, 1994.

[28] IBRL-Web. 2009, 2006. [Online]. http://db.lcs.mit.edu/labdata/labdata.html

[29] Moshtaghi M, Leckie C, Karunasekera S, Bezdek JC, Rajasegarar S, Palaniswami M. Incremental elliptical boundary estimation for anomaly detection in wireless sensor networks. In: Proceedings of the Eleventh IEEE International Conference on Data Mining (ICDM), Vancouver; December 2011Canada. pp. 467–476.

[30] Moshtaghi M, Bezdek JC, Havens TC, Leckie C, Karunasekera S, Rajasegarar S, Palaniswami M. Streaming analysis in wireless sensor networks. Wireless Commun Mob Comput 2014;14(9):905–21.

[31] Moshtaghi M, Havens TC, Bezdek JC, Park L, Leckie C, Rajasegarar S, Keller JM, Palaniswami M. Clustering ellipses for anomaly detection. Pattern Recognit 2011;44:55–69.

IoT RELIABILITY, SECURITY, AND PRIVACY

SECURITY AND PRIVACY IN THE INTERNET OF THINGS

10

V. Chellappan, K.M. Sivalingam

Department of Computer Science and Engineering, Indian Institute of Technology Madras, Chennai, India

10.1 CONCEPTS

The Internet of Things leads to a new computing paradigm. It is the result of shifting computing to our real-time environment. The IoT devices, besides connecting to the Internet, also need to talk to each other based on the deployment context. More precisely, IoT is not only about bringing smart objects to the Internet, but also enabling them to talk to each other. This will have direct implications to our life, and change the way we live, learn, and work. Thus, it provides a huge opportunity for hackers to compromise security and privacy. Note that we should not only secure IoT systems from dangers that might attack it over the public Internet, but also protect a coopting device or well-behaved node from a bad node in the same network.

Today, we have reasonably secure and safe online financial transactions, e-commerce, and other services over the Internet. Core to these systems is the use of advanced cryptographic algorithms that require substantial computing power. Smart objects have limited capabilities in terms of computational power and memory, and might be battery-powered devices, thus raising the need to adopt energy-efficient technologies. Among the notable challenges that building interconnected smart objects introduces are security, privacy, and trust. The use of Internet Protocol (IP) has been foreseen as the standard for interoperability for smart objects. As billions of smart objects are expected to come to life and IPv4 addresses have eventually reached depletion, the IPv6 protocol has been identified as a candidate for smart-object communication. The challenges that must be overcome to resolve IoT security and privacy issues are immense. This is primarily because of the many constraints attached to the provision of security and privacy in IoT systems. The deployment of the IoT raises many security issues arising as a result of the following aspects:

- the very nature of smart objects, for example, the adoption of lightweight cryptographic algorithms, in terms of processing and memory requirements
- the use of standard protocols, for example, the need to minimize the amount of data exchanged between nodes
- the bidirectional flow of information, for example, the need to build an end-to-end security architecture.

This chapter provides a detailed overview of the security challenges related to the deployment of smart objects. Security protocols at the network, transport, and application layers are discussed, together with lightweight cryptographic algorithms to be used instead of conventional and demanding ones, in terms of computational resources. Security aspects, such as key distribution and security bootstrapping, and application scenarios, such as secure data aggregation and service authorization, are also discussed.

10.1.1 IoT REFERENCE MODEL

Today, there is no standardized conceptual model that characterizes and standardizes the various functions of an IoT system. Cisco Systems Inc. has proposed an IoT reference model [1] that comprises seven levels. The IoT reference model allows the processing occurring at each level to range from trivial to complex, depending on the situation. The model also describes how tasks at each level should be handled to maintain simplicity, allow high scalability, and ensure supportability. Finally, the model defines the functions required for an IoT system to be complete. The seven levels and their brief characteristics are shown in Table 10.1. The fundamental idea is to present a level of abstraction and appropriate functional interfaces to provide a complete system of IoT. It is the coherence of an end-to-end IoT architecture that allows one to process volume of context specific data points, make meaningful information, manage intrinsic feature of large scale, and ultimately design insightful responses.

The important design factor is that IoT should leverage existing Internet communication infrastructure and protocols. Level 3 is famously referred to as *Edge Computing or Fog Computing*. The primary function is to transform data into information, and perform limited data-level analytics. Context-specific information processing is done at this level so that we obtain actionable data. An important feature of fog computing is its capability of real time processing and computing. More precisely, levels 1, 2, and 3 are concerned with data in motion, and the higher levels are concerned with information derived from the data items. It leads to an unprecedented value zone wherein people and the processes are empowered to take meaningful action from the underneath world of IoT. The core objective is to automate most of the manual processes, and empower people to do their work better and smarter.

At each level of the reference model, the increasing number of entities, heterogeneity, interoperability, complexity, mobility, and distribution of entities represent an expanding attack surface, measurable by additional channels, methods, actors, and data items. Further, this expansion will necessarily increase the field of security stakeholders and introduce new manageability challenges that are unique to the IoT.

Table 10.1 IoT World Forum Reference Model

IoT Reference Model	
Levels	**Characteristics**
Physical devices and controllers	End point devices, exponential growth, diverse
Connectivity	Reliable, timely transmission, switching, and routing
Edge computing	Transform data into information, actionable data
Data accumulation	Data storage, persistent and transient data
Data abstraction	Semantics of data, data integrity to application, data standardization
Application	Meaningful interpretations and actions of data
Collaboration and processes	People, process, empowerment, and collaboration

10.1.2 IoT SECURITY THREATS

There are three broad categories of threats: *Capture, Disrupt, and Manipulate*. *Capture* threats are related to capturing the system or information. *Disrupt* threats are related to denying, destroying, and disrupting the system. *Manipulate* threats are related to manipulating the data, identity, time-series data, etc. The simplest type of passive threats in the IoT is that of eavesdropping or monitoring of transmissions with a goal to obtain information that is being transmitted. It is also referred to as capture attacks. Capture attacks are designed to gain control of physical or logical systems or to gain access to information or data items from these systems. The ubiquity and physical distribution of the IoT objects and systems provide attackers with great opportunity to gain control of these systems. The distribution of smart objects, sensors, and systems results in self-advertisements, beacons, and mesh communications, providing attackers greater opportunity to intercept or intercede in information transmission within the environment. Moreover, the frequency of the data transmissions, data models, and formats help attackers in cryptanalysis.

Some of the well-known active threats are as follows: *Masquerading*: an entity pretends to be a different entity. This includes masquerading other objects, sensors, and users. *Man-in-the-middle*: when the attacker secretly relays and possibly alters the communication between two entities that believe that they are directly communicating with each other. *Replay attacks*: when an intruder sends some old (authentic) messages to the receiver. In the case of a broadcast link or beacon, access to previous transmitted data is easy. *Denial-of-Service (DoS) attacks*: when an entity fails to perform its proper function or acts in a way that prevents other entities from performing their proper functions.

Active threats such as masquerading, replay attacks, DoS attacks are, in general, comparatively easy in an IoT environment. One example is the implementation of cloned beacons from an untrusted source. Beacons are small wireless devices that continuously transmit a simple radio signal saying, "I am here, this is my ID." In most cases, the signal is picked up by nearby smartphones using Bluetooth Low Energy (BLE) technology. When the mobile device detects the beacon signal, it reads the beacon's identification number (ID), calculates the distance to the beacon and, based on these data, triggers an action in a beacon compatible mobile app. In the literature [2], the IoT threats are enumerated as cloning of smart objects by untrusted manufacturers, counterfeiting/substitution of the IoT devices by the third parties, malicious firmware replacement, and attacks on relatively unprotected devices by eavesdropping or extraction of credentials or security properties, in addition to the standard threat vectors such Man-in-the-middle and DoS attacks. The security and privacy requirements are determined by the nature of attacks in an IoT environment.

10.1.3 IoT SECURITY REQUIREMENTS

This section presents an overview on the security requirements of the IoT. The basic security properties that need to be implemented in IoT are listed next. *Confidentiality*: transmitted data can be read only by the communication endpoints; *availability*: the communication endpoints can always be reached and cannot be made inaccessible; *integrity*: received data are not tampered with during transmission, and assured of the accuracy and completeness over its entire lifecycle; *authenticity*: data sender can always be verified and data receivers cannot be spoofed and authorization: data can be accessed only by those allowed to do so and should be made unavailable to others. The requirements for securing the IoT are complex, involving a blend of approaches from mobile and cloud architectures, combined with industrial control, automation, and physical security. Many of the security requirements for the IoT are similar to the requirements for the IP protocol-based Internet. The technologies and services that have been used to secure the Internet are applicable in most cases with suitable adaptation required at each level of the IoT reference model. Besides the standard security requirements, and from the threats discussed, the following security requirements can be derived.

10.1.3.1 Scale

The important requirement is the scale in which an IoT environment is expected to grow. The population of entities is expected to grow exponentially as users embrace more smart and connected objects and devices, more sensors are deployed, and more objects are embedded with intelligence and information. Each entity, depending on its nature, characteristics, carries with it an associated set of protocols, channels, methods, data models, and data items, each of which is subject to potential threat. This increased scale has the effect of expanding the target surface. As noted earlier, the scale and complexity at each level of the IoT model determine the amount of compute and storage requirements, and hence the cost and power budget. The trade-off between cost and resources determines the availability of resources for system security, cryptographic algorithms, key size, and methods.

10.1.3.2 IP Protocol-Based IoT

The use of IP technologies in IoT brings a number of basic advantages such as a seamless and homogeneous protocol suite, and proven security architecture. It also simplifies the mechanisms to develop and deploy innovative services by extending the tested IP-based frameworks. It leads to a phenomenon called "expansion of attack surface." It implies that when we connect the previously unconnected—by introducing new devices that stream context sensitive data, by placing data in mobile cloud, or by pushing computing to edge devices—new points of ingress for security threats inevitably materialize. As the networks of smart objects and IP merge, there is a high probability of security vulnerabilities due to protocol translations, incompatible security infrastructures, etc. The enterprise security model has been marked by two chief tenets:

- Security has been focused on best-of-breed applications and appliances: solutions for firewall, for network security, for data security, for content security, and so forth.
- Security has been perimeter-based, meaning organizations secured the end device and the server, and reacted to recognized intrusions or threats such as viruses or DoS attacks.

In the context of IoT, perimeter-based security mechanisms have little relevance. The attack surface is much broader, often borderless, and involves heterogeneous systems.

10.1.3.3 Heterogeneous IoT

Another important design consideration in the IoT is how the connected things can work together to create value and deliver innovative solutions and services. IoT can be a double-edged sword. Although it provides a potential solution to the innovation imperative, it can also significantly boost operational complexity if not properly integrated with key organizational processes. Security processes should also be properly designed to align with the organization processes. The complex operational technologies make it difficult for designing a robust security architecture in IoT. It is a common opinion that in the near future IP will be the base common network protocol for IoT. This does not imply that all objects will be able to run IP. In contrast, there will always be tiny devices, such as tiny sensors or Radio-Frequency Identification (RFID) tags, that will be organized in closed networks implementing very simple and application-specific communication protocols and that eventually will be connected to an external network through a proper gateway. In short, the heterogeneous characteristics of the networks make it harder to implement certain IP-based security systems such as symmetric cryptosystems.

10.1.3.4 Lightweight Security

The unprecedented value of IoT is realized only when smart objects of different characteristics interact with each other and also with back-end or cloud services. IPv6 and web services become the fundamental building blocks of IoT systems and applications. In constrained networked scenarios, smart objects may require additional protocols and some protocol adaptations in order to optimize Internet communications and lower memory, computational, and power requirements. The use of IP technologies in IoT brings a number of basic advantages such as a seamless and homogeneous protocol suite, and proven security architecture. It also simplifies the mechanisms to develop and deploy innovative services by extending the tested IP-based frameworks. However, it also introduces new challenges in adopting certain frameworks as is. The IoT provides interconnectedness of people and things on a vast scale with billions of devices. It is at once a huge opportunity for better efficiency and better services, as well as a huge opportunity for hackers to compromise security and privacy.

It may be noted that one of the key elements of the state-of-the-art security in the Internet is the use of advanced cryptographic algorithms needing substantial processing power. Many, if not most, IoT devices are based on low-end processors or microcontrollers that have low processing power and memory, and are not designed with security as a priority design goal. Privacy enforced through encryption, authentication to conform identity, and Information authentication by using digitally signed certificates are the key security mechanisms in the Internet today. These mechanisms rely on the following:

- Cryptographic ciphers such as Advanced Encryption Standard (AES), Secure Hash Algorithm (SHA2), and the public-key ciphers RSA and elliptic-curve cryptography (ECC).
- Transport Layer Security (TLS) protocol, and predecessor Secure Sockets Layer (SSL) protocol, which provide authentication and information encryption using the ciphers mentioned.
- Public-Key Infrastructure (PKI) provides the building blocks for authentication and trust through a digital certificate standard and Certificate Authorities (CA).

Current IoT implementations have gaps in terms of implementing the above security mechanisms, even though these mechanisms have widespread adoption in the IP networks. For example, there are multiple commercial and open-source TLS implementations that can be adopted in an IoT device. These libraries typically consume more than 100 KB of code and data memory, which is not a lot for a conventional computing device, but is impractical for an IoT device such as a medical sensor. The cryptographic ciphers used by the TLS protocol are a source of significant computational load on the low end CPU of the typical IoT device. This computational load results in higher power consumption as well. For example, the data rate supported by a 32 bit MCU implementing AES-128 may fall from 3 Mbps to 900 Kbps if the MCU is substituted with a 16 bit processor. Note that this in turn leads to indirect effects like longer active time, more power drain, and a shorter battery life. Essentially the challenge is to make the resource constrained IoT networks interoperate with the resourceful IP networks.

The current principles of IT security need to be deconstructed by reevaluating and redesigning protocols, algorithms, and processes in light of the evolving IoT architecture. More precisely, network scale, heterogeneous, power constraints, and mobility alter the attack surface on a much larger scale and in greater breadth. It necessitates reinvention and adaption of IP-based protocols and introduction of IoT specific protocols.

Table 10.2 Security Mechanisms to Mitigate the Threats in the IoT Networks

Threats/Security Mechanism	Data Privacy	Data Freshness	Source Authentication	Data Integrity	Intrusion Detection	Identity Protection
Capture						
Physical systems						X
Information	X			X		X
Disrupt						
DoS Attack		X	X		X	
Routing attack					X	
Manipulate						
Masquerading	X		X	X		X
Replay attack		X	X	X	X	
Man-in-the-middle			X	X	X	

10.2 IoT SECURITY OVERVIEW

This section presents necessary background on the IoT control protocols such as ZigBee, IPv6 over Low-power WPAN (6LoWPAN), Constrained RESTful Environments (CoRE), CoAP, and security protocols such as IKEv2/IPSec, TLS/SSL, Datagram Transport Layer Security (DTLS), Host Identity Protocol (HIP), Protocol for Carrying Authentication for Network Access (PANA), and Extensible Authentication Protocol (EAP). It also discusses the key concepts on IoT security that includes identity management, authentication, authorization, privacy, trust, and governance for IoT networks. The taxonomy of security attacks, threats, and security mechanisms is presented in Table 10.2.

10.2.1 IoT PROTOCOLS

Bonetto et al. [3] discussed the security procedures for constrained IoT devices with use cases. It starts with the description of general security architecture along with its basic procedures, and then discusses how its elements interact with the constrained communication stack and explores pros and cons of popular security approaches at various layers of the ISO/OSI model. Similarly, the applicability and limitations of existing Internet protocols and security architectures in the context of IoT are discussed in Ref. [4]. It gives an overview of the deployment model and general security needs. It presents the challenges and requirements for IP-based security solutions and highlight specific technical limitations of standard IP security protocols (IPSec). There are currently IETF working groups focusing on extending existing protocols for resource-constrained networked environments. These are: CoRE [5], 6LoWPAN [6–8], Routing Over Low power and Lossy networks (ROLL) [9], and the Light-Weight Implementation Guidance (LWIG) working groups. Significant reasons for proper protocol optimizations and adaptations for resource-constrained objects are targeted toward protocol compression to fit into smaller Maximum Transmission Units (MTU), thereby reducing power consumption with smaller packets, elimination of fragmentation, and reducing the handshake messages. A typical IoT layer for a Bluetooth smart enabled device protocol stack is shown in Table 10.3.

Table 10.3 Bluetooth Smart Device Protocol Stack	
Application layer	CoAP MQTT
Transport layer	UDP TCP
Network layer	IPv6 ICMPv6 RPL
Adaptation layer	Bluetooth Smart 6LoWPAN
Physical and link layer	IPSP

IPv6 significantly expands the number of available IP addresses for use by providing 2128 addresses. This means that, if necessary, every device can have its own unique IPv6 address. Standards such as 6LoWPAN have made it possible to integrate sensors in a transport agnostic manner. 6LoWPAN enables sensors to talk to IP Protocols natively. Furthermore, new application layer protocols such as CoAP and Message Queue Telemetry Transport (MQTT) [10] ensure optimal use of bandwidth and resources of constrained IoT devices. Bluetooth Smart is an open standard that is specifically designed for the needs of battery powered sensors and wearables. Now powered with the 6LoWPAN IETF draft, Bluetooth Smart is well placed to address evolving needs of sensors connecting to the cloud without the need for intelligent gateways. The Internet Protocol Service Profile (IPSP) defines establishing and managing the Bluetooth logical link control and adaptation protocol (L2CAP) connection oriented channel. IPSP and Bluetooth Smart 6LoWPAN standard ensures optimal IP stack performance over Bluetooth Smart as a physical layer. 6LoWPAN defines the creation of an IPv6 address of a device from its Bluetooth Smart device address. It also compresses the IP header where possible to ensure optimal use of RF bandwidth for power saving purposes.

A static profile of an IoT object represents the knowledge by an endpoint of its own resources (such as identity, battery, computing power, memory size, etc.) and the security settings it intends to use or needs from the network. The static profile can be read-only (preset by vendor), write-once (set by manufacturer), or rewritable (user enabled). Note that certain security primitives may be computationally prohibitive for IoT objects; a negotiation is thus required before the establishment of a secure channel so that the concerned endpoints can agree upon a cryptographic suite.

10.2.2 NETWORK AND TRANSPORT LAYER CHALLENGES

The IPSec [11] uses the concept of a Security Association (SA), defined as the set of algorithms and parameters (such as keys) used to encrypt and authenticate a particular flow in one direction. To establish a SA, IPSec can be preconfigured (specifying a preshared key, hash function, and encryption algorithm) or can be dynamically negotiated by the IPSec Internet Key Exchange (IKE) protocol. The IKE protocol uses asymmetric cryptography, which is computationally heavy for resource-constrained devices. To address this issue, IKE extensions using lighter algorithms should be used. Data overhead is another problem for IPSec implementations in IoT environments. This is introduced by the extra header encapsulation of IPSec AH and/or Encapsulating Security Payload (ESP) [12], and can be mitigated by using header compression.

CoAP proposes to use the DTLS protocol [13] to provide end-to-end security in IoT systems. The DTLS protocol provides a security service similar to TLS, but on top of UDP. This is highly suitable for IoT environments due to its usage of UDP as transport protocol. This results in avoidance of problems from the use of TCP in network-constrained scenarios that are caused due to the extremely variable transmission delay and loss links. DTLS is a heavyweight protocol and its headers are too long to fit in a single IEEE 802.15.4 MTU. 6LoWPAN provides header compression mechanisms to reduce the size of upper layer headers. 6LoWPAN header compression mechanisms can be used to compress the security headers as well. Raza et al. [14] proposed a new 6LoWPAN header compression algorithm for DTLS is proposed. It links the compressed DTLS with the 6LoWPAN standard using standardized mechanisms. It is shown that the proposed DTLS compression significantly reduces the number of additional security bits. Kothmayr et al. [15] introduced a two-way authentication security scheme for the IoT based on DTLS. The proposed security scheme is based on the widely used public-key based RSA cryptography protocol and works on top of standard low power communication stacks.

10.2.3 IoT GATEWAYS AND SECURITY

Connectivity is one of the important challenges in designing the IoT network. The diversity of end points makes it very difficult to provide IP connectivity. It is important that non-IP devices too have a mechanism to connect with IoT. The IoT gateways can simplify IoT device design by supporting the different ways nodes natively connect, whether this is a varying voltage from a raw sensor, a stream of data over an inner integrated circuit (I2C) from an encoder, or periodic updates from an appliance via Bluetooth. Gateways effectively mitigate the great variety and diversity of devices by consolidating data from disparate sources and interfaces and bridging them to the Internet. The result is that individual nodes do not need to bear the complexity or cost of a high-speed Internet interface in order to be connected. There are several ways that an IoT gateway can extend connectivity to nodes as described below.

- The network nodes connect to the IoT via a gateway. The nodes themselves are not IP-based and thus cannot directly connect to the Internet/WAN. Rather, they use either wired or wireless PAN technology to connect to the gateway with a less expensive and less complex mode of connectivity. The gateway maintains an IoT agent for each node that manages all data to and from nodes. In this case, application intelligence can also be located in the gateway.
- The nodes can also connect directly to the Internet using a WAN connection such as Wi-Fi or Ethernet. The gateway serves primarily as a router; in fact, it can be simply a router when nodes have their own IoT agent and autonomously manage themselves.
- Alternatively, the nodes can connect directly to the Internet using a PAN connection such as 6LoWPAN. In this case, the gateway serves as a translation point between the PAN and WAN.

Many IoT applications handle potentially sensitive data. Data collected from location services, for example, need to be protected from hacking. Similarly, medical devices need to maintain the privacy of individuals. In the context of the IoT gateway architecture, the security processing and mechanisms can be offloaded from nodes to the gateway to ensure proper authentication, protecting exchanges of data, and safeguarding intellectual property. This enables IoT nodes to implement greater security than could be economically implemented in individual end points.

10.2.4 IoT ROUTING ATTACKS

Threats arising due to the physical nature of IoT devices can be mitigated by appropriate physical security safeguards, whereas secure communication protocols and cryptographic algorithms are the only way of coping with the fact that they arise due to IoT devices communicating with each other and the external world. For the later, IoT devices can either run the standard TCP/IP protocol stack, if their computational and power resources allow, or can run adaptions which are optimized for lower computational and power consumption. There are some well-known routing attacks that can be exploited by attackers. The 6LoWPAN networks or an IP-connected sensor networks are connected to the conventional Internet using 6LoWPAN Border Routers (6LBR). The Routing Protocol for Low-Power and Lossy Networks (RPL) [9] is a novel routing protocol standardized for 6LoWPAN networks. RPL creates a destination-oriented directed acyclic graph (DODAG) between the nodes in a 6LoWPAN. It supports unidirectional traffic toward DODAG root and bidirectional traffic between 6LoWPAN devices and between devices and the DODAG root (typically the 6LBR). RPL enables each node in the network to determine whether packets are to be forwarded upwards to their parents or downwards to their children.

Attacks on sensor networks that are applicable to IoT are discussed in Refs. [16,17]. Some well-known routing attacks on IoT are as follows:

- Selective-forwarding attacks
- Sinkhole attacks
- Hello flood attacks
- Wormhole attacks
- Clone Id and Sybil attacks

With selective-forwarding attacks, it is possible to launch DoS attacks where malicious nodes selectively forward packets. This attack is primarily targeted to disrupt routing paths. For example, an attacker could forward all RPL control messages and drop the rest of the traffic. This attack has severer consequences when coupled with other attacks such as sinkhole attacks. One of the solutions to guard against selective-forwarding attacks is to create disjoint paths between the source and the destination nodes. Another effective countermeasure against selective-forwarding attacks is to make sure the attacker cannot distinguish between different types of traffic, thus forcing the attacker to either forward all traffic or none.

In sinkhole attacks, a malicious node advertises a fraudulent routing path with a seemingly favorable route metric and attracts many nearby nodes to route traffic through it. An intrusion detection system could be hosted in the 6LBR and can utilize information from multiple DODAGs to detect sinkhole attacks.

In the hello-flood attack, The HELLO message refers to the initial message a node sends when joining a network. By broadcasting a HELLO message with strong signal power and a favorable routing metric, an attacker can introduce himself as a neighbor to many nodes, possibly the entire network. A simple solution to this attack is for each HELLO message the link is checked to be bidirectional.

A wormhole is an out-of-band connection between two nodes using wired or wireless links. Wormholes can be used to forward packets faster than via normal paths. A wormhole created by an attacker and combined with another attacks, such as sinkhole, is a serious security threat. One approach is to use separate link-layer keys for different segments of the network. This can counteract the wormhole attack, as no communication will be possible between nodes in two separate segments. Also, by binding geographic information to the neighborhoods it is possible to overcome a wormhole.

In a clone-ID attack, an attacker copies the identities of a valid node onto another physical node. This can, for example, be used in order to gain access to a larger part of the network or in order to overcome voting schemes. In a Sybil attack, which is similar to a clone ID attack, an attacker uses several logical entities on the same physical node. Sybil attacks can be used to take control over large parts of a network without deploying physical nodes. By keeping track of the number of instances of each identity it is possible to detect cloned identities. It would also be possible to detect cloned identities by knowing the geographical location of the nodes, as no identity should be able to be at several places at the same time.

10.2.5 BOOTSTRAPPING AND AUTHENTICATION

Bootstrapping and authentication controls the network entry of nodes. Authentication is highly relevant to IoT and is likely to be the first operation carried out by a node when it joins a new network, for instance, after mobility. It is performed with a (generally remote) authentication server using a network access protocol such as the PANA [18]. For greater interoperability, the use of the EAP [19] is envisioned. Upon successful authentication, higher layer security associations could also be established (such as IKE followed by IPSec [20]) and launched between the newly authenticated endpoint and the access control agent in the associated network.

The Internet Key Exchange (IKEv2)/IPSec and the HIP [21] reside at or above the network layer. Both protocols are able to perform an authenticated key exchange and set up the IPSec transforms for secure payload delivery. Currently, there are also ongoing efforts to create a HIP variant called Diet HIP [22] that takes loss low-power networks into account at the authentication and key exchange level.

10.2.6 AUTHORIZATION MECHANISMS

The present day services that run over the Internet, such as popular social media applications, have faced and handled privacy-related problems when dealing with personal and protected data that might be made accessible to third parties. In the future, the IoT applications will face similar issues, and others that may be unique to the domain. The OAuth (Open Authorization) protocol has been defined to solve the problem of allowing authorized third parties to access personal user data [23]. OAuth2.0 [24] is an authorization framework that allows a third party to access a resource owned by a resource owner without giving unencrypted credentials to the third party. For example, assume that a healthcare sensor or mobile app wants to access a Facebook profile to post status updates. There is no need to provide the Facebook credentials to the app; instead, the user logs into Facebook, and as a result the app is authorized to use Facebook on the user's behalf. The user can also revoke this authorization any time by deleting the privilege in the Facebook settings. The OAuth 2.0 protocol defines the following four roles.

10.2.6.1 Resource Owner
It is an entity capable of granting access to a protected resource. When the resource owner is a person, it is referred to as an end user. In the above example, this could be the end user of the healthcare device.

10.2.6.2 Resource Server (Service Provider, SP)
It is the server hosting the protected resources, capable of accepting and responding to protected resource requests using access tokens. In the example, this is the Facebook server.

10.2.6.3 Client (Service Consumer, SC)
It is the application making protected resource requests on behalf of the resource owner and with its authorization. The term client does not imply any particular implementation characteristics (eg, whether the application executes on a server, a desktop, or other devices). In this case, it is the healthcare sensor or mobile application.

10.2.6.4 Authorization Server
It is the server issuing access tokens to the client after successfully authenticating the resource owner and obtaining authorization. In this example, it would be the Facebook authorization server.

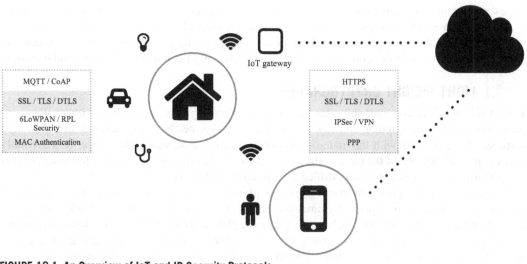

FIGURE 10.1 An Overview of IoT and IP Security Protocols

10.2.7 IoT OAS

Note that the IoT devices may have challenges in implementation of OAuth due to the CPU intensive nature of cryptographic computations. Cirani et al. [25] proposed a modified architecture called IoT-OAS. In this approach, authorization-related functions are delegated to an external IoT-OAS authorization service, in order to minimize the memory and CPU requirements on the IoT device itself. An incoming OAuth secured request is forwarded to an IoT-OAS service for verification of the access token contained in the request. The IoT-OAS service computes the digital signature of the incoming request using the appropriate scheme (PLAINTEXT/HMAC/RSA) and matches it with its internal store to verify the user and client credentials and permissions for resource access. It then provides an *appropriate* response back allowing or denying the requested access from the client. This approach enables the IoT device to focus on its own service logic and frees up computational resources from being overwhelmed by security and cryptographic implementations. The security protocols at each layer between different networks are shown in Fig. 10.1.

10.3 SECURITY FRAMEWORKS FOR IoT

In this section, we discuss some of the specific frameworks used for realizing a secure IoT system. The low capabilities of IoT devices in terms of their energy and computing capabilities, wireless nature, and physical vulnerability are discussed to be the contributing factors to some unique security vulnerabilities. In particular, we cover the tight resource constraints, protocol translation such as HTTP ↔ CoAP, and end-to-end Security. Other important topics include the architecture framework aspects: Distributed vs Centralized approach, bootstrapping identity and key interchange, privacy aware identification, mobility, and IP network dynamics.

In the era of pervasive computing with large networks of resource constrained IoT devices, Moore's law can be interpreted differently [26]: rather than a doubling of performance, we see a halving of the price for constant computing power every 18 months. Since many foreseen applications have extremely tight cost constraints over time, such as RFID in tetra packs, Moore's law will increasingly enable such applications. Many applications will process sensitive health monitoring or biometric data, so the demand for cryptographic components that can be efficiently implemented is strong and growing.

10.3.1 LIGHT WEIGHT CRYPTOGRAPHY

The term lightweight cryptography refers to a family of cryptographic algorithms with smaller footprint, low energy consumption, and low computational power needs. Every designer of lightweight cryptography must cope with the trade-offs between security, cost, and performance. It is generally easy to optimize any two of the three design goals: security and cost, security and performance, or cost and performance; however, it is very difficult to optimize all three design goals at once.

When we compare lightweight cryptographic implementations, we can make a distinction between symmetric and asymmetric ciphers. Symmetric ciphers serve mainly for message integrity checks, entity authentication, and encryption, whereas asymmetric ciphers additionally provide key-management advantages and nonrepudiation. Asymmetric ciphers are computationally far more demanding, in both hardware and software. The performance gap on constrained devices such as 8-bit microcontrollers is huge. For example, an optimized asymmetric algorithm such as ECC performs 100–1000 times more slowly than a standard symmetric cipher such as the AES algorithm, which correlates with a two to three orders of-magnitude higher power consumption [26].

Symmetric-key cryptographic algorithms use the same key for encryption of a plain text and decryption of a message. The encryption key represents a shared secret between the parties that are involved in the secure communication.

10.3.1.1 Symmetric-Key LWC Algorithms

- The Tiny Encryption Algorithm (TEA) is a block cipher renowned for its simplicity of description and implementation, typically a few lines of code [27]. TEA operates on two 32-bit unsigned integers (could be derived from a 64-bit data block) and uses a 128-bit key. TEA relies only on arithmetic operations on 32-bit words and uses only addition, XORing, and shifts. For IoT devices with small memory footprints, TEA is very suitable since its algorithm uses a large number of iterations, rather than a complicated program, in order to avoid preset tables and long setup times. TEA defines a simple and short cipher that does not rely on preset tables or precomputations, thus saving on memory resources.
- The Scalable Encryption Algorithm (SEA) is targeted for small embedded applications [28]. The design explicitly accounts for an environment with very limited processing resources and throughput requirements. A design principle of SEA is flexibility: the plaintext size n, key size n, and processor (or word) size b are design parameters, with the only constraint that n is a multiple of $6b$; for this reason, the algorithm is denoted as SEA$n;b$. The main disadvantage is that SEA$n;b$ trades space for time and this may not be trivial on devices with limited computational power.
- PRESENT is an ultra-lightweight block cipher algorithm based on a Substitution-Permutation Network (SPN) [29]. PRESENT has been designed to be extremely compact and efficient in hardware. It operates on 64-bit blocks and with keys of either 80 or 128 bits. It is for use in situations where low-power consumption and high chip efficiency are desired, thus making it of particular interest for constrained environments.
- The HIGh security and lightweigHT (HIGHT) [30] encryption algorithm is a generalized Feistel network with a block size of 64 bits, 128-bit keys, and 32 rounds. HIGHT was designed with

an eye on low-resource hardware performance. HIGHT uses very simple operations, such as XORing, addition mod 28, and bitwise rotation.

10.3.2 ASYMMETRIC LWC ALGORITHMS

Public-key (asymmetric) cryptography requires the use of a public-key and a private key. Public keys can be associated with the identity of a node by including them into a public certificate, signed by a Certification Authority (CA) that can be requested to verify the certificate. Public-key cryptography requires the significant effort of deploying a PKI. Moreover, asymmetric cryptography requires higher processing and long keys (at least 1024 bits for RSA [31]) to be used. Alternative public-key cryptographic schemes, such as ECC [32], might require shorter keys to be used in order to achieve the same security than RSA keys. However, because of these reasons, symmetric cryptography is preferred in terms of processing speed, computational effort, and size of transmitted messages. Public key can be used to setup symmetric keys to be used in subsequent communications. Lightweight cryptography algorithms are suitable for environments that do not have stringent security requirements and where the constraints on available hardware and power budget cannot be relaxed.

10.3.3 KEY AGREEMENT, DISTRIBUTION, AND BOOTSTRAPPING

A mechanism for key distribution and management has to be in place when security mechanisms have to be adopted. Asymmetric (public-key) cryptographic algorithms are usually used in key agreement protocols. However, other mechanisms that do not involve the adoption of asymmetric cryptography have been proposed, to address the challenges of resource-constrained devices. A polynomial-based key predistribution protocol has been defined [33] and applied to Wireless Sensor Networks in Ref. [34]. A possible alternative key agreement protocol is SPINS [35], which is a security architecture specifically designed for sensor networks. In SPINS, each sensor node shares a secret key with a base station, which is used as a trusted third party to set up a new key, with no need of public-key cryptography. The authors of Ref. [36] present three efficient random key predistribution schemes for solving the security-bootstrapping problem in resource-constrained sensor networks, each of which represents a different tradeoff in the design space of random key protocols.

10.3.3.1 Security Bootstrapping

The key agreement protocols require that some type of credentials such as symmetric keys, certificates, and public–private key pairs are preconfigured on the nodes, so that the key agreement procedure can occur. Bootstrapping refers to the sequence of tasks that need to be executed before the network can interwork, requiring the correct configuration at all layers of the OSI model from link layer to application layer. It can be viewed as a process of creating a security domain from a set of previously unassociated IoT devices. Current IoT architectures are fully centralized in most cases, so that a central party handles all the security relationships in an administrative domain. In the ZigBee standard, this entity is the trust center. Current proposals for 6LoWPAN/Core identify the 6LoWPAN Border Router (6LBR) as such an entity. A centralized architecture allows for central management of devices and key associations. The limitation is that there is a single point of failure; a decentralized approach will allow creating ad-hoc security domains that might not require a centralized online management entity and will allow subsets of nodes to work in a stand-alone manner. The ad-hoc security domains can be synced to centralized entity later, allowing for both centralized and distributed management.

10.4 **PRIVACY IN IoT NETWORKS**

This section discusses the privacy aspects and frameworks relevant to IoT. The smart, connected objects will interact with both humans and other smart objects by providing, processing, and delivering all sorts of information and signals. All of these objects and their communications with the environment carry with them a risk to privacy and information leakage. Healthcare applications represent the most outstanding application of IoT. The lack of confidence regarding privacy results in decreased adoption among users and is therefore one of the driving factors in the success of IoT. The ubiquitous adoption of the wireless medium for exchanging data may pose new issue in terms of privacy violation. In fact, wireless channel increases the risk of violation due to the remote access capabilities, which potentially expose the system to eavesdropping and masking attacks.

IoT devices and applications add a layer of complexity over the generic issue of privacy over the Internet, for example due to generation of traceable characteristics and attributes of individuals. IoT devices in healthcare present a major concern, since these devices and applications typically generate large volumes of data on individual patients through continuous monitoring of vital parameters. In this case, it is crucial to delink the identities of the device from that of the individual, through mechanisms such as data anonymization. Data anonymization is the process of either encrypting or removing personally identifiable information from data sets, so that the originator of the data remains anonymous. Similar to the preceding discussion of the OAuth protocol, digital shadows enable the individual's objects to act on their behalf, storing just a virtual identity that contains information about their parameters. Identity management in IoT may offer new opportunities to increase security by combining diverse authentication methods for humans and machines. For example, bio-identification combined with an object within the personal network could be used to open a door.

10.4.1 **SECURE DATA AGGREGATION**

Homomorphic encryption is a form of encryption that allows specific types of computations to be executed on cipher texts and obtain an encrypted result that is the cipher text of the result of operations performed on the plain text. Applying the standard encryption methods presents a dilemma: If the data is stored unencrypted, it can reveal sensitive information to the storage/database service provider. On the other hand, if it is encrypted, it is impossible for the provider to operate on it. If data are encrypted, then answering even a simple counting query (for example, the number of records or files that contain a certain keyword) would typically require downloading and decrypting the entire database content.

A homomorphic encryption allows a user to manipulate without needing to decrypt it first. An example of homomorphic encryption is the RSA algorithm. Other examples of homomorphic encryption schemes are the ECC encryption [32], the ElGamal cryptosystem [37], and the Pailler cryptosystem [38]. Homomorphic encryption has a lot of relevance to IoT networks, since privacy can be preserved at all stages of the communication, especially without the need for intermediate nodes to decrypt the information. For example, a lot of processing and storage can be eliminated at intermediate nodes by data aggregation with operations such as sums and averages. This in turn results in lower power consumption, which is relevant for constrained environments. However, note that this type of homomorphic cryptosystems is more compute-intensive and needs longer keys to achieve a comparable security level than typical symmetric-key algorithms.

Typically, secure data aggregation mechanisms require nodes to perform the following operations [2]:

- at the transmitting node, prior to transmission, data are encrypted with some cryptographic function E

- at the receiving node, all received data packets are decrypted with the inverse cryptographic function $D = E^{-1}$ to retrieve the original data;
- data are aggregated with an aggregation function;
- prior to retransmission, aggregated data are encrypted through E and relayed to the next hop.

10.4.2 ENIGMA

MIT Researchers, Guy Zyskind and Oz Nathan, have recently announced a project dubbed Enigma that makes a major conceptual step toward this Holy Grail of a fully homomorphic encryption protocol. Zyskind, et al. [39] proposed a peer-to-peer network, enabling different parties to jointly store and run computations on data while keeping the data completely private. Enigma's computational model is based on a highly optimized version of secure multiparty computation, guaranteed by a verifiable secret-sharing scheme. For storage, it uses a modified distributed hash table for holding secret-shared data. An external block chain is utilized as the controller of the network, manages access control, identities, and serves as a tamper-proof log of events. Security deposits and fees incentivize operation, correctness, and fairness of the system. Similar to Bitcoin, Enigma removes the need for a trusted third party, enabling autonomous control of personal data. For the first time, users are able to share their data with cryptographic guarantees regarding their privacy.

The typical use case of Enigma would be for interactions between hospitals and health-care providers who store encrypted patient data as per HIPAA regulations. Research organizations and pharmaceutical companies would benefit from access to these data for clinical analysis. For example, a hospital can encrypt its data and store it in the cloud, where potentially other universities, pharma companies, and insurance companies could access it with permission from the originating hospital. With the usage of Enigma, note that there is no need for the originating hospital to first decrypt and anonymize the data, it only needs to authorize the third party for access.

10.4.3 ZERO KNOWLEDGE PROTOCOLS

Zero-knowledge protocols allow identification, key exchange and other basic cryptographic operations to be implemented without leaking any secret information during the conversation and with smaller computational requirements than using comparable public-key protocols. Thus Zero-knowledge protocols seem very attractive especially in the context of IoT networks, especially for some applications like smart cards. Zero-knowledge protocols have been claimed to have lighter computational requirements than, for example, public-key protocols. The usual claim is that zero-knowledge protocols can achieve the same results than public-key protocols with one to two orders of magnitude less (1/10, 1/100) computing power. A typical implementation might require 20–30 modular multiplications (with full-length bit strings) that can be optimized to 10–20 with precalculation. This is much faster than RSA. The memory requirements seem to be about equal: to have very high security with zero-knowledge protocols, we need very long keys and numbers, so in memory terms, the requirements may not be very different [40].

10.4.4 PRIVACY IN BEACONS

Beacon in wireless technology is the concept of broadcasting small pieces of information. The information may be anything, ranging from ambient data to vital signs such as body temperature, blood pressure, pulse, and breathing rate or microlocation data such as asset tracking. Based on the context, the transmitted data maybe static or dynamic and change over time. The Bluetooth beacon opens a new world of possibilities for location awareness, and countless opportunities for smart applications. Beacons are becoming one of the key enablers of the IoT. One kind of beacon is a low energy Bluetooth transmitter or receiver. The power efficiency of Bluetooth Smart makes it perfect for devices needing to run off a tiny battery for long periods. The advantage of Bluetooth Smart is its compatibility to work with an application on the smartphone or tablet you already own. An important use case of beacons is to obtain context-specific observations and repeated measurements over time. Most data collected from beacons are correlated in time, which might cause serious threats to data security and user privacy.

Security and privacy issues specific to beacons and time series data transmitted from them are emerging areas of research interest. There are both advantages and disadvantages of security based on the difficulty of an underlying computation problem and information theoretic security, which is based on lack of information content. A more basic measure of the information-theoretic security is the inherent information available for exploitation by an adversary, independent of how the adversary exploits it or indeed any assumed computational limitations of the adversary. In Ref. [41], a new measure of information theoretic measure such as conditional entropy is shown to be suited for evaluating the privacy of perturbed real-world time-series data, compared with other existing measures.

Much of the research and study of privacy issues in ubiquitous computing systems is applicable to the IoT. Establishing meaningful identity, using trusted communication paths, and protecting contextual information is all very important to ensure the protection of user privacy in this environment. Beresford and Stajano [42] have explored anonymous communication techniques and the use of pseudonyms to protect user privacy while also working on metrics to assess user anonymity. Their work takes a novel approach by hiding identity from the applications that utilize it in order to better protect the user consuming those services.

In their work on Decentralized Trust Management, Zhao et al. [43] propose new technologies that enable the bootstrapping of trust, and subsequently, the calculation of trust metrics that are better suited to mobile, ad-hoc networks. Their model showcases the inherent problems with establishing trust in ad-hoc networks like those in the IoT where new sensors, services, and users are constantly introduced and asked to share data.

Finally, applications in the IoT, which will be enabled by a ubiquitous computing and communications infrastructure, will provide unobtrusive access to important contextual information as it pertains to users and their environment. Clearly, the successful deployment of such applications will depend on our ability to secure them and the contextual data that they share.

One example of sensitive contextual information is location. When location-aware systems track users automatically, an enormous amount of potentially sensitive information is generated and made available. Privacy of location information is about both controlling access to the information and providing the appropriate level of granularity to individual requestors. The Location Services Handbook [44] explores a variety of location-sensing technologies for cellular networks and the coverage quality and privacy protections that come with each.

10.5 SUMMARY AND CONCLUSIONS

The IoT brings to the fore issues on privacy that were seen as less impactful on the World Wide Web. For example, people have been sharing personal profile information on Social media sites such as Facebook, and this in turn enables the business model of these applications through targeted advertising in lieu of subscriptions. This context has meant that the privacy issues are largely ignored. However, the smart IoT devices expose much more sensitive information, and provide much less scope for this type of commercial model as it is largely back-end data. Hence users are likely to be both vulnerable and sensitive to privacy concerns. These challenges make it very complex to operationalize IoT in a secure way, while fully preserving privacy. There are a number of promising approaches that are being investigated to solve for each aspect of the privacy issues, and there is still some distance to go before we can see production ready commercial implementations that are standardized and widely adopted.

REFERENCES

[1] Green J. IoT reference model. http://www.iotwf.com/resources/72; 2014.

[2] Cirani S, Ferrari G, Veltri L. Enforcing security mechanisms in the IP-based Internet of Things: an algorithmic overview. Algorithms 2013;6(2):197–226.

[3] Bonetto R, Bui N, Lakkundi V, Olivereau A, Serbanati A, Rossi M. Secure communication for smart IoT objects: protocol stacks, use cases and practical examples. In: IEEE International Symposium on a World of Wireless, Mobile and Multimedia Networks (WoWMoM), San Francisco; 2012. p. 1–7.

[4] Heer T, Garcia-Morchon O, Hummen R, Keoh S, Kumar S, Wehrle K. Security challenges in the IP-based Internet of Things. Wirel. Pers Commun 2011;61(3):527–42.

[5] Shelby Z. Constrained restful environments (CoRE) link format. RFC 6690, RFC Editor; 2012.

[6] Montenegro G, Kushalnagar N, Hui J, Culler D. Transmission of IPv6 packets over IEEE 802.15.4 networks. RFC 4944, RFC Editor; 2007.

[7] Hui J, Thubert P. Compression format for IPv6 datagrams over IEEE 802.15.4 based networks. RFC 6282, RFC Editor; 2011.

[8] Shelby Z, Chakrabarti S, Nordmark E, Bormann C. Neighbor discovery optimization for IPv6 over low-power wireless personal area networks (6loWPANs). RFC 6775, RFC Editor; 2012.

[9] Winter T, Thubert P, Brandt A, Hui J, Kelsey R, Levis P, Pister K, Struik R, Vasseur J, Alexander R. RPL: IPv6 routing protocol for low-power and lossy networks. RFC 6550, RFC Editor; 2012.

[10] Hunkeler U, Truong HL, Stanford-Clark A. In: Choi S, Kurose J, Ramamritham K, editors. Mqtt-s—a publish/subscribe protocol for wireless sensor networks. IEEE COMSWARE; 2008. p. 791–8.

[11] Kent S, Seo K. Security architecture for the Internet protocol. RFC 4301, RFC Editor; 2005.

[12] Kent S. IP encapsulating security payload (ESP). RFC 4303, RFC Editor; 2005.

[13] Rescorla E, Modadugu N. Datagram transport layer security version 1.2, RFC 6347, RFC Editor; 2012.

[14] Raza S, Trabalza D, Voigt T. 6loWPAN compressed DTLS for CoAP. In: Eighth IEEE Distributed Computing in Sensor Systems (DCOSS), Hangzhou, China; 2012. p. 287–89.

[15] Kothmayr T, Schmitt C, Hu W, Brunig M, Carle G. A DTLS based end-to-end security architecture for the Internet of Things with two-way authentication. In: Thirty Seventh IEEE Conference on Local Computer Networks Workshops, FL; 2012. p. 956–63.

[16] Karlof C, Wagner D. Secure routing in wireless sensor networks: attacks and countermeasures. Ad Hoc Netw 2003;1(2):293–315.

[17] Wallgren L, Raza S, Voigt T. Routing attacks and countermeasures in the RPL-based Internet of Things. Int J Distr Sensor Netw 2013;2013:11.

[18] Forsberg D, Ohba Y, Patil B, Tschofenig H, Yegin A. Protocol for carrying authentication for network access (PANA). RFC 5191, RFC Editor; 2008.

[19] Aboba B, Blunk L, Vollbrecht J, Carlson J, Levkowetz H. Extensible Authentication Protocol (EAP). RFC 3748, RFC Editor; 2004.

[20] Frankel S, Krishnan S. IP security (IPSec) and internet key exchange (like) document roadmap. RFC 6071, RFC Editor; 2011.

[21] Moskowitz R, Nikander P, Jokela P, Henderson T. Host Identity Protocol. RFC 5201, RFC Editor; 2008.

[22] Chan H, Perrig A, Song D. Random key predistribution schemes for sensor networks. In: Proceedings of the IEEE Symposium on Security and Privacy, Oakland; 2003. p. 197–213.

[23] Hammer-Lahav E. The OAuth 1.0 protocol. RFC 5849, RFC Editor; 2010.

[24] Hardt D. The OAuth 2.0 authorization framework. RFC 6749, RFC Editor; 2012.

[25] Cirani S, Picone M, Gonizzi P, Veltri L, Ferrari G. IoT-OAS: an OAuth-based authorization service architecture for secure services in IoT scenarios. IEEE Sens J 2015;15(2):1224–34.

[26] Eisenbarth T, Kumar S. A survey of lightweight-cryptography implementations. IEEE Des Test Comput 2007;24(6):522–33.

[27] Wheeler DJ, Needham RM. TEA, A tiny encryption algorithm. Proceedings of fast software encryption, 2nd internation workshop, vol. 1008. Leuven, Belgium; 1995. p. 363–66.

[28] Standaert F-X, Piret G, Gershenfeld N, Quisquater J-J. SEA: A scalable encryption algorithm for small embedded applications. Proceedings of 7th IFIP WG 8.8/11.2 international conference, CARDIS 2006. Tarragona, Spain; 2006. p. 222–36.

[29] Bogdanov A, Knudsen LR, Leander G, Paar C, Poschmann A, Robshaw MJ, Seurin Y, Vikkelsoe C. PRESENT: An ultra-lightweight block cipher. Proceedings of 9th international workshop. Vienna, Austria; 2007. p. 450–66.

[30] Hong D, Sung J, Hong S, Lim J, Lee S, Koo B-S, Lee C, Chang D, Lee J, Jeong K, et al. Hight: a new block cipher suitable for low-resource device. Cryptographic hardware and embedded systems. Springer; 2006. p. 46–59.

[31] Rivest RL, Shamir A, Adleman L. A method for obtaining digital signatures and public-key cryptosystems. Commun ACM 1978;21(2):120–6.

[32] Koblitz N. Elliptic curve cryptosystems. Math Comput 1987;48(177):203–9.

[33] Blundo C, De Santis A, Herzberg A, Kutten S, Vaccaro U, Yung M. Perfectly-secure key distribution for dynamic conferences. Inform Comput 1998;146(1):471–86.

[34] Liu D, Ning P, Li R. Establishing pairwise keys in distributed sensor networks. ACM Trans Inform Syst Secur 2005;8(1):41–77.

[35] Perrig R, Szewczyk JD, Tygar V, Wen DE, Culler. SPINS: security protocols for sensor networks. Wirel Netw 2002;8(5):521–34.

[36] Chan H, Perrig A, Song D. Random key predistribution schemes for sensor networks. In: IEEE Symposium on Security and Privacy; 2003. p. 197–213.

[37] ElGamal T. A public key cryptosystem and a signature scheme based on discrete logarithms. Advances in cryptology. Proceedings of CRYPTO 84. Santa Barbara, USA; 1984. p. 10–18.

[38] Paillier P. Public-key cryptosystems based on composite degree residuosity classes. In: Advances in Cryptology—EUROCRYPT'99. Springer; 1999. p. 223–38.

[39] Zyskind G, Nathan O, Pentland A. Enigma: decentralized computation platform with guaranteed privacy. CoRR, abs/1506.03471; 2015.

[40] Aronsson HA. Zero knowledge protocols and small systems. http://www.tml.tkk.fi/Opinnot/Tik-110.501/1995/zeroknowledge.html; 2015.

[41] Ma CY, Yau DK. On information-theoretic measures for quantifying privacy protection of time-series data. In: Proceedings of the Tenth ACM Symposium on Information, Computer and Communications Security. New York: ACM; 2015. p. 427–38.

[42] Beresford AR, Stajano F. Location privacy in pervasive computing. IEEE Pervasive Computing; 2003;2(1): 46–55.

[43] Zhao Meiyuan, Li Hong, Wouhaybi Rita, Walker Jesse, Lortz Vic, Covington Michael J. Decentralized trust management for securing community networks. Intel Technol J 2009;13(2):148–69.

[44] Martin E, Liu L, Covington M, Pesti P, Weber M. Chapter: 1 Positioning technology in location-based services. In: Ahson SA, Ilyas M, editors. Location based services handbook: applications, technologies, and security. CRC Press; 2010.

INTERNET OF THINGS— ROBUSTNESS AND RELIABILITY

S. Sarkar

Department of CSIS, Birla Institute of Technology and Science Pilani, K.K.Birla Goa Campus, Goa, India

11.1 INTRODUCTION

Building a reliable computing system has always been an important requirement for the business and the scientific community. By the term *reliability*, we mean how long a system can operate without any failure. Along with reliability, there is another closely related quality attribute, called *availability*. Informally, availability is the percentage of time that a system is operational to the user. An internet of things (IoT) system deploys a massive number of network aware devices in a dynamic, error-prone, and unpredictable environment, and is expected to run for a long time without failure. To commission such a system and to keep it operational, it is therefore essential that the system is designed to be reliable and available. Let us understand these two attributes in detail.

Since the exact time of a failure of any operational system is not known a priori, it is appropriate to model the time for a system to fail as a (continuous) random variable. Let $f(t)$ be the failure probability density function, which denotes the instantaneous likelihood that the system fails at time t. Next, we would like to know the probability that the system will fail within a time t, denoted by $F(t)$. Let T be the time for the system to fail. The function $F(t) = \Pr\{T \le t\} = \int_0^t f(u)\,du$, also known as the failure function, is the cumulative probability distribution of T. Given this distribution function, we can predict the possibility of a system failing within a time interval $(a,b]$ to be $\Pr\{a < T \le b\} = \int_a^b f(t)\,dt = F(b) - F(a)$. The reliability of a system $R(t)$ can be formally defined as the probability that the system will not fail till the time t. It is expressed as $R(t) = \Pr\{T > t\} = 1 - F(t)$.

The mean time to failure (MTTF) for the system is the expected value $E[T]$ of the failure density function $= \int_0^\infty tf(t)\,dt$ which can rewritten as $-\int_0^\infty tR'(t)\,dt = -[tR(t)]_0^\infty + \int_0^\infty R(t)\,dt$

When t approaches ∞, it can be shown that $tR(t)$ tends to 0. Therefore, MTTF, which intuitively is the long-run average time to failure, is expressed as: $\int_0^\infty R(\tau)\,d\tau$

With this MTTF value, availability A can be computed as: $A = \dfrac{\text{MTTF}}{\text{MTTF} + \text{MTTR}}$ where MTTR denotes the average time the system takes to be operational again after a failure. Thus, the definition of availability takes reliability also into account.

Availability has been one of the most important quality attributes to measure the extent of uninterrupted service that a distributed and more recently a cloud-based system provides. It has also been an important metric to define the service level agreement (SLA) between the service provider (a SaaS or an IaaS provider) and the service consumer.

From the definition, it is obvious that a system which is highly reliable (high MTTF) will tend to be highly available as well. However, the mean time to recover or MTTR brings another alternative means to achieve high availability. One can design a highly available system even with components having relatively poor reliability (not very large MTTF), provided that the system takes a very little time to recover when it fails. Although the hardware industry has always strived to make the infrastructure reliable (ie, increase MTTF), today it has possibly reached its limit. Increasing MTTF beyond a certain point is extremely costly, and sometimes impossible. In view of this, it becomes quite relevant to design a system equipped with faster recovery mechanisms[a]. This observation has led to the emergence of recovery oriented computing (ROC) [20] paradigm, which has now been considered to be a more cost-effective approach to ensure the service continuity for distributed and cloud-based systems. The fundamental principle of ROC is to make MTTR as small as possible. For an IoT-based system, the participating components can have high failure possibilities. In order to ensure that an IoT system always remains operational, the ROC becomes an attractive and feasible approach.

Along with reliability and availability, the term serviceability coined by IBM (https://en.wikipedia.org/wiki/Serviceability_(computer)) is frequently used to indicate the ease with which the deployed system can be repaired and brought back to operation. Thus, serviceability implies reduction of the MTTR using various failure-prevention methods (prediction, preventive maintenance), failure detection techniques (through monitoring), and failure handling approaches (by masking the impact of an error, recovery). The goal of serviceability is obviously to have a zero repair time, thereby achieving a near 100% availability.

In the remainder of this chapter we will discuss suitable serviceability techniques to improve the reliability and availability of IoT systems.

11.2 IoT CHARACTERISTICS AND RELIABILITY ISSUES

With the advancement in infrastructure and wireless communication, proliferation of new communication aware devices of various form factors, and with the introduction of cloud computing paradigm, Internet of Things-based applications are emerging [1,4,6,7,14]. Such an application, distributed on multitude of devices, is more embedded into the business environment than ever before. For instance, smart, network accessible cameras can be placed at strategic locations in a cluster of buildings or on streets, smart meters may be installed in a power-grid, tiny embedded devices can be used for health monitoring, vehicles in a city can be equipped with GPS-based sensors, and static wireless sensors can be embedded in modern appliances like a television or a refrigerator. These network-enabled devices can run distributed processes, which in turn can coordinate, exchange data, and take critical decisions in real time. Such a system is expected to be deployed once and be operational forever.

11.2.1 IoT ARCHITECTURE IN BRIEF

Though there is no consensus of what the standard architecture of an IoT-based system should be, we find a general adoption of the following IoT architecture reference model shown in Fig. 11.1

---

[a]The High Cost of Achieving Higher Levels of Availability—Gartner Report G0099122, June 2001.

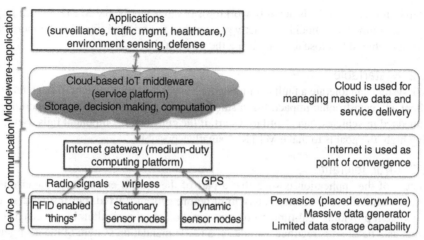

FIGURE 11.1 Layered Architecture Reference Model

Device layer: The lowest layer in Fig. 11.1 consists of devices with a low to moderate compute and communication capability. These devices are typically battery operated, and can execute tiny OS like RIOT [17] or Contiki. They typically receive data from the environment, perform local processing on the data, and then transmit the result.

Communication layer: The devices transmit data through WIFI, GSM/GPRS, Bluetooth, and radio frequency for RFID-enabled devices [5]. The communication layer comprises devices (routers, signal transceivers, etc.) that are responsible for reliable transmission of data.

Application layer: In this layer, an IoT middleware resides, with which the devices interact to exchange data. We refer to this middleware as the "service platform" in this chapter. The service platform can be hosted on the cloud to exploit the on-demand and scalable infrastructure capability of the cloud. In order to make the application layer flexible and extendible, well-known architecture patterns like hub and spoke, microkernel, and blackboard-based design can be adopted. The smart devices can join the network on-demand, and the platform, acting as a hub, processes a massive amount of data from the network of devices. On top of this middleware, the IoT specific application can reside which can perform various on and offline tasks which can be low-latency real-time responses or heavy-duty data-analysis activities [10]. Such an approach is beneficial from two perspectives. For the cloud, the overall reach of the system becomes far more deep as the real-world devices get embedded in the application domain. For the devices, their limited compute and storage capabilities are compensated by virtually unlimited resources in the cloud, and the cloud becomes a point of convergence for the devices [52].

11.2.1.1 *Different Categories of Applications*
We can classify IoT applications into the following categories from reliability and availability perspective:

11.2.1.1.1 Zero tolerance
When an IoT system is placed in a mission critical scenario, specifically in the health care domain, where network aware devices monitor the health of the patient, or a network-enabled pacemaker device that interacts with a larger health-care platform, the system components do not tolerate any failure

during its mission time (when it is actively working). In other words, the MTTF (which impacts reliability) for these components should be strictly greater than the mission time. Furthermore, the MTTR for such a system should be close to zero during the mission time.

11.2.1.1.2 Restartable

Here the IoT system can tolerate a faulty component or event the entire system (though undesirable) to restart without any catastrophic impact. For instance, an IoT system for urban transport, having components embedded in vehicles, can afford to restart, if the embedded component fails. Here, more than MTTF being high, the goal is to make MTTR as small as possible.

11.2.1.1.3 Error Tolerant

Here the nature of the application is such that a part of the system can tolerate the erroneous input for some time, within the user-defined safety limit before getting it fixed. For instance, an unmanned surveillance system providing real-time routine information of an agricultural land, can afford to send poor/incorrect data before it is rectified. Similarly, a recommendation system of the next generation e-commerce system reading a real-time input data-feed can accept erroneous data (and obviously generate erroneous recommendations) for a small time before the error conditions are rectified.

11.2.2 FAILURE SCENARIOS

Like any mission critical system, we say that an IoT-based system becomes unreliable or unavailable when the system either fails to respond to a request or provides an unexpected, incorrect service [28]. A service failure happens when faults are not handled properly. Researchers and practitioners have extensively studied various faults and remedial actions to keep software operational in a business critical scenario. Broadly, these faults are categorized as (i) development fault (ii) infrastructure fault, and (iii) interaction faults. Development faults are induced by incorrect implementation of the software, whereas infrastructure faults are caused due to unanticipated faults in the hardware. Interaction faults occur due to interaction with other software modules or incorrect data format. Let us analyze how they are relevant in the IoT context.

11.2.2.1 Infrastructure Fault

The cluster of network-enabled devices in an IoT-based system are expected to operate in unanticipated scenarios. Some of these scenarios can lead to infrastructure failures. For instance:

1. In a given IoT application scenario, the network-enabled devices ought to be embedded in a specific environment to gather and process data stream. The devices can fail due to the physical condition and interference with the environment in which they operate. Such an operating condition can reduce the life of such devices drastically due to the physical deterioration. Consider the scenario of electronic tracking of animals [2,26,27], which is an important business problem in Norway. The sensor attached on an animal has an extremely high chance of a failure, resulting in poor or erroneous data transmission, or a complete data loss. This may not result in an imminent failure of the service platform but it can certainly lead to corruption of data, incorrect interpretation, and an eventual failure of service.
2. The external environment may provide unexpected inputs to IoT entities resulting in a computation failure in the device.

3. The processors of these devices have been designed keeping a small form-factor in mind rather than making them highly fault-tolerant. Thus these devices can be much more fault-prone than a normal computer.
4. Many a times these devices run on a battery which can severely limit their compute time and can cause unexpected termination of a computation.

The overall reliability and availability of the system will obviously depend on the extent to which these devices can withstand these unexpected scenarios.

11.2.2.2 Interaction Fault

Network-enabled devices and appliances have widely varying compute capabilities. When these devices are made to communicate with each other and share data, there can be operational failures due to several reasons:

1. The entire network or the communication components can fail. Consider the same scenario of electronic tracking of animals [2,26,27]. Now consider a likely situation where the GPRS backbone fails in the IoT system that is supposed to be used to report the animal tracking data. Such an event can certainly impact the overall system functionality.
2. Due to the heterogeneity of the devices, there could be an "impedance mismatch" of the data being exchanged. Such a scenario can occur when the IoT system allows a device to join the network in real time. An example of such a scenario is the management of vehicular network in a city where the vehicles joining dynamically may not comply with the protocol. In such a situation, it will not be possible to interpret the data and take the appropriate action.
3. Interaction faults are also caused by unexpected workload coming from various IoT components.

11.2.2.3 Fault in Service Platform

Consider the architecture reference model shown in Fig. 11.1 where the service platform acts as a hub that collects data from various network aware sensor objects and processes the data. It is unlikely that the platform will be built from the scratch. It will integrate many third party products and will be integrated with external partner systems. Even if we assume that this middleware has been thoroughly tested for its own functionality, many transient faults can be due to off-the-shelf components. The reliability of these third party components may be questionable and can often be a cause of failure of the main system. Additionally, the external partner systems of the IoT application middleware can fail or provide incorrect data, which can result in a failure of the middleware. When the platform fails due to these faults, it will not be able to process the incoming messages and route them.

11.2.3 RELIABILITY CHALLENGES

11.2.3.1 Making Service Available to User

The aim of an IoT application is to provide an immersive service experience through a tightly coupled human–device interaction in real time. Therefore, it is highly important that the availability of the system be judged from the user perspective. This is known as "user perceived availability" [21] where the perceived availability is about delivering the service to the user, not just surviving through a failure. A relatively old study on Windows server [22] shows that though the server was available for 99% of the time (obtained from the server log), but the user perceived it to be just 92%. To improve the user perceived availability, the IoT service platform has an important role to play where it needs to ensure that the user service requests (coming from the application layer on top of the middleware as shown in Fig. 11.1) are always responded to even in extreme circumstances.

11.2.3.2 Serviceability of IoT System

We discussed earlier that it is quite likely for an IoT system to have a set of devices that can dynamically come and join the system. In such a case, ensuring serviceability without disrupting the ongoing activities is more difficult in the case of IoT devices. In a traditional high-available system, nodes as well as the software running on them go through a scheduled maintenance when the software and patches are upgraded to prevent any upcoming failure. Such a traditional maintenance may not be feasible for an IoT system. For instance, a device is located in a mission critical location where one cannot simply perform a shutdown (for instance, smart healthcare devices like network aware pacemaker). The devices may operate on a relatively low network bandwidth and on a limited battery power where over-the-wire large data (such as a software patch) transmission may not be practical all the time. For this reason, the software, protocols, and applications that are created in the IoT framework need to be tested not only for functionality, and traditional nonfunctional features, but also for their fault-tolerance so that it can remain operational for a longer duration without any repair.

11.2.3.3 Reliability at Network Level

Most Internet of Things applications for buildings, factories, hospitals, or the power grid are long-term investments that must also be operable for a long time. The networks can also be unmanaged (eg, home automation, transport applications). This implies that the network must be able to configure itself as environmental conditions or components in the network itself change so that the information can always be transmitted from one application to the other reliably. There can be further complexities in using sensor devices. The links used in most sensor networks today use completely unregulated bands of frequency. As a result, it is very easy that the signals from a sensor device interfere with another and make the links unreliable. For instance, if a newly deployed IoT sensor network starts using the same channel as someone's existing WLAN access point, the interference can disable critical sensor data reporting. Links in sensor networks are often more unreliable than the Internet due to the lack of regulation. Therefore, it is highly desirable to have some form of reliable transport protocol for IoT that is as power-saving as UDP and as reliable as TCP.

11.2.3.4 Device Level Reliability

From the network level, let us now focus on the embedded devices that are connected via network. Even when the network is reliable, there are scenarios when the applications running on these devices may generate poor quality data, which makes the entire computation unreliable. Consider a scenario when the device needs to gather image from the physical world where it is embedded. Due to the environmental condition, the quality of the images captured can be below the acceptable level; as a result the associated inferences drawn from the captured images become unreliable. For sensor devices, the environmental condition can result in a bit error.

Computing devices are now being deployed in medical monitoring and diagnostic systems. Such a system that not only performs monitoring but also provides recommendation to the physicians, is safety critical. Similarly devices used in fire safety scenarios need to be zero tolerant (as we have mentioned earlier) [2]. However, a sensor device embedded in a fire alarm system also has a high chance of malfunctioning during the critical time. The reliability challenge in this case is to ensure the timely diagnosis and alert generation during the critical time, even when some part of the system (for instance, the fire sensor) malfunctions or sends poor quality information. The security threats of these safety critical systems can adversely impact reliability to a large extent.

Smart mobile phones of today have a good amount of computing capability, and they are becoming an intrinsic part of IoT applications. The study by Cinque et al. [23] shows that for cell-phone-based communication, it is the inexpensive and power constrained mobile phone that poses the reliability challenges than the communication infrastructure.

11.2.4 PRIVACY AND RELIABILITY

Data privacy is an important part of IoT, specifically when an IoT system allows a machine-to-machine interaction, where machines can join the network dynamically [3]. In this context, identity management, and proving identity on-demand has been considered an important mechanism to ensure the authenticity of the communicating parties [11]. For instance consider an IoT-based vehicle management system, which expects vehicles to reveal their identity in a vehicular network. The system can create an alarm and can trigger actions if the deployed sensors on a street sense that a car has not revealed the identity. However, this alarm can be a false one if the car is a police car, which can reveal its identity to another police car and to the designated staff at the police station, but keep its identity hidden during undercover work otherwise. Under such a scenario, the real-time surveillance system's reliability of detecting intrusion becomes questionable due to the inaccuracy. In this chapter we refrain from discussing detailed issues related to identity preservation, anonymization, and use of pseudonyms (using alternate identity) since they strictly belong to the security. Interested readers can refer to the recently established car-to-car consortium[b] and the work by Papadimitratos et al. [54] for further details.

11.2.5 INTEROPERABILITY OF DEVICES

Since IoT allows heterogeneity of devices interacting with each other, there is always a possibility that the participating devices cannot exchange information due to the lack of standardization. As of today, the standardization of the communication among the devices has not been enforced in IoT. In the article from Telenor group [12] the interoperability issues of communicating devices in the context of IoT have been discussed in detail. Traditionally, system reliability is often associated with various other quality attributes like performance, availability, and security. Interoperability, an important quality attribute by itself, has not traditionally been considered in conjunction with reliability. However, with the emergence of IoT, we now find that if an IoT infrastructure has devices that are not interoperable, and if the IoT system requires that the devices can come and join dynamically, the overall reliability of the infrastructure to perform the intended service is bound to suffer significantly unless the dynamically participating devices are interoperable.

11.2.6 RELIABILITY ISSUES DUE TO ENERGY CONSTRAINT

Autonomous devices of an IoT system such as automated surveillance system need to collect and process data in real time from the environment for a long duration. The data stream is transmitted from a set of embedded sensors, which are running on battery power. Even in an ideal scenario, when the environmental condition does not interfere with the functioning of the sensors, the reliability of the

---

[b]Car-to-Car Communication Consortium (C2C-CC) http://www.car-2-car.org/

overall system can still be impacted due to the limited power supply. It is therefore essential that the IoT infrastructure ensures both reliability and low energy consumption [also referred to as energy efficient reliability (EER) in the literature] [13].

11.3 ADDRESSING RELIABILITY

Traditionally, the designers of a reliable system take the approach of either *fault prevention* or *fault-tolerance* to ensure reliability and availability. To prevent a failure, proactive actions are taken to stop the imminent failure of a running system. In the case of an IoT-based system, prevention many a times becomes quite difficult, as there are many unanticipated external as well as transient faults due to reasons often beyond the realm of our control. Fault-tolerance on the other hand implies that the system is able to operate in the presence of faults. Fault-tolerance is achieved mainly through *nullifying the impact of an error* (also known as error masking), *error detection, and recovery*. The system can nullify the impact of an error mostly through employing a set of redundant components—expecting that while the primary component fails due to an unanticipated error, the other clones still survive the impact to render the service. ROC, introduced earlier in this chapter, essentially consists of detecting an error early, taking the corrective actions, and performing a speedy recovery. The article by Roman et al. [11] provides a high-level guideline of making an IoT system fault-tolerant. They suggest three broad guidelines for sensor objects namely (i) making the objects participating in the IoT network robust, by default (ii) build capability to make the operational state of the objects observable, and (iii) incorporate self-defense and recovery mechanism in the participating objects.

We believe that these guidelines are not only applicable for the sensor objects, but also for the service platform, as well as the communication infrastructure. The following table summarizes the applicability:

Guideline	Applicability	Technique
Making objects robust	IoT objects as well as service platform	Failure prevention, nullifying impact of error through redundancy, and software design
Observable operational state	IoT objects	Error detection techniques that can analyze the operational state to trigger the recovery action
Self-defense	IoT objects as well as service platform	Graceful degradation and recovery through restart

We discuss these techniques in the next section.

11.3.1 NULLIFYING IMPACT OF FAULT

A common approach for a traditional high-availability cluster is to reduce the impact of a fault as much as possible by eliminating the single point of failure (SPOF) both at the hardware and at the software level. A common technique for this is to increase redundancy at various levels such as the infrastructure, the network, and in the software.

A simplified model to calculate the reliability of a system with redundancy having N components (a hardware or a software), of which it is sufficient to have K components operational, can be expressed as $R_{KN} = \sum_{j=K}^{N} \binom{N}{j} R^j (1-R)^{N-j}$ where R denotes the reliability of a component. If it is sufficient to have one out of N redundant components operational, then the overall reliability becomes $R_N = 1 - (1 - R)^N$ or $R_N = 1 - \prod_{i=1}^{N}(1-R_i)$ in case the reliability of the individual component is different. The first model is relevant when we have exactly identical copies of software modules whereas the second model is for different versions of the software or hardware components. The equation becomes more complex when we assign different reliability values to active (K) and standby ($N-K$) components. Such a technique of reliability estimation is quite common in the case of hardware-based redundancy for HA clusters, though it is equally applicable for software components as well.

The report in Ref. [2] has illustrated a specific IoT case study called Connected Object platform where various reliability issues of the CO platform have been highlighted. In these case studies, the traditional redundancy-based solution has been applied at the sensor object level as well as at the service platform level.

11.3.1.1 Redundancy in Service Platform Design

A good design to build a robust IoT service platform is to introduce a set of loosely coupled components so that the failure of one component does not bring the entire platform down. Depending on the application scenario, one can then deploy multiple copies of the critical components.

Many times database systems become an integral part of the platform where the data from different communicating objects are collected for analysis. In such a case, the database system can also be a SPOF. Depending on the nature of the application one can adopt the following redundancy strategies:

1. *Load balancing across multiple databases:* The load of the incoming data can be shared across multiple databases
2. *Data replication:* Multiple copies of data can be stored in the vast storage areas of clouds.

11.3.1.2 Redundancy in M2M Topology

In some application domains such as a large scale environment monitoring system, the IoT devices can be scattered and decentralized. Unlike a hub and spoke model, these devices may require to interact with each other to exchange their local computation. In order to increase the redundancy in such a scenario, researchers have suggested storing replicas of the local data and computation on the neighboring devices [35] so that a device failure does not result in a data loss. In a recent work, a fault-tolerant middleware has been proposed [34] where the applications (called services) are replicated across multiple nodes, with one being active at a time. Each device computes its own application, and also knows where its own local applications have been replicated. Furthermore, it monitors another device(s) through a heartbeat mechanism. For this purpose, the device maintains a copy of the application deployment information of the device it is monitoring. This topology ensures that there is no SPOF for any application. The failures are detected in a decentralized manner and failure recovery is performed autonomously.

11.3.1.3 Graceful Degradation

In order to make the autonomous objects as well as the service platform of an IoT system survive for long, a graceful degradation (also known as fail-safe) capability should be built-into the components.

When an unexpected event occurs, a gracefully degradable system can remain partly operational, rather than failing completely. However, as the system designer, it is important to define what degradation means in a given application context. For instance, in an autonomous power-grid management system, the monitoring system can selectively stop power transmission to a certain region keeping the main controlling unit unimpacted. In the case of office automation system, the elevators can run at a lower speed when the system falls back to a degraded mode. For a component-based software system, a fault in a particular component can result in nonavailability of the service provided by the failed component rather than bringing the entire system down.

11.3.1.3.1 Software Design

Building a gracefully degradable system requires careful planning and design. SaaS platforms today are building applications that are failure resilient. These design practices have been presented as a collection of design patterns by the practitioner community (http://techblog.netflix.com/2011/12/making-net-flix-api-more-resilient.html; http://www.infoq.com/news/2012/12/netflix-hystrix-fault-tolerance; http://martinfowler.com/bliki/CircuitBreaker.html)[36,49,50]. Although the references contain more details, here we briefly discuss how some of these design patterns can be applied in the IoT context.

Patterns	Applicability	Description
Circuit breaker	Service platform	In the event of failure, the calls are not allowed to reach the failed component and an alert is raised.
Timeout	Service platform and devices	If a call takes too long, assume that the call has failed and continue with the appropriate next step.
Bulkhead	Service platform	Distribute the component in multiple servers so that the failure of one component does not impact other. This technique can also be applied in designing the database for IoT service platform using the following rules: a. Distribute different tables in different database servers, so that if one server fails, the platform is still operational b. Partition tables horizontally and distribute records: Older records can be kept in a separate database and the main database handles the current information and the recent history
Fail-fast	Service platform and devices	The component is designed not to go ahead with execution if certain preconditions are violated.
Blocked thread		Ability to detect execution threads that are blocked or consuming resource beyond a threshold
State decrement Maximum subtrahead	Service platform and devices	As a part of the fail-safe design, the state decrement pattern models various partially failed states. Here the assumption is that the system has the ability to make different services unavailable to deal with an error. Minimum subtrahead proposes a monitor that detects the failure and decides the next state.

11.3.1.3.2 Performability Model

A well-known technique to evaluate the graceful degradation, specifically the State decrement pattern, is to build a performability model of the system. The work by Trivedi et al. [47] proposes a Markov model to capture the steady degradation from no-failure state to total failure situation and computes the performability. We briefly explain the idea here. Assuming that it is possible to characterize the extent of service loss l (possibly through the analysis of failure log) as different parts of the system fail, the performability value indicates the relative amount of useful service per unit time by the system in the steady state and is proved to be equal to $Y = \sum_{i=0}^{N} \rho_i (1 - l_i)$ where ρ_i is the probability that the system is in degraded state i ($i = 0$ means no failure at all and no service loss, ie, $l_0 = 0$; $i = N$ means total failure with complete loss of service, ie, $l_N = 1$).

11.3.2 ERROR DETECTION

Use of heartbeat and watchdog timers are traditional approaches to make the operational state visible to the outside world, which can help in detecting the failure of any node in a networked, real-time system. These techniques are certainly applicable in the context of an IoT system. We briefly discuss them here.

11.3.2.1 Watchdog

This is a lightweight timer (often implemented by the hardware, as in traditional fault-tolerant VAX 11/780 or Pluribus reliable multiprocessor), which runs separately from the main process. If the main process does not periodically reset the timer before it expires, the process is assumed to have a control-flow error (the correct flow of control would have reset the timer). In such a case, a hardware-implemented timer can generate an interrupt that can trigger a recovery routine. The recovery procedure can

1. Restart the process or the system from its checkpointed state
2. Invoke an appropriate recovery routine

Popular open-source IoT middleware today such as RIOT [17] or Contiki[c] has a watchdog timer support. Snappy Ubuntu Core (http://www.ubuntu.com/internet-of-things) for IoT devices also reports that a watchdog mechanism is supported in the OS. Intel has recently announced their IoT infrastructure solution known as Intel IOT gateway [29], which promises hardware watchdog support.

Although a watchdog is easy to implement, the main problem with a watchdog-based approach is that it does not adhere to any specific fault-model. Therefore, it is not possible to figure out the reason why a watchdog-based trigger was activated. For a reasonably less complicated process running on an IoT device with a deterministic runtime, the watchdog is an effective mechanism for error detection.

It is important to note that a watchdog is useful when availability is more important than correct functioning (reliability). Therefore, IoT scenarios where zero tolerance is expected, watchdog may not be a proper solution.

---

[c]Contiki: The Open Source Operating System for the Internet of Things, http://www.contiki-os.org/

11.3.2.2 Heartbeat

In this approach, a node in the network sends a message with a payload (ie, meaningful results, execution progress) to indicate that it is alive. If the heartbeat signal is not received within the prescribed time, the monitoring component assumes that the application running on the node has failed. Heartbeat-based communication has been used over a couple of decades in distributed systems. In the IoT context, heartbeat-based detection can be employed when the interacting devices are computing complex time-consuming tasks, or the devices are expected to respond only to some aperiodic events. In such a case, it is important to know whether the device is fault-free and is ready to process any upcoming event. However, for devices that send data streams in a periodic manner, heartbeat-based technique can be an overhead. In such a case, watchdog-based approach is more appropriate.

Identifying the correct time interval for a heartbeat is tricky. Many modern distributed systems use adaptive heartbeat mechanism where the heartbeat monitoring component estimates the heartbeat message roundtrip time (RTT). A popular roundtrip estimation technique is $T = \omega T_\mathrm{p} + (1 - \omega)D$ where T denotes the estimated round trip time, which is a factor of the previously computed round trip time T_p and the time-delay D to receive the acknowledgment after sending the heartbeat message. Following the architecture reference model in Fig. 11.1, the heartbeat monitoring component can reside in the gateway module. For a distributed set of components without any central hub, the heartbeat monitoring needs to be implemented in the crucial components, who are responsible for data collection and processing from other nodes.

11.3.2.3 Exception Handling

The basic premise behind an error detection technique is that an application satisfies a set of properties for all correct executions of the application. If the property is not satisfied for any run of the program due to a fault, exception occurs in the program. Use of exception handling mechanism in the program (using language level features, or through checking error codes) is a recommended guideline for a reliable software design. Such a design practice needs to be adopted in an IoT-based system as well.

11.3.2.4 Recovery Through Restart

In conjunction with error detection, it is essential to implement a recovery mechanism for IoT components. At a minimum, autonomous devices as well as network devices need to have a basic restart mechanism [33], which can be triggered by the watchdog timer, or by the service platform. Restart is a useful technique for autonomous devices to recover from any transient error. However, it is often costly to have the entire system restart. Recently, a technique known as micro-reboot has been proposed where a module can be selectively restarted rather than the entire system. Such a technique has been first put into practice for the J2EE system where an EJB container can be restarted rather than the entire application server. A component needs to be specially designed to have the micro-reboot capability. In the context of an IoT system, the software written for an autonomous agent as well as the IoT service platform can be designed based on a principle called crash-only-design [37]. Here the architecture of the system is not only based on loosely coupled components but micro-reboot enabled as well. A micro-reboot capable component needs to maintain its own states in a state repository. Such a model has the functionality to create, read, and update the states. This functionality is invoked just before the component execution to load its most recent state.

To implement the micro-reboot feature in the IoT service platform, the platform should adopt the micro-kernel architecture pattern such that the components dealing with failure prone external entities are decoupled from the platform core. In addition, the failure resilient driver model [38] design can be adopted where the main service platform remains fault-resilient even when the modules that interact with various devices and other partner systems fail.

11.3.3 FAULT PREVENTION

Fault prevention implies that faults are prevented from occurring on the runtime system. In traditional high availability systems, it is a common practice to detect an imminent failure possibility and remove a part of the system that can potentially fail. Although the basic idea is applicable in IoT, it is necessary to adapt these ideas in IoT-based systems. Another approach to prevent failures in high-availability system is to perform scheduled maintenance and timely software upgrades. Such a technique cannot always be applicable for the IoT devices.

11.3.3.1 Failure Prediction

A generic approach for any failure prediction is to define a set of invariants the application must satisfy when it is in operation. If these invariants are broken, the application can encounter an imminent failure. If these invariants are modeled properly, it is possible to implement a monitor that can watch for a failure of any invariant and can take a preventive action. The invariants can be designed at various levels:

Program level: Assertions in a program are invariants that need to be satisfied for a correct execution of a program. Program level assertions can be used for autonomous agents to detect an incorrect input at an early stage and prevent the error propagation. Program level invariants can be defined for the service platform software specifically at the places where the platform integrates with external subsystems, which are extremely vulnerable. There are automated control-flow-based assertion creations techniques [51] that can detect (i) if there is an unexpected branch from the middle of a basic block or (ii) it is branching to any illegal block. Such techniques use control flow analysis of the compiled program to insert the assertions. However, such an automated insertion of assertions can significantly impact the performance of the system.

Infrastructure level: For autonomous devices, one can define a set of system resource usage thresholds as invariants. An external monitor can observe if those thresholds are violated and triggers a preventive action. This is a common practice for a traditional HA system.

Process level: Another class of noninvasive detection and enforcement of invariants has been proposed for a running system, specifically when the system is complex and it is not easy to insert assertions at design time or perform code analysis. These approaches do not deal with the source code but tries to collect invariant properties of the running processes from the operation logs. For such invariants to be meaningful, the challenge is that the invariants should not have many false-positive cases, ie, the invariant violations really do not indicate an erroneous behavior. The invariants should be at a reasonably high level so that the operations team can validate the invariant violations. These invariants, created from the past operational data, can be useful for the service platform. Specifically the flow invariants, which are relevant for detecting anomalies in the case of stream of data or a set of transactions, can be applied in the context of IoT service platform monitoring. A few flow invariant-based anomaly detection techniques for SaaS platforms based on statistical models have been indicated in Ref. [30–32]. The work presented in Ref. [48] proposes a monitoring agent to monitor the infrastructure usage related invariants as well as use a stochastic failure model to predict an upcoming failure of a running SaaS system. Such an approach can be adapted in the context of an IoT system.

11.3.3.2 Improving Communication Reliability

In many IoT application scenarios, the communication of machines and sensors without human intervention is a key requirement. To achieve this goal without failure, the reliability of the communication system that connects the sensors together plays a key role in the overall system reliability [7]. Unlike traditional systems, various IoT application scenarios such as environmental monitoring and office automation demand that the communication infrastructure be reliable and sustain for a long time in an energy constrained environment. For traditional system, use of redundant communication paths such as multihop networking [15] has been a common design practice for better availability. Although such a communication protocol provides the needed redundancy in IoT, it is also important to optimize the number of hops, without sacrificing the reliability so that the energy consumption is under control. Optimizing the energy consumption in wireless network through optimal area coverage has been an important and active area of research [39–42] for a long time. In particular, the energy conserving protocols such as UDP would be a better choice than TCP-based communication for the embedded devices. However, UDP comes at a cost that it is not as reliable as TCP. To address the reliability problem, the Zigbee protocol (IEEE 802.15.4e) has been proposed recently which uses multihop communication to avoid a single point of failure and it is energy efficient. This has now been adopted in several IoT operating systems like RIOT, Contiki, TinyOS, and several others [18,19]. Further discussion on the reliability of wireless sensor networks in general has been discussed in Ref. [53].

Recently, Maalel et al. [16] have proposed a new reliable protocol for IoT where the broadcast nature of the wireless protocol is exploited to "overhear" a packet by the neighboring node even when the neighbor is not the intended recipient. As a result, the necessity to send the additional ACK signal is alleviated. This in turn reduces the traffic in network, resulting in an overall improvement of the total energy consumption. Researchers have attempted to model various quality of service requirements of a wireless sensor network (which includes sensors, actuators, and the network)—namely the lifetime of a sensor, throughput, delay, and accuracy of data transmission [8] which can be used to evaluate the reliability of a WSN.

11.3.3.2.1 Service Degradation Support

In the event of network failures, the network protocol may incorporate mechanisms to alert the autonomous objects participating in the interaction. Such objects can then trigger their in-built graceful degradation mechanism in response to the alert information received from the network.

11.3.3.3 Failure Prevention by Service Platform

The service platform in the architecture reference model can help in making the IoT system failure resilient. The project MiLAN [9] describes an environmental monitoring system comprising several embedded sensors and a central service platform. Although a sensor topology can introduce redundancy to reduce the single point of failure, the sensors may not have the overall sense of the topology to improve their longevity or to modify the next course of action based on the collective information generated out of the topology. The service platform, equipped with the knowledge of the overall topology, can take a better decision to prevent any failure. In MiLAN [9], the middleware assumes the responsibility of improving the overall longevity of the sensor topology by regulating the quality of service of different sensor devices. The quality of the service for a sensor device is mapped to a reliability value to determine the state of the variable from the sensor data. For instance, in an IoT-based healthcare scenario a blood pressure sensor with QoS 0.9 indicates 90% reliability with which the sensor data can be used to determine the exact blood pressure. Depending on the overall state of the monitored patient, the middleware can switch off the blood-pressure sensor or can instruct the sensor to collect data at a QoS level of 0.9

11.3.3.4 Improving Energy Efficiency

Since an IoT-based system is supposed to be operational for a long time, it is important that the autonomous devices can run on a battery power for a long time. To achieve this, a holistic approach to optimize the energy consumption needs to be considered to prevent any failure due to the unavailability of the battery power [24,25].

11.3.3.4.1 Device Power Management

It is highly important to optimize the energy consumption by the device as the battery power can severely limit the device longevity. Dynamic management of power through dynamic voltage and frequency scaling (DVFS) is a common technique to reduce the power consumption of a device. However, it has been observed that scaling down the voltage can increase the rate of occurrence of transient faults on the embedded device [45]. A recent task scheduling strategy by Wei [44] considers a fault model related to DVS and schedules tasks under varying voltage scales for real-time jobs.

CPUs in the mobile embedded devices are becoming increasingly powerful where multicore processors are being used in smartphones. In addition, these CPUs are equipped with various power management mechanisms such as offlining a CPU core or dynamic voltage and frequency scaling (DVFS) which reduces the CPU frequency to reduce the power consumption but compromises the performance. In a recent study by Carroll and Heiser [46] it was shown that a policy that combines frequency scaling and core offlining can result in reduction of power without compromising the performability. In this approach, the frequency of a core is increased to a threshold and then switches on another core, but drops the frequency to half for both the cores. This has been implemented as a new frequency governor in the Linux kernel, meant for embedded devices. Such techniques can be introduced in today's modern sensor devices that are capable of running IoT operating systems for better energy management.

11.3.3.4.2 Communication Power Management

We have already discussed earlier that the communication protocols are becoming energy aware. Additionally, energy efficiency can also be improved by adjusting transmission power (to the minimal necessary level), and carefully applying algorithms and distributing computing techniques to design efficient routing protocols.

11.3.3.4.3 Service Platform

Researchers have focused on building the energy optimization capability at the IoT service platform level. The article by Sundar Prasad and Kumar [13] discussed energy optimization by scheduling various activities judiciously where a selected set of nodes can be switched to sleep mode and only a subset of connected nodes remains active without compromising the quality of sensing and data gathering. The MiLAN project [9] proposes an energy aware middleware to orchestrate the activities of the sensor networks. For example, the middleware can decide that even though the sensor topology contains redundancy, it may be more energy efficient to turn off a few redundant sensors so as to improve the overall longevity of the network under normal circumstances. Next, the middleware can reduce the overall load of the critical sensors in a particular application scenario so as to extend the battery life of the critical sensor. In yet another scenario, the middleware can reduce the quality of data (such as signal resolution) of healthcare devices in a normal situation. The article by Liu et al. [43] discusses the quality of information (QoI) and energy efficiency in IoT network through a special purpose energy management module in the service platform, which can take an informed decision to switch on or off sensor nodes. The scheduler that is run by this module is aware of the QoI.

11.3.3.4.3.1 *Data Quality vs Energy Usage.*
In the context of IoT, the data quality management has become all the more relevant specifically when the quality of data collected by the sensors has a direct impact on the energy consumption. The QoI present in the data broadly implies whether the data (image, environmental data stream, audio) are fit for using the intended purpose. Defining QoI metric is context specific. In general, factors like latency, accuracy, and other physical contexts (like coverage) can be used to create a QoI metric. The article by Liu proposes an IoT middleware having a specific energy management module that provides an optimal covering of a set of sensor network devices without compromising the QoI using a greedy approach. Such an approach essentially aims to improve the overall reliability of the system and also increases the system longevity.

REFERENCES

[1] Botterman M. for the European Commission Information Society and Media Directorate General, Networked Enterprise & RFID Unit—D4, Internet of Things: An Early Reality of the Future Internet, Report of the Internet of Things Workshop, Prague, Czech Republic; 2009.

[2] Grimsmo SB. Reliability issues when providing M2M services in the Internet of Things. MS Thesis Report, Norwegian Institute of Science and Technology; 2009.

[3] Weber RH. Internet of Things—new security and privacy challenges. Comput Law Secur Rev 2010;26(1):23–30.

[4] Weiser M, Gold R, Brown JS. The origins of ubiquitous computing research at PARC in the late 1980s. IBM Syst. J. 1999;38(4):693–6.

[5] Finkenzeller KR. RFID Handbook: Fundamentals and Applications in Contactless Smart Cards and Identification. John Wiley & Sons, Ltd; 2003.

[6] Atzori L, Iera A, Morabito G. The Internet of Things: a survey. Comput Netw 2010;54(15):2787–805.

[7] Gubbi J, Buyya R, Marusic S, Palaniswami M. Internet of Things (IoT): a vision, architectural elements, and future directions. Fut Gen Comput Syst 2013;29(7):1645–60.

[8] Ming Z, Yan M. A modeling and computational method for QoS in IOT. IEEE Third International Conference on Software Engineering and Service Science (ICSESS); 2012.

[9] Heinzelman W, Murphy A, Carvalho H, Perillo M. Middleware to support sensor network applications. IEEE Netw 2004;18(issue I):6–14.

[10] Shi W, Liu M. Tactics of handling data in internet of things. In: IEEE International Conference on Cloud Computing and Intelligence Systems (CCIS); 2011, p. 515–517.

[11] Roman R, Najera P, Lopez J. Securing the internet of things. Computer 2011;44(9):51–8.

[12] Grønbæk I. Connecting objects in the Internet of Things (IOT). Telenor R&I; 2008.

[13] Sundar Prasad S, Kumar C. An energy efficient and reliable Internet of things. IEEE International Conference on Communication, Information & Computing Technology (ICCICT); 2012.

[14] Kyriazis D, Varvarigou T. Smart, autonomous and reliable Internet of Things. Procedia Comput Sci 2013;21:442–8.

[15] Al-Karaki J, Kamal A. Routing techniques in wireless sensor networks: a survey. IEEE Wirel Commun 2004;11:6–28.

[16] Maalel N, Natalizio E, Bouabdallah A, Roux P, Kellil M. Reliability for emergency applications in Internet of Things. In: IEEE International Conference on Distributed Computing in Sensor Systems (DCOSS); 2013.

[17] Baccelli E, Hahm O, Petersen H, Gunes M, Wählisch M, Schmidt T. RIOT OS: towards an OS for the Internet of Things. IEEE INFOCOM; 2013.

[18] ARM mbed OS, http://mbed.org/technology/os/

[19] Ubuntu wants to be the OS for IoT, http://www.zdnet.com/article/ubuntu-wants-to-be-the-os-for-the-internet-of-things/

[20] Patterson D, et al. Recovery oriented computing (ROC): motivation, definition, techniques. Technical Report. University of California at Berkeley, Berkeley, CA; 2002.

[21] Siewiorek DP, Chillarege R, Kalbarczyk ZT. Reflections on industry trends and experimental research in dependability. IEEE Trans Depend Secur Comput 2004;1(2):109–27.

[22] Murphy B, Levidow B. Windows 2000 dependability. Microsoft Research Technical Report MSR-TR-2000-56; 2000.

[23] Cinque M, Cotroneo D, Kalbarczyk Z, Iyer RK. How do mobile phones fail? a failure data analysis of Symbian OS smart phones. Thirty Seventh Annual IEEE/IFIP International Conference on Dependable Systems and Networks, 2007. DSN '07, June 25–28, 2007, p. 585–594

[24] Thiagarajan N, Aggarwal G, Nicoara A, Boneh D, Singh JP. Who killed my battery?: analyzing mobile browser energy consumption. in Proceedings of the Twenty First International Conference on World Wide Web, ACM; 2012, p. 41–50.

[25] Hao S, Li D, Halfond WG, Govindan R. Estimating mobile application energy consumption using program analysis. Thirty Fifth International Conference on Software Engineering (ICSE). IEEE; 2013, p. 92–101.

[26] The Council of The European Union. COUNCIL DIRECTIVE 98/58/EC of July 20, 1998 concerning the protection of animals kept for farming purposes; 1998.

[27] Telespor AS. Telespor. http://telespor.no/; 2009 [Online].

[28] Avizienis A, Laprie J-C, Randell B, Landwehr C. Basic concepts and taxonomy of dependable and secure computing. IEEE Trans Depend Secure Comput 2004;1(1):11–33.

[29] White Paper, Intel® IOT Gateways: Enabling and Configuring Watchdog Timer; 2015, #332842-002US.

[30] Jiang G, et al. Discovering likely invariants of distributed transaction systems for autonomic system management. Cluster Comput. 2006;9(no. 4):385–99.

[31] Sarkar S, Ganesan R, Cinque M, Frattini F, Russo S, Savignano A. Mining invariants from saas application logs. In: European Dependable Computing Conference (EDCC); 2014.

[32] Perkins JH, Ernst MD. Efficient incremental algorithms for dynamic detection of likely invariants. In Twelfth Symposium on Foundations of Software Engineering; 2004.

[33] Internet Engineering Task Force. RFC 5187, OSPFv3 Graceful Restart; 2008.

[34] Su PH, Shih C-S, Hsu JY-J, Lin K-J, Wang Y-C. Decentralized fault tolerance mechanism for intelligent IoT/M2M middleware. IEEE World Forum on Internet of Things (WF-IoT); 2014.

[35] Neumann J, Hoeller N, Reinke C, Linnemann V. Redundancy Infrastructure for Service-Oriented Wireless Sensor Networks. In: Ninth IEEE International Symposium on Network Computing and Applications (NCA, 2010); 2010, p. 269–74.

[36] Saridakis T. Design patterns for graceful degradation. In: Noble J, Johnson R, editors. Transactions on Pattern Languages of Programming I. Springer-Verlag Berlin, Heidelberg; 2009, p. 67–93.

[37] Candea G, Kawamoto S, Fujiki Y, Friedman G, and Fox A. Microreboot: a technique for cheap recovery. In: Proceedings of the Sixth Symposium on Operating Systems Design and Implementation (OSDI); 2004.

[38] Herder N, Bos H, Gras B, Homburg P, Tanenbaum AS. Failure resilience for device drivers. In: Proceedings of the Thirty Seventh Annual IEEE/IFIP International Conference on Dependable Systems and Networks (DSN); 2007.

[39] Santi P. Topology control in wireless ad hoc and sensor networks. ACM Comput Surv (CSUR) 2005;37(2):164–94.

[40] Cheng X, Narahari B, Simha R, Cheng MX, Liu D. Strong minimum energy topology in wireless sensor networks: Np-completeness and heuristics. IEEE Trans Mob Comput 2003;2(3):248–56.

[41] Stojmenovic I. Localized network layer protocols in wireless sensor networks based on optimizing cost over progress ratio. IEEE Netw 2006;20(no. 1):21–7.

[42] Gallais A, Carle J, Simplot-Ryl D, Stojmenovic′ I. Localized sensor area coverage with low communication overhead". IEEE Trans Mob Comput 2008;7(no. 5):661–72.

[43] Liu CH, Fan J, Branch JW, Leung KK. Toward QoI and energy-efficiency in Internet-of-Things sensory environments. IEEE Trans Emerg Top Comput 2014;2(4):473–487.

[44] Wei T, Mishra P, Wu K, Zhou J. Quasi-static fault-tolerant scheduling schemes for energy-efficient hard real-time systems. J Syst Softw 2012;85(6):1386–99.

[45] Zhu D, Melhem R, Mosse D. 2004. The effects of energy management on reliability in real-time embedded systems. In: Proceedings of the IEEE International Conference on Computer-Aided Design (ICCAD); 2004.

[46] Carroll A, Heiser G. Unifying DVFS and offlining in mobile multicores, 20th IEEE Real-Time and Embedded Technology and Applications Symposium (RTAS); 2014.

[47] Trivedi KS, Muppala JK, Woolet SP, Haverkort BR. Composite performance and dependability analysis. Perform. Eval. Elsevier Science Publishers B.V. 1992;14(3):192–215.

[48] Roy A, Ganesan R, Sarkar S. Keep it moving: proactive workload management for reducing SLA violations in large scale SaaS clouds. Twenty Fourth IEEE International Symposium on Software Reliability Engineering (ISSRE); 2013.

[49] Shore J. Fail Fast, IEEE Software; 2004.

[50] Nygard MT. Release It! Design and Deploy Production-Ready Software, Pragmatic Programmers; 2007.

[51] Bagchi S. Hierarchical error detection in a SIFT environment. PhD Thesis, University of Illinois at Urbana-Champaign; 2000.

[52] Botta A, Donato W, Persico V, Pescape A. On the integration of cloud computing and Internet of Things. International Conference on Future Internet of Things and Cloud; 2014.

[53] Adeel Mahmood Muhammad, Seah WKG, Welch I. Reliability in wireless sensor networks: a survey and challenges ahead. Comput Netw 2015;79:166–87.

[54] Khodaei M, Jin H, Papadimitratos P. Towards deploying a scalable & robust vehicular identity and credential management infrastructure. In: IEEE VNC, Paderborn, Germany; 2014.

GOVERNING INTERNET OF THINGS: ISSUES, APPROACHES, AND NEW PARADIGMS

M. Maheswaran*, S. Misra**

*School of Computer Science, McGill University, Montreal, Quebec, Canada;
**Ericsson Canada, Montreal, Quebec, Canada

12.1 INTRODUCTION

The popularity and problems of Internet of Things (IoT) [1] are rising very fast. Various projections are estimating that IoT will reach about 50 billion devices by 2020. However, already approximately 2 billion smartphones are on the Internet, which means that well over 2 billion connected devices should be operating on the Internet. A smartphone has many sensors including video cameras, which enables users to easily shoot videos and share them with others over the Internet. This facility has already created many privacy breaches [2] where unauthorized videos have harmed the reputation of many people. The grander vision of IoT is to have a much larger number of sensors and actuators in the environment that can be called upon to monitor and manage physical spaces. Therefore, we need to have methodical governance mechanisms to regulate the activities of the smart objects (things) in future networked societies.

One of the most anticipated problems of IoT is the management of the vast amount of data IoT can generate [3]. This creates a huge networking and storage issue to get the data to a stable computing platform from tiny devices where the data are captured and an even bigger problem from a data security and privacy point-of-view [4]. In addition to generating data, IoT also heavily depends on data for its operation. For example, a HVAC system of a smart building would depend on the temperature and humidity data to properly maintain the living conditions within the building. If the temperature and humidity data feeding into the HVAC control system are corrupted, the operation of the HVAC could be unpredictable.

Although satisfactorily addressing the data management issues is crucial for the success of IoT, there are important *operation control* issues as well. For instance, a computer needs to have a proper access control scheme to prevent unauthorized users and malicious programs intruding it. Similarly, IoT needs proper management framework to authorize its operations. For example, a drone may need to get permissions from a property owner before crossing a private property much like an airplane requesting clearance to cross a sovereign airspace. Such requirements posed by IoT bring many interesting research issues to fore.

This chapter presents an argument for developing a governance framework for tackling the data confidentiality, data integrity, and operation control issues faced by IoT. We argue that an IoT governance framework should be developed that is styled after the governance structures we have in the real world.

Such a framework can deviate quite substantially in its architecture from the network management systems [5] developed for enterprises due to the cyber-physical nature of IoT.

With a well-defined IoT governance framework, citizens and other stakeholders can hold the framework accountable for breaches in data confidentiality, violations of data integrity, or irregularities in operation control. Unlike an enterprise network management system which is driven by information technology (IT) legislations or corporate ideals, an IoT governance framework needs to be driven by the requirements of potentially large number of stakeholders [6]. Therefore, as favored by the respondents of a recent EC study [7], the IoT governance framework should be architected such that it will provide equal opportunity for all stakeholders to provide their input toward the evolution of the governance procedures. Another interesting concern expressed by the respondents of the EC study is the slow and weak enforcement of policies by existing governance structures in the Internet space. Clearly, with IoT, we need frameworks that are agile to changing user requirements. Otherwise, citizens will be living in environments that do not operate according to their expectations.

One of the unique challenges of IoT governance is the need to accommodate a variety of different stakeholders with nonaligned goals. For instance, citizens or consumers want to protect their data [7] whereas service providers want to use consumer data to know more about their behavior. Similarly, device manufacturers want less or self-regulatory oversight such that they have the least hindrance for introducing new technologies into the marketplace. Another challenge is that we need a common vocabulary for expressing the requirements to reach a consensus among the different stakeholders in IoT. Yet another challenge is to deal with the massive scale [1] of IoT and cope with the large number of interactions among the constituting elements of the IoT.

At this time, IoT is still a vision that is yet to penetrate the lives of ordinary citizens. However, massive deployment of computing elements in the form of smartphones has already taken place and other IoT devices such as drones are gaining popularity. Therefore, the IoT management problem is already gaining the attention of many researchers [8, 9]. So far four different ways have been postulated for managing IoT: (1) Do Nothing, (2) Self-Regulation, (3) Co-Regulation, and (4) Binding Law. In most of the current engagement scenarios, data acquisition by the digital services occurs through a voluntary release of information by the owner of the data. Therefore, *Do Nothing* in terms of regulation is an option because the person can be assumed to make an informed choice [4] when releasing the data. However, with IoT, data about a person could be captured involuntarily. Therefore, Do Nothing is not a feasible option. Similarly, Self-Regulation is a popular model for many Internet-based services. For instance, online social networking sites and other online portals that gather significant amount of user data use Self-Regulation [10]. The policies they follow as part of their Self-Regulation process is made known to the customers who can take this into consideration while making a decision to stay with or leave the service. Co-Regulation is another option that is mostly used by online services. In Co-Regulation a service could use well accepted standards or a trusted third party to validate its data handling processes. The third party (eg, a service such as TRUSTe) validates the data handling processes of an online service portal and assures its customers on the safety of their data. The choice of the third party and the extent of its involvement in managing data security at the site can be under the service provider's discretion. Further, the third party does not have any enforcement capabilities to intervene at a finer level. The fourth approach is Binding Law. In this approach, the law dictates how the data should be handled by a service provider. Again, implementing the law at a finer level (ie, ensuring each transaction is safe) is very difficult. Applications that handle sensitive data such as health-care data are subjected to Binding Law.

12.2 **BACKGROUND AND RELATED WORK**
12.2.1 **OVERVIEW**

IoT governance is a problem that is beginning to gain the attention of the researchers in the area of IoT [8]. However, many of the problems addressed under IoT governance are similar to the issues faced while governing or managing other large-scale systems such as the Internet. In the background part of this section, we highlight the management issues in the Internet and enterprise networks. Although the Internet is a public infrastructure that spans the globe, enterprise networks are deployed and managed by a particular organization or a group of closely related organizations. Examining the governance that takes place in these two cases sheds some important insights that could be used in the future development of IoT governance systems. Also, in the background part of this section, we discuss surveillance which is considered a top problem posed by IoT. We discuss various types of surveillance techniques and how they could be amplified by IoT. Although IoT governance is a recent concern, many researchers have already started examining this issue. In the related part of this section, we discuss some related initiatives.

12.2.2 **BACKGROUND**

12.2.2.1 *Governance*

Governance is a complex notion that is very difficult to capture using a single definition. Different stakeholders tend to think of governance in different ways. The need for governance emerges when a large group of people with different objectives come to coexist in a community. With a group size that is too large to reach efficient consensus on the course of action on important matters, the group members can delegate majority of the decision-making responsibility to an entity made of few members. These members referred to as board of directors, committee, project management, or equivalent are responsible for "steering" the community by setting the rules. The decision makers that constitute the governing entity are responsible for taking into consideration all the contextual information and make appropriate decisions with regard to governance for which they will be held accountable by the broader community [11].

What constitutes good governance and the principles that should be adhered to ensure such process has been widely studied. As the definition of governance, there is little agreement on the principles of good governance. Here are some of the important principles put forward by a UNDP study [12].

- *Broader participation*: The governing entity should facilitate everyone in the community to contribute to the governing process without bias. The members of community could create intermediate entities to represent them in the governing process and should have the freedom to associate and speech.
- *Strategic vision*: The governing process must take the long-term well being of the community while accommodating the short-term needs.
- *Effectiveness and efficiency*: The governing entity should be able reach timely decisions while consuming minimal amount of resources.
- *Transparency and accountability*: Free flow of information is necessary for good governance. The community members should be able to rationalize the decisions arrived by the governing entity using the information that led to such decisions. Another related principle of good governance is accountability. The community should be able to hold the governing entity responsible for the decisions they make.

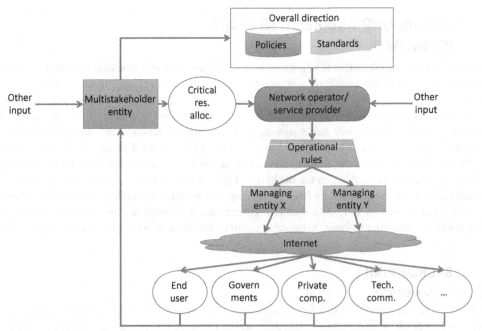

FIGURE 12.1 High-Level Block Diagram of the Multistakeholder Model in Internet Governance

- *Equity and rule of law*: The governing entity should act without bias in their decision making. It should also take into consideration the laws of the land and long-term traditions of the community.

12.2.2.2 Internet Governance

Internet is one of the most successful initiatives that is collaboratively governed by a large number of stakeholders of different types: private enterprises, government agencies, public, and academic or technical communities. While the different stakeholders have nonaligned objectives at a finer level, their overall objective is to develop and maintain a network that will provide pervasive connectivity—that is, they want the Internet to remain connected. In Ref. [13], DeNardis and Raymond provide an in-depth analysis of Internet governance and its connection to multistakeholder models (MSMs). The paper explains the pros and cons of MSMs vis-a-vis Internet governance. MSMs can help meet broader objectives such as Internet interoperability, security, stability, and openness. However, MSMs also could be used by crafty private enterprises and oppressive governments to stall the progressive evolution of the Internet. Despite popular perception that Internet governance is dominated by the United States, the reality is much different. Only a narrow but important functionality is within the purview of United States—name and address space management. The rest of the governance is distributed among MSM bodies, private stakeholders, and other sovereign states.

Fig. 12.1 shows a high-level block diagram of the MSM that is associated with the Internet governance. The purpose of the block diagram is to illustrate the complex information exchanges that take place among the different participates in the governance process.

In Ref. [13], the authors disaggregate the Internet governance into six areas: (1) control of *critical Internet resources,* (2) setting Internet standards, (3) access and interconnection coordination, (4) cybersecurity governance, (5) information intermediation, and (6) architecture-based intellectual property right enforcement. Various functions are performed under the control of critical Internet resources. For instance, central oversight of numbers and names, technical design of address formats, domain name assignment, root certificates for trust bootstrapping, and domain name resolution. Some of these functions such as central oversight of numbers and names are under US influence and others such as root certificates are handled by private enterprises (eg, VeriSign). Setting Internet standards is another important area of governance that involves designing core Internet and Web standards, and establishing low-level or high-level communication and storage standards. Many institutions controlled by MSM bodies such as IETF and ITU play a major role in this aspect of the Internet governance [14].

Access and interconnection coordination is important to get information flowing from one point to another point on the Internet particularly when these two points are located on networks that are controlled by different network operators. To get networks that are independently owned and operated to talk to each other, we need interoperable protocols. So the protocol standardization is carried out by an MSM body such as the IETF. Further, multilateral network interconnection points called Internet exchange points are managed and operated for the purposes of facilitating interconnectivity. Network quality of service and end user access policies are concerns that are handled by the operators of each network by appropriately provisioning or setting the local access policies. One of the most controversial aspects of interconnection governance has been *network neutrality* [15]. Network neutrality is centered around the debate whether network operators are entitled to give some content service providers preferential treatment over others for a fee. The Internet community sprung up advocates for either side of the argument and expected the government regulators to step in and arbitrate.

With the importance of the Internet for day-to-day human activities, security and protection of the Internet infrastructure is a major concern. Part of Internet security is detecting security vulnerabilities and coordinating the response to the vulnerabilities such that the damages could be minimized. Multilateral institutions (eg, Computer Emergency Response Teams) along with end users and software companies organize to detect the vulnerability, create patches, and deploy the patches. Another part of Internet security is the secure operation of the Internet infrastructure itself. To achieve this, secure protocols standards should be created and the infrastructure should be made to deploy acceptable standards while interoperability is maintained across the Internet. To secure the Internet infrastructure, it is not sufficient to have secure software and hardware, the system should be physically secure as well. This is the responsibility of many Internet stakeholders. Also part of the Internet infrastructure security is trust management. If trust is not properly managed a malicious attacker can interpose their equipment into the Internet infrastructure and cause significant damage while the proper Internet is not subverted. Therefore, trust governance on the Internet is an important problem that involves agreeing on a trust certification protocol, certificate format, and operating the trust maintenance infrastructure [16].

The governance of *information intermediation* is quite different from other areas of Internet governance. For one, it directly involves the Internet users unlike other issues that impact the Internet users indirectly through the availability and trustworthiness of the services offered by the Internet. Issues such as privacy from one another, privacy from government-backed surveillance, cyberbullying, censorship, and freedom of speech have many people taking contentious positions with regard to their governance. With government-backed surveillance programs [17], Internet stakeholders become suspicious of one another, which can reduce the overall trust on Internet governance.

One issue that has shot to prominence due to the popularity of the Internet is digital intellectual property management. Therefore, significant amount of governance effort is spent on quelling the problems that arise due to intellectual property infringement concerns. Intellectual property governance could involve dealing with disputes over domain name trademarks, removal of copyrighted material from Internet-based repositories, and removing copyrighted material from Internet search engines. Due to the international reach of the Internet, sometimes the party responsible for a particular violation may be beyond reach in a sovereign state. In such situations, the Internet governance could dictate corrective measures to isolate the offending party from the rest of the Internet.

Despite the lack of solid understanding of the way MSMs work [13, 14], MSMs bring broader participation into Internet governance. Some of the benefits obtained through the broad participation include: openness, transparency, accessibility, credibility, accountability, and measurement. Due to its openness and transparency, MSMs are also resistant to capture by interested parties. Further, MSMs while wanting to remain independent from sovereign governments, still facilitate the governments to contribute toward Internet governance.

12.2.2.3 Enterprise Network Management

Modern enterprises manage their IT assets using policy-based approaches [18, 19], where activities are guided by rules of the form "if condition than action." Set of such rules are known as policies, and policies can be created to shape different behaviors for different types of systems (eg, technical or social).

Policies can be first expressed as high-level goals and then refined to operational rules that implement the original goals. The original goals can emerge from corporate ideals or privacy legislations. The process of refining the policies from high level specifications (possibly in natural language) to low level operational rules is challenging due to conflicts, ambiguities because of different interpretations of context, incompleteness of the specifications, and the difficulty of ensuring that the operational rules obtained after the refinement implement the original intent. The last challenge is known as the *gulf of execution* [20] between the original intent and what is actually accomplished by the implemented rules. For instance, a confidentiality control policy might restrict the access of a data object to a selected set of trusted individuals, which does not always ensure the confidentiality of the data.

In enterprise network management, policy formulation is not automated [18]. However, significant amount of research has been done in policy validation, ratification, and runtime analysis. Policy validation determines whether a policy is valid given the available capabilities and the computing context. For example, a policy that calls for the use of an encryption that is not supported by the software stack will be considered an invalid policy. The policy ratification can involve a formal process that can be used by policy managers and authors to ascertain the suitability of a policy before deploying it. Runtime analysis is performed once the policy is in force. This includes monitoring, auditing, and dynamic conflict resolution.

In an enterprise network there are two types of end users: data users (accessing data) and data subjects (data are about them). The policy should be understood by both types of users. To make users understand the policies, the policies should be presented in human-friendly format (eg, in a high level language) instead of the machine-friendly language that is used while it is being interpreted by programs.

Another interesting enterprise network management problem that is closely connected to the IoT governance problem is the bring your own device (BYOD) problem [21]. BYOD introduces many players into the enterprise network management process and weakens the control network managers have on data privacy [22]. The biggest problem is the placement of data in devices that are not under the direct control of the network managers of the company. There is lot of debate on the best way of managing BYOD. In Ref. [21], Frank Andrus from Bradford Networks (a market leader in Network Access Control) argues that users need to be engaged as responsible stakeholders in creating and enforcing management regimes with BYOD. The level of compliance with the governance schemes can be very high if they already have user requirements factored into them. One of the key observations made by him is the need for effective information flow between the users and the corporate network operators—this he argues can lead to mutually beneficial governance schemes for *all* parties.

12.2.2.4 Management Versus Governance

Like the definition of governance itself the difference between governance and management is blurred. From the example scenarios we discussed in Internet governance and enterprise networking, it is evident that governance is carried by an entity that has a broad membership (ie, a multistakeholder participation) and that entity is accountable for the whole community. In a management scenario, the management team has a narrow membership often selected by the governing body. The management team is responsible for efficiently implementing the policies and goals of the enterprise and may not be accountable for the whole community. Further, the governing entity is responsible for strategic decision making and the outcome of this could create policies and rules that could guide the management team.

A governance entity cannot function by itself. It relies on a management team to actuate its policies or guidelines. The management team needs to take the high-level specifications and make operational decisions to achieve certain objectives. The details of the implementation are often left for the management team and they could be held accountable for devising weaker forms of implementations that do not meet all the objectives.

A management team, on the other hand, can exist without a governance entity. Small scale organizations will use management alone. In the Internet governance, we have several small entities such as network service providers that could solely depend on management. They would be taking the parameters defined by the Internet governance structures as guidance in their management process.

12.2.2.5 Surveillance and Internet of Things

Ever since computers enabled automatic data processing, concerns about different forms of surveillance have escalated. Although surveillance is possible using old-school techniques that do not include computers at all, automatic data processing and the associated data storage and retrieval techniques allow surveillance of massive scale to happen across long time ranges. With the introduction of IoT, surveillance regimes that were once the domain of governments could be within the reach of small profit making ventures. In such a scenario, surveillance would not be a concern with regard to government sanctioned policies but a broader concern with many active surveillance initiators and the general public that is affected by it. We believe a proper IoT governance framework is the best approach to manage such surveillance capabilities afforded by the IoT.

Smart surveillance [17] is a term coined by Langheinrich et al. to describe the assemblage of surveillance schemes one could create using individual schemes that are enabled by the advancements in sensors, networking, cloud computing, and intelligent data processing algorithms. It enormously augments the capacities of the parties that want to gather intelligence in a strategic and opportunistic manner. With smart surveillance [17], application-specific intelligence from captured data (eg, the presence of people or vehicles in a video) can be extracted with ease. The intelligence could be archived, correlated, shared, or used to deduce high-level decisions.

In Ref. [17], Langheinrich et al. identify six stakeholders relevant for smart surveillance: governments and public authorities, industry representatives, academics, policy makers, the media, and citizens. *Governments and public authorities* often champion the introduction of smart surveillance regimes in the context of ensuring public safety. *Industry representatives* are interested in pushing their technologies for implementing surveillance regimes and as a result often highlight the efficiencies such regimes could bring to the society. For instance, immigration control, safety in public places from acts of terrorism are some of the applications that trigger the installation and operation of surveillance schemes at different levels of sophistication. *Academics* have engaged in researching various technologies for surveillance (eg, image recognition algorithms) and at the same time debating policy and social ramifications of surveillance. *Policy makers* are often part of a government agency (eg, defence departments) or part of a multistakeholder institution that has a broad composition. With large amount of data gathering and storing done by private enterprises (eg, online social networks) some of the policy making is falling within their purview as well. For instance, what type of data to gather and how long to store them is part of the policy followed by the private enterprises that could determine the role such data could play in smart surveillance. *Media* could be playing an active role promoting surveillance by propagating information regarding the perceived threats for public safety and at the same time the media could give a voice for the negative aspects of surveillance. *Citizens and citizen groups* often favor the introduction of surveillance to combat terrorism and other criminal activities but change their allegiance when they learn that the scope of surveillance could be much broader and it could impact their freedom.

The position of these stakeholders is often mixed [17] with regard to the different forms of surveillance: some supporting and others opposing and sometimes changing their positions. However, academics, media, and citizen groups (eg, civil liberties union) play important roles in analyzing the impact of surveillance on individual freedom and disseminate them to the public for appropriate response.

12.2.3 RELATED WORK

In Ref. [8], Almeida et al. present the most recent discussion on IoT governance. In this paper, the authors observe that the privacy and data protection measures that are often instituted are dependent on the function and scale of the data gathering mechanisms. For instance, when automated data processing became feasible due to the introduction of the Internet, many of the existing privacy legislations became necessary. Although the introduction of Internet and cloud-based back ends enable the automation of data analysis, IoT can bring in automated data capture. If proper safeguards are not put in, people can be subjected to massive automated surveillance as they go about doing their day-to-day activities. The paper argues the adoption of four principles for data protection: (1) notice and choice, (2) data minimization, (3) access to personal data, and (4) accountability. Notice and choice is a popular approach to address the data collection concerns in many Internet-centric systems (eg, online social networks). Implementing this idea on IoT might be challenging due to user interface restrictions and the shear number of devices and services one would encounter with IoT. Access to personal data mandates that the end user has the right to access the data that were collected on him/her. Many online portals are beginning to implement some form of this principle to address the mounting privacy concerns. In IoT, the volume of data could be so huge that merely having access to the collected data might not be very helpful.

The paper also notes that IoT governance could be an extension of the Internet governance which is already very well developed. Some issues such as standardization, interoperability, security, and privacy could leverage the frameworks that are already in place for Internet governance. Certain aspects of IoT governance such as multistakeholder involvement might need extensions of the existing frameworks.

In Ref. [6], Almeida et al. examine multistakeholder model and their connection to Internet governance. This paper defines *stakeholders* as individuals or groups who have interest in a particular decision because they can influence it or can be affected by it. The MSM described in the paper has five major components: goals, participants, scope, timelines, and connection to decision makers. The cooperation elicited by a successful MSM among its participants can yield a system that is not achievable by a single stakeholder. The Internet brings together diverse participants: governments, technical community, civil society, and private sector. An MSM can have stakeholders that operate at different scopes. For example, the Internet can have international organizations such as ICANN and regional organizations such as Regional Internet Registries. The MSM can be connected to the decision makers in two different ways: on a purely informational basis or developing best practices. When MSM is engaging with the decision makers in a purely information manner, the decision makers are not compelled to take the ideas of MSM into consideration. On the other hand, by generating best practices, the MSM can exert some pressure on the decision makers to follow the set guidelines.

One of the key activities in MSM bodies is consensus building. The process of consensus building is often very difficult and messy. The different stakeholders will arrive at an agreement only if their viewpoints or grievances are reasonably accommodated in the final decision. An agreement of the stakeholders indicates their willingness to accept and implement the final decision.

The paper identifies many research issues that should addressed for designing and implementing successful MSM bodies: (1) identifying the right set of stakeholders to participate in a particular decision-making process, (2) the mechanisms for selecting participants for the different groups, (3) inclusion of crowdsourcing in the MSM dialog, (4) technologies for the representative to stay connected to their constituencies, (5) technology support for achieving and accelerating consensus in MSM bodies, and (6) theoretical models for consensus development in MSM bodies.

In Ref. [9], Weber discusses IoT governance problem in depth. It starts off with a discussion of EC sponsored user study [7] on IoT. It then describes some IoT-specific issues by comparing IoT governance to Internet governance. Two major issues are identified in Ref. [9]: naming differences and issues requiring regulatory frameworks. In the Internet, domain names are used whereas object names such as RFID tags are used in IoT networks. Governing the object name space so that it would provide an interoperable facility for naming and discovering smart objects is an important problem. As issues requiring regulatory frameworks, the paper discusses privacy, security, ethics, and standardization of IoT architecture. Continuing further, the paper identifies important pillars of IoT governance. One of the ideas heavily discussed is the idea of setting up a regulator for IoT along the lines of existing ones for trade (World Trade Organization). The paper posits that it is still premature to float this idea and does not envision it to be a viable approach in the near future. Although setting up a regulator is deemed infeasible, the paper is favorable for regulation. It goes into a discussion of what would be the best approach to regulation: top-down or bottom-up. Another interesting idea floated in the paper is open mechanisms for coordination. The paper is of the opinion that depending on the underlying social structure we should adopt different coordination mechanisms to achieve an efficient regulatory mechanism.

The paper identifies the following set of *substantive* principles for IoT governance as part of exposition of the topic: (1) legitimacy and representation, (2) transparency, (3) accountability, and (4) IoT infrastructure governance. Everyone in a society could be affected by the way IoT is managed. Therefore, it is important that everyone has an opportunity to influence the IoT governance. Like the idea of transparency in the Internet, the IoT transparency involves the ability to identify the elements of the management structure, information pertaining to management, and the right to access information. Accountability is an important substantive principle which dictates that the governing body should be held responsible for its actions. For instance, governing regimes could be subject to sanctions for irregular practices.

A cloud-based management framework called GovOps (Governance and Operations) is presented in Ref. [23] for IoT. The objective of GovOps is to make operational governance of IoT cloud systems easier by seamlessly integrating the governance objectives into IoT cloud operation processes. Instead of defining a new methodology for governing IoT, GovOps attempts to obtain high efficiencies in the overall IoT cloud management by providing a facility to integrate governance policies into operation processes. Two example applications used in the paper are building automation systems (BASs) and fleet management systems (FMS). In both applications, we can have variety of different stakeholders: end users, managers, and government policy makers. The paper identifies three forms of governance: environment-centric, data-centric, and infrastructure-centric. In a BAS environment, residents, building managers, and regulatory policy makers (government) are concerned about governing the environment created within and outside the buildings. In data-centric governance, measures for securing data and enforcing privacy requirements are carried out. Infrastructure-centric governance focuses on issues related to installing, configuring, and deploying IoT cloud systems.

One of the example governance objectives used to illustrate GovOps is implementing the legal requirements with respect to sensory data in BAS or FMS environments. The corresponding operation process would be spinning up a secure aggregator gateway in the cloud for sensor data stream and setting it up properly. Another important component of the GovOps is the GovOps manager. It is a dedicated manager that is responsible for bridging the gap between the governance strategies and the operations processes.

An implementation of the GovOps concept presented in Ref. [23] is given in Ref. [24] and referred to as the runtime framework for GovOps (rtGovOps). It provides the first known large scale implementation of a governance framework. Following the philosophy of GovOps, the purpose of their framework is not to evolve the management policies, but to implement a given governance policy across a large cloud-based IoT system. An experiment involving an FMS was carried out in Ref. [24], where golf carts were controlled using a cloud-based rtGovOps framework. One of the experiments demonstrated in the paper was to switch the golf cart management from normal mode to emergency mode. The authors claim that without their rtGovOps framework such a switch is cumbersome particularly for a large fleet of golf carts. With the rtGovOps framework, golf cart renting agency can easily manage the operation by setting the policies using a cloud interface.

12.3 IoT GOVERNANCE

12.3.1 OVERVIEW

The IoT governance is a very new problem. In fact, the full extent of the problem is still unknown because IoT itself is still a developing phenomenon [25]. IoT is very closely intertwined with space and time because the fundamental problem is the injection of computing intelligence into the space. Such injection can be carried out by static or dynamic (mobile) installations. The dynamic means changes with time because they could be tied to the movement of people.

The IoT governance models discussed here highlight the need to consider different variations of the governance structures to accommodate the different ways of injecting intelligence. In this section, we also discuss several IoT governance issues and existing approaches. Finally, we highlight some new paradigms that could be examined for IoT governance.

12.3.2 AN INTEGRATED GOVERNANCE IDEA

Governance in a modern society is a feedback-based process, where the composition of the governing entity and the policies it adopts can change with time based on the feedback from the larger community that is being governed. The Internet governance described in a previous section fits this model. In this model, the composition of the governing entity could change in response to emerging scenarios. For example, when a new technology (eg, software defined networking) emerges, IETF may create working groups to initiate and study standardization efforts on that technology. Such working groups would have participants from interested organizations and individuals reflecting the broad and open participation model of the Internet governance. As the community loses interest in a technology, working groups on the technology may cease their activities.

The IoT governance could be called upon to tackle even broader set of issues than Internet governance. It could, however, be styled after the Internet governance—as an MSM entity. With the scale of IoT and the expected dynamism of the system, we may need an automated governance framework. The best way to create such a governance framework is to leverage the strength of IoT. In particular, IoT is expected to bring tremendous improvements in terms of efficiency for existing physical processes.

12.3.3 GOVERNANCE MODELS

One of the unique aspects of IoT is its massive scale [1]. Therefore, we do not envision a single governance process to apply to the whole system. There will be many governance processes concurrently working within the system. The governance model defines how these concurrent governance processes relate to each other. They could all be running completely independent of each other or there could be a hierarchical relationship among the governance processes. With a hierarchical relationship, a child governance process would inherit the parameters established by the parent governance process.

12.3.4 IMPORTANT GOVERNANCE ISSUES

In the EC user study [7], curiously, some of the industrial players registered themselves as "other" to keep their affiliations private, which highlights a need for privacy in governance. Like the *secret ballot* enabling governance with broad participation, we need privacy preserving participation mechanisms to create an agile governance framework for IoT. In particular, user input should be securely registered without associating it with user identification. User identification could be a crucial and contentious issue in developing a secure framework for obtaining user input. For instance, if users are identified by the IoT they own, users without the particular device will feel disenfranchised. On the other hand, tying user input to biometric markers would be considered highly intrusive and cause much privacy concerns. Therefore, developing a broadly acceptable user identification that is deployable with minimum startup cost at a massive scale is the key for the creation of a novel governance framework for IoT.

An IoT governance framework will receive input from potentially large number of stakeholders and need to find consensus among their positions. Although we need unrestricted input for an agile governance process, the framework must adhere to the following principles to realize fair governance:

- *Transparency*: Despite the massive scale and potentially heterogeneous composition of an IoT system, we need open mechanisms for policy generation and enforcement as part of governance. This would allow the participants to verify that the governance process is operating without bias or malice.
- *Proportionality*: It is inevitable that an IoT governance process would make decisions that go against the wishes of certain users at certain times. Such decisions would be made to maximize the overall welfare of the system. Therefore, it is important to take actions that are proportional to the problems. Suppose an IoT governance framework creates policies disabling certain actions based on privacy concerns. We expect the privacy concerns to be severe enough to offset the utility lost due to disabling the given actions.
- *Accountability*: IoT governance processes would be very long running processes. At any given time, there could be dispute about decisions or operating policies applied in the past. So it is necessary to maintain a verifiable record of the decisions and the factors that contributed to those decisions. Offending parties should be held accountable despite privacy preserving measures and the framework must ensure that factors contributing to bias or malice are removed (if possible retroactively).

Fig. 12.2 shows a layered model for IoT. It has four layers including the physical world components. The *Gadget Layer* consists of all the components that capture physical processes or create the physical processes that are fed into the smart system. The gadgets in the Gadget Layer are connected by the *Communication Layer*. The Communication Layer can be realized using wireless, ad hoc, or wireline networks. The data captured or created by the gadgets are passed over to powerful compute nodes in the cloud for intelligence extraction. The intelligence extraction itself is managed or dictated by the applications that run on the compute nodes. From the governance perspective it is interesting to note the separation of the model into two realms: *Physical Realm* and the *Cyber Realm*. A data generator or owner can have two different identities in the two realms and linking them in a secure and privacy preserving manner in all situations is a major challenge. For example, when Alice takes a video that includes Bob, the stored or streamed video would not have Bob unless he is tagged, which can be error prone even if done automatically. An IoT governance framework will be subject to the data attribution problem depending on the granularity of policy enforcement. Suppose it uses a data-oriented governance then it needs to discern the type and criticality of the data.

12.3.5 EXISTING APPROACHES

IoT and ubiquitous computing share the frightening vision of Orwellian-nightmare-come-true [4], where the world is full of spying devices that are watching each and every activity of a person. Therefore, not surprisingly, privacy is a problem that has been studied very carefully by many researchers in ubiquitous computing [26]. In Ref. [4], Langheinrich discusses several important design principles

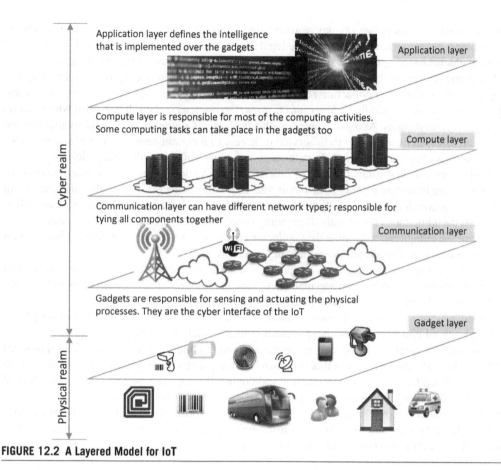

Application layer defines the intelligence that is implemented over the gadgets — Application layer

Compute layer is responsible for most of the computing activities. Some computing tasks can take place in the gadgets too — Compute layer

Communication layer can have different network types; responsible for tying all components together — Communication layer

Gadgets are responsible for sensing and actuating the physical processes. They are the cyber interface of the IoT — Gadget layer

Cyber realm

Physical realm

FIGURE 12.2 A Layered Model for IoT

and guidelines to implement privacy in ubiquitous computing: notice, choice and consent, anonymity and pseudonymity, proximity and locality, adequate security, and access and recourse. It is interesting to note that the scope of much of the work in privacy aware ubiquitous computing is limited to stopping opportunistic privacy invasions than stopping a determined adversary with potentially unlimited amount of resources (eg, a government spy agency). The scope of the privacy aware design of IoT is still unknown and will become evident as the field matures.

Notice is a fundamental principle which requires the data collector to notify the subject about its intention to collect data. While such a notifying protocol would not help in thwarting illegal surveillance operations, it would prevent mass-market devices being turned into surveillance equipment by interested parties. One of the implementations of the *notice* principle is the Platform for Privacy Preferences (P3P) [27] project. In P3P, websites describe their data collection activities in a machine readable format. This specification is parsed by the web browser and compared with the privacy requirements of the user. If conflicts are detected (ie, the data collection practices are contravening the privacy requirements of the user), the user is alerted otherwise not. A device in a ubiquitous computing system could use a declaration format like P3P to announce its requirements to other elements.

As ubiquitous systems gather privacy sensitive data, it becomes necessary to get explicit consent from the subject before gathering to satisfy the legal requirements. *Choice and consent* is the protocol proposed in ubiquitous computing systems to obtain such explicit consent. One of the tricky problems with choice and consent is the amount of work users could be subjected to by over eager collectors wanting consent for their data collection regimes. For instance, when a user enters a ubiquitous computing environment, she would find *Choice and Consent* too onerous if she is bombarded with requests from many collector devices. Another problem with *Choice and Consent* is the possibility that consent might be tied to the delivery of a certain service or access to a certain resource. For example, a user could be denied access to a building if she refuses to accept certain data collection policies.

With advancements in the development of precise indoor locationing and GPS assisted outdoor locationing, there are mounting locality or proximity-based privacy concerns. Although many users roam around and access services anonymously, to obtain specific services they need to authentic themselves using at least pseudonymous credentials. Depending on other information that could be gleaned from the context of the computing activity, a data collector could try to link user's activities to information from other sources (eg, sites visited) to reconstruct a user profile.

The initiatives within the ubiquitous computing umbrella are focused in safeguarding individual users from institutions that may setup and manage ubiquitous computing environments. With IoT, very diverse patterns of highly distributed computing are emerging.

The popularity of smartphones is making them indispensable tool for large number of people including high-school children. Parents have various concerns such as online pornography, cyber-bullying, and excessive gaming when giving smartphones to their children. Smart Sheriff [28] sponsored by the South Korean government is a tool that provides the parents an oversight into the smartphone activities of their children. Parents can monitor and control the applications and other parameters of the smartphone by setting appropriate management policies. The remote control of Internet connected smartphones by parents is not unlike the management of enterprise networks by system administrators. Although the system administrators are enforcing IT policies of the enterprise over all computers, Smart Sheriff allows the parents to control their children's smartphones according to their family values.

Drone control is another problem that is gaining considerable attention. There is debate on whether drones should be controlled and if so, how they should be controlled [29]. Industry representatives and enthusiasts who are keen in the development of the drone industry do not favor excessive regulations. However, due to privacy and nuisance concerns, efforts are underway to regulate drone operations. First of its kind is the Senate Bill 142 in California State Legislature, which prohibits trespassing in a drone through a private property at or below 350 feet [30]. The mechanisms devised to enforce such a law is a challenging problem. The Federal Aviation Agency (FAA) that has the oversight of the airspace over United States for all forms of civil aviation is also getting ready with its own set of regulations for drones. One of the biggest problems with regulations is that the drone operators may not be aware which space is restricted and which is not. To address this problem, FAA is developing a smartphone application called B4UFLY that can be used to verify whether a flight plan is allowed or determine the restrictions (if any) that are associated with it. At this time, the flight control software of the drone does not abide by the regulations. So transgressions of the drone operator with respect to the regulations are not stopped by the flight control system nor detected by an automated enforcement system.

Connected cars maintain a continuous connection to a vehicle control center through which they could be controlled thus overriding some of the inputs of the drivers (if necessary). Although such a

Table 12.1 Comparison of the Different Governance Schemes

Example Scenario	What is Being Controlled?	Who is the Controller?	Control Type
Ubiquitous computing scenario	Data release	Device operator	Mandatory
Drone regulations	Device operation	Central agency	Regulatory
Drone application (B4UFLY)	Device operation	Central agency	Advisory
Ford MyKey	Device operation	Parent	Mandatory
Smart Sheriff	Device operation	Parent	Mandatory

facility is a massive security concern, it could help with the management of a fleet of vehicles according to some set policies. The Ford MyKey is one such remote vehicle control system that allows a parent to set the limits on performance and functionality of the car when a teen driver is operating the vehicle. The Ford MyKey provides various control functions through which the parent could control the operation to suit their intentions. For example, speed could be hard limited and warning chimes could alert the driver for excessive speed even within the hard limit. MyKey could also be used to remind the occupants about the seatbelt and disable some functions unless seatbelts are worn.

In Table 12.1, we summarize the approaches we have discussed so far. We are particularly interested in eliciting the major factors that are involved in managing a large smart environment. We use three factors in this analysis: what is being controlled, who is the controller, and the type of control. In ubiquitous computing, we control private data release. The environment notifies the incoming device about the types of data that will be collected and the device could either opt in or out of the environment. So we denote the type of control as mandatory because the device is not going to release the data if it does not agree to the terms of data collection. In connected car and Smart Sheriff, the device operation is controlled. In ubiquitous computing, the device operator is the controller whereas in the other examples we have a remote controller. The type of control could be either mandatory or advisory. For instance, with Ford MyKey Smart Sheriff, the control is mandatory. The equipment is designed so that the parent's control cannot be circumvented.

12.3.6 NEW PARADIGMS

One of the important problems highlighted by the EC study [7] on IoT governance is the gap that exists between the different stakeholders that contribute to the development of IoT. The industrial players wanted least regulation so that the industries involved in IoT will have the freedom to innovate. Also, they heavily favored a self-regulated setup much like what is happening with data privacy in online social networks. The citizen groups and other civil societies were heavily concerned about privacy and related issues so they heavily favored some form of governance. However, interestingly, existing forms of governance in the Internet did not find much favor among many of the respondents due to their "slow and weak enforcement" of policies. Although the respondents agreed that IoT needs some form of governance, they were in strong disagreement with regard to the way in which such a mechanism could be realized.

The immediate need with regard to IoT governance is to improve the information flow among the stakeholders to narrow the gap among them with regard to the major issues. For example, policy makers should have up-to-date information on citizen's reaction to new technologies, their needs, and the environmental impact, or social effect. Similarly, manufacturers should have the most recent information on social impact and anticipated policy decisions with regard to emerging technologies. This creates an environment where all parties are cognizant of the concerns and needs of the other parties. Although improving the information flow improves the situation, we cannot expect it alone to completely narrow the gap and create cooperation among the parties.

The ultimate purpose of IoT is to deeply integrate the physical and cyber worlds such that day-to-day objects become part of smart systems. It is anticipated that such smart systems will yield much higher levels of *user experiences* and gain popular support of the users. The user experience can be described as the "sum of our relationship with technology." Therefore, a smart system should go well beyond supporting sophisticated sensory inputs and providing exciting outputs; it should make an emotional connection. One way of ensuring this emotional connection is to have a governance regime that takes the users' wishes into consideration.

The biggest benefit IoT brings to physical systems such as electric power grid is agility, where the smart variation of the system is able to sense various environmental factors and adapt very quickly to the emerging conditions. The smart system is expected to provide higher levels of efficiencies by being agile. Applying the similar mechanisms for governance and taking into consideration users wishes as environmental factors should be part of the new paradigm for IoT governance.

12.4 FUTURE RESEARCH DIRECTIONS

Governance of IoT is a topic full of many interesting research problems. Many initiatives are still underway at major industrial labs, startups, and open-source projects to realize the full vision of IoT. As these initiatives materialize and IoT gets deployed in a massive scale in the real world, we are going to experience the real governance problems. This will trigger an urgency to address these problems and manage the disruptions caused by this exciting technology to human life. Following is a list of research problems, we believe, should be addressed to realize an efficient governance framework for IoT.

- *User studies*: One of the well-known user studies regarding IoT was carried out by EC [7]. In this study, 600 questionnaires were answered by participants from a variety of different demographics. One improvement is to repeat such studies for a period of time and also track the infusion of technology into the group of people that are being studied. This way we can get an idea of how user opinions change with time and penetration of technology. User opinions are important for governance. The ultimate objective of governance of IoT is to manage the injection of the technology such that humans would not start rejecting the technology due to privacy, security, and other intrusion concerns.
- *Case studies*: Although the user studies mentioned earlier are targeting how user perceptions change with time, we also need feedback on actual user interactions in smart environments created by IoT. Although many studies have measured user behavior from a usability point-of-view in smart homes and buildings [31, 32], we are yet to have significant studies from a governance point-of-view. For governance studies, we need deployments in the scale of cities to gauge user actions in a realistic manner. With the anticipated advancements in real world adoptions of IoT, we are not far away from such large-scale studies. To carry out such real world studies, we also need to establish hypotheses to test, interesting experiments, and parameters to measure.

- *Secure device designs*: The reliability of the governance framework would be very low if we rely on the end user to comply with the governing policies formulated by the framework. Instead, we need a holistic framework that includes enforcement. The enforcement step requires support at the end devices so that the policies are mandatorily followed. The biggest problem to tackle here is the design and implementation of tamper-proof devices that are still cheap and easy to maintain. One of the core requirements of IoT is to keep the hardware cost very low due to the massive number of devices that can be deployed at the edge. Along with the power constraints the cost constraints can severely limit the design options one can have for the devices. The advantage is the possibility of building on top of the tremendous advancements already made in developing highly trustworthy devices such as smartphones at massive scale. However, unlike smartphones, which are personal devices, the IoT devices would be shared much like the physical infrastructure.
- *Secure software designs*: Software plays an important role in implementing the governance framework. We need hardened software that is hard to subvert. Although it is still a challenge to develop highly complex software system that is impervious to subversion, significant advancements have been made in creating hardened large-scale software systems. IoT needs hardened software systems that cannot be subverted and can be relied upon to implement the governance policies whatever they are. The biggest challenge in this regard will be the end user. Because the policies formed by the governance framework could run counter to the requirements of the end user, we need to have software and hardware systems that can withstand the efforts of a local end user to subvert the system.
- *Accountability and sanctioning mechanisms*: We cannot rely on the hardware and software mechanisms to implement the governance policies in a fault-proof manner. Therefore, we need fallback mechanisms that will detect violations of the expected governance policies and sanction the parties that are causing the violations. As part of detecting the violations, we need to attribute the governance policy violations to the correct party. This requires a trusted user identification mechanism that has accountability support. One of the challenges in realizing this goal is the need to preserve user privacy as they engage with IoT. This calls for research into privacy preserving identification schemes that can support accountability while running on resource constrained IoT devices.

12.5 CONCLUSIONS

IoT is a vision that is expected to bring significant changes to every aspect of human life. Given its pervasive nature, one of the important problems with regard to IoT is its governance. Governance is a complex concept that is often defined in many different ways. For the purposes of this chapter, we consider governance as way of delegating the authority of managing a large-scale system to an entity and holding the entity accountable for the decisions it makes.

We discussed the concept of governance and management (particularly enterprise network management) and contrasted between the two in the context of large-scale systems. We reviewed many initiatives that are examining the IoT governance or related problems and highlighted their contributions. The advent of various forms of service-oriented computing made data security and privacy a major concern because service-oriented computing facilitates the application of automated techniques for extracting intelligence from data. IoT introduces another new dimension—this time automated data capture. When automated data processing is coupled with automated data capture, we have a lethal combination that is ideally suited for smart surveillance by parties that are interested in gathering intelligence on other people.

In this chapter we motivated the need for an IoT governance framework and discussed some of the research issues with respect to such a framework and approaches for realizing such a vision. We posit that an IoT governance framework could play a key role in data privacy management in addition to setting the policies governing the operation of lot of Internet connected devices (eg, smartphones, cars) in smart spaces (eg, homes, cities, etc).

REFERENCES

[1] Gubbi J, Buyya R, Marusic S, Palaniswami M. Internet of Things (IoT): a vision, architectural elements, and future directions. Fut Gen Comput Syst 2013;29(7):1645–60.
[2] Xu N, Zhang F, Luo Y, Jia W, Xuan D, Teng J. Stealthy video capturer: a new video-based spyware in 3G smartphones. Presented at the Second ACM Conference on Wireless Network Security; 2009, p. 69–78.
[3] In: Bessis N, Dobre C, editors. Big data and Internet of Things: a roadmap for smart environments, vol. 546. Cham: Springer International Publishing; 2014.
[4] Langheinrich M. Privacy by design—principles of privacy-aware ubiquitous systems. Presented at the Third International Conference in Ubiquitous Computing, Berlin, Heidelberg; 2001. p. 273–291.
[5] Benson T, Akella A, Maltz DA. Unraveling the complexity of network management. Presented at the Sixth USENIX Symposium on Networked Systems Design and Implementation; 2009. p. 335–348.
[6] Almeida V, Getschko D, Afonso C. The origin and evolution of multistakeholder models. IEEE Internet Comput 2015;19(1):74–9.
[7] E. Commission, Report on the Public Consultation on IoT Governance. European Commission; 2013.
[8] Almeida VAF, Doneda D, Monteiro M. Governance challenges for the Internet of Things. IEEE Internet Comput 2015;19(4):56–9.
[9] Weber RH. Internet of things—governance quo vadis? Comput Law Secur Rev Aug 2013;29(4):341–7.
[10] Tang Z, Hu YJ, Smith MD. Gaining trust through online privacy protection: self-regulation, mandatory standards, or caveat emptor. J Manag Inform Syst 2008;24(2):153–73.
[11] Simonsson M, Johnson P. Defining IT governance – a consolidation of literature. EARP Working Paper MS103. Stockholm, Sweden: Royal Institute of Technology (KTH); 2005.
[12] Qudrat K, Elahi I. UNDP on good governance. Int J Soc Econ 2009;36(12):1167–80.
[13] DeNardis DL, Raymond M. Thinking clearly about multistakeholder Internet governance. Eighth Annual Conference of the Global Internet Governance Academic Network (GigaNet), Bali, Indonesia; 2013.
[14] Waz J, Weiser P. Internet governance: the role of multistakeholder organizations. J Telecomm High Technol Law 2013;10(2).
[15] Krämer J, Wiewiorra L, Weinhardt C. Net neutrality: a progress report. Telecommun Policy 2013;37(9): 794–813.
[16] Butler K, Farley TR, Mcdaniel P, Rexford J. A survey of BGP security issues and solutions. Proc IEEE 2010;98(1):100–22.
[17] Langheinrich M, Finn R, Coroama V, Wright D. Quo vadis smart surveillance? How smart technologies combine and challenge democratic oversight. In: Gutwirth S, Leenes R, De Hert P, editors. Reloading data protection. Dordrecht: Springer; 2014.
[18] Karat J, Karat CM, Bertino E, Li N, Ni Q. Policy framework for security and privacy management. IBM R&D J; 2009.
[19] Bertino E, Brodie C, Calo S, Cranor LF, Karat C-M, Karat J, Li N, Lin D, Lobo J, Ni Q, Rao P, Wang X. Analysis of privacy and security policies. IBM R&D J 2009;53(2):3:1–13.

[20] Norman D. The design of everyday things. New York, NY: Basic Books, Inc; 2002.

[21] Mansfield-Devine S. Interview: BYOD and the enterprise network. Comput Fraud Secur 2012;2012(4):14–7.

[22] Morrow B. BYOD security challenges: control and protect your most sensitive data. Netw Secur 2012;2012(12):5–8.

[23] Nastic S, Inzinger C, Truong HL, Dustdar S. GovOps: the missing link for governance in software-defined IoT cloud systems. Presented at the Workshop on Engineering Service-Oriented Applications; 2014.

[24] Nastic S, Vögler M, Inzinger C, Truong H-L, Dustdar S. rtGovOps: a runtime framework for governance in large-scale software-defined IoT cloud systems. Presented at the Third IEEE International Conference on Mobile Cloud Computing, Services, and Engineering (MobileCloud); 2015. p. 24–33.

[25] Van Kranenburg R, Bassi A. IoT challenges. Commun Mob Comput 2012;1(1):9.

[26] Langheinrich M. A privacy awareness system for ubiquitous computing environments. Presented at the Fourth International Conference on Ubiquitous Computing; 2002. p. 237–245.

[27] Cranor LF. P3P: making privacy policies more useful. IEEE Secur Priv 2003;1(6):50–5.

[28] Smart Sheriff, Wikipedia [Online]. https://en.wikipedia.org/wiki/Smart_Sheriff

[29] Majoo F. Giving drone industry leeway to innovate. *The New York Times* [Online]. http://www.nytimes.com/2015/02/05/technology/personaltech/giving-the-drone-industry-the-leeway-to-innovate.html?ref=technology&_r=0

[30] Perry T. California's no drone zones. IEEE Spectrum [Online]. http://spectrum.ieee.org/view-from-the-valley/robotics/aerial-robots/californias-no-drone-zones/?utm_source=techalert&utm_medium=email&utm_campaign=021215

[31] Krioukov A, Fierro G, Kitaev N, Culler DE. Building application stack (BAS). Presented at the ACM BuildSys (in conjunction with ACM SenSys), New York, New York; 2012. p. 72–79.

[32] Dawson-Haggerty S, Krioukov A, Taneja J, Karandikar S, Fierro G, Kitaev N, Culler D. BOSS: building operating system services. Presented at the 10th USENIX Conference on Networked Systems Design and Implementation; 2013.

TinyTO: TWO-WAY AUTHENTICATION FOR CONSTRAINED DEVICES IN THE INTERNET OF THINGS

13

C. Schmitt, M. Noack, B. Stiller

Communication Systems Group CSG, Department of Informatics IFI, University of Zurich, Zurich, Switzerland

13.1 INTRODUCTION

Atzori et al. already stated in 2010 that the Internet of Things (IoT) consists of manifold devices, ranging from IP networks and servers to small devices such as Wireless Sensor Network (WSN) devices (e.g., Radio-Frequency IDentification (RFID) tags or sensor nodes) [1]. Throughout the years, especially WSN consisting of constrained devices with limited resources in memory, energy, and computational capacity, rapidly gained popularity. Thus, the questions raised of how to integrate them into the IoT and what challenges occur when looking at their constrained resources [2–4]. The number of possible deployments of such networks rises, and more applications have a need for confidential and authenticated communication within the network. This security issue must be addressed, due to the fact that sensitive information (e.g., identity (ID), names, or Global Positioning System (GPS) information) is linked almost everywhere to all kinds of collected data, such as temperature, sound, and brightness [5–7]. Hence, collected data is no longer anonymous and is often desired to be kept confidential. Fig. 13.1 illustrates this case for a building scenario, where environmental data is collected in rooms and transmitted over multiple hops to the gateway in order to make the data available to applications, such as climate control, security office, and room calendar (Section 13.5). If room information can be retrieved by eavesdropping due to missing security in the communication, then an attacker would be aware of sensitive information and could plan, for example, a burglary. Therefore, collected data must be transmitted in a secure manner and/or over a secure channel providing end-to-end security, giving only authorized entities (e.g., gateway, security system, or company members) access to this confidential information. But how is this supposed to be done? Keeping in mind that WSNs are part of the IoT and consist of constrained devices with limited resources, any security risks are aggravated by WSN design and security requirements of the IoT. Ultimately, an end-to-end security solution is required to achieve an adequate level of security. Protecting data only after it leaves the scope of the local network (e.g., WSN) is not sufficient.

Using existing technologies (e.g., Secure Sockets Layer (SSL)/Transport Layer Security (TLS) [8] or cryptography [9,10]) is the easiest way to achieve the goal of secure data- transmission. But this becomes increasingly challenging when looking at WSN devices used today (e.g., RFIDs, heart beat monitor, or environmental sensors), as their resources are strictly limited in memory, power, and

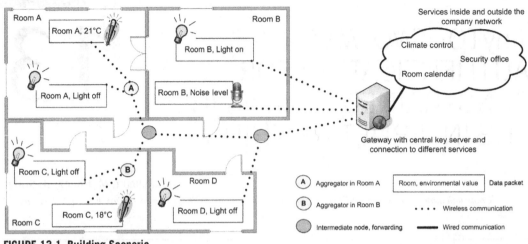

FIGURE 13.1 Building Scenario

computational capacity [11,12]. Those WSN devices are divided into constrained classes corresponding to their computational capacity and memory resources (Table 13.1) [11]. Security support is very challenging when assuming they are Class 1 devices (e.g., TelosB [13]), as done for the proposed solution TinyTO, because they offer only about 10 kByte RAM and 100 kByte ROM. A standard approach for securing communications in the Internet is SSL/TLS [8], relying on asymmetric cryptography such as RSA, which requires many resources and computational capacity, and, thus, is only feasible for at least Class 2 devices (which have approximately 50 kByte RAM and 250 kByte ROM) [14]. Additional challenges are the device diversity in today's WSNs, the network size itself, and multiple requirements (e.g., lifetime or security support) due to the target application [3]. Developing a proper solution is still a challenge, especially for security issues under consideration of the aforementioned challenges and constraints. Depending on the application, it might be prohibited to reuse existing solutions (e.g., military area). In general, it is preferred to either reuse standards or to develop a generic solution that can be integrated without major modifications and would not require hardware features such as cryptographic coprocessors [14], certain radio modules, or specific processors. On the software side, it would not require a specific protocol stack, but it would rely on the most basic interfaces, and be kept separate from applications in order to allow simple integration into any used protocol-stack with a limited number of connection points (i.e., interfaces). Furthermore, all additional features have to avoid affecting excessive performance- and memory-consumption.

Table 13.1 Device Classes (1 KiB = 1024 Byte) [11]				
Name	**RAM**	**ROM**	**IP Stack**	**Security**
Class 0	≪10 KiB	≪100 KiB	NO	NO
Class 1	~10 KiB	~100 KiB	CoAP [15], BLIP [16,17]	YES
Class 2	~50 KiB	~250 KiB	HTTP, TLS	YES

Based on the aforementioned hardware and application requirements, the proposed security solution TinyTO, an optimized two-way authentication solution for tiny devices, provides confidential data transfer with an additional integrity protection and data authentication, as well as a two-way authentication between sender and receiver of messages, delivering end-to-end security even for Class 1 devices. This is achieved by introducing an efficient handshake with a direct authentication and key exchange between pairs of nodes in the network, thus setting up an encrypted data transfer with an integrated encryption scheme. To minimize overall hardware requirements, the Elliptic Curve Cryptography (ECC) is used for key generation, key exchange, encryption, decryption, and signature generation.

Initially, each node is only familiar with the gateway. This relationship is authenticated with an individual shared key (in TinyTO of 16 Byte length), which is only known to the gateway and to the node, and is deployed to all nodes during the initial programming routine. Individual keys between nodes are either established during the handshake performance or can be requested by a node from the gateway (e.g., in case of communication with the aggregator).

TinyTO is designed to fit WSN requirements, is application-independent, and allows for an easy integration into existing applications due to its modular nature. TinyTO explicitly supports in-network aggregation by enabling a full and secure end-to-end communication without the need for a network-wide shared secret.

In the following, all data that is transmitted in data packets is considered to be confidential. The remainder of this chapter is structured as follows. Section 13.2 introduces relevant work in the area of pre-shared keys (PSK), ECC usage, and authentication without any special requirements to infrastructure. Afterward, Section 13.3 presents the design decisions for TinyTO, followed by a detailed description of the proposed solution TinyTO within Section 13.4. The approach is evaluated in Section 13.5 with respect to resource consumption, runtime performance, and security aspects. Finally, Section 13.6 summarizes the chapter.

13.2 SECURITY ASPECTS AND SOLUTIONS

The necessity of providing an end-to-end security solution in WSNs is not entirely new. Over the years, different approaches have emerged that address various security issues.

Thus, an often-quoted solution is to predistribute symmetric keys. However, flexibility of the deployment, connectivity between nodes, and resilience against attackers is limited significantly [18]. Instead, Du et al. proposed a solution that applies public key authentication to smaller-resource-demanding symmetric key operations, where a one-way hash function is used to authenticate public keys. The basic idea is to allow for individual nodes to verify that a transmitted public key matches the claimed identity, without relying on a trusted third party (e.g., Certificate Authority (CA)). For an exhausting mapping among all keys and identities, a large number of keys and certificates must be stored on every node, which is not feasible. Hence, a hash function, mapping from identity to the hash value of the corresponding public key, is preshared. Thus, only hash values and identities must be compared, which requires only a fraction of the memory and computational power. This can be optimized further by using Merkle Trees, in which nonleaf nodes are labeled with the hash of the labels of its children [19].

ECC determines a promising option for WSN security solutions, in particular, for message encryption, because ECC can deliver strong security with only a small amount of resources needed, as denoted in [20–22]. A 192-bit ECC key provides the same level of security as an RSA-key in the range of 1024 bit to 2048 bit [23]. ECC is viable for key generation, key exchange, encryption, decryption, and signatures, especially in resource-constrained applications.

Nie et al. developed the HIP DEX protocol for hop-by-hop secure connections using a Diffie–Hellman key exchange for public keys and the AES encryption for the session key-exchange [24]. Computational requirements are reduced by limiting cryptographic primitives to a minimum (e.g., removing expensive signature algorithms and any form of cryptographic hash functions). Cryptographic challenges are included in the first messages of the handshake proposed, in order to avoid flooding attacks. Identity authentication is achieved by password verification within the handshake, where nodes need to know their respective passwords in advance.

The PAuthKey protocol for application-level end-to-end security overcomes the problem of two-way authentication (i.e., mutual authentication) between sensor nodes [25]. It provides pervasive lightweight authentication and keying mechanisms, allowing nodes to establish secure and authenticated communication channels with each other. PAuthKey employs ECC-based implicit certificates, using a trusted central CA to handle authentication security. Thus, it stands in contrast to other authentication approaches, as certificates are generally considered to be resource-challenging for WSNs, and they require additional hosting infrastructure (e.g., CA) or hardware (e.g., Trusted Platform Module (TPM)) that can be integrated on the gateway or as an external network entity.

The UbiSec&Sens project offered a toolbox of security-aware components. The proposed Zero Common Knowledge (ZCK) protocol for authentication can establish well-defined pairwise security associations between entities, even in the absence of a common security infrastructure and pre-shared secrets [26]. ZCK authentication is based on re-recognition between entities, allowing entities to authenticate any other entity known from the past. This approach does not provide full security, as required, for instance, for financial transactions because the first contact between entities cannot be authenticated. However, in a scenario without any form of preestablished knowledge or a trusted third party, ZCK provides the best level of security that can be achieved under those limitations given. The ZCK protocol itself does not cater to a key exchange, but can be used in combination with any form of cryptography, such as Diffie–Hellman [27].

TinyDTLS—a DTLS-based solution for constrained (tiny) devices—provides end-to-end security, but targets Class 2 devices with additional memory resources [14]. In this case the platform used includes a TPM, offering additional dedicated memory and computational power for costly security functions. TinyDTLS performs a TLS handshake, using X.509 certificates for authentication and Advanced Encryption Standard (AES) for encryption, but still exceeds most alternatives, due to the high amount of available resources on its target devices. An advantage of using this solution is its compatibility with established standard protocols such as SSL/TLS [8].

The security aspects addressed by TinyTO are a direct result of the aforementioned existing solutions and of the final design-decisions taken in the upcoming Section 13.3, especially to counter Unknown Key-Share Attacks (UKSA) and Man-In-The-Middle (MITM) attacks. Therefore, TinyTO's goals are summarized as:

1. TinyTO brings end-to-end security to Class 1 devices by providing two-way authentication.
2. The TinyTO's handshake design with two-way authentication adds immensely to the security level without an involvement of certificates and CA in the network's infrastructure, or special hardware components such as TPM on the device.
3. TinyTO is protected against MITM attacks, in contrast to other solutions, such as UbiSec&Sens and ZCK, for Class 1 devices.

4. TinyTO allows for adding devices dynamically to the secure network, in contrast to static Merkle Trees.

5. TinyTO uses the Routing Protocol for Low power and Lossy Networks (RPL) [17,28], which offers various measurements to improve routing, which, in turn, can be used for an attack detection and defense.

In order to address these goals, TinyTO requires preprogrammed master keys for authentication between devices and the gateway, RPL routing, and support of an ECC functionality for encryption and signing.

13.3 DESIGN DECISIONS

An ideal solution for the two-way authentication should work generically on WSN nodes of all classes, especially because the trend goes toward heterogeneous WSNs. However, because WSN nodes are primarily designed to collect data, they prioritize frugality and longevity over processing-power and memory size. Section 13.1 has outlined that Class 1 devices are, by definition in RFC 7228 [11], very constrained to run security schemes beyond the very specific implementations mentioned in Section 13.2. Thus, the newly proposed end-to-end security solution in this chapter targets Class 1 devices as a minimum requirement. Even though Class 1 devices can connect to the Internet without additional proxies or gateways, they are limited in communication with peers, if those peers have a full protocol-stack employed [11], which would overwhelm available resources of Class 1 devices. Therefore, Class 1 devices require a specifically designed protocol-stack for constrained devices, such as the Constrained Application Protocol (CoAP) over User Datagram Protocol (UDP) [15]. Consequently, traditional security concepts for wireless networks, such as Wired Equivalent Privacy (WEP) or TLS in their native form, are unsuitable for WSNs, as pointed out in [29].

One approach to adapt the traditional Public-Key Cryptography (PKC) to WSNs (cf. Section 13.2) is the integration of extra hardware into nodes [18], for performing security operations and operations that are separate from the main application and the node processor. At first glance, Class 2 devices have more resources and can be used for this purpose [11]. Among other functionalities, Class 2 devices can deliver Internet-level security by providing confidentiality and message authentication at high speed [14]. Hu et al. have shown that a TPM chip outperforms most alternative solutions of similar resource levels [30]. But at second glance, as a drawback, all nodes in a WSN need to be equipped with an appropriate amount of resources (e.g., more RAM/ROM or using a TPM) to apply the security scheme network-wide.

A Class 1 device cannot build and maintain an RFC-compliant PKI while executing its main task—data collection and data forwarding—that is already resource-consuming in itself. One commonly used OpenSSL X.509 RSA-1024 certificate alone has a size of about 800 Byte [31], and adding the corresponding RSA key pair to this takes an additional 800 Byte [32]. Assuming an aggregation support, $n + 2$ certificates and $n + 2$ key pairs for a degree of aggregation (DOA) of n must be stored, quickly filling the available memory. For example, following those calculations, an aggregator with $DOA = 5$ needs to store an additional 11.2 kByte of data, only for certificates and corresponding key pairs.

This extreme memory consumption can be avoided by utilizing PKC only between designated node pairs (cf. Section 13.2), so that every node (aggregator or collector) only has to store its own key pair and the public key of the given recipient (ie, gateway or next hop). Gura et al. showed the general feasibility of PKC on simple 8-bit processors, as typically found within WSN nodes [33]. Therefore, TinyTO's security solution is based on PKC. Furthermore, memory and energy-consumption savings are gained by applying ECC instead of RSA (Rivest, Shamir, and Adleman) for key generation, key exchange, signatures, and encryption. The National Institute of Standards and Technology (NIST) recommends that SP 800-57 explains that an RSA key in the range of 1024–2048 bit delivers the same security level as a 160-bit ECC key, that is, the same amount of resources is required to break them [23]. Even more, Arvinderpal et al. showed that ECC implementations are faster and require less energy compared to equally secure RSA algorithms [32].

In general, standardization bodies and researchers agree on a set of security objectives that are necessary to achieve information security: confidentiality, integrity, authenticity, availability, and accountability of all messages, as defined in [34–36]. Furthermore, a set of requirements that are particular to WSNs and to the development goals for TinyTO must be considered: (1) End-to-end security to prevent eavesdropping and spoofing attacks, meaning risk for the communication because the underlying network infrastructure is only partially under the user's control and might be compromised. Especially in a WSN, where multi-hop communications are common, authentication and key exchange are essential design goals. (2) In WSNs, connections are often not lossless. Transmission Control Protocol (TCP) erroneously invokes congestion-control mechanisms to counter the loss of packets, which drastically impact the performance, and results in the UDP to serve as a better choice for WSNs [37]. (3) Two-way authentication denotes two entities authenticating each other at the same time [38]. In the scope of WSNs, it is not sufficient to authenticate only the sender to the receiver, but the sender has to be sure also about the identity and authorization of the potential receiver of confidential information. (4) ECC is promising to save resources, when performing PKC in TinyTO. For message encryption an Integrated Encryption Scheme (IES) is applied, especially to harness the speed-advantage of symmetric encryption for large amounts of data without the drawback of a repeated key-exchange for every transmission, which otherwise is necessary so that no secret credential would be used more than once.

Diffie et al. argued that an authentication protocol should always be linked to the key exchange for later encryption, otherwise an attacker might just wait until the authentication is completed to compromise the established communication channel thereafter [39]. Canetti et al. summarized the objective of a key-exchange protocol in a very intuitive way: A key-exchange protocol is secure, if it is impossible or at least infeasible for an attacker to distinguish the generated key from a random value [40]. The same fundamental concept can be applied to the Authenticated Key Exchange (AKE) protocol. But additionally, entity (or party) authentication has to guarantee the identity of communicating parties in the current communication session, and, therefore, has to prevent impersonation [41]. A good authentication protocol combines several properties, as explained by various researchers [39,42–45], and is relevant to TinyTO's design: (1) Forward secrecy guarantees, such that, if a generated private key of one or more of the participating entities is compromised, the security of previous communications is not affected. (2) Asymmetry of messages is required to prevent reflection attacks, where one entity simply replays the same message back to the sender; it is desirable to avoid symmetries. In other words, the authentication responses of two different parties must not be identical. (3) Direct authentication is provided by a protocol if the authentication is completed in a successful handshake, that is, if both parties have proven knowledge of the shared secret. (4) Timestamps are to be avoided, because not every participating entity can be expected to maintain a reliable local clock, which must be synchronized periodically, too.

13.4 TinyTO PROTOCOL

Due to TinyTO's main goal of supporting an end-to-end security with two-way authentication on Class 1 devices, the authentication protocol has to always include a key exchange, such that several possible handshake candidates can be considered in practice, leading to the final design and implementation of TinyTO. First, handshake candidates for TinyTO and their drawbacks are introduced. Second, the resulting TinyTO handshake, including two-way authentication purposes and aggregation support, are described. Finally, key information on the respective implementation is presented.

13.4.1 POSSIBLE HANDSHAKE PROTOCOL CANDIDATES

Handshake protocol candidates considered in this section support a two-way authentication of two independent entities without prior information exchange, which make them highly appropriate for TinyTO. From this stage on, the traditional naming pattern of cryptography is applied to protocol descriptions, assuming two communication parties—Alice and Bob—which are instantiated as sensor nodes.

At first glance the Station-to-Station protocol (STS) seems to be an ideal candidate for TinyTO because STS is based on a Diffie–Hellman's key exchange, followed by an exchange of authentication signatures [41]. Both parties, Alice (A) and Bob (B), compute their private key x and a public key X in the beginning. Next, Alice sends her public key X_A to Bob. Once Bob receives X_A, he can compute a shared secret K_{AB} with X_A and x_B, according to the Diffie–Hellman's key-exchange algorithm [38]. Bob can now encrypt any message to Alice using K_{AB}. For decryption purposes Bob sends X_B back to Alice, so that she can compute the same shared secret K_{AB}. Additionally, Bob sends a token consisting of both public keys, signed with his own private key to authenticate himself. Alice can use X_B to verify that Bob was indeed the same person who had signed the message and computed the shared secret. Bob is now authenticated to Alice. As the last step of the two-way authentication, Alice constructs an authentication message and sends it to Bob to authenticate herself to Bob. To avoid unnecessary communication overhead, the second key-exchange message is combined with the first authentication message. As a result, STS entails the establishment of a shared-secret key between two parties, with mutual entity-authentication and mutual implicit key-authentication [38]. The forward secrecy can be provided by deriving a new ephemeral key from the shared secret for the encryption of every message in that exchange [46]. The signatures are used to obtain protection against impersonation during the exchange.

However, there are two main shortcomings: (1) Although the STS is relatively simple to execute, it does not include any explicit key-confirmation. Neither Bob nor Alice inherently can be sure that the other party has actually computed a shared secret without additional messages. (2) Furthermore, STS is vulnerable to UKSAs and the MITM attack [41]. To prevent UKSAs and to provide explicit key-authentication, the signatures used can be encrypted additionally with the successfully computed K_{AB} [39]. Thus, Bob is assured that he shares K_{AB} only with one single party, namely Alice. Because he has created X_B specifically for this handshake and Alice has signed X_B and X_A, her signature is now tied to this particular handshake. By encrypting the message with the resulting K_{AB}, Alice assures Bob that she was indeed the entity who had created X_A. Similar assumptions can be made from the position of Alice [39]. This modification requires more computational capacity, due to parallel execution of signature and symmetric encryption algorithms. Hence, for WSN devices below Class 2, it is desirable to avoid this sort of overhead. The need for encryption can be resolved by including the identity of both parties in the exchanged signatures, resulting in the adapted STS protocol [46]. When combining the adapted STS with identities in signatures it becomes almost functionally identical to the Bellare–Canetti–Krawczyk protocol (BCK) [42,43,46]. The only difference in BCK is the absence of the sending parties' identities. According to Basin et al., it is generally desirable to include identities of both parties, to avoid the spoofing of identities [47]. But in a bidirectional exchange, as is the case for BCK, it is only required to include the receiver's identity [47]: at least in one direction, the receiving party is presented with an invalid signature that does not contain its own identity, and as a result it immediately aborts the handshake.

At this point, BCK is computationally relatively inexpensive, but still vulnerable to MITM attacks [46]. This weakness boils down to the fact that it is impossible to reliably map a public key to a specific entity, that is, to derive their public key from their identity. Any party can claim any public key as its own. To counteract, it is essential to strongly couple a public key with the respective identity. The prevalent solution for this is to introduce a PKI with certificates and trusted CAs, as proposed for TLS [48]. A certificate contains the identity and the corresponding public key. Entities can be assured of the correct coupling between key and identity, because trusted CAs had constructed the certificate. However, BCK itself does not suit the given requirement of Class 1 devices, but can be used as a baseline, as justified in the upcoming section.

13.4.2 BCK WITH PRESHARED KEYS FOR TINYTO

Badra et al. have outlined that PSK is suitable to provide authentication [49], while requiring only a small amount of computational power and memory. Thus, it is selected for TinyTO to verify the identity of an entity. The distribution of PSKs is simple in the context of WSN devices: Adding a unique PSK to the programming procedure introduces practically no overhead because nodes need to be programmed before deployment in any case, and the key generation and management can be moved to the software programming the nodes. Compared to approaches where every node is equipped with a set of keys for encryption between peers before deployment, TinyTO assumes that every node has only one PSK, solely for authentication toward the gateway. The developed handshake for TinyTO compares to BCK, with preshared keys that form master keys for an initial authentication between the node and the gateway. Fig. 13.2 illustrates the resulting handshake, where Alice and Bob can represent any one of the following device types in the WSN:

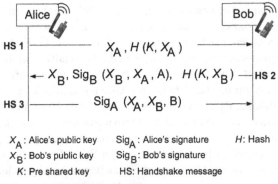

FIGURE 13.2 Extended BCK Protocol With PSK for TinyTO

- A *collector* is a device-collecting sensor, which forward them directly to the next device within communication range.
- An *aggregator* works with the data received, either as aggregating several messages into one large message, or preprocessing data (e.g., average, max, min calculation of values) before forwarding them to the next device within communication range.
- The *gateway* defines the gate to the world, connecting the WSN to other applications in the IoT domain.

Under the assumption that only the two parties under investigation have knowledge of the PSK, each party can be assured that indeed the other communication party uses this PSK. It is vital not to transmit the PSK in plaintext during the authentication, in order to keep the PSK a secret between the two parties. Otherwise any attacker who picks up that message containing the PSK can use the PSK. Thus, it must be avoided to send any form of information that can (1) be used to retrieve the PSK or (2) be replayed to achieve authentication for any other entity. Traditionally, those two goals are met by transmitting a cryptographic hash digest of the PSK together with a cryptographic nonce [50]. Including a different nonce in every message makes it impossible to reuse an authentication message (e.g., replay attack). In comparison, TinyTO desires to couple a unique public key with the PSK (and, thus, the identity), which may be replayed several times, but never for another public key, which makes it very hard to recalculate the PSK by an attacker. Hence, it is possible to use the public key instead of a random nonce and to create a hash from the PSK and from this public key, that is, $H(K, X_A)$. This ensures Bob that X_A is indeed Alice's public key [51,52]. A cryptographic hash function is infeasible to be reverted, even with a partially known input (the public key is obviously publicly known). But the PSK is not recoverable [52]. At the same time, a spoofed hash digest for a different public key can be produced only with the knowledge of the PSK. To provide mutual authentication in the TinyTO protocol, those digests must be computed from both parties, with their respective public keys. To avoid transmission overhead, these digests can be included in the first and second handshake messages (HS1 and HS2 in Fig. 13.2) in order to avoid any transmission overhead by additional messages.

In accordance with the requirements for TinyTO, this approach determines the two-way authentication protocol, which includes, as the key agreement, delivering a direct and explicit key authentication [53]. Messages do not include timestamps, they are completely asymmetrical, and they cannot be used for a replay or for reflection attacks. Appropriate encryption techniques (e.g., RSA or AES) of subsequent messages are required to guarantee the forward secrecy beyond the handshake.

As explained in Section 13.3, two flexible roles—collector and aggregator—are possible for a node. The gateway, in contrast, is unique and static. Collectors and aggregators use TinyTO to establish a secure communication channel with the gateway. Aggregators introduce additional performance-overhead to TinyTO and the WSN, because the handshake is more complicated (Fig. 13.3). Also, the collectors need to switch the destination of their data stream from the gateway to the aggregator, which, in turn, needs to process the information. Therefore, the aggregator sends a presence announcement via a broadcast to collectors that redirect their streams upon receipt. Schmitt et al. stated that four conceptual steps are required for an aggregator introduction, if no authentication is required [12]. The TinyDTLS solution [14] inspired the development of TinyTO. [14] specifies four steps that must be taken in order to establish a two-way authentication, and those steps must be slightly adapted for the proposed TinyTO solution in the following manner: (1) Collectors complete their TinyTO handshake with the gateway (Fig. 13.2) and transmit data over a secure channel. (2) In turn, the aggregator can be activated, contacting the gateway immediately, and executing the TinyTO handshake, resulting in a secure channel. (3) The aggregator broadcasts its presence to collectors in range that are

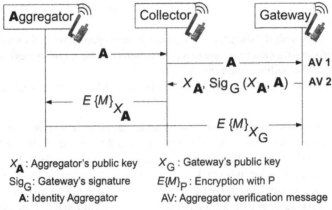

$X_\mathbf{A}$: Aggregator's public key X_G: Gateway's public key

Sig_G: Gateway's signature $E\{M\}_P$: Encryption with P

$\mathbf{A}$: Identity Aggregator   AV: Aggregator verification message

FIGURE 13.3 Secure Aggregation Support

programmed to wait for such a specific message type (e.g., simple echo request, counter, or nonce). The aggregator's public key is included in the broadcast message to avoid additional message exchanges. (4) Finally, collectors redirect their streams, encrypted with the aggregator's public key ($E\{M\}_{X_A}$), to the aggregator. The aggregator decrypts incoming streams, processes messages, encrypts the results again, and sends the new message securely to the gateway ($E\{M\}_{X_G}$) or to the next hop.

Although the previously described approach of aggregator integration provides an encryption of messages among all parties, and, therefore, a protection against eavesdropping between collectors and the aggregator as well as the aggregator and the gateway, it entails one important drawback, which we will now explain. Collectors have executed the complete TinyTO handshake with the gateway, resulting in a two-way authentication of both parties. However, in the aforementioned steps (3) and (4), collectors sacrifice all assertions about identities, if they blindly react to the aggregator's broadcasts. Attackers just need to broadcast an aggregator announcement to reach access to data streams from every collector in range that is conveniently encrypted with the attacker's own public key. Because such a situation breaks the entire security concept, collectors are requested to establish a new secure channel to aggregators, which fulfill TinyTO's design principles without blindly trusting aggregator broadcasts. Consequently, the authentication needs to be extended by an authorization: collectors need the confirmation that a broadcasting aggregator is a valid aggregator and not an intruder who is trying to access confidential information.

Assuming that collectors or aggregators communicate only with the gateway, the request for secure communication is implicitly covered by the exchange of preprogrammed PSKs. Intuitively, it is possible to preprogram aggregators and collectors with pairwise PSKs in the same way, followed by a handshake execution, including the authentication and the key exchange. But this workaround does not fulfill the flexibility requirement for TinyTO: in this case, aggregators can only aggregate data streams from predefined collectors and will further need to hold $n + 1$ PSKs for n collectors. A more flexible and less resource-demanding solution is to lever the already fully authenticated and secured channels between both aggregator and collector, and the gateway (Fig. 13.3). Upon receipt of an aggregator announcement, collectors need to check only with the fully authenticated gateway, whether the broadcast sender is an authorized aggregator. If so, the gateway can reply with the aggregator's public key, signed by his own trusted private key. This is similar to a PKI, where the gateway takes the role of the certificate authority as a trusted third party. For TinyTO it is assumed that all parties have completed previously and successfully their handshakes with the gateway. The signature is used in order to verify the mapping between the aggregator's public key and its identity, which makes spoofing attacks on the public key impossible. This stands in contrast to the previously exchanged authentication messages, where the identity of the receiving party must be included instead of the key owner's identity because the channel between gateway and collector is already authenticated. The aggregator's identity is not encrypted between the collector and the gateway, allowing for spoofing attacks on the identity because expensive computations would be required for this additional encryption. Hence, it is substituted with the identity in the signature from the next message, computed by the more powerful gateway. The gateway might reply with the public key for a spoofed identity, but it is detectable by the collector due to the invalid signature, resulting in the process' abortion.

13.4.3 HANDSHAKE IMPLEMENTATION

From now on, it is assumed that TinyTO is implemented in TinyOS, where different components are "wired" to each other and use the offered set of functionality. Thus, the TinyTO handshake is implemented in the component HandshakeHandler, which is exclusively responsible for handshake-message handling, including message composition and reply handling. HandshakeHandler is wired to components called in for cryptographic functions. The three TinyTO handshake messages HS1 to HS3 (Fig. 13.2) are implemented in a similar manner. Listing 13.1 shows a model of the structure of handshake message HS2, where *nx_uint8_t* stands for the network-serializable unsigned integer type.

The *msgType* field is used to distinguish between handshake messages and other types of control messages that are sent via the same port. *hsType* identifies different handshake messages HS1, HS2, and HS3. Furthermore, public ECC keys are broken down into *x*- and *y*-coordinates [39,41] for easy handling on the node's side. Elliptic Curve Digital Signature Algorithm (ECDSA) signatures are defined as integer key pairs, written as (r, s), and, therefore, difficult to include in a fixed-length packet, because the bit length of the hexadecimal representation of large integers may vary. Actual length detection and signature processing is not complicated, but the TinyECC library is very selective on input parameters and requires accurate length information before a signature validation. As a consequence, the signature in HS2 is encoded in the Abstract Syntax Notation One (ANS.1), inherently including length information for r and s [53].

The reply can be sent with two plain fixed-length arrays for the signatures, because the powerful gateway can handle the necessary computations to strip any padding and to encode the signature correctly. Thus, the computation time on the node is minimized. Similar to the three handshake messages, the two necessary authentication messages of the aggregator to the collectors are implemented (Fig. 13.3). The

```
// Handshake Message 2 (HS2):
typedef nx_struct to_hsm2_t{
    nx_uint8_t msgType;
    nx_uint8_t hsType; // 0x02
    nx_uint8_t public_x[24];
    nx_uint8_t public_y[24];
    nx_uint8_t digest[20];
    //variable length, ANS.1 encoded
    nx_uint8_t signature[];
} to_hsm2_t;
```

LISTING 13.1 Example of Handshake Message

aggregator's verification message 1 (AV1), sent from the collector to the gateway upon receipt of the aggregator announcement, includes *msgType*, *hsType*, and the aggregator *address*. Additionally, AV2, sent from the gateway to the collector, includes the *public agg x*, *public agg y*, and a *signature* from the previously authenticated gateway, confirming the aggregator's public key with the given address. [53]

13.5 EVALUATION

TinyTO is evaluated for memory and energy consumption, and its ability to fit those requirements of Class 1 devices. Furthermore, the performance is analyzed and the security level is compared to related work. In order to show the feasibility of TinyTO for Class 1 devices, TelosB nodes are used exclusively in a testbed for evaluation purposes. TinyOS is the operating system chosen for the current implementation. A simplified setup for the testbed is shown in Fig. 13.1, and the following situation is assumed: In Rooms A, C, and D the light is turned off and the room temperature is low. Sensors in Room B report lights being switched on and the microphone shows a high noise-level. All data collected is sent either directly (see Room B—use-case 1) or via multiple hops (see Rooms A, C, and D—use-case 2) to the gateway. Software on the gateway can analyze the data collected and sends corresponding information to other systems (e.g., climate control or room-booking system). The analysis result for Room B indicates that a conference takes place, and, thus, the climate control is activated and an entry is made in the room's calendar that Room B is currently occupied. For Rooms A, C, and D the internal room-lock system is informed that these rooms are empty and shall be locked automatically. In this example, the addressing of inconspicuous data can lead to the claim that confidential information collected allows for conclusions about room occupancy. Additionally, this introduces security risks in the application, as in the case of room information being retrieved by eavesdropping due to missing security in the communication of those sensors, an attacker can become aware of this situation and could plan for a burglary.

13.5.1 MEMORY CONSUMPTION

TinyTO's main challenge was to require only a small part of the resources available, allowing applications (e.g., TinyIPFIX [12]) to run, in addition to the security solution. The memory consumption of applications can be determined for TinyOS directly from the compiling tool, because resources are already known at the time of compilation. Deactivation of components (e.g., RPL or TinyECC optimizations) via the compiling tool or by removing components (e.g., TinyTO component or HandshakeHandler) in the code allows for a recording of the individual memory consumption of TinyTO components, shown in Table 13.2. The small memory difference between conceptually identical components (handshake and cryptography) in the collector's and aggregator's implementation originates from marginally different use-cases, as described previously and as illustrated in Fig. 13.1. For example, collectors only need to store one message at a time, but aggregators need additional memory to buffer data before that aggregation can be performed [12]. Because the memory is statically reserved, the detailed memory footprint depends on the DOA. Furthermore, collectors only need code for an encryption, whereas aggregators need code for both the decryption and the encryption. In comparison to aggregators, collectors periodically read their sensor values, which requires additional memory. Overall, this leads to a ROM consumption of 37,590 Byte purely for the collector and 33,174 Byte for aggregator applications (including data handling [12] and RPL [17,28]), as shown in Table 13.2, and yields slightly more than

Table 13.2 Memory Consumption of Components [53]

Operation	Aggregator		Collector	
	ROM (Byte)	RAM (Byte)	ROM (Byte)	RAM (Byte)
Handshake	1,636	602	1,138	612
Cryptography	11,406	406	9,378	406
TinyTO total	**13,042**	**1,018**	**10,516**	**1,018**
Data handling [12]	26,904	6,964	31,144	5,478
RPL [17,28]	6,270	498	6,228	1,498
Total	**46,216**	**8,470**	**48,114**	**7,994**

Table 13.3 Memory Consumption of TinyECC Optimizations [53]

Operation	ROM (Byte)	RAM (Byte)	Aggregator	Collector
Barrett reduction	780	114	—	—
Hybrid multiplication	12	0	X	—
Hybrid square	114	0	X	X
Secpt optimization	414	0	X	—
Projective coordinates	850	0	X	X
Sliding window	206	2350	—	—

4 kByte of additional free memory for aggregators, which can be used to enable ECC optimizations. Table 13.3 shows that optimizations have a direct impact on memory consumption and whether they are used (indicated by X) on TinyTO.

13.5.2 RUNTIME PERFORMANCE

In terms of performance, the slow microcontroller and limited memory have a high impact on all results. A message size of 116 Byte was assumed, because it is typically used for the application TinyIPFIX supported [12]. Further collectors do not need to decrypt data. For measurements performed, a timer was read before and after an operation was executed. The resolution was at 65.53 ms, allowing accurate measurements within the scope of several seconds. Table 13.4 shows the execution times for various cryptographic operations in TinyTO's aggregators and collectors. Aggregators are generally almost twice as fast as collectors, which is mainly due to more activated ECC optimizations (see Table 13.3). Liu et al. give a performance evaluation for TelosB, showing the speed for ECC operations, when all optimizations are used [22]: ECDSA signing takes only about 1.6 s (TinyTO aggregator needs about 5.14 s; TinyTO collector, about 9.28 s), and verification, about 2 s (TinyTO aggregator needs about 10.20 s; TinyTO collector, about 18.51 s). This is much faster than TinyTO, and proves the performance limitations due to the restricted memory of chosen hardware (here, TelosB).

Table 13.4 Execution Times for ECC Operations [53]

ECC Operation	Aggregator (s)	Collector (s)
EC Key Generation	4.77	8.77
SHA-1	≤0.10	≤0.10
ECDSA Sign	5.14	9.28
ECDSA Verify	10.20	18.51
ECIES Encrypt	5.98	9.41
ECIES Decrypt	4.96	—

Table 13.5 Energy Consumption of Composite Operations [53]

Operation	Time (s)	Energy (mJ)
Handshake Aggregator	20.14	85.90
Handshake Collector	36.59	154.99
Aggregator verification	18.52	78.58
Message aggregation ($DOA = 2$)	15.90	68.28

Table 13.5 shows the execution times of composite operations, including transmission times in both directions and response-calculation times. The fact that the gateway performs faster than nodes has no influence on the overall result. The value for a message aggregation with $DOA = 2$ is calculated based on two decryption operations and one encryption operation on the aggregator.

Based on those results, it is possible to determine the minimal interval t, where collectors send their encrypted messages and aggregators can still catch up with incoming packets. Once the handshake is executed, collectors send data after $t = 9.41$ s, which is the minimal time needed for encryption, even if data is immediately available. Assuming sufficient memory on an aggregator's device is available for caching packets of degree DOA—plus an aggregate computation—an aggregator requires $t = DOA * 4.96$ s + 5.89 s to decrypt incoming messages of the degree DOA and to encrypt the aggregate. For $DOA = 2$, the aggregator needs $t = 15.81$ s. This equation does hold for a small degree of aggregation and small networks (e.g., 20 nodes). The formula for t must be adapted with the required time for ECIES encryption and decryption, if the aggregator: (1) is more powerful, (2) can support a greater degree of aggregation, and (3) can perform faster operations, and if the network becomes larger.

13.5.3 ENERGY CONSUMPTION

WSN devices are usually battery-powered and depend on the deployment, which makes an exchange not very easy. Hence, TinyTO must be energy efficient to avoid a fast battery depletion. TelosB nodes in the testbed are powered by two off-the-shelf batteries, each with a capacity of 2000 mAh and voltage of 1.5 V, in total delivering $U = 3.0$ V. Wireless data transmissions and computations in the microcontroller show the largest impact on energy consumption. Auxiliary components, such as LEDs or serial connectors, are not taken into consideration, as they are typically deactivated during a final deployment.

TelosB nodes are equipped with a CC2420 RF chip on the IEEE 802.15.4 2.4 GHz band [54], which has a maximum output power of −25 to 0 dBm for data transmissions [13]. Assuming 0 dBm, the current draw for sending (Tx) is at $I_{Tx} = 17.4$ mA and at $I_{Rx} = 19.7$ mA for receiving (Rx) [55,56]. The theoretical transmission rate of the CC2420 is at 250 kbps, but some practical measurements are as low as 180 kbps. For the purposes of the calculation being as close to reality as possible, it can be assumed that the full transmission rate R is never actually reached, and $R = 220 ± 20$ kbps. Knowing the transmission rate and implementation details of messages (see Section 13.4) allows for the calculation of the transmission time for each message and the total energy consumption ER as follows: ER depends on the message size S for a given voltage, a current draw, and a transmission rate, resulting in $ER(S) = U * I * S$. In particular, this concerns the data handling with TinyIPFIX [12], the three handshake messages (HS1 to HS3), and the aggregator verification (AV1 and AV2) [53]. In comparison to ECC operations, TinyIPFIX operations are almost instantaneous and negligible in the light of the overall energy consumption of TinyTO. Furthermore, messages as outlines in the handshake design consider only the size of individual data fields in an unencrypted message (see Section 13.4). In reality, the packets transmitted are much larger than supported by IEEE 802.15.4 on the MAC layer (102 Byte out of the total frame size of 127 Byte [54]). Hence, packet fragmentation support for TinyTO is essential. Because 12 Byte are used by TinyOS and the cyclic redundancy check (CRC) for error detection is added, 90 Byte remain for the actual payload in every message on the MAC layer.

TinyTO handshake messages are not transmitted as plaintext, but in larger Elliptic Curve Integrated Encryption Scheme (ECIES) cipher texts, requiring 69 Byte [1 Byte to indicate the point compression type, 24 Byte for each Elliptic Curve (EC) point component, and 20 Byte for the message authentication more than the pure message size]. For example, an HS1 message has a size of 70 Byte and a size of 139 Byte after encryption with ECIES. Given the maximum payload size of 90 Byte, HS1 is fragmented to fit into MAC layer packets. Every fragment requires additional headers and other fields (e.g., fragment number and header field indicating fragmentation). Thus, the effective data size DS, which is transmitted to convey a payload of size $ps = 139$ Byte, is calculated as $DS = ps + \lceil ps/90 \text{ Byte} \rceil * 37 \text{ Byte} = 213$ Byte. Table 13.6 shows the results of these considerations for different message types and the energy consumption for their transmissions. It can be stated that the energy consumption for HS2 is the highest, with 6.34 mJ, compared to HS1 and HS3, due to its enormous message size of 189 Byte. If a message size is approximately 100 Byte then the energy-consumption levels are around 0.3 mJ.

Table 13.6 Energy Consumption of the Radio Transmission [53]

Message	ps (Byte)	DS (Byte)	Time (ms)	Energy (mJ)
HS 1 (Tx)	139	223	8.11	0.42
HS 2 (Tx)	189	300	10.91	0.64
HS 3 (Tx)	114	203	7.38	0.38
AV 1 (Tx)	82	171	6.22	0.32
AV 2 (Tx)	168	242	8.80	0.52

Table 13.7 Energy Consumption of Cryptographic Operations [53]

Operation	Aggregator		Collector	
	Time (s)	Energy (mJ)	Time (s)	Energy (mJ)
EC Key Generation	4.77	20.03	8.77	36.83
ECDSA Sign	5.14	21.59	9.28	38.98
ECDSA Verify	10.20	42.84	18.51	77.74
ECIES Encrypt	5.98	25.12	9.41	39.52
ECIES Decrypt	4.96	20.83	—	—

Similarly to energy calculations for radio transmissions, the energy consumption of the microcontroller (MSP430F1611 16-bit Ultra-Low-Power Micro-Controller Unit (MCU) from Texas Instruments [57]) for different cryptographic operations can be calculated. The current draw in active mode (i.e., only MCU and no radio transmissions) is given as 1.8 mA [55,58]. However, experimental measurements show that the relevant difference between idle and a fully utilized MCU is only at $I_{AM} = 1.4$ mA. The formula used to calculate the energy consumption E_{MCU} of the MCU, depending on the computation time t subsequently, is $E_{MCU}(t) = U * I_{AM} * t$. As shown in Table 13.7, the energy consumption differs for the aggregator and the collector, due to different activations of these ECC optimizations. Given the cost of a radio transmission (see Table 13.6) and the computation of single cryptographic operations (see Table 13.7), the energy consumption for the entire handshake, and similarly for more complex sequences of operations, can be calculated. According to the design shown in Fig. 13.2, the handshake requires six operations: EC Key Generation, sending of HS 1, reception of HS 2, ECDSA signature verification, ECDSA signature signing, and sending of HS 3. Similarly, the verification of an aggregator needs three operations (see Fig. 13.3): sending of the aggregator's identity in AV1, the reception of the signed message containing the public key in AV2, and an ECDSA signature verification. Aggregation with $DOA = 2$ requires a combination of the reception of two data packets, including data collected, two times an ECIES decryption, the ECIES encryption, and the sending of one aggregated data packet. Table 13.5 shows the corresponding times and energy consumptions.

The battery-powered TelosB requires a minimal voltage of 1.8 V [13], meaning a battery cannot be depleted to an energy level below 60% of the original charge, otherwise the voltage will drop below that threshold. Thus, it can be calculated that 12.96 kJ are available in one set of batteries. Measurements show that TelosB nodes draw on average of 70.7 mA, while remaining idle when no sleep modes for MCU and radio are activated. Thus, the expected runtime without any application is about 12.96 kJ = 61,103 s, or roughly 16 h and 58 min for one 3 V * 70.7 mA set of batteries. If collectors are programmed to collect, encrypt, and send data in the format proposed by [12], then every interval t, the impact on the runtime of collectors, and their aggregators can be calculated accordingly. Assuming every tenth transmission contains the TinyIPFIX template (only metainformation) instead of a TinyIPFIX record (data values) and an aggregation with $DOA = 2$ is performed [12], the same batteries will last for 16 h and 53 min in aggregators (which compares to a reduction of 0.5% or 5 min) and 16 h and 55 min in collectors (reduction of 0.3% or 3 min), given $t = 1$ min^{-1}.

13.6 SUMMARY

In this chapter, a new handshake for two-way authentication and key-exchange has been introduced, which provides end-to-end security for Class 1 devices in the IoT domain. The newly developed protocol TinyTO is based on the Bellare–Canetti–Krawczyk protocol, with an additional PSK extension for secure authentication. In order to match major resource constraints, TinyTO applies energy-efficient ECC operations for cryptographic functions and uses preshared master keys (with a length of 16 Byte) for an authentication toward the gateway only. Furthermore, TinyTO supports secure data aggregations with a small overhead, which is the key for today's IoT applications. Transferring TinyTO to more resourceful devices will enhance performance, because additional ECC optimizations can be activated and the responsiveness of the network will increase. Finally, the maximum degree of aggregations can be increased in these cases, as more memory for buffering data will be available.

ACKNOWLEDGMENTS

This work was partially supported by the FLAMINGO [59] and the SmartenIT [60] projects, funded by the EU FP7 Program under Contract No. FP7-2012-ICT-318488 and No. FP7-2012-ICT-317846, respectively.

This chapter's content is based on the Master Thesis [53] performed at the Communication Systems Group of the University of Zurich, Switzerland.

REFERENCES

[1] Atzori L, Iera A, Morabito G. The Internet of Things: a survey. Comput Netw, Elsevier, Atlanta, GA, USA. 2010;54:2787–805.
[2] Alcaraz C, Najera P, Lopez J, Roman R. Wireless sensor networks and the Internet of Things: do we need a complete integration? In: Proceedings of the first international workshop on the Security of the Internet of Things (SecIoT). Tokyo, Japan; 2010. p. 1–8.
[3] Akyildiz I, Su W, Sankarasubramaniam Y, Cayirci E. Wireless sensor networks: a survey. Comput Netw, Elsevier, Atlanta, GA, USA. 2002;38(4):393–422.
[4] Perrig A, Stankovic J, Wagner D. Security in wireless sensor networks. Commun ACM 2004;47(No. 6):53–57.
[5] Hausmann S. Internet of Things—a risk-reward proposition for security professionals, SecurityInfoWatch, [Online] http://www.securityinfowatch.com/article/11714106/navigating-security-threats-posed-by-internet-of-things-technology; 2014.
[6] Weber R. H. Internet of Things—new security and privacy challenges. Comput Law Secur Rev, Elsevier, Atlanta, GA, USA. 2010;26(No. 1):23–30.
[7] Medaglia C, Serbanati A. An overview of privacy and security issues in the Internet of Things. The Internet of Things, Giusto D, Iera A, Morabito G, and Atzori L (Eds.). New York, NY, USA: Springer; 2010. p. 389–395.
[8] Rescorla E. SSL and TLS: building and designing secure systems. Amsterdam, The Netherlands: Addison-Wesley Longman; 2000.
[9] Schmeh K. Kryptografie: Verfahren - Protokolle - Infrastrukturen, vol. 5. Heidelberg, Germany: dpunkt.verlag GmbH; 2013.
[10] Katz J, Lindell Y. Introduction to modern cryptography, vol. 2. Boca Raton, FL, USA: CRC Press; 2014.
[11] Bormann C, Ersue M, Keranen A. Terminology for constrained-node networks, RFC 7228, IETF, Internet Engineering Task Force, Fermont, CA, USA, [Online] http://www.ietf.org/rfc/rfc7228.txt; 2014.

[12] Schmitt C, Kothmayr T, Ertl B, Hu W, Braun L, Carle G. TinyIPFIX: an efficient application protocol for data exchange cyber physical systems. J Comput Commun, Elsevier, Atlanta, GA, USA, 2016;74(2):63–76 DOI: 10.1016/j.comcom.2014.05.012, January 2016.

[13] Advantic Sistemas y Servicios S.L. TelosB CM5000-SMA, [Online] http://www.advanticsys.com/shop/mtmcm5000sma-p-23.html; 2016.

[14] Kothmayr T, Schmitt C, Hu W, Brünig M, Carle G. DTLS-based security and two-way authentication for the Internet of Things. Ad Hoc Netw., Elsevier, Atlanta, GA, USA. 2013;11(No. 8):2710–2723.

[15] Shelby Z, Hartke K, Bormann C. The constraint application protocol (CoAP), RFC 7252, IETF, Internet Engineering Task Force; 2014, Fermont, CA, USA, [Online] http://www.ietf.org/rfc/rfc7252.txt; 2014.

[16] TinyOS: BLIP tutorial [Online]. http://tinyos.stanford.edu/tinyos-wiki/index.php/BLIP_Tutorial; 2016.

[17] Ko J. G., Dawson-Haggerty S, Culler D. E., Hui J. W., Levis P. Connecting low-power and lossy networks to the Internet. IEEE Communications Magazine, New York, NY, USA, vol. 49, No. 4. New York, NY; 2011. p. 96–101.

[18] Du W, Wang R, Ning P. An efficient scheme for authenticating public keys in sensor networks. In: Sixth ACM international symposium on mobile ad hoc networking and computing (MobiHoc). Urbana-Champaign, IL, USA; 2005. p. 58–67.

[19] Devanbu P, Gertz M, Martel C, Stubblebine S. G. Authentic third-party data publication. Data and application security, Thuraisingham B, van de Riet R, Dittrich K, and Tari Z, (Eds.). vol. 73. New York, NY, USA: Springer; 2001. p. 101–12.

[20] Chang Q, Zhang Y. P., Qin L. L. A node authentication protocol based on ECC in WSN. In: Proceedings of the 2010 international conference on computer design and applications (ICCDA). Qinhuangdao, Hebei, China; 2010. p. 606–609.

[21] Jeong Y. S., Lee S. H. Hybrid key establishment protocol based on ECC for wireless sensor network. Ubiquitous intelligence and computing. Lecture notes in computer science, vol. 4611. Heidelberg, Germany: Springer; 2007. p. 1233–1242.

[22] Liu Y, Li J, Guizani M. PKC based broadcast authentication using signature amortization for WSNs. IEEE Trans Wireless Commun, New York, NY, USA: 2012;11(6):2106–15.

[23] Barker E. B., Barker W. C., Burr W. E., Polk W. T., Smid M. E. Recommendation for key management, Part 1: general (revised). SP 800-57. Gaithersburg, MD, USA: National Institute of Standards and Technology (NIST); 2007.

[24] Nie P, Vähä-Herttua J, Aura T, Gurtov A. Performance analysis of HIP diet exchange for WSN security establishment. In: Seventh ACM symposium on QoS and security for wireless and mobile networks (Q2SWinet). Miami, FL, USA; 2011. p. 51–56.

[25] Porambage P, Schmitt C, Kumar P, Gurtov A, Ylianttila M. PAuthKey: a pervasive authentication protocol and key establishment scheme for wireless sensor networks in distributed IoT applications. Int J Distr Sens Netw, New York, NY, USA, 2014;2014:1–14.

[26] Westhoff D, Girao J, Sarma A. Security solutions for wireless sensor networks. NEC J Adv Technol, vol. 1, no. 3/2016, pp. 106–111.

[27] Weimerskirch A, Westhoff D. Zero common-knowledge authentication for pervasive networks. Selected areas in cryptography. Lecture Notes in Computer Science (LNCS), vol. 3006. Heidelberg, Germany: Springer; 2004. p. 73–87.

[28] Winter T, Thubert P, Brandt A, Hui J, Kelsey R, Levis P, Pister K, Struik R, Vasseur JP, Alexander R. RPL: IPv6 routing protocol for low-power and lossy networks, RFC 6550, IETF, Internet Engineering Task Force, Fermont, CA, USA, [Online] https://tools.ietf.org/html/rfc6550; 2012.

[29] Saleh M, Al Khatib I. Throughput analysis of WEP security in ad hoc sensor networks. In: Proceedings of the second international conference on innovations in information technology. Dubai, United Arab Emirates; 2005. p. 26–28.

[30] Hu W, Tan H, Corke P, Shih W, Jha S. Toward trusted wireless sensor networks. ACM Trans Sensor Netw, New York, NY, USA, 2010;7(1),5:1–5:25.

[31] Linn J. Privacy enhancement for Internet electronic mail: part I: message encryption and authentication procedures, RFC 1421, IETF, Internet Engineering Task Force, Fermont, CA, USA, [Online] http://www.ietf.org/rfc/rfc1421.txt; 1993.

[32] Wander A, Gura N, Eberle H, Gupta V, Shantz S. Energy analysis of public-key cryptography for wireless sensor networks. In: Proceedings of the third international conference on pervasive computing and communications. New York, NY, USA; 2005. p. 324–328.

[33] Gura N, Patel A, Wander A, Eberle H, Shantz S. Comparing elliptic curve cryptography and RSA on 8-bit CPUs. Cryptographic hardware and embedded systems. Lecture Notes in Computer Science (LNCS), vol. 3156. Heidelberg, Germany: Springer; 2004. p. 119–132.

[34] Xiaojiang D, Hsiao-Hwa C. Security in wireless sensor networks. IEEE Wireless Commun, New York, NY, USA, 2008;15(4):60–66.

[35] Karlof C, Wagner D. Secure routing in wireless sensor networks: attacks and countermeasures. Ad Hoc Netw, Elsevier, Atlanta, GA, USA, 2003;1(2):293–315.

[36] Stoneburner G. Underlying technical models for information technology security, Tech. Rep. SP 800-33. Washington, DC, USA: National Institute of Standards and Technology (NIST), Washington, DC, USA, [Online] http://csrc.nist.gov/publications/nistpubs/800-33/sp800-33.pdf; 2001.

[37] Balakrishnan H, Padmanabhan V, Seshan S, Katz R. A comparison of mechanisms for improving TCP performance over wireless links. IEEE/ACM Trans Netw, New York, NY, USA, 1997;6(5):756–769.

[38] Menezes A, Van Oorschot P, Vanstone S. Handbook of applied cryptography. Boca Raton, FL, USA: CRC Press; 2010.

[39] Diffie W, Van Oorschot P, Wiener M. Authentication and authenticated key exchanges. Design Code Cryptogr, Springer, Heidelberg, Germany, 1992;2(No. 2):107–125.

[40] Canetti R, Krawczyk H. Analysis of key-exchange protocols and their use for building secure channels. Advances in cryptology—EUROCRYPT. Lecture Notes in Computer Science (LNCS), vol. 2139. Heidelberg, Germany: Springer; 2001. p. 453–474.

[41] Delfs H, Knebl H. Introduction to cryptography: principles and applications. Information security and cryptography. Heidelberg, Germany: Springer; 2007.

[42] Bellare M, Canetti R, Krawczyk H. A modular approach to the design and analysis of authentication and key exchange protocols (extended abstract). In: 13th annual ACM symposium on theory of computing (STOC). Dallas, TX, USA; 1998. p. 419–428.

[43] Blake-Wilson S, Menezes A. Authenticated Diffie–Hellman key agreement protocols. Selected areas in cryptography. London, UK: Springer; 1999. p. 339–361.

[44] LaMacchia B, Lauter K, Mityagin A. Stronger security of authenticated key exchange. Provable security. Lecture Notes in Computer Science (LNCS), vol. 4784. Heidelberg, Germany: Springer; 2007. p. 1–16.

[45] Blake-Wilson S, Johnson D, Menezes A. Key agreement protocols and their security analysis. Cryptography and coding. Lecture Notes in Computer Science (LNCS), vol. 1355. Heidelberg, Germany: Springer; 1997. p. 30–45.

[46] Boyd C, Mathuria A. Protocols for authentication and key establishment. Information security and cryptography. Berlin, Heidelberg, Germany: Springer; 2010.

[47] Basin D, Cremers C, Meier S. Provably repairing the ISO/IEC 9798 standard for entity authentication. Principles of security and trust. Lecture Notes in Computer Science (LNCS), vol. 7215. Heidelberg, Germany: Springer; 2012. p. 129–148.

[48] Boeyen S, Howes T, Richard P. Internet X.509 public key infrastructure operational protocols—LDAPv2, RFC 2559, IETF, Internet Engineering Task Force, Fermont, CA, USA, [Online] http://www.ietf.org/rfc/rfc2559.txt; 1999.

[49] Badra M, Hajjeh I. Key-exchange authentication using shared secrets. IEEE Comput J 2006;39(3):58–66.

[50] Franks J, Hallam-Baker P, Hostetler J, Lawrence S, Leach P, Luotonen A, Stewart L. HTTP authentication: basic and digest access authentication, RFC 2617, IETF, Internet Engineering Task Force, Fermont, CA, USA, [Online] http://www.ietf.org/rfc/rfc2617.txt; 1999.

[51] Preneel B. Analysis and design of cryptographic hash functions. PhD Thesis, KU Leuven, Leuven, The Netherlands, [Online] http://homes.esat.kuleuven.be/~preneel/phd_preneel_feb1993.pdf; 1993.

[52] Rogaway P, Shrimpton T. Cryptographic hash-function basics: definitions, implications, and separations for preimage resistance, second preimage resistance, and collision resistance. Fast software encryption. Lecture Notes in Computer Science (LNCS), vol. 3329. Heidelberg, Germany: Springer; 2004. p. 371–388.

[53] Noack M. Optimization of two-way authentication protocol in Internet of Things. Master thesis, University of Zurich, Communication Systems Group, Department of Informatics, Zurich, Switzerland, [Online] https://files.ifi.uzh.ch/CSG/staff/schmitt/Extern/Theses/Martin_Noack_MA.pdf; 2014.

[54] Texas Instruments: 2.4 GHz IEEE 802.15.4/ZigBee-ready RF transceiver, [Online] http://www.ti.com/lit/ds/symlink/cc2420.pdf; 2016.

[55] Nguyen H. A., Forster A, Puccinelli D, Giordano S. Sensor node lifetime: an experimental study. In: Proceedings of the 2011 IEEE international conference on pervasive computing and communications workshops (PERCOM). New York, NY, USA; 2011. p. 202–207.

[56] Sadler C, Martonosi M. Data compression algorithms for energy-constrained devices in delay tolerant networks. In: Proceedings of the fourth international conference on embedded networked sensor systems (SenSys). New York, NY, USA: ACM; 2006. p. 265–278.

[57] Texas Instruments: MSP430F161x mixed signal microcontroller datasheet. http://www.ti.com/lit/ds/symlink/msp430f1611.pdf; 2016.

[58] Polastre J, Szewczyk R, Culler D. Telos: enabling ultra-low power wireless research. In: Proceedings of fourth international symposium on information processing in sensor networks (IPSN). Piscataway, NJ, USA: IEEE Press; 2005. p. 364–369.

[59] FLAMINGO consortium. FLAMINGO: Management of the Future Internet, [Online] http://www.fp7-flamingo.eu/; 2015.

[60] SmartenIT consortium. SmartenIT: Socially-aware Management of New Overlay Application Traffic combined with Energy Efficiency in the Internet, [Online] http://www.smartenit.eu/; 2015.

OBFUSCATION AND DIVERSIFICATION FOR SECURING THE INTERNET OF THINGS (IoT)

S. Hosseinzadeh, S. Hyrynsalmi, V. Leppänen

Department of Information Technology, University of Turku, Finland

14.1 INTRODUCTION

Information sharing in Internet of Things (IoT) is the element that makes the cooperation of the devices feasible, but on the other hand, it raises concerns about the security of the collected data and the privacy of the users. Some of the collected data contain (sensitive) personal and business information about the users. Therefore, it is highly significant to appropriately protect this data while it is stored and transmitted.

Nonetheless, the IoT service providers principally are tackling the availability and interoperability of the IoT services, so the security of the devices and services has never been the main focus. A report by [1] claims that nearly 70% of the devices participating in IoT are vulnerable to security exploits, which make the network prone to security attacks. Therefore, there should be effective techniques to protect these devices and the shared information over the network, in order to ensure the liability of the system in addition to the availability of it.

Due to the fact that IoT is based on the Internet, it is subject to the traditional security threats existing for the Internet. The dynamic nature of the IoT environment, along with the heterogeneity and large scale of devices, make the traditional security issues more critical and also present new security challenges. Additionally, devices in IoT are exceedingly constrained in capacity and computational power. Hence, the security measure considered is required to be lightweight, to be tolerable by the devices, and to be compatible with the limitations of the participating nodes in IoT.

To the best of our knowledge, there is no research existing that studies the security of IoT through the potential techniques of obfuscation and diversification. In this chapter, we propose two novel approaches to address the security threats in IoT based on these two promising techniques. Obfuscation and diversification have been successful in mitigating the risk of malware in various domains [2]. We propose: (1) applying the two techniques, obfuscation and diversification, for protecting the operating systems and APIs of the IoT devices, and (2) applying the two techniques on the communication protocols among the devices.

This chapter is structured as follows: Section 14.2 discusses the characteristics and security challenges in IoT. Considering the fact that our proposal focuses on securing the operating systems related to the sensors and devices participating in the IoT and their access protocols, we study different types of operating systems (in Section 14.2.1) and the access protocols (in Section 14.2.2), designed and used in

IoT. We continue by discussing the security challenges in IoT that need to be tackled. In Section 14.3, we introduce the terms and techniques, obfuscation and diversification, that our proposed ideas are based on. We discuss how these techniques have been used to protect operating systems and software in other environments. In Section 14.4, we present our proposed techniques in detail, our motivations behind our ideas, the limitations, and the possible drawbacks of the proposed techniques. Section 14.5 considers applying IoT-related software diversification in different use-case scenarios from the viewpoint of various stakeholders and discusses the validity considerations. Finally, "Conclusions and Future Work" come in Section 14.6.

14.2 DISTINGUISHING CHARACTERISTICS OF IoT
14.2.1 OPERATING SYSTEMS AND SOFTWARE IN IoT

IoT is made up of a wide variety of heterogeneous components, including sensors, devices, and actuators. Some of these components are supplied by more powerful 32-bit processors (eg, PCs and smartphones), whereas some others are equipped with only lightweight 8-bit micro-controllers [2]. On that account, the chosen software should be compatible with all ranges of devices, including the low-powered ones. Moreover, the software should not only be able to support the functionality of the devices, but also should be compatible with the limitation of the participating nodes of this network, in terms of computational power, memory, and energy capacity [3]. Baccelli et al. [2] discuss that the following items are the generic prerequisites of software running on IoT devices:

- *Heterogeneous hardware constraints*: The chosen software for IoT should require a fairly low amount of memory, and operate with low complexity, so that the IoT devices with limited memory and computational power would be able to support the operations. Additionally, due to the variety of the hardware in IoT, the software should be able to support a wide range of hardware platforms, including the constrained ones.
- *Programmability*: From the development point of view, the chosen software should provide a standard application-program interface (API), and should also support the standard programming languages. For example, the operating system should make C and C++ available, as high-level languages, for the application developers.
- *Autonomy*: For energy efficiency means, (1) the software should allow sleep cycles for saving energy when the hardware is in the idle mode; (2) the network stack should be adaptive to the constrained characteristic of the devices in IoT, and also should allow the protocols to be replaced at each layer; and (3) the chosen software should be sufficiently robust and reliable.

These factors motivated the developers to construct generic software and operating systems that are compatible with all ranges of devices in IoT that have diverse capacities and capabilities. This means that the software, on one hand, is capable of leveraging the capabilities of the more powerful devices, and, on the other hand, can run on the power-restricted devices. Table 14.1 lists some of the embedded operating systems that are designed to meet the requirements of the heterogeneous constrained nodes (sensors and devices) in this network [4].

Among all, Contiki [6] and TinyOS [7] are the most commonly used operating systems for IoT devices [5]. *Contiki* [8] is an open-source operating system developed in C programming language and designed to operate on low-power memory-restricted devices. Contiki is considered to be a lightweight

Table 14.1 Operating Systems for Embedded Systems

Operating System	Overview	Characteristics	Language	Open Source
Contiki	An open-source multitasking OS designed for wireless sensor network (WSN) and memory-efficient embedded systems network.	Modular structure, multithreading, event-driven.	C	✓
TinyOS	An open-source OS, intended for the low-power wireless devices	Monolithic structure, multithreading, event-driven, support for TOS threads.	NesC	✓
RIOT OS	Real time	Modular structure, multithreading	C and C++	✓
Mantis	An open-source operating system designed for WSN. It presents C API with Linux and Windows development environments.	Threads	C	✓
Nano-RK	This OS has a lightweight embedded resource kernel (RK) and networking support to be used in WSN.	Threads	C	✗
LiteOS	An open-source UNIX-like OS for WSN	Threads and events	LiteC++	✓
FreeRTOS	A real-time OS designed for embedded devices		C	✗
Linux		Monolithic structure, event-driven	C and C++	✓

operating system and reasonably memory efficient, requiring only a few kilobytes of memory [8]. By supporting various networking standards, such as IPV4, IPV6, and CoAP, it connects the low-power microcontrollers to the Internet. For energy efficiency means, it has a set of mechanisms that enables the system to run in a lower-power mode, which consumes less power but is still able to send and receive messages. For memory-efficiency purposes its design is based on a protothreads model, which is a combination of a multithreading and event-driven approach. Protothreads provide blocking event-handlers. Therefore, this demonstrates that multithreading does not always have to be on the kernel's lowest levels, but can be at the application library on top of the event-driven kernel. Moreover, Contiki has a dynamic nature, that is, it allows the dynamic loading and unloading of applications at runtime.

TinyOS [7] is an open-source operating system developed in nesC [9], which is an extension of the C language. Similar to Contiki, TinyOS is multithreading and event-driven, and it is designed according to a component-based programming model and monolithic structure. TinyOS is specifically designed for the devices distributed in the sensor networks with limited resources, for example, 512 bytes of RAM and 8 Kbytes of program memory.

14.2.2 IoT NETWORK STACK AND ACCESS PROTOCOLS

IoT is built up of a large number of objects, including sensors, devices, and applications, connected to one another. There are three different types of links for connecting these objects to each other [5,10]:

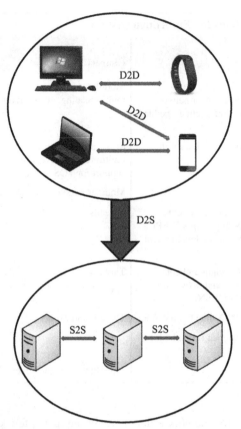

FIGURE 14.1 Communication Links

There are three different types of communication links among the different components of IoT. (A) *D2D*, device to device; (B) *D2S*, device to server; (C) *S2S*, server to server.

Adapted from Ref. [12].

(1) device-to-device (D2D), which is the connection between the devices; (2) device-to-server (D2S), which is the connection between the devices and the servers, and (3) server-to-server (S2S), which is the connection between different servers to share collected data (see Fig. 14.1). For making the connections feasible, various communication protocols are employed.

Considering the TCP/IP as the de facto standard for the communication networks, some are in the opinion that it could be used also for IoT in the future, to provide flexible IP based architecture. Currently, the low capacity of the resource-constrained devices makes it challenging to deploy IPv6 in IoT and in Low power and Lossy Networks (LLNs). LLNs are types of networks in which both routers and nodes are constrained in terms of memory, energy, and processing power. These networks are characterized as being unstable, having a high rate of loss, and having a low data-rate [11]. On that account, the Internet Engineering Task Force (IETF) has presented protocols adaptable to this environment, such as Constrained Application Protocol (CoAP) [12] and IPv6 Routing Protocol for Low power and Lossy

Networks (RPL) [11]. With the help of these standard protocols, the normal IP-based devices (eg, PCs and smartphones) can connect to the sensor devices [13]. The developed protocols are designed in accordance with the requirements and characteristics of IoT. Users select the proper set of protocols based on the requirements of their applications. Due to the fact that components in IoT utilize various protocols to communicate to the network (eg, CoAP, MQTT, DDS, XMPP), to enable them to communicate to each other the protocols need to be translated to a standard protocol through XML, JSON, or RESTful APIs. These standard protocols support the scalability, interoperability, and the low power and lossy behavior of the nodes in IoT. The scalability deals with the issues of adding an extra node to the network, and interoperability ensures that the devices in IoT are able to communicate with each other [14].

Fig. 14.2 depicts the network stack that is currently used in IoT, with some examples of the communication protocols at each layer.

The following are the most commonly used protocols:

- CoAP [12] is an application-layer protocol that is built on UDP and is used in resource-constrained nodes. As HTTP is fairly complex for the LLNs, CoAP is proposed as a web-transfer protocol, which is simply translated to HTTP and simplifies the integration with the Web. Due to the fact that CoAP is designed over UDP and not TCP, the common SSL/TLS cannot be used for providing security. For this purpose, Datagram Transport Layer Security (DTLS) is available to provide the same services as TLS.
- User Datagram Protocol (UDP) and Transmission Control Protocol (TCP) are the protocols that are used on the Internet. TCP has proven to be quite complex for the LLNs. Thus, UDP is the most common protocol used at this layer for the LLNs [4].
- On the traditional Internet IP diagram, IPv4 and IPv6 are used for controlling the messaging at the network layer. In IoT architecture, in order to allow IPv6 packets to be transmitted over IEEE 802.15.4-based networks, 6LoWPAN [15] comes as an adaptation layer between the link layer and the network layer. It presents packet fragmentation and header compression to decrease the datagram size [4].
- RPL is a routing protocol standardized for the LLNs. It supports the traffic flow between the devices of a network (point-to-point), the devices and a central node (multipoint-to-point), and the central node with devices (point-to-multipoint) [11].
- The MAC/PHY layers that had been traditionally used on the Internet (eg, WiFi and Ethernet) typically had high bandwidth and required high power, which made them incompatible for IoT.

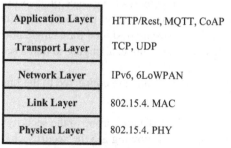

FIGURE 14.2 IoT Network Stack and Some of the Communication Protocols Used at Each Layer

IEEE 802.15.4 is the standard that is mainly used for IoT to specify the MAC layer and the physical layer. It has lower bandwidth that supports smaller packet size [16].

- Message Queue Telemetry Transport (MQTT) [17] is a publish/subscribe messaging protocol for communicating the collected data from the devices to the servers (D2S). MQTT is considered to be a many-to-many protocol that passes the messages from one client to another through a central broker. MQTT is designed on top of the TCP/IP, so the connection could be encrypted with SSL/TLS.
- Extensible Messaging and Presence Protocol (XMPP) [18] is a protocol to connect the devices and their users to the server (D2S). It is based on XML (Extensible Markup Language) and provides services for instant messaging and presence functionality.
- Data Distribution Service (DDS) [19] is a fast bus for connecting the publisher to the subscriber (D2D) in real-time systems. It is known as interoperable, dependable, scalable, and having high performance.
- Advanced Message Queuing Protocol (AMQP) [20] is an application-layer protocol with features of flexible routing and a queuing system for connecting one server to another (S2S). It can reuse the underlying transport models, such as TCP/IP and UDP [21].

In the following, we will discuss the security and privacy aspects of IoT devices and networks.

14.2.3 SECURITY AND PRIVACY IN IoT

Considering the fact that IoT is founded on the Internet, it is susceptible to the traditional security attacks threatening the Internet. Furthermore, the key characteristics of IoT not only make the traditional security challenges more severe, but they also introduce new challenges. The characteristics are [22]:

- *Heterogeneity:* IoT embraces a diverse set of devices with different capabilities that communicate with each other. An extremely constrained device should open up a secure communication channel with a more powerful device, for example, a smartphone. Therefore, the security mechanism used (such as a cryptography approach or key management scheme) needs to be compatible with both communicating parties.
- *Low capacity:* The devices in IoT are fairly limited in terms of computational power, memory, and battery capacity, which make them unable to handle complex security schemes.
- *Scale:* The number of participating nodes in IoT is exceedingly growing, which makes it harder to control the collected data.
- *Wireless connection:* Devices connect to the Internet through various wireless links (eg, ZigBee, Bluetooth). The wireless connection increases the chance of eavesdropping. Thus, the links need to be secured so that the intruders cannot intercept the communication.
- *Embedded use:* most of the IoT devices are designed for a single purpose with different communication patterns. This makes it quite challenging to find a security scheme compatible with these varied patterns.
- *Mobility:* The devices in IoT are mobile and are connected to the Internet through various providers.

The aforementioned properties make IoT more prone to the security threats compared to the Internet and traditional sensor networks. The following are the security challenges in IoT that need to be tackled [23]:

The tiny sensors and devices of IoT are typically unable to handle the traditional *authentication and authorization* techniques. Furthermore, the existing authentication mechanisms proposed previously for the sensor networks assume that sensors are part of a network that connect to the Internet through a central gateway; however, the idea in IoT is that the nodes connect to the Internet directly. This makes the authentication more challenging, as the nodes need to be authenticated individually. *Communication security* is an important factor in any communication network to ensure the integrity of the transmitted data and to guarantee that the data will not fall into the wrong hands. Cryptography is a successful technique always used for securing the communication; however, typical cryptographic algorithms take up a high amount of computational power and bandwidth.

The programming bugs caused by the developers at the development stage cause software *vulnerabilities*. Software vulnerabilities, if exposed, can result in security attacks. Program analysis is a way of discovering these vulnerabilities before the software is released, which, however, requires computing power that is not compliant with the constraints of the IoT. *Malware (malicious software)* is a set of instructions injected in the user's computer to manipulate the system maliciously toward the attacker's desires [24]. The connectivity of the devices in IoT makes it easier for the attackers to widely propagate the malware over the network. The first malware instance against IoT was reported by Symantec in November 2013, which indicated the significance of having solutions to address this security issue. To the best of our knowledge, there has not been much research work on the malware targeting IoT.

Privacy is another issue in IoT to be addressed. Because of the increase in the use of IoT in people's daily lives, more and more (personal) data is collected. Additionally, IoT captures the behavioral pattern of the daily actions that a user takes, in order to provide customized services based on the user's preferences. Hence, it is highly significant to protect all of this information, while it is either stored or transmitted over the network, in order to maintain the privacy of the user. Nonetheless, the existing privacy-preserving approaches, such as data anonymity and location privacy, require high-powered equipment and higher bandwidth that are not always adaptable to the IoT network [25].

14.3 OBFUSCATION AND DIVERSIFICATION TECHNIQUES

Code obfuscation [26] is to transform the program's code into another version, which is syntactically different but semantically the same. That is, the program still produces the same output although its implementation differs from the original one. The purpose of this transformation is to make the code more complex and difficult to understand, in order to make the malicious reverse-engineering of the code harder and costlier for the attacker.

Fig. 14.3 illustrates a piece of obfuscated code, which is scrambled in a way so that the purpose of the code is not easy to understand. Certainly, with given time and resources, the attacker may succeed in comprehending and breaking the obfuscated code; however, it requires more time and energy compared to breaking the original version. There have been several different obfuscation mechanisms proposed [27]. Each of these mechanisms applies the obfuscation transformations at various parts of the code, and also at various phases of the program development. For instance, obfuscation through opaque predicates [27] is a technique used to alter the control flow of the program. Opaque predicates are Boolean expressions that are always executed in the same way, and the outcome is always known for the obfuscator, but not for the attacker in priori. Evaluating these Boolean expressions at runtime makes the analysis of the code harder.

```
(A)
    function setText(data) {
    document.getElementById("myDiv").innerHTML = data;
    }
```

```
(B)
    function ghds3x(n) {
    h = "\x69\u006En\u0065r\x48T\u004DL";
    a="s c v o v d h e , n i";x=a.split(" ");b="gztxleWentBsyf";
 r=b.replace("z",x[7]).replace("x","E").replace("s","").replace("f","I")
    ["repl" + "ace"]("W","m")+"d";
c="my"+String.fromCharCode(68)+x[10]+"v";
    s=x[5]+x[3]+x[1]+"um"+x[7]+x[9]+"t";d=this[s][r](c);if(+!![])
    { d[h]=n; } else { d[h]=c; } }
```

FIGURE 14.3

(A) Original version of a piece of JavaScript code, and (B) obfuscated version of the same code.

Diversification aims to make diverse unique instances of a program that are syntactically different but functionally equivalent. This idea was pioneered by [28] in 1993, to protect the operating systems through generating diversified versions of them [29–36]. Following that, there has been a large body of research on obfuscating and diversifying the program interfaces, and on applications to protect them against the malicious software.

Currently, the software and operating systems are developed and distributed in a monocultural manner. Their identical design makes them suffer from the same types of vulnerabilities, and they are prone to the same security attacks. An intruder, by exploiting these vulnerabilities, can simply undertake a vast number of systems. Diversification, by introducing multiculturalism to the software design, aims at impeding the risk of massive-scale attacks. The way that a program is diversified is unique, and it is kept secret. Assuming that the attacker discovers the diversification secret of one instance of the program, it can possibly attack against that specific version, whereas the others would still be safe. That is to say, a single-attack model does not work on several systems, and the attacker needs to design system-specific attack models. For this reason, diversification is considered to be a promising technique to defend against massive-scale attacks and protect the largely distributed systems. Fig. 14.4 shows the distribution of the uniquely diversified replicas of Program P among its users. The attacker, by designing an attack model, can only undertake one replica, and the other replicas are safe.

Program bugs caused by the developers at the time of development are unavoidable and lead to software vulnerabilities. In theory, the injected malware uses the knowledge it has picked up from the system's vulnerabilities to run its code. Diversification of the internal system interfaces makes it difficult for the malware to gain knowledge about the vulnerabilities of the system and exploit those vulnerabilities to perform an attack, as code-injection attacks are based on using some knowledge of the internal implementation details. Moreover, after diversification, because the malware does not have enough knowledge about the interfaces, it is harder for it to call them and execute its malicious code. Thus, eventually, the malware becomes ineffective. The general idea in code obfuscation and program diversification is not to remove the vulnerabilities of the software, but to elude the attacker from taking advantage of them. Some of these vulnerabilities are not even known at the time of the software release. These techniques help with preventing the zero-day type of attacks that take advantage of the unknown vulnerabilities.

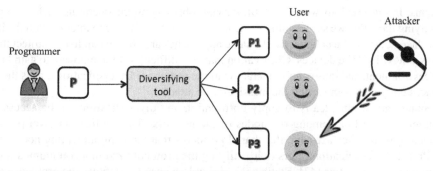

FIGURE 14.4 Diversification Generates and Distributes Unique Replicas of a Program

Thus, if an attacker manages to attack one copy of the software, the other copies are safe.

14.4 ENHANCING THE SECURITY IN IoT USING OBFUSCATION AND DIVERSIFICATION TECHNIQUES

The majority of the security threats in IoT base their exploits on the vulnerabilities that exist at the application layer and the network layer. As we discussed earlier, the vulnerabilities caused at the development phase of the applications and software are unavoidable, and some of them remain unknown until an attack occurs (ie, zero-day attacks). Therefore, there should be security measures considered to prevent intruders from taking advantage of these vulnerabilities. To this end, we propose two novel techniques that make it difficult for an attacker to exploit the system's vulnerabilities to conduct a successful attack. We propose (1) obfuscating/diversifying the operating systems and APIs used in the IoT devices, and (2) obfuscating/diversifying some of the access protocols among nodes of this network. The earlier approach secures the IoT at the application layer, whereas the later introduces security at the network layer.

The sensors and devices participating in IoT function with the help of the operating systems and software on them, and, like any other software system, they have vulnerabilities that make them prone to security attacks. An intruder seeks to exploit existing vulnerabilities on the system by finding his or her entry to the system. For instance, a piece of malware can capitalize on these vulnerabilities to inject its malicious code to spy on or manipulate the targeted system. In our proposed approach, we do not aim at removing these vulnerabilities, but we aim at preventing or making it difficult for the attacker to learn about these vulnerabilities and to utilize them. We achieve this goal by applying obfuscation and diversification techniques on the operating systems and APIs of the devices in IoT. Obfuscation of the operating systems and APIs make them complicated to comprehend, thus an attacker needs to spend more time and effort to understand the program in order to design an attack model. Diversification of the operating systems and APIs used on the devices improve the security of the devices by creating a unique internal structure for them. This implies that even if an attacker finds out the diversification secret for the software of one of the devices, it can undertake only that specific device, and other devices are safe. This is because their operating systems and APIs are diversified with a different diversification secret, that is, although devices might have similar software with similar functionality, their interfaces are uniquely diversified and the attacker needs to design various attack models for each of these systems. In our previous work [37–46], through obfuscating the operating systems (eg, Linux) and diversifying the APIs, we successfully made it harder for the malware to interact with the interfaces and access the resources. We believe that the same approaches are effective in IoT to protect the operating systems and APIs of the devices. Obfuscation makes it difficult for the malware to gain knowledge about the environment, and thus cannot interact with the resources. Diversification makes the software of the devices unique, thus thwarting the massive-scale attacks.

The second part of our idea is to apply obfuscation and diversification on the access protocol of the communication links among the nodes of the network. The application level protocol of a network identifies the interfaces and the shared protocols that the communicating nodes use in the network. Protocol identification refers to identifying the protocol used in a communication session by the communicating parties [47]. Static analysis could be used to capture the protocol used in the communication and compare it to the common existing protocols. The knowledge gained about the protocol used can be misused by an intruder to break into the communication, to eavesdrop, or to manipulate the data being sent over the network. Our idea is to make it hard for an attacker to gain this knowledge and identify the protocol used. We propose to obfuscate the protocols, in order to make the protocol unintelligible and difficult to identify. Protocol obfuscation removes/scrambles the characteristics that make the protocol identifiable, such as byte sequence and packet size (eg, by making them look random). Cryptography is a common way to obfuscate the protocol. Upon the security need and the capacity of the network, different levels of encryption could be employed [47]. For instance, in *Plain* mode, only the headers are encrypted and the payload is transmitted unencrypted, whereas in *RC4*, stronger cryptography is applied, for which a more powerful attack model is required to break. Certainly, RC4 is a stronger approach than Plain, but consumes more CPU time.

We propose to obfuscate the communication protocol of a subset of nodes (eg, communicating devices in a home). The way in which the obfuscated protocol is kept is a secret among these nodes, in a manner that the nodes need to know the obfuscation secret, in order to be able to communicate with each other. Changing/complicating the form of the protocol makes it dissimilar from the typical format. With the help of obfuscation, we aim at generating a large number of unique, diversified protocols that function the same as, but look different from, the reference protocol. We have already applied this to the SQL query protocol in [48].

14.4.1 MOTIVATIONS AND LIMITATIONS OF THE PROPOSED IDEAS

The techniques, obfuscation and diversification, have been shown to bring a high level of security in various domains. This motivated us to propose the use of these techniques in an IoT environment to boost the security of the participating nodes of this network and also the communication links among them. We believe our approaches are fairly successful in impeding the risk of malicious reverse-engineering, unknown zero-day attacks, targeted attacks, and massive-scale types of attacks. In the following, we consider the advantages of the proposed ideas, and we will continue with the limitations and drawbacks that these approaches may bring along.

- *Additional security at the device level*: The existing security measures in IoT mainly focus on securing the network. The proposed ideas present security at the device level, which is an orthogonal proactive security measure. In this manner, even if the malware makes its way to one node, it is stopped at that point and has no way to propagate to the whole network. This is because, in order to communicate with the other nodes, it has to know the obfuscation method, which is secret. Therefore, the malware that is unable to talk to the other nodes becomes ineffective.

- *Energy efficiency*: The sensors and devices in IoT are quite resource-constrained, meaning that they are extremely limited with regard to computational power, memory, and energy capacity. The considered security measure is required to be lightweight and compatible with these limitations. For this reason, the strong cryptography mechanisms and the anti-virus programs cannot be used on these devices, due to their high complexity, energy consumption, and the impact on performance. API diversification will not have any substantial execution overhead, whereas protocol diversification and also obfuscation may slow down the execution to some extent.

- *No complexity for the manufacturer*: The sensors and devices in IoT contain tiny chips embedded in them, which are intolerant to a complex design. Our proposed security techniques do not introduce any additional complexity to the manufacturing process.

- *Mitigates the risk of malware*: the participating devices in IoT function with the help of lightweight operating systems on them. In order to handle the operations, the operating systems execute codes. Similar to any other software, code execution is a potential attack surface for malicious software to access the code, read, or modify it as the attacker desires. To this end, the operating systems of the devices should be protected from the malicious software. We believe that obfuscation and diversification of the operating systems are effective techniques to render the malware ineffective to interact with the environment and execute its code. To make our approach compatible with the limitations of the devices, we employ the less complicated obfuscation and diversification mechanisms, such as identifier renaming.

- *Mitigates the risk of massive-scale attacks*: The sensors, actuators, and devices are designed, manufactured, and distributed identically in "monoculture" manner. This means that they are produced with similar layout, and therefore, with similar security vulnerabilities. Thus, an attacker, by getting knowledge about the vulnerabilities of a component, and then designing an attack model, can simply invade a large number of devices. We believe that diversification presents a "multicultural" behavior in software deployment, and is a potent security mechanism for a largely distributed environment such as IoT.

- *Amend the update limitation in embedded devices*: Typically, the software on the embedded devices cannot be updated or receive the security patches. We believe that obfuscation and diversification techniques can protect these devices so as to be prepare them for the zero-day type of attacks, because the basic idea of these two techniques does not try to remove the vulnerabilities and security holes of the software, but it avoids (or makes it hard for) an attacker to take advantage of them.

In spite of the security advances that our proposed approach presents to the system, it has some limitations and also brings along some costs. Code obfuscation protects the code through scrambling and complicating it, which causes costs in terms of code-size increase and execution overhead, thus affecting the performance of the system to some extent. Protocol obfuscation is done by changing/complicating the form of the protocol and making it different from the default format (for instance, by changing the datatypes, states, and number of message exchanges). Therefore, when obfuscating the communication protocol, it is required that the communicating parties are capable of supporting the obfuscated protocol, that is, that they know the obfuscation secret and how the protocol is obfuscated. Diversification of the applications makes the development and distribution of the software more challenging. At the deployment phase, there comes an additional phase to diversify the software to make unique versions. Also, at the distribution level, managing the update patches might be a challenge [49].

Considering these challenges, limitations, and costs, depending on the need of the system, different levels of obfuscation and diversification could be applied to achieve the security. The more obfuscation/diversification is applied, the higher security and for sure the more overhead we will attain. There is always a trade-off between the level of security and performance. Taking the low capacity of the IoT devices into account, lightweight obfuscation/diversification mechanisms are the most suitable to apply, such as renaming the identifiers of callable entities in APIs and propagating the changes to legal applications of IoT devices.

14.5 DIFFERENT USE-CASE SCENARIOS ON SOFTWARE DIVERSIFICATION AND OBFUSCATION

In the following, we will discuss two use-case scenarios in which program diversification and code obfuscation are applied together with protocol obfuscation. The first use-case scenario describes a security sensor network used to monitor public spaces. The second use-case illustrates a medical sensor network used to observe patients.

Most of our modern cities are already overlooked by a legion of sensors. Nowadays most of these are digital video recorder (DVR) cameras mounted in the walls to monitor public streets and parks. Nevertheless, in the future, it is likely that a wide range of sensors will be used to observe and adjust cities. For example, air- and water-quality sensors can be installed into the population centers. Similarly, it is likely that traffic and transportation will be monitored closely in the future. In public areas, some sensors could be used for environmental monitoring, and some others could be used for detecting explosives [50].

A public monitoring system is a tempting target for a hacker. Whereas hacking a public security-sensor network would be an easy way to achieve great publicity, it is also a strategically important objective for cyberterrorists as well as criminals. One recent example of a security breach in these cameras was announced recently. The security cameras were hijacked and used to mine bitcoins [51]. Thus, it is highly significant to protect these kinds of surveillance-device networks.

As with all IoT devices, the security-surveillance-device networks are prone to attacks due to their limited hardware and computational capabilities. Hence, there is a great need for security measures that are tolerable by these constraint devices. Diversification of the operating systems of the devices is an achievable way to break device monoculturalism. With this, for example, the previously described bitcoin-mining attack could have been easily avoided: although the attackers would still have been able to capture a single device, they would not have been able to paralyze the whole network. Furthermore, if the program code and interfaces of sensor devices are obfuscated, then creating an attack against those devices would be an arduous task.

Another interesting possibility enabled by IoT technologies is remote health-monitoring. The technology offers a wide range of different vital signs that can be monitored. For example, blood pressure, heart rate, blood glucose level, and other signs can be remotely observed. These kinds of systems could, for example, send a notification in case of an emergency or collect information to a database for later use. In countries where the average age of citizens has been constantly growing, the remote health-monitoring would be able to bring efficiency and cost savings to the healthcare districts and societies.

In the domain of healthcare, privacy and security are crucial. In remote health monitoring, securing the confidentiality of information is an important aspect. Although diversification and obfuscation help to protect the monitors against large-scale attacks, securing the privacy of the communication between the end-points is still an open question. In our use case, we propose utilizing the protocol obfuscation in addition to other techniques to secure the communication. The protocol obfuscation makes the communication between end-points more arbitrary and harder to break than using only, for example, cryptography.

There are, however, certain open problems that need to be addressed when utilizing diversification in IoT networks. First, what must be resolved is how the controlling unit knows and stores the way that each monitor is diversified, and how it should be contacted. Second, although the program code diversification adds only a little, if any, performance penalty, it is currently not known as to what these penalties might be, which are caused by the protocol obfuscation.

14.6 CONCLUSIONS AND FUTURE WORK

In this chapter, we discussed that the use of IoT is considerably growing in both the personal and business lives of people, in a way that the connected devices are outnumbering the population of the world. All of these physical objects work together by collecting information about the people and the environment, and sharing these data. Therefore, it is highly significant to protect these data while they are being transmitted and stored. However, the specific characteristics of IoT compared to the traditional networks makes the security in IoT more challenging. These characteristics are: the large scale, the heterogeneity, and the low capacity of the devices in IoT. There is a huge number of devices and sensors in IoT that capture large amounts of data. The security mechanism needs to ensure the integrity of these data throughout the whole network. The physical objects in IoT are fairly heterogeneous, that is, they connect to the network through various means and have different capacities. Therefore, the security mechanism under consideration should be compatible with all of these objects. Furthermore, the sensors and devices are extremely limited in resources, for example, memory, battery, and computational power. Thus, the security mechanism should be supported by an entire range of devices, including the least powerful ones.

In this chapter, we proposed two novel approaches for securing IoT at the application and network layer, using two potential techniques: obfuscation and diversification. The proposed ideas were: (1) applying obfuscation and diversification techniques to the software, operating systems, and APIs of the devices in IoT, and (2) applying obfuscation and diversification techniques to the communication protocols among a set of devices. We believe this approach is compatible with the limitations of the participating nodes in IoT.

For our future work, we will focus on implementing the proposed ideas, by obfuscating and diversifying the operating systems that are dominantly used in IoT (eg, Contiki) and in the application layer protocols (eg, CoAP). Nevertheless, the methods discussed in this chapter may already be taken into use by the IoT device manufacturers, and thus harden their device networks against malicious attackers.

REFERENCES

[1] Internet of Things research study—HP report, http://www8.hp.com/h20195/v2/getpdf.aspx/4aa5-4759enw.pdf/; 2015.

[2] Larsen P, Homescu A, Brunthaler S, Franz M. Sok: automated software diversity. In: 2014 IEEE Symposium on Security and privacy (SP); 2014. p. 276–291.

[3] Baccelli E, Hahm O, Gunes M, Wahlisch M, Schmidt TC. Operating systems for the IoT—goals, challenges, and solutions. Workshop Interdisciplinaire sur la Sécurité Globale (WISG2013). France: Troyes; 2013.

[4] Baccelli E, Hahm O, Gunes M, Wahlisch M, Schmidt T. RIOT OS: towards an OS for the Internet of Things. In: Conference on computer communications workshops (INFOCOM WKSHPS), IEEE; 2013. p. 79–80.

[5] Postscapes, tacking the Internet of Things, http://postscapes.com/; 2015.

[6] Dunkels A, Gronvall B, Voigt T. Contiki—a lightweight and flexible operating system for tiny networked sensors. In: Twenty ninth annual international conference on local computer networks, IEEE; 2004. p. 455–62.

[7] Levis P, Madden S, Polastre J, Szewczyk R, Whitehouse K, Woo A, Gay D, Hill J, Welsh M, Brewer E, Culler D. TinyOS: an operating system for sensor networks. In: Weber W, Rabaey JM, Aarts E, editors. Ambient intelligence. Berlin Heidelberg: Springer; 2005. p. 115–48.

[8] Contiki: The open source OS for the Internet of Things, http://www.contiki-os.org/; 2015.

[9] nesC: a programming language for deeply networked systems, http://nescc.sourceforge.net/; 2015.

[10] Electronic design, http://electronicdesign.com/; 2015.

[11] RPL: IPv6 routing protocol for Low-power and Lossy Networks (RPL), https://tools.ietf.org/html/rfc6550/; 2015.

[12] Shelby Z, Hartke K, Bormann C. The Constrained Application Protocol (CoAP), RFC 7252; 2014.

[13] Sheng Z, Yang S, Yu Y, Vasilakos A, McCann J, Leung K. A survey on the IETF protocol suite for the Internet of Things: standards, challenges, and opportunities. IEEE Wireless Commun 2013;20(6):91–8.

[14] Embedded computing design, http://embedded-computing.com/; 2015.

[15] IPv6 over low power WPAN (6LowPAN), https://tools.ietf.org/wg/6lowpan/; 2015.

[16] IEEE 802.15: wireless personal area networks (PANs), http://standards.ieee.org/about/get/802/802.15.html/; 2015.

[17] Hunkeler U, Truong HL, Stanford-Clark. MQTT-S—a publish/subscribe protocol for wireless sensor networks. In: Third International conference on communication systems software and middleware and workshops, COMSWARE; 2008. p. 791–798.

[18] Extensible messaging and presence protocol (XMPP), http://tools.ietf.org/html/rfc6121/; 2015.

[19] Pardo-Castellote G. Omg data-distribution servitd: architectural overview. In: Proceedings of the 23rd international conference on distributed computing systems workshops; 2003. p. 200–206.

[20] Vinoski S. Advanced message queuing protocol. IEEE Internet Comput 2006;10(6):87–9.

[21] O'Hara J. Toward a commodity enterprise middleware. Queue 2007;5(4):48–55.

[22] Babar S, Mahalle P, Stango A, Prasad N, Prasad R. Proposed security model and threat taxonomy for the Internet of Things (IoT). In: Meghanathan N, Boumerdassi S, Chaki N, Nagamalai D, editors. Recent trends in network security and applications of communications in computer and information science, 89. Berlin, Heidelberg: Springer; 2010. p. 420–9.

[23] Zhang ZK, Cho MCY, Wang CW, Cheng CK, Hsu CW, Shieh S. IoT security: ongoing challenges and research opportunities. In: 2014 IEEE seventh international conference on service-oriented computing and applications (SOCA); 2014. p. 230–234.

[24] Skoudis E, Zeltser L. Malware: fighting malicious code. New Jersey, NJ: Prentice Hall Professional: 2004.

[25] Bandyopadhyay D, Sen J. Internet of things: applications and challenges in technology and standardization. Wireless Personal Commun 2011;58(1):49–69.

[26] Collberg C, Thomborson C, Low D. A taxonomy of obfuscating transformations. Technical report, Department of Computer Science, The University of Auckland, New Zealand; 1997.

[27] Collberg C, Thomborson C, Low D. Manufacturing cheap, resilient, and stealthy opaque constructs. In: Proceedings of the 25th ACM SIGPLANSIGACT symposium on principles of programming languages. POPL '98. ACM, New York, NY, USA; 1998. p. 184–196.

[28] Cohen FB. Operating system protection through program evolution. Comput Secur 1993;12(6):565–84.

[29] Anckaert B, De Sutter B, De Bosschere K. Software piracy prevention through diversity. In: Proceedings of the 4th ACM workshop on digital rights management. DRM 2004. ACM, New York, NY, USA; 2004. p. 63–71

[30] Franz M. E unibus pluram: massive-scale software diversity as a defense mechanism. In: Proceedings of the workshop on new security paradigms, NSPW '10. ACM, New York, NY, USA; 2010. p. 7–16.

[31] Homescu A, Neisius S, Larsen P, Brunthaler S, Franz M. Profile-guided automated software diversity. In: IEEE/ACM international symposium on code generation and optimization (CGO); 2013.

[32] Larsen P, Brunthaler S, Franz M. Security through diversity: are we there yet? IEEE Secur Privacy 2014;12(2):28–35.

[33] Low D. Protecting Java code via code obfuscation. Crossroads 1998;4(3):21–3.

[34] Majumdar A, Thomborson C. On the use of opaque predicates in mobile agent code obfuscation. In: Kantor P, Muresan G, Roberts F, Zeng DD, Wang F, Chen H, Merkle RC, editors. Intelligence and security informatics, volume 3495 of lecture notes in computer science. Berlin, Heidelberg: Springer; 2005. p. 648–9.

[35] Murphy M, Larsen P, Brunthaler S, Franz M. Software profiling options and their effects on security based diversification. In: Proceedings of the first ACM workshop on moving target defense. MTD. ACM, New York, NY, USA; 2014. p. 87–96.

[36] Schrittwieser S, Katzenbeisser S. Code obfuscation against static and dynamic reverse engineering. In: Filler T, Pevn T, Craver S, Ker A, editors. Information hiding, volume 6958 of lecture notes in computer science. Berlin, Heidelberg: Springer; 2011. p. 270–84.

[37] Rauti S, Holvitie J, Leppänen V. Towards a diversification framework for operating system protection. In: Proceedings of the 15th international conference on computer systems and technologies. CompSysTech. ACM, New York, NY, USA; 2014. p. 286–93.

[38] Rauti S, Laurén S, Hosseinzadeh S, Mäkelä JM, Hyrynsalmi S, Leppänen V. Diversification of system calls in linux binaries. In: Proceedings of international conference on trustworthy systems (InTrust2014). LNCS (9473); 2015. p. 15–35.

[39] Laurén S, Mäki P, Rauti S, Hosseinzadeh S, Hyrynsalmi S, Leppänen V. Symbol diversification of Linux binaries. In: Shonigun CA, Akmayeva GA, editors. Proceedings of world congress on Internet security (WorldCIS-2014). IEEE; 2014. p. 75–80.

[40] Uitto J, Rauti S, Mäkelä JM, Leppänen V. Preventing malicious attacks by diversifying Linux shell commands. In: Proceedings of 14th symposium on programming languages and software tools (SPLST'15); 2015. p. 206–220.

[41] Laurén S, Rauti S, Leppänen: V. Diversification of System Calls in Linux Kernel. In: Proceedings of international conference on computer systems and technologies (CompSysTech); ACM Press, ACM ICPS, Dublin, Ireland. 2015. p. 284–291.

[42] Leppänen V, Rauti S, Laurén S. Wide application security by low-level program code obfuscation techniques. In: MATINE Report 2014; 2015. p. 7.

[43] Rauti S, Leppänen V. A proxy-like obfuscator for web application protection. Int J Inform Technol Secur 2014;6(1):39–52.

[44] Rauti S, Parisod H, Aromaa M, Salanterä S, Hyrynsalmi S, Lahtiranta J, Smed J, Leppänen V. A proxy-based security solution for web-based online eHealth services. In: Saranto K, Castrén M, Kuusela T, Hyrynsalmi S, Ojala Stina, editors. Safe and secure cities, communications in computer and information science, 450. Switzerland: Springer International Publishing; 2014. p. 168–76.

[45] Rauti S, Leppänen V. Browser extension-based man-in-the-browser attacks against ajax applications with countermeasures. In: Rachev Boris, Smrikarov Angel, editors. Proceedings of the thirtenth international conference on computer systems and technologies. New York, NY: ACM Press; 2012. p. 251–8.

[46] Rauti S, Leppänen V. Man-in-the-browser attacks in modern web browsers. In: Akhbar B, Arabnia H, editors. Emerging trends in ICT security, emerging trends in computer science & applied computing. Waltham, MA: Morgan Kaufmann Publishers; 2014. p. 169–480.

[47] Hjelmvik E, John W. Breaking and improving protocol obfuscation. Technical report 123751, Chalmers University of Technology; 2010.

[48] Rauti S, Teuhola J, Leppänen V. Diversifying SQL to prevent injection attacks. In: Proceedings of the 14th IEEE international conference on trust, security and privacy in computing and communications (IEEE TrustCom-15); Helsinki, Finland; 2015. p. 344–351.

[49] Nagra J., Collberg C. Surreptitious software: obfuscation, watermarking, and tamper proofing for software protection. Pearson Education; 2009.

[50] Ma R-H, Ota S, Li Y, Yang S, Zhang X. Explosives detection in a lasing plasmon naocavity. Nature Nanotechnol 2014;9:600–4.

[51] McMillan R. Hackers turn security camera DVRs into worst bitcoin miners ever, http://www.wired.com/2014/04/hikvision/; 2014.

IoT APPLICATIONS

APPLIED INTERNET OF THINGS

15

S.J. Johnston, M. Apetroaie-Cristea, M. Scott, S.J. Cox

Faculty of Engineering and the Environment, University of Southampton, Southampton, United Kingdom

15.1 INTRODUCTION

In this chapter we work through an Internet of Things (IoT) example scenario, beginning with data collection and working through to data transmission and analysis [1]. This example is designed to be generic to ensure that the techniques are transferable, particularly as IoT devices become more commonplace [2]. Where possible, we utilize commodity hardware and established technologies, explaining design decisions as the chapter progresses.

An in-depth knowledge of electronics or computer science is not required, and the discussed architecture is designed as a generic blueprint to facilitate other applied IoT solutions. It is intended to be simple and overcome the most common pitfalls in setting up an IoT infrastructure.

The key requirements for the proposed architecture are:

- The hardware must be commodity and available
- The software and hardware must be low cost
- It must provide enterprise scalability
- A minimal level of electronics and computing experience is required
- Higher-level programming languages are preferred

We consider the decisions behind building a prototype for the IoT example scenario, and do not focus on specific sensors or on their capabilities. Specific analysis tools or techniques are considered out-of-scope. Instead, we design and build a generic prototype which is applied to an example scenario. Building an IoT device is an iterative process, resulting in multiple prototypes and a final *production* version. There are two objectives when building a prototype:

- To demonstrate that the scenario concept is viable; for example, to ensure that the data collected is appropriate to validate a hypothesis.
- To test that the hardware will perform as expected; for example, ensuring the data precision and that all of the hardware can coexist.

The number of IoT devices required will dictate the development cycle. For example, as the volume of devices increases, more emphasis is attached to the hardware costs. For low volumes, building custom devices in-house is appropriate, but for high-volume devices professional design and assembly is required.

Before beginning production of a large volume of devices, a well-thought-out and thoroughly tested prototype is required. In our chosen scenario we are interested in low volumes of devices, but will ensure that there is a path to higher-volume production. For example, we can ensure that development hardware designs are open sourced, to enable redesign and manufacture without incurring licensing costs.

Throughout the design cycle it is important to consider how the final IoT device will be used, and to ensure that it complies with local and international regulations, especially if made commercially available. This is particularly important if the device incorporates wireless technologies or controls high AC current.

In this chapter, we focus on low-volume custom IoT devices that are possible with commodity hardware, and consider IoT device-certification and local regulatory requirements out-of-scope.

15.2 SCENARIO

Imagine you would like to know the weather outside in your garden. In an ideal IoT world, you would have a range of sensors, for example, a temperature sensor that can talk directly to the Internet. This would be achieved by sending the temperature data from the sensor directly to a backend service via the Internet. The backend service would probably display the data on a web page and would ideally offer the ability to display and analyze the data.

There are a few complexities associated with such a simple example. The most obvious is that most sensors cannot communicate via the Internet to backend services. In part this is due to the cost of having Wi-Fi or wired Ethernet connections to *every* sensor, and in part also due to the electrical power required. Supporting a full TCP/IP networking stack on every sensor is not required if a low-power wireless network is available. It is for these reasons that local sensors often communicate via a gateway, which can broker or relay messages across the Internet.

Adding a single Wi-Fi or wired Ethernet Internet connection to a gateway which communicates to a group of sensors or actuators is more cost-effective. The Internet connection can then be shared by using either local wired or wireless connections between the gateway and local devices.

The aim of this chapter is to design, build, and test an environmental-sensing IoT architecture for weather monitoring. The architecture must use commodity hardware and software to produce a system that is secure, reliable, and low cost.

It must be generic and applicable to alternative application areas by swapping the sensors/actuators. The weather station will reside outdoors in a suitably exposed location and will need to record values from various sensors at regular time-intervals, mainly temperature, humidity, wind speed and direction. This data needs to be reliably stored and transmitted for use in analysis, graphs, and for consumption by external services.

15.3 ARCHITECTURE OVERVIEW

There are three key components to an IoT architecture: the sensors and actuators, the gateway, and the backend services. These three components communicate via a wide variety of interfaces and protocols, and, as a whole, enable the functionality of an IoT device, as shown in Fig. 15.1.

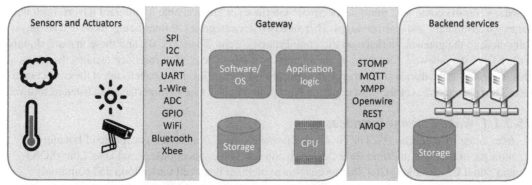

FIGURE 15.1 IoT Architecture Key Components and Example Protocols

- *The sensors and actuators* are application-specific and will require some thought to ensure that the data collected meets the accuracy and sampling frequency required for analysis.
- *The gateway* is responsible for communicating with the sensors and actuators as well as the backend services; it is a translator between localized interfaces, such as hard-wired sensors and remote backend systems. It basically adds TCP/IP capability to sensors, and, although it could be part of a sensor, we separate the gateway to allow a many-to-one mapping with sensors, as well as additional functionality, such as data persistence for unreliable Internet connectivity. The gateway is optional in IoT sensor-devices that can communicate directly with the Internet; either the sensor becomes very lightweight and has minimal functionality, or some of the desired gateway functions such as data persistence and security are incorporated into the sensor.
- *The backend services* are predominantly used to store the IoT device data but can include additional functionality such as individual device configuration and analysis algorithms. It is beneficial to also consider data analysis as part of the backend, since the data is only useful if it can be analyzed. As the volumes of data grow, this becomes critically important, for example, low bandwidth between a data store and compute cluster will reduce the ability to process all the data in a timely fashion.

Communication between these three components ensures that data collected by an IoT device can be transported via the Internet to backend services. The communication must be bidirectional so that the configuration of the gateway can be updated, for example, to change the polling frequency of sensors or to manipulate actuators.

15.3.1 SENSOR TO GATEWAY COMMUNICATION

The sensors themselves usually have low-level electronic interfaces for communication. For example, I^2C and SPI are common serial-communication buses capable of linking multiple electronic components.

Connecting one or more sensors to the serial bus of a gateway device is a simple way of creating an IoT device. The transmission distance of many hard-wired interfaces can be an issue. For example, a few meters for I^2C and up to 1 km for RS-485. In its simplest form, the gateway is a converter from these lower-level electronic interfaces to Internet-compatible interfaces.

Many sensors come with multiple electronic interfaces or are available in different flavors, each with their own advantages and disadvantages. There are two key categories of interfacing, those that are physically close to the gateway, perhaps on the same Printed Circuit Board (PCB), and those that are slightly farther from the gateway, for example, on a length of cable. The chosen interface dictates the physical characteristics of the device and is therefore application-specific. It is important to select the correct interface. The characteristics of the most common wired and wireless gateway interfaces are listed as follows.

15.3.1.1 *Wired Gateway Interfaces*

- *Inter-Integrated Circuit* (I^2C) or *Two Wire Interface* (TWI) is a serial bus capable of hosting multiple master and multiple slave devices using just two connections: Serial Data Line (SDA) and Serial Clock Line (SCL). It is an easy-to-implement bus, well understood and commonly used, making it a good choice for IoT sensor communications. Although often considered slow, it is capable of 3.4 Mbit/s in fast mode, but is generally limited to 400 kbit/s for most implementations. As the name indicates, it is intended for communication between integrated circuits, so it is ideal for sensors on the same PCB as the gateway, but it will also run over wires. The clock frequency and total bus capacitance will generally limit the range to a few meters, but in theory, distances in excess of 100 m are possible.

  Since one of the connections is transmitting the clock signal, it supports any arbitrary data-transmission speed, including pausing the data transmission through a process called *clock stretching*, for example, to give a component time to process the received data. Devices that do not support clock stretching are often referred to as TWI or just "2-wire" [3]. Many I^2C devices have their address set by the manufacturer, which can cause problems if multiple devices are put on the same bus because it is possible to get an address clash; this can be solved by using an additional I^2C bus.

- *Serial Peripheral Interface* (SPI) is a serial bus capable of hosting a single master with multiple slave devices per bus. It uses three connections plus one connection per slave device: Serial Clock (SCLK); Master Output, Slave Input (MOSI); Master Input, Slave Output (MISO); and Slave Select (SS).

  SPI is very common and has a lower power consumption than I^2C, but requires more connections; most notably every slave requires a slave-select pin so that it knows when to listen to the bus transmission. Some SPI implementations daisy-chain the slave-select pins to create a shift register, so that only one slave-select pin is required.

  The maximum clock speed is determined by the components, usually the slave devices, and controlled by the master. Often clock speeds can reach 32 MHz, but there is no theoretical maximum; combined with full-duplex communication, this provides SPI with a higher throughput than I^2C.

- *Pulse-Width Modulation* (PWM) is not an interface, but is rather a technique to encode a message by varying the power supplied by a digital pin. It works by turning the PWM pin on and off at different frequencies to lower the average voltage supplied to the load. It is often implemented in hardware to ensure accurate timings of each pulse, permitting switching frequencies of up to 1 MHz. The duty-cycle (the percentage of time the output is high/on) resolution is the number of discrete values that the PWM pin can output, for example, a 10-bit resolution on a 5-V digital pin will allow for 1024 different voltage outputs between 0 and 5 V. This could relate to motor speed or servo angle.

The PWM technique is common for dimming LEDs or for creating analog outputs, and is commonplace for controlling variable-speed motors.

- *Universal Asynchronous Receiver/Transmitter* (UART) refers to the hardware that converts parallel to serial communications, and is often simply called *serial*, rather confusingly; it is actually the communication standards over UART to which people are generally referring; the most common are RS-232 and RS-485.

  RS-232 connectors are no longer commonplace on computers but are easily added using a USB-Serial chip from manufacturers such as FTDI. Speeds of up to 1 Mbit/s are achievable, but this is often limited by the slave device. Cable lengths are limited to 15 m at 19.6 kbit/s, depending on the quality of the cable. There are two variants, a 3-wire and a 5-wire, with the 5-wire variant providing hardware flow-control for improved speed.

  RS-485 is well suited to longer distances, and enables data transmissions of 35 Mbit/s up to 10 m, but can be used for distances in excess of 1 km at lower speeds. It is commonplace in building automation and for protocols such as MODBUS. It also permits up to 256 devices on a single connection.

- A *Controller Area Network* (CAN) is a message-based protocol defined by ISO 11898-1 that allows multiple-master device communication. It was designed over the last 30 years for in-vehicle electronic networking, and has been adopted by automotive, railway, and aerospace industries.

  Every device on the network has a CAN controller chip. All the devices in the network can see the transmitted messages, on which they can perform message filtering. Each message has an ID that is used for filtering and bus prioritization. The bus also has an error-handling scheme which allows for messages that are not transmitted properly to be retransmitted. This network structure allows modifications to the network with minimal impact, for example, the addition of nontransmitting nodes. The access to the bus is controlled by a nondestructive bit-wise arbitration.

  The physical layer is not specified, but is generally two wires for communication and two for power, allowing speeds of 1 Mbit/s for over 40 m.

- *Analog to Digital-Converter* (ADC) is a device that converts a continuous analog voltage to a digital number. The number of bits used to store this number relates to the accuracy of the ADC, for example, an 8-bit ADC is capable of 256 discrete values, which for an analog voltage range of 0–5 V would give a resolution of 0.019 V.

  The most common ADC devices range from 8-bit to 16-bit, but they can easily exceed 24-bit. It is important to ensure that the analog signal that is being encoded is sampled at a high enough resolution to ensure that analog variations are not lost.

  It is possible to create an ADC using a GPIO pin by emulating the way some microcontroller ADCs work. The nonlinear ramp-compare ADC uses a capacitor that charges with the input analog signal and then discharges across a resistor. By monitoring the time it takes for the capacitor to discharge, it is possible to calculate the input voltage.

- *General Purpose Input Output* (GPIO) is a general-purpose pin whose behavior can be controlled by the user at the runtime. Some of these GPIO pins can be configured to function as Interrupt Request (IRQ) inputs. The GPIO interrupts are implemented using electronic alerting signals that are sent to the interrupt controller from a GPIO pin, to communicate that it requires attention from the operating system. The GPIO can be set to interrupt on either a rising, falling, or on both edges of the incoming signal. The interrupt controller sends the signal to the CPU, which suspends its current operation to execute the process associated with the interrupt. A device connected to the GPIO IRQ pin drives a pulse onto the interrupt line, when signaling an interrupt would otherwise leave it floating.

The alternative of using interrupts is polling—the system checks for changes periodically. However, in this case the processing time and power are increased, and there is a risk of introducing lags between occurrence and detection of an event.

- *1-Wire* is a device communications bus-system capable of hosting multiple slave devices connected to one single master, using a serial protocol for communication with a single data-line plus ground reference. The data line can also be used to provide power to the slave devices (parasitic power mode), or they can be powered up externally, in which case, an extra wire per slave would be required. The 1-Wire concept is similar to I^2C, having a longer range but lower data rates. It has two serial communication speeds: Standard (15.4 kbit/s) and Overdrive (125 kbit/s), and can be used to communicate with small devices, such as weather instruments.

  Each device has a factory-programmed unique ID that serves as its address on the 1-Wire bus, allowing for multiple devices to share the same bus. A single pull-up resistor is common to all devices, used to pull up the bus to 3 V or 5 V and to provide power to the slaves. The communication occurs when the master or the slave connects the pull-up resistor to the ground.

- *X10* is a protocol for communication between automated home-electronic devices. It controls any device plugged into an electric powerline by signaling digital information in the form of short radio-frequency bursts. The X10 standard is a well-known protocol, easy to use, inexpensive, and highly available, which makes it very popular within the home automation environment, although a number of higher bandwidth alternatives exist.

  The packets transmitted using the X10 protocol consist of a 4-bit house code followed by one or more 4-bit unit codes, finally followed by a 4-bit command. There are two types of X10 devices: one-way devices and two-way devices. The one-way devices are inexpensive, but they can only receive commands and are not able to transmit them to the whole network. The two-way device allows for more complex network communication, but it is much more expensive.

15.3.1.2 Wireless Gateway Interfaces

Wiring sensors to a gateway device is not always practical; it is for this reason that wireless technologies are often used. Wi-Fi 802.11a/b/g/n consumes a lot of power, so there are other wireless technologies which are also commonplace and applicable. For example:

- *Bluetooth Low Energy* is a wireless personal-area-network technology that aims to provide similar capabilities to classic Bluetooth, but at lower power consumption and cost. Due to its low-power consumption, it can be used by small devices, such as watches and toys, and in areas such as healthcare, beacons, and fitness. This makes it very useful for IoT wireless communication. It has a master/slave topology, the number of active slaves being implementation-dependent. The Bluetooth Low Energy can send up to 1 Mbit/s of data over distances greater than 100 m.

- *IPv6 over Low-Power Wireless Personal Area Networks* (6LowPAN) is a networking technology that allows IPv6 packets to be sent and received within small link-layer frames, such as the ones based on IEEE 802.15.4. It provides low-power networking support for mesh networks using an end-to-end IP-based infrastructure, making it a very useful technology for IoT applications. It has low data-transfer rates, being able to transmit up to 250 kbit/s over distances of up to 200 m. It operates in the 2.4 GHz frequency range only, and it can support up to 100 nodes per network.

- *INSTEON* is a home-automation technology that enables electrical devices to interoperate through power cables, radio-frequency communications, or both, using a dual-mesh networking topology. For example, it can be used to control LED bulbs, wall switches, sensors, or remote controls. The RF physical layer can transmit up to 2.88 kbit/s for up to 46 m [3].
- *Infrared* is not often an immediate consideration when looking at wireless networks, but can be useful for interacting with existing devices, such as heating controllers, air conditioners, and television receivers. The Infrared Data Association (IrDA) claims speeds of 1 Gbit/s over distances of up to 3 m [4].
- *Z-Wave* is a wireless-based home-automation system designed for controlling electrical devices within a household such as heating and lighting. It uses an open-routed mesh networking topology and can support up to 232 devices per network. Z-Wave has low power consumption, and can be used by battery-powered devices, being able to transmit small data-packets at rates of up to 100 kbit/s for average ranges of up to 100 m [3].
- *ZigBee* is a wireless-based open, global standard used for personal-area networks targeted at low-power applications with infrequent data transmission needs. It operates on the 802.15.4 standard and enables wireless mesh networks with low-cost and low-power solutions. It can transmit 250 kbit/s over distances of up to 100 m, and supports up to 65,000 nodes per network. It has many applications, for example, in lighting control, healthcare devices, and electrical meters [3].
- *Xbee* is not a standard, but rather a communication-module product that provides wireless end-point connectivity to devices using the IEEE 802.15.4 protocol. It is partially compatible with ZigBee. It is one of the most popular communication modules for low-power applications, being able to offer fast point-to-multipoint or peer-to-peer networking. It can send data at rates of up to 250 kbit/s over distances of up to 11.6 km.

15.4 SENSORS

We will now discuss the sensors required to build the environmental-sensing IoT gateway device for weather monitoring, as introduced in Section 15.2.

The IoT application area will drive the sensor selection and specification. In the current section, we select a range of different sensors with a variety of capabilities as examples. The sensors have a reasonable accuracy for an external weather station, and will all be connected simultaneously, although many IoT requirements will have fewer sensors. Table 15.1 provides a summary of the sensors, their electronic interface, and hardware specifics.

The ultraviolet (UV) intensity sensor uses an ML8511 [5] detector, which is most effective between 280 and 390 nm, and will detect both UVA and UVB. The output is a linear voltage relating to the UV intensity (mW/cm^2), which can be read using an analog pin and then converted to a UV index.

The wind vane has eight magnetic reed switches arranged in a dial; each reed switch is connected to a different-sized resistor. As the vane changes direction a magnet moves, making and breaking the switches, and therefore changing the resistance of the circuit. The magnet is sized such that when it is halfway between two reed switches both will be connected. This will give a total of 16 distinct circuit

Table 15.1 Summary of Weather-Station Sensors

Sensor	Interface	Processor/Hardware	Power
Wind vane	Analog	Switched resistors	—
Anemometer	GPIO interrupt	Reed switch	—
Rain gauge	GPIO interrupt	Reed switch	—
UV intensity	Analog	ML8511	1,000 μW
Humidity and temperature	2-wire serial	SHT15	80 μW
Barometric pressure	I^2C	BMP180	30 μW
Luminosity	I^2C	TSL2561	720 μW
Lightning sensor	SPI + GPIO interrupt	AS3935	100 μW
Geiger counter	RS-235	LND712	147,000 μW
Weather board	I^2C	Si7020	540 μW
Weather board	I^2C	BMP180	30 μW
Weather board	I^2C	Si1132	1,419 μW

resistances, hence 16 positions indicating wind direction, as shown in Fig. 15.2. This is a crude sensor and with a resolution of 22.5 degrees, but is an excellent example of a simple analog circuit. A 5-V supply is connected to the wind vane, and the enabled resistors act as a voltage divider; by reading the voltage using an analog pin, it is simple to tell which resistors are enabled in the circuit, and hence establish the wind direction.

The three-cup hemispherical anemometer is used to calculate the wind speed. As the anemometer cups rotate, a single magnet on the device closes a reed switch, completing the circuit. This particular device has two reed switches, resulting in the circuit closing twice per revolution. Connecting one end

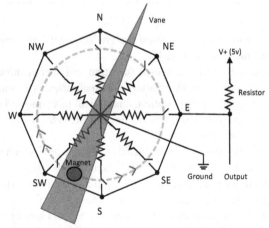

FIGURE 15.2 Wind-Vane Voltage Divider Circuit, Reading the Output With an Analog to Digital Converter Can Give Up to 16 Distinct Wind Directions

of the circuit to ground and the other to a GPIO pin pulled high, we will get an interrupt every time the magnet passes. Counting the interrupts will provide a wind speed, for example, a wind of 2.4 km/h will result in a single rotation of the cups and two interrupts every second.

The rain gauge is a self-emptying tipping bucket; each time the bucket empties it moves a magnet past a reed switch, which will close the circuit. In the same way as the anemometer, we can count these interrupts over time and calculate the rainfall. In this particular gauge the bucket tips with every 0.28 mm of rain.

The SHT15 temperature and humidity sensor is a very reliable low-cost sensor, with an accuracy of ±0.3°C and relative humidity at ±2.0%. The SHT1X range of sensors are precalibrated and provide a serial 2-wire interface, which can coexist with I^2C but cannot be addressed. The easiest way to communicate with this sensor is to use two GPIO pins: one for the clock and one for the data. By manipulating the GPIO pins we can clock commands into the sensor and read the data back.

The BMP180 is a digital pressure-sensor, which can measure atmospheric pressure between 950 and 1050 hPa, with an accuracy of 0.12 hPa. An accurate temperature reading is needed to measure the pressure so that the BMP180 can also be used as a temperature sensor. The pressure readings can be converted into altitude using the international barometric formula. The BMP180 has an I^2C serial output and a fixed address, and it can be connected to an I^2C bus together with other sensors, providing there is not an address clash.

The TSL2561 luminosity sensor detects infrared and full-spectrum light, and has an I^2C serial output. The sensor can be used for lux calculations and has a configurable slave address (a total of three different address combinations are possible).

The AS3935 Franklin lightning sensor detects lightning within a 40-km range and estimates the distance to the head of a storm. It can detect cloud-to-cloud and cloud-to-ground lightning, as well as identify and reject interferences, for example, from fluorescent lighting, microwave ovens, switches, and mobile phones. It offers both I^2C and SPI serial interfaces, and will provide a GPIO interrupt when lightning is detected. By querying the device via the I^2C or SPI bus, you can obtain information about the type of detection, and, in the case of lightning, the distance.

The Geiger counter board is based on a LND712 Geiger tube, with an ATmega328 to process the results. The data is output over a serial RS-232 connection via an FTDI serial over a USB processor. This is an excellent example of a sensor which is complex enough to require a coprocessor, in this case, the ATmega328. The ATmega328 is commonly used in the Arduino development platform [6], and is an excellent starting point for beginner electronics projects. This sensor with coprocessor is a model worth considering for custom sensor development.

All the previous sensors have been single-sensor modules, but it is also common to group sensors together on a single PCB. This reduces costs and eliminates some of the wiring, but limits the sensor selection. The physical-form factor can also be an issue, as sensor positioning is critical for accurate measurements. For example, a lux sensor needs to be exposed to light, whereas a barometer should not be exposed to wind—having them on the same board complicates the physical design.

In the case of a weather station, there are plenty of single-board options; we are using a weather board with the following three sensors:

- The Si1132 is a UV index and ambient-light sensor with I^2C interface, and is comparable to the TSL2561 luminosity sensor.
- The BMP180 is the same sensor described previously.
- The Si7020 temperature and humidity sensor is less accurate than the SHT15.

15.5 THE GATEWAY

Next we consider the IoT gateway device, which can be split into the hardware and the software.

Selecting the hardware to sit between sensors and an Internet connection requires careful thought. In its simplest form, the gateway reads data from the sensor's electronic interface and transmits it to a destination across the Internet. For this to take place, the gateway must have the appropriate electronic interfaces, a processor with memory, and either wired or wireless Internet capability. Often, using a small microprocessor such as those used by Arduino would be perfect. However, such a simple design omits some of the critical IoT features such as Secure Sockets Layer (SSL) or Transport Layer Security (TLS), a cryptographic protocol that provides communication security over TCP.

The specific IoT application area will drive the hardware selection, for example, if it has to operate in a low-power, off-grid location, or if electromagnetic interference or radiation are a concern. If we were to focus on application-specific functionality or power consumption, the result would be a heavily customized device (eg, with custom firmware). This would provide little option for extensibility or adaptability to other applications, since all noncritical functionality would be removed to save power. If an application area requires specific hardware, such as Digital Signal Processing (DSP) or hardware video-encoding, or has a real-time requirement, this needs to be taken into consideration.

In this example IoT device, the following features are identified as requirements, and are used to select the gateway hardware:

- *Electronic interface*: All of the required electronic interfaces for the sensors must be present, for example, SPI, ADC, and I^2C. This includes the correct bandwidth, number of connections, and, in the case of an ADC, the correct resolution.
- *Data persistence*: The IoT gateway will transmit data to the Internet, but Internet connections are unreliable, especially in mobile IoT applications. Losing data is unacceptable, so the IoT gateway needs to be able to cache the unsent data, even if it has to hibernate or it loses power. Durable storage is required with sufficient capacity to collect data at the maximum rate at which it is generated.
- *Wired or wireless Internet stack*: The Internet connection can be provided by either Wi-Fi or an Ethernet cable, depending on the location of the IoT device. It should support a standard TCP/IP stack and preferably support IPv6 for future compatibility.
- *Data encryption*: It is good practice to ensure that all data transmitted is encrypted, regardless of its perceived value. The IoT device requires sufficient processing power to encrypt transmissions without impacting sensor operation.
- *Data-processing capability*: The more sensors that get added, the more data will be produced. The gateway needs sufficient processing power and bandwidth to cope with peak demands. In addition, it may be necessary to preprocess the data from a sensor to either filter or aggregate readings before transmission.
- *Programmability*: The hardware needs to be simple to program, preferably in a high-level language or by using nonhardware-specific libraries.
- *Low cost and commercially available*: The hardware needs to be available, but cost also needs to be considered. The IoT ethos indicates that there will be large numbers of devices, which puts a greater emphasis on the cost.

- *Device security*: It is difficult to secure a device which can be physically compromised. A basic level of security should be offered to ensure that, for example, false data cannot be injected from a compromised gateway.
- *Future proof*: Hardware prices are constantly falling and electronic-power performance is improving. Reducing costs and improving performance by updating hardware is only an option if the software is easily portable.

15.5.1 GATEWAY HARDWARE

As new hardware is constantly appearing, we divide the available hardware into groups and select the preferable hardware for the gateway, based on the previously outlined requirements. It is worth revisiting the hardware market frequently to identify better-suited hardware.

A microprocessor usually only offers processing power and requires RAM and storage to be added as separate chips on a PCB. This results in a lot of additional work and power, whereas a microcontroller has most of the basics embedded on a single chip; it is for this reason that we consider microcontrollers for the gateway hardware. Table 15.2 shows a selection of common microcontrollers. They tend to have a low clock-speed and are suitable for real-time applications. Programming requires low-level languages such as C or assembly.

More powerful microcontrollers exist, and are often referred to as a System on a Chip (SoC), although the distinction between them is blurred. The term microcontroller often refers to low-memory, low-performance, single-chip devices, whereas a SoC usually supports an operating system such as Linux or Windows, although this is not a definition. Table 15.3 shows a selection of common SoC processors.

Both a microcontroller and a SoC are of little use on their own; they need to be assembled on a PCB with other components, for example, power regulators, pin headers, and peripheral interfaces. The easiest way to build a prototype is to use a development board. The development board, often called an evaluation board, will expose all the electronic interfaces, and provide a way to program and power the chosen chip. For example, the Arduino UNO shown in Fig. 15.3 is a development board for the ATmega328.

Table 15.2 Common Microcontroller Details

Microcontroller	Clock (MHz)	RAM/Flash/ EEPROM KB	I/O
MSP430	25	66/512/0	12-bit ADC, 74 GPIO, SPI, I2C, UART/USART, USB, LCD, DAC, RTC
ATSAM3X8E	84	100/512/0	12-bit ADC, 54 GPIO, SPI, UART/USART, USB, DAC, RTC, PWM, CAN, SDIO/SD/MMC, NFC, TWI
ATtiny828	20	0.512/8/0.256	10-bit ADC, 28 GPIO, SPI, I2C, UART/USART, PWM
PIC32MX	80	32/512/0	10-bit ADC, 16 GPIO, SPI, I2C, UART, JTAG USB, CAN, Ethernet, DMA controller

Table 15.3 Example System on a Chip (SoC) Hardware

SoC	Cores/Clock	GPU	I/O
Exynos5422	4 × 2.1 and 4 × 1.5 GHz	ARM Mali-T628MP6	ADC, GPIO, I2C, SPI, UART, USB, HDMI, SDIO/SD/MMC, PWM, LCD, MIPICSI2, eDP, PCM, I2S, S/PDIF, PMIC, DMA Controller, MCT
S805	4 × 1.5 GHz	ARM Mali-450	ADC, GPIO, SPI, I2C, UART, USB, DDIO/SD/MMC, PWM, SDXC/SDHC/SD, I2S, SPDIF, HDMI, PCM, Ethernet
AM3358	1 × 1 GHz	SGX530	ADC, GPIO, SPI, I2C, UART, CAN, USB, SDIO/SD/MMC, McASP RTC.
BCM2836	4 × 900 MHz	Broadcom Video Core IV	GPIO, SPI, I2C, UART, USB, PWM, PCM/I2S, DMA, Timers, Interrupt Controller.
E3845	4 × 1.91 GHz	Intel HD Graphics	USB, I2S, SIO, eDP, DP/HDMI, VGA, SIO
i.MX6Solo	1 × 1 GHz	VivanteGC880 for 3D and VivanteGC320 for 2D	ADC, GPIO, SPI, I2C, UART, USB, ESAI, I2S/SSI, Ethernet, FlexCAN, NANDCntrl, PCIe, MIPIHSI, S/PDIFTx/Rx, HDMI, LVDS
IntelQuark-SoCX1000	1 × 400 MHz	N/A	ADC, 16GPIO, SPI, I2C, UART, USB, SDIO/SD/eMMC, DMA, RTC, PCIe, Ethernet, CSMSA/CD

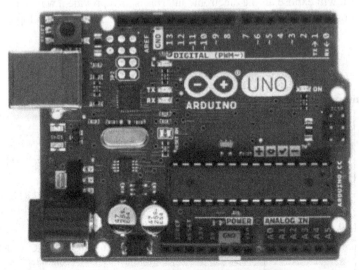

FIGURE 15.3 Arduino UNO Development Board With ATmega328 Microcontroller

If the IoT device is to be made in low volumes, then the development board can be used in the final design, whereas for larger numbers it is best to get custom boards manufactured. It is important to understand any royalties or licensing restrictions associated with manufacturing custom boards, for example, disclosing derived works.

15.5.2 GATEWAY SOFTWARE

The more powerful a microcontroller or SoC, the more complicated the software becomes, for example, there will be more interrupts and electronic interfaces. To manage the processing power efficiently, supporting libraries are required, for example, for threading.

In Table 15.4, we look at how different platforms meet the IoT requirements for this specific weather-station gateway example.

The Arduino platform offers a great deal of libraries for all sorts of hardware, but ultimately the CPU and processing capabilities, combined with the lack of a full TCP/IP stack, make it unsuitable for a gateway.

The .NetMF platform is open source and supports high-level programming languages such as C# and Visual Basic, and provides libraries for SSL, but it only runs on a limited set of hardware. Overall, .NetMF would be a good contender for the weather-station gateway.

The Mbed platform is excellent for IoT devices, it supports SSL, and there is a good selection of supported hardware. Programming is done with C, which may be difficult for beginners. Commercial licensing must be considered, depending on the libraries and hardware utilized. The Mbed operating system is designed specifically for IoT, making it an excellent choice if you are comfortable programming in C.

The Microsoft Windows 10 IoT platform is a full OS that is targeted toward IoT devices. It runs the Windows 10 kernel and supports high-level programming languages such as C#. There are libraries to support most electronic interfaces, and it is designed to interoperate with cloud backend services. The supported hardware is currently very limited, making it unsuitable for the weather-station gateway.

There are many variants of Linux available for embedded systems. They are generally well supported, and are capable of interfacing with a wide range of hardware. Many programming languages,

Table 15.4 Platform Capability for Different IoT Requirements

	Arduino Platform	.NetMF	Mbed	Windows IoT	Linux
Electronic interfaces	×	×	×	×	×
Data persistence	×	×	×	×	×
Wired or Wireless Internet stack		×	×	×	×
Data encryption		×	×	×	×
Programmability		×		×	×
Low cost commercially available	×	×	×		
Device security				×	×
Future proof	×				×

environments, and libraries are available, and software programs are easily ported to new hardware. If the "device security" requirement is to be met, then storage encryption and specialist hardware such as a Trusted Platform Module (TPM) chip should be used. Linux is the most versatile option for the weather-station gateway, as it offers a range of development environments and languages, has good hardware support, and has extensive libraries. It is the easiest for beginners, supports high-level languages such as Python [7], and is simple to lock down with disk encryption.

Hardware capable of running a full Linux operating system is more expensive than a simple microcontroller, for example, the memory requirements mean that off-chip memory is required. The processor needs to be more powerful, and the total electronic power consumption of the IoT device will be considerably greater than that of a custom microcontroller device. Platforms such as Mbed may be better suited to this.

There are many variants of Linux that run on ARM-based single-board computers, such as Android, Slackware, Gentoo, openSUSE, Fedora, and Arch Linux, to name a few. Although they are all similar, selecting a variant is down to personal preference and compatibility with the chosen hardware. The variant which particularly stands out is Snappy Ubuntu Core. It has support for fault-tolerant upgrades and APIs for cloud service- providers. We will base the weather-station example on Snappy Ubuntu Core.

15.5.3 SUMMARY

Based on the requirements for the weather-station example and the collection of sensors, we have opted for a single-board Linux computer, powered by a System on a Chip (SoC). The main driving force behind this is to make an easily transferable example rather than a custom-built device. The implications of this are that the hardware is relatively expensive and the power consumption will be considerably higher compared to a microprocessor. The weather-station example will be easily transferable to other application areas as well as to newer hardware. Table 15.5 shows a range of single-board computers compatible with Linux variants, as well as the supported electronic interfaces. We decided to use the Snappy Ubuntu Core Linux distribution as the main OS.

15.6 DATA TRANSMISSION

The sensor data needs to be transmitted to the backend services via the Internet. To do this we have an IoT gateway with either wired or wireless Internet access. The data is packaged for transmission and received by an online service. Traditionally the online service would use Remote Procedure Calls (RPC) [6] or Simple Object Access Protocol (SOAP) [8], but these are rather heavyweight and have been superseded by protocols such as Representational State Transfer (REST) and frameworks such as Apache Thrift [9].

SOAP transmits messages over different application protocols such as HTTP [9]. It is designed to allow interoperability between different services by exchanging messages, but is considered rather verbose. The default message transmission is XML but this can be substituted by binary encoding to reduce the message size.

REST uses HTTP to transmit messages at the application layer. This way, any device which can communicate via HTTP can interact with a REST backend service. HTTP is well understood, and widely supported in many languages on many different hardware platforms, providing a greater level of flexibility for IoT devices. It is lightweight and supports different message payloads, for example, JSON and MIME [10,11].

Table 15.5 Comparison of Low-Cost, Single-Board Computer Development Boards

Mainboard (SoC)	RAM	Storage	USB	Interfaces	Size (mm)	Cost ~USD 2016
ODROID-XU4 (Exynos 5422)	2 GB, 933 MHz	MicroSD, eMMC	1 × USB 2.0, 2 × USB 3.0	ADC, 42 GPIO, SPI, I2C, UART, PWM, RTC I2S, HDMI, PMIC.	82 × 58 × 22	70
ODROID-C1 (S805)	1 GB DDR3 SDRAM	MicroSD Card Slot, eMMC module socket	4 × USB 2.0 Host, 1 × USB 2.0 OTG	ADC, 40 GPIO, SPI, I2C, UART, HDMI, RTC, IR Receiver, DMC, PLL/OSC.	85 × 56	60
BeagleBone Black(AM3358)	512 MB DDR3	MicroSD Card Slot, 4GB 8-bit eMMC on-board flash storage	1 × USB host, 1 × USB miniB	ADC, 66 GPIO, SPI, I2C, UART, CAN, PWM, LCD, GPMC, MMC1, 4 Timers.	86.4 × 53.3	50
Raspberry Pi 2 Model B (BCM-2836)	1 GB (shared with GPU)	MicroSD Card Slot	4 × USB	ADC, 17 GPIO pins, UART, SPI, I2C.	85.6 × 56.5	30
SECOpITX-BT (E3845)	Up to 8 DDR3L-1333	MicroSD, eMMC (optional), S-ATA connector	2 × USB 3.0 Host, 2 × USB 2.0 host (header), 1 × USB 2.0 host (miniPCI-e), RS-232, RS-422, RS-485	1 × RS-232/RS-422/RS-485	100 × 72	300
Udoo Neo (i.MX 6SoloX)	512 MB or 1 GB DDR3	SPI Flash onboard, MicroSD, 8-bit SDIO interface	1 × USB 2.0 A Host, 1 × USB OTG	ADC, 36 × GPIO pins, UART, 2X CAN Bus, PWM, I2C, SPI	85 × 59.3	80–110
Intel Galileo Gen 2 (Intel Quark SoC 1000)	256 MB DDR3	8MB Flash, 8KB EEPROM, SD	1 × USB 2.0 host type A, 1 × USB 2.0 client type B	ADC, 20 GPIO, SPI, I2C, UART, PWM, JTAG, RTC, JTAG	123.8 × 72	70

Both SOAP and REST were not created with IoT devices in mind. By looking at these and other technologies, we can list the top IoT data-transmission requirements:

- *Efficient data-transmission packet size*: Remote IoT devices using either mobile phone or satellite Internet connections need to preserve bandwidth and data-transmission costs.
- *Reliable transmission*: Messages need to be resent or batched, for example, where Internet connectivity is intermittent.
- *IoT message persistence*: Unsent messages need to be stored on the IoT device to survive crashes and power outages.
- *Supported by a wide range of programming languages*: The message needs to be easy to build, using a wide range of languages, and hardware suitable for IoT devices.

Based on these requirements, it is clear that we need more than just a messaging protocol: we need a message framework. Message Queue Telemetry Transport (MQTT), Messaging and Presence Protocol (XMPP), Data Distribution Service (DDS), and Advanced Message Queuing Protocol (AMQP) [12] are good examples.

15.6.1 ADVANCED MESSAGE QUEUING PROTOCOL

We have chosen to use the Advanced Message Queuing Protocol (AMQP) as our messaging protocol, as it is supported by many different server implementations, and the client is available across platforms and programming languages. The main advantage is that AMQP is a wire-level protocol, not requiring a verbose HTTP packet. This means that data is sent more efficiently in smaller, specifically encoded packets. Our IoT device sends AMQP messages to a broker (server), which then passes them on to the readers (weather-station application code). There are many AMQP-supported architectures, ranging from publish/subscribe to content-based routing, and they are worth investigating for more complex scenarios (we are using a simple publish and subscribe architecture).

We could run any AMQP-compatible server, such as Apache Qpid [13], RabbitMQ [14], or Apache ActiveMQ [15], but we have chosen to use the Windows Server AMQP-compatible service, called Windows Service Bus v1.0, which can run on any Windows server on-site installation.

We selected the Windows Server Service Bus because it is identical to the cloud-based Windows Azure Service Bus, a fully hosted commercial service. We now have the option to use the on-site solution until performance becomes an issue, and then switch over to a hosted service if required. The Microsoft Azure Service Bus has a Service Level Agreement (SLA) of 99.9%, which is approximately 8.7 h of downtime per year. Retry and error management is still required, but the uptime should be greatly improved over an on-site installation.

The weather-station application code is implemented in Python, and so we use the Apache Qpid library to post messages to the Service Bus. Currently, all sensor data is stored on the IoT device in an SQL database, which acts as a buffer before the data is transmitted. It should be possible to use an AMQP broker to automatically persist messages until transmission is possible, however, this proved to be problematic and made debugging difficult.

Be aware that not all AMQP broker implementations are the same. For example, RabbitMQ has some custom features, and Apache ActiveMQ supports multiple messaging protocols but has limited client-library support. Some implementations of an AMQP broker do not implement TLS/SSL, making it more difficult to secure the data. The recommendation is to use a Virtual Private Network (VPN), but if one IoT device is compromised this could have security implications for the remaining IoT devices; running a Secure Shell (SSH) tunnel may be an alternative.

15.6.2 BACKEND PROCESSING

Sending data to a backend service is not the end of the IoT data story: some sources predict that the number of IoT devices will exceed 26 billion by the year 2020, excluding PCs, smartphones, and tablets [16]. This means that any IoT backend service will need to be able to scale and maintain a high level of availability, just to receive and store the data produced by IoT devices.

This can cause issues. Let's assume you run a custom backend server to receive the IoT data streams. During application or operating-system updates the service may be offline, wasting valuable IoT data bandwidth. It is possible to run a failover service on enterprise-grade software and hardware to improve reliability, but this increases the complexity of the setup. We have made two key decisions for the backend services: (1) the messages will be orchestrated using a service bus supporting the Advanced Message Queuing Protocol (AMQP) [17], and (2) the processing will be orchestrated using the Hadoop platform and supporting infrastructure [18].

15.6.2.1 Overview

The objective of the backend services varies according to the application; generally there will be both compute and storage components. Fig. 15.4 shows the backend requirements for just the SHT15 sensor (temperature and humidity). The data is received from the service bus, which is written to by all IoT

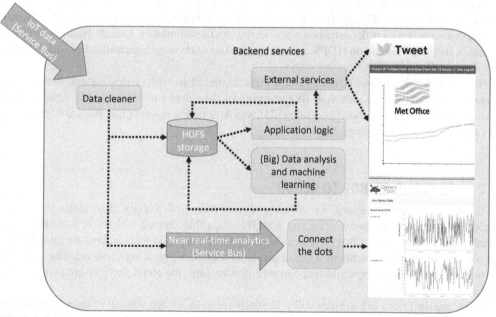

FIGURE 15.4 Backend Processing for the Weather Station SHT15 Sensor, Showing a Variety of Services Supported

devices. The data is cleaned, to ensure basic validation, and to separate data from multiple sensors into a format suitable for storage. The data is then forked into two streams:

- One stream ensures that near-real-time critical data is put on a second service bus for consumption. In our example, the temperature and humidity data are formatted on a service bus ready for consumption by a *Connect the Dots* service, which displays near-real-time data graphs on a web page [19].
- Another stream persists the data to storage, ensuring it is available for postprocessing.

The postprocessing is split into two categories: data analytics/machine learning and application logic. The data analytics and machine learning is used to explore the datasets and locate anomalies, for example, to detect sensor failure. This is very much work-in-progress, and uses the Microsoft Azure Machine Learning Studio for analysis [20].

The application logic in this example processes and filters the data to calculate the daily/weekly/ monthly minimum and maximum temperature values. The data is also formatted and pushed to external services, such as Twitter and the Weather Observations Website (WOW) [21].

15.6.2.2 Data Processing Framework

Managing the compute and storage requirements of an IoT infrastructure will get more complex as the number of devices, users, and supported services increases. This can be made easier by using an existing framework; we have selected Apache Hadoop.

Apache Hadoop is a versatile software framework which can utilize a cluster of computers for distributed storage and distributed compute [22]. There is a strong ecosystem of supporting modules for data analysis, but more importantly, it is supported by multiple cloud providers (Amazon Elastic MapReduce and Microsoft HDInsight), as well as an on-site solution, for example, HortonWorks. All our IoT weather-station data is deposited on a service bus and consumed by a single Hadoop instance. All the data is stored in Hadoop on HDFS, and the application code is orchestrated using Apache STORM [23], a near real-time data-processing engine.

There is a huge amount of Hadoop-related projects that assist with processing and storing data; for example, Apache Hive provides SQL-like querying of data stored in Hadoop [24], Apache STORM provides fast near-real-time data-processing [23], and Apache Pig is a scripting platform for processing large datasets stored in Hadoop [25].

15.6.3 TO CLOUD OR NOT TO CLOUD

For the messaging infrastructure, we have chosen the Microsoft Service Bus, although we are not locked to any particular vendor since any AMQP-compatible service will work, including a cloud-hosted solution. This ensures that there is a simple progression to and from a cloud-based solution, and that we can harness the benefits of a cloud-managed service. Comparing these benefits to an on-site solution depends on your expertise and current infrastructure; the cloud services are commercial and have a monetary cost.

Collecting data from IoT devices will potentially result in a large volume of data being produced; although not officially *Big Data*, it still takes compute resources to process. Processing data is more ef-

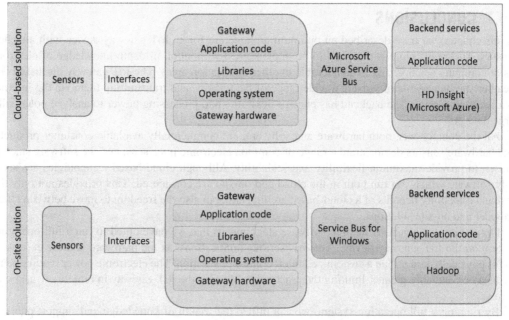

FIGURE 15.5 The Chosen Architecture is Designed to Operate Equally Well On-Site and With a Cloud Provider

The technologies selected have equivalents that will allow either full or partial migration to a cloud provider.

ficient if the compute resources are *computationally close* to the data store. Sizing an on-site infrastructure for the expected or optimal level of compute resources is difficult and costly, especially during low demand; hence a cloud-based solution offers benefits.

A cloud-based infrastructure provides the ability to purchase compute resources as, and when, they are required, even for short durations. This is particularly cost-efficient for cyclic or peak-demand data analytics. Cloud providers have fast interconnects between the data stores and compute resources, making them ideal for data processing/analytics.

The Cloud-provider market is a fast-developing space and clearly offers benefits, especially to an IoT architecture. We are keen to harness these benefits, but fear vendor lock-in; redesigning an IoT solution to migrate a Cloud provider is unacceptable.

Hadoop is offered by multiple cloud providers, has a wide range of powerful add-ons/tools, and can easily be run on-site using a wide range of nonspecialist hardware, making it an ideal choice.

For this example, we have selected HDInsight, hosted by Microsoft Azure, to store and process the IoT data, and the hosted Azure Service Bus for message transmission. For testing, debugging, and experimentation we use an on-site install of Hortonworks HDInsight for computation and processing, and an on-site install of Service Bus for Windows. A comparison can be seen in Fig. 15.5.

15.7 CONCLUSIONS

In this chapter, we have described an optimum architecture for an IoT gateway device with attached sensors. The architecture is designed to be implemented without an in-depth knowledge of electronics or computer science, and is transferable to other application areas. The IoT gateway discussed is a weather station capable of sensing a wide range of parameters, and transmitting them via the Internet to a backend service. The backend has enough flexibility and processing power to analyze potentially large datasets.

All the components, both hardware and software, are commercially available consumer products. The hardware sensors demonstrate a range of common electronic interfaces, and the software stack is chosen to provide maximum flexibility and scalability. Although cloud-based technologies are used, only software which can run both in the cloud and on-site are considered. This provides not only the cost and scalability benefits of a cloud-based architecture, but also the freedom to move between cloud provider and on-site solutions.

Optimizing for a generic flexible software-stack means that we have opted to run a full operating system on the IoT gateway device. This has serious implications, as the hardware is more expensive and is physically larger than a customized microcontroller solution. The electronic power requirements are also considerably greater, limiting the practicality of using the IoT gateway in remote off-grid scenarios.

By running a full operating system, we can utilize the wealth of knowledge and support publicly available, and easily incorporate existing libraries and functionality. Users can select from a range of programming and scripting environments, and migration to newer hardware is simpler. With the emergence of low-cost SoC single-board computers, we can expect to see many more IoT gateway devices running an OS.

The sensor data is first stored in an SQL database on the IoT gateway to ensure persistence through power outages. The data is then sent via AMQP messages to the backend, via the Internet, as the connectivity and bandwidth becomes available.

AMQP provides a framework for sending messages, which simplifies the architecture and minimizes the amount of custom code on the IoT gateway device. AMQP is supported by a cloud-based service bus, which is commercially available as part of the Microsoft Windows Azure cloud offering. Using the service bus is optional and can be removed by running an AMQP server as part of the backend services. We include the service bus to increase the backend availability to 99.9%, as we identify the IoT bandwidth as a limited, costly resource.

The data is stored as part of a Hadoop cluster, which provides a distributed data-store and compute resource. Hadoop enables us to harness the power of compute clusters on-site, and is supported by multiple cloud-providers. Hadoop has an ecosystem of modules and packages which provide, for example, stream processing (STORM), data storage (HDFS), and querying (HIVE). Hadoop is a very active framework; once the IoT streams are stored, there are enough tools to support detailed analysis, and scalability sufficient to process large datasets. Fig. 15.6 shows the complete architecture of the weather-station hardware and software, as detailed in this chapter.

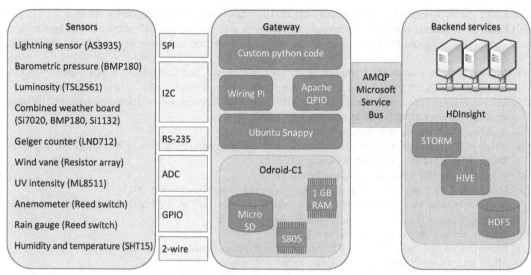

FIGURE 15.6 IoT Weather-Station Device and Supporting Backend Services

ACKNOWLEDGMENTS

Much of this work was made possible by the University of Southampton summer internship program, Microsoft, and Microsoft Research. We are particularly grateful to the following interns: Ethan Harris—cloud services and Marian Daogaru—weather-station hardware.

REFERENCES

[1] Telecommunication standardization sector of ITU, series Y. 2060 overview of the Internet of Things; 2012.

[2] Rivera J, Van der Meulen R. Gartner's 2014 Hype Cycle for emerging technologies maps the journey to digital business. http://www.gartner.com/newsroom/id/2819918; 2014.

[3] Gomez C, Paradells J. Wireless home automation networks: a survey of architectures and technologies. IEEE Commun Mag 2010;48(6):92–101.

[4] Millar I, Beale M, Donoghue BJ, Lindstrom KW, Williams S. The IrDA standard for high-speed infrared communications. HP J 1998;49(1):10–26.

[5] LAPIS Semiconductor. ML8511 UV sensor with voltage output. Datasheet FEDL8511-05. https://cdn.sparkfun.com/datasheets/Sensors/LightImaging/ML8511_3-8-13.pdf; 2013.

[6] Birrell AD, Nelson BJ. Implementing remote procedure calls. ACM Trans Comput Syst (TOCS) 1984;2(1):39–59.

[7] Dalheimer MK, Welsh M. Running Linux, 5th ed. O'Reilly Media, Sebastopol, CA; 2006.

[8] Box D, Ehnebuske D, Kakivaya G, Layman A, Mendelsohn N, Nielsen HF, Thatte S, Winer D. Simple object access protocol (SOAP) 1.1, 2000. World Wide Web Consortium (2001) (W3C); 2001.

[9] I. RFC, 2616, hypertext transfer protocol—HTTP/1.1. http://www.rfc.net/rfc2616html/; 1999.

[10] Pautasso C, Zimmermann O, Leymann F. Restful web services vs. big web services: making the right architectural decision. In: Proceedings of the seventeenth international conference on World Wide Web, ACM; 2008.

[11] Aho AV, Sethi R, Ullman JD. Compilers: Principles, Techniques, and Tools. Boston, MA: Addison-Wesley Publishing Company; 1986. Addison-Wesley series in computer science and information processing.

[12] International organization standardization, ISO/IEC 19464:2014 information technology—advanced message queuing protocol (AMQP) v1.0 specification. ISO/IEC; 2014.

[13] Apache, Qpid [Online]. http://qpid.apache.org/; 2015.

[14] Videla A, Williams JJW. RabbitMQ in Action: Distributed Messaging for Everyone. Manning Pubs Co Series. Shelter Island: Manning Publications Company; 2012.

[15] Apache, ActiveMQ. http://activemq.apache.org/; 2011.

[16] Middleton P, Kjeldsen P, Tully J. Forecast: the Internet of Things, worldwide; 2013.

[17] OASIS Advanced Message Queuing Protocol (AMQP) Version 1.0. OASIS Standard. http://docs.oasis-open.org/amqp/core/v1.0/os/amqp-core-complete-v1.0-os.pdf; 2012.

[18] Apache, Hadoop. https://hadoop.apache.org/; 2015.

[19] Bloch O. Connect the Dots [Online]. https://github.com/Azure/connectthedots; 2015.

[20] Microsoft. Microsoft Azure Machine Learning. https://studio.azureml.net/; 2016.

[21] MetOffice. Weather Observations website; site ID 938516001. http://wow.metof http://ce.gov.uk/; 2015.

[22] Cox SJ, Cox JT, Boardman RP, Johnston SJ, Scott M, O'Brien NS. Iridis-pi: a low-cost, compact demonstration cluster. Cluster Comput 2014;17(2):349–58.

[23] Apache, STORM. https://storm.apache.org/; 2015.

[24] Apache, Hive [Online]. http://hive.apache.org/; 2015.

[25] Apache, Pig [Online]. http://pig.apache.org/; 2015.

INTERNET OF VEHICLES AND APPLICATIONS

16

W. Wu*, Z. Yang*, K. Li**

*Department of Computer Science, Sun Yat-sen University, Guangzhou, China;
**Department of Computer Science, State University of New York, NY, United States of America

16.1 BASICS OF IoV

16.1.1 BACKGROUND AND CONCEPT

The new era of the Internet of Things is driving the evolution of conventional vehicular ad-hoc networks (VANETs) into the Internet of Vehicles (IoV). IoV refers to the real-time data interaction between vehicles and roads, vehicles and vehicles, as well as vehicles and cities, using mobile-communication technology, vehicle navigation systems, smart-terminal devices, and information platforms to enable information exchange/interaction and a driving–instruction–controlling network system.

IoV enables the gathering and sharing of information regarding vehicles, roads, and their surroundings. Moreover, it features the processing, computing, sharing, and secure release of information onto information platforms, including Internet systems. Based on such information, information platforms can effectively guide and supervise vehicles, and provide abundant multimedia and mobile Internet application services. IoV is an integrated network for supporting intelligent traffic management, intelligent dynamic information services, and intelligent vehicle control, representing a typical application of IoT technology in intelligent transportation systems (ITS).

The concept of IoV has been recognized by more and more people in recent years, and it is currently in a stage of evolving from concept to reality. ITS in Europe and Japan have adopted certain forms of IoV technology. In New Delhi, all 55,000 licensed rickshaws have been fitted with GPS devices so that drivers can be held accountable for their questionable route selection. China's Ministry of Transport had ordered that GPS systems be installed and connected on all long-haul buses and hazmat vehicles by the end of 2011, to ensure good driving habits and reduce the risk of accidents and traffic jams. The Brazilian government has set a goal for all cars in circulation to be fitted with electronic ID chips from its National Automated Vehicle Identification System (Siniav).

IoV is a complex integrated network system, which connects different people within vehicles, different vehicles, and different environmental entities within cities. With the rapid development of computation and communications technologies, IoV promises huge commercial interest and research value.

16.1.2 NETWORK ARCHITECTURE

IoV consists of complex and heterogeneous wireless-network components. A general network architecture is shown in Fig. 16.1. From the viewpoint of system, IoV consists of three layers: vehicles, connections, and servers/clouds.

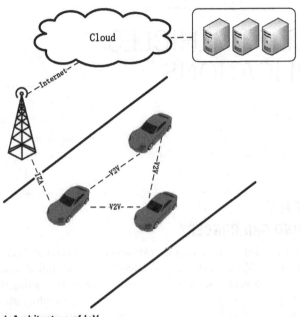

FIGURE 16.1 The Network Architecture of IoV

16.1.2.1 Vehicles in IoV

Vehicles in IoV are smart-vehicles with complex intravehicle systems. In particular, there are various sensors to collect vehicle and driving status, and communication devices to communicate with other vehicles and/or the Internet. Of course, an embedded software platform (also known as a vehicular operating system) is necessary to process status information and control all devices.

More and more efforts are being made on research and development of vehicle intelligence. Almost all major vehicle manufacturers have started their intelligent-vehicle projects, including Toyota, Ford, GM, BMW, Volvo, etc. Also, major IT corporations such as Google, Apple, Baidu, and Huawei are working on intelligent-vehicle systems. Quite a number of vehicles running on the highway have been equipped with intelligent systems, although the functionalities related to IoV are still very simple.

In IoV, vehicles play a dual role: they are clients to consume the service from the Internet and at the same time they are peers to perform distributed computing. Obviously, IoV is a hybrid system with both peer-2-peer and client–server computing paradigms. With a peer-2-peer paradigm, vehicles can cooperate and collaborate with each other to realize distributed-computing functionalities, such as file sharing and cooperative driving. With the client–server paradigm, vehicles can use the resources at servers from the Internet. A server can be either an ordinary computing node or a cloud data center. With servers, IoV can conduct many more complex applications and tasks.

16.1.2.2 Connections in IoV

From the view of communications, IoV consists of two different types of wireless connections. Vehicle-to-Vehicle (V2V) communication is used to exchange information among vehicles directly. Wireless links of V2V connect vehicles in an ad-hoc way and construct VANETs. The recently defined standard IEEE 802.11p for intervehicular communication, designed according to the specific requirements of

V2V interaction, constitutes an essential step toward this next phase. However, V2V communication is subject to major network effects. The second type of connection is Vehicle-to-Road (V2R), also called Vehicle-to-Infrastructure (V2I). V2R refers to the information exchange between vehicles, and to the roadside infrastructure equipped with wireless communication technology, such as traffic lights or warning signs for roadwork. Unlike V2V, V2R can reach long distances and achieve high scalability. V2R facilitates the interaction of vehicles and roadside units to enhance the aforementioned application scenarios. Moreover, those units may be used as additional hops to augment the reach, and thus the overall value, of intervehicular communication.

With V2V and V2R communications, IoV can realize information exchange among vehicles, roadside infrastructure, and also the Internet. Then, various applications can be supported by IoV, including ITS and Internet services.

16.1.2.3 Servers/Clouds in IoV

Servers or cloud data centers may provide various services to vehicles. Servers have powerful computing resources, storage resources, and also more information/data outside of vehicles, so advanced or complex IoV applications must involve servers at the Internet.

Besides traditional servers, cloud-computing based on data centers are becoming more and more popular. In cloud data centers, various computing and communication resources, including CPU cycles, memory, storage, and even network bandwidth, can all be scheduled and consumed in a flexible and on-demand way. Resources allocated to a specific user can be scaled automatically, according to workload levels. Such a new computing paradigm can significantly improve capacity/efficiency, and at the same time reduce the cost of IoT information processing. For example, driving-status data can be collected from vehicles and sent to cloud data centers for congestion analysis. During rush hour there are many vehicles on the road; therefore more data may be collected, and then more computing resources may be allocated to conduct the processing. Then, at midnight, the computing resource for congestion analysis may be released automatically by the cloud management system.

16.2 CHARACTERISTICS AND CHALLENGES
16.2.1 CHARACTERISTICS OF IoV

Vehicular networks are mainly composed of vehicle nodes, which behave quite differently from other wireless nodes. Therefore, a vehicular network has several characteristics that may affect the design of IoV technologies. Some of the characteristics will bring challenges to IoV technological development, whereas some others may bring benefit.

1. *Highly dynamic topology*: Compared to common mobile nodes, vehicles may move at quite a high speed. This causes the topology of a vehicular network to change frequently. Such high dynamicity in network topology must be carefully considered in IoV development.
2. *Variable network density*: The network density in IoV varies, depending on the traffic density, which can be very high in the case of a traffic jam, or very low, as in suburban traffic. At either extreme the network may frequently disconnect.
3. *Large-scale network*: The network scale could be large in dense, urban areas, such as city centers, highways, and at entrances to big cities.
4. *Geographical communication*: Compared to other networks that use unicast or multicast where the communication endpoints are defined by ID or group ID, the vehicular networks often have

a new type of communication, which addresses the geographical areas where packets need to be forwarded (eg, in safe-driving applications).

5. *Predictable mobility*: Vehicular networks differ from other types of mobile ad-hoc networks in which nodes move in a random way. Vehicles, on the other hand, are constrained by road topology and layout, by the requirement to obey road signs and traffic lights, and by responding to other moving vehicles, leading to predictability in terms of their mobility.

6. *Sufficient energy and storage*: A common characteristic of nodes in vehicular networks is that nodes have ample energy and computing power (including both storage and processing), since nodes are cars instead of small handheld devices.

7. *Various communication environments*. Vehicular networks are usually operated in two typical communication environments. In highway traffic scenarios, the environment is relatively simple and straightforward (eg, constrained one-dimensional movement), whereas in city conditions it becomes much more complex. The streets in a city are often separated by buildings, trees, and other obstacles; therefore, there is not always a direct line of communication in the direction of intended data communication.

16.2.2 CHALLENGES IN IoV

The objective of IoV is to integrate multiple users, multiple vehicles, multiple things, and multiple networks, to always provide the best connected communication capability that is manageable, controllable, operational, and credible. It composes a truly complex system. Moreover, the applications of IoV are quite different from those of other networks, and, consequently, many special requirements arise. Both of these two aspects bring new technical challenges to IoV research and development.

1. *Poor network connectivity and stability*: Due to the high mobility and rapid changes of topology, which lead to frequent network disconnections and link failures, message loss should be common. Then, how to elongate the life of communication links is always challenging.

2. *Hard delay constraints*: Many IoV applications have hard delay constraints, although they may not require a high data rate or bandwidth. For example, in an automatic highway system, when a brake event happens, the message should be transferred and arrive in a certain time to avoid a car crash. In this kind of application, instead of an average delay, a minimal delay would be crucial.

3. *High reliability requirements*: Transportation and driving-related applications are usually safety-sensitive. Obviously, such an application requirement is high reliability. However, due to complex network architecture, large network scale, and poor stability of network topology, achieving high reliability in IoV is far from trivial. A special design should be conducted in various layers, from networking protocols to applications.

4. *High scalability requirements*: High scalability is another big challenge in IoV. As mentioned before, IoV is usually very large in terms of node number and deployment territory. Such a large scale certainly requires high scalability in IoV technology.

5. *Security and privacy*: Keeping a reasonable balance between the security and privacy is one of the main challenges in IoV. The receipt of trustworthy information from its source is important for the receiver. However, this trusted information can violate the privacy needs of the sender.

6. *Service sustainability*: Assuring the sustainability of service providing in IoV is still a challenging task, calling for high intelligence methods, as well as a user-friendly network-mechanism design. There are challenges in adjusting all vehicles to provide sustainable services over heterogeneous

networks in real-time, as they are subject to limited network bandwidth, mixed wireless access, lower service platforms, and a complex city environment.

16.3 ENABLING TECHNOLOGIES

IoV is a large-scale and complex system with heterogeneous network components and diverse applications. Therefore, various technologies, especially networking technologies, are necessary to make IoV applications workable. In the following, we introduce these enabling technologies according to network layers: MAC layer and routing layer. In the routing layer, we introduce both unicast-oriented routing protocols and broadcast-based dissemination algorithms. Of course, broadcast-based information dissemination can also be viewed as application-layer protocols. In any respect, this does not affect the understanding of these algorithms.

16.3.1 MAC PROTOCOLS AND STANDARDS

There is quite a lot of research on designing special MAC protocols for IoV, or more precisely, on VANETs. Almost all VANET MAC protocols are based on the basic wireless-communication standard IEEE 802.11. Therefore, we introduce IEEE 802.11 first, and then discuss the extension to its variants for VANETs.

16.3.1.1 IEEE 802.11

According to the IEEE's technical paper, a wireless LAN (WLAN or WiFi) is a data transmission system designed to provide location-independent network access between computing devices by using radio waves rather than a cable infrastructure.

The IEEE LAN committee raised a series of Wireless Local Area Network (WLAN) standards. Collectively, these wireless standards are identified as the 802.11 standard [1]. Initially, this specification was ratified by IEEE in 1997. Subsequently, various amendments have been made to the 802.11 standard, as shown in Table 16.1.

Table 16.1 IEEE 802.11 Standards

Protocol	Release Date	Frequency (GHz)	Maximum Data Rate	Modulation	Approximate Range	
					Indoor (m)	Outdoor (m)
801.11	1997	2.4	2 Mbit/s	DSSS/FHSS	20	100
802.11a	1999	5	54 Mbit/s	OFDM	35	120
802.11b	1999	2.4	11 Mbit/s	DSSS	35	140
802.11g	2003	2.4	54 Mbit/s	OFDM/DSSS	38	140
802.11n	2009	2.4/5	600 Mbit/s (40 MHz, 4 MIMO)	OFDM	70	250
802.11ac	2011	5	867 Mbps, 1.73 Gbps, 3.47 Gbps, 6.93 Gbps (160 MHz, 8 MIMO)	OFDM	35	
802.11ad	2012	60	Up to 6912 Mbit/s	SC/OFDM	60	100

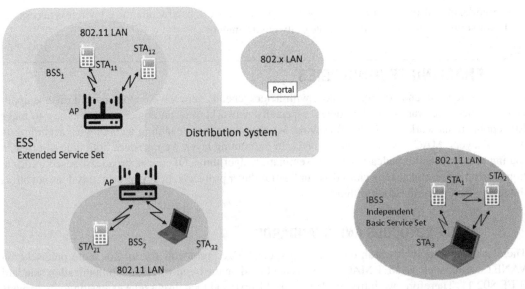

FIGURE 16.2 The Network Architecture of IEEE 802.11

As shown in Fig. 16.2, an IEEE 802.11 network consists of two types of entities: mobile station (STA) and access point (AP). AP refers to the device integrated into the wireless LAN and the distribution system. STA refers to the client terminal, with access mechanisms to the wireless medium and radio contact to the AP. There may be also a "portal," which bridges a WLAN to other (wired) networks. A Basic Service Set (BSS) is the basic building functional-block of an IEEE 802.11 LAN, which consists of an AP and a set of STAs. Multiple BSSs may be connected into one LAN to extend the coverage to a large area; such a set of BSSs is called Extended Service Set (ESS). An IBSS is a special type of IEEE 802.11 LAN, where wireless clients can connect with each other via point-to-point mode.

IEEE 802.11's frequency band is either the 2.4-GHz (specifically, 2.4000–2.4835 GHz) or the 5.0-GHz (specifically, 5.150–5.825 GHz) spectrum bands. The 2.4-GHz band supports a total of 14 channels, although the FCC limits this to 11 channels in the US. The 5-GHz band is regulated and thus generally free of interference. However, signals at this frequency suffer from poor range and are easily obstructed by intermediary objects. The less-often-used 5-GHz band supports up to 12 nonoverlapping channels (in the US), and is further separated into 3 sub-bands (with 4 channels each).

16.3.1.2 IEEE 802.11p/WAVE

Vehicular networks have attracted more and more attention, without a doubt, as the number of vehicles on the road grows so quickly. Therefore, several working groups have been set up to make the communication protocols, such as the IEEE 1609 working group and the IEEE 802.11p task group.

IEEE 802.11p is known as an amendment to the IEEE Std 802.11 for wireless access in vehicular environments. Because of the high mobility of vehicles, the original protocols in IEEE Std 802.11 are no longer suitable to this environment. To address this issue, the IEEE working group has come up with

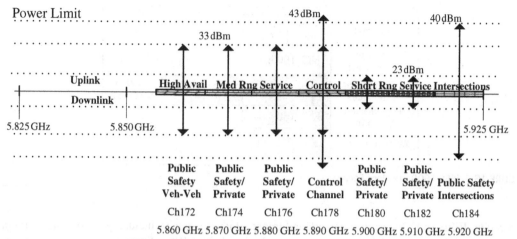

FIGURE 16.3 Channel Allocation in WAVE

a protocol stack known as IEEE 802.11p Wireless Access in Vehicular Environment (WAVE) [2] to handle the problem of a reliable connection.

WAVE extends the ASTM Standard E2213-03 (known as DSRC) to operate in a rapidly varying environment, and to exchange messages without joining a BSS. It uses the Enhanced Distributed Channel Access (EDCA) MAC sublayer protocol design, based on that of the IEEE 802.11e, with some modifications, whereas the physical layer is OFDM (Orthogonal Frequency Division Modulation), as used in IEEE 802.11a. In addition, it defines the signaling techniques and interface functions used by stations communicating outside of the context of a BSS that are controlled by the IEEE 802.11MAC.

Fig. 16.3 shows the channel allocation in IEEE 802.11p. The 75-MHz band is divided into one Control Channel (CCH) and six Service Channels (SCHs). Two small- and two medium-zone service channels are designated for extended data transfer. Two service channels are designated for special safety-critical applications. Public safety applications and messages have priority in all channels. First, RSU announces to OBUs 10 times per s the applications it supports and on which particular channels. OBU listens on Channel 172, then authenticates the RSU digital signature. OBU should execute safety apps first, and then switch channels, and then, in turn, should execute nonsafety apps. At last OBU returns to Channel 172 and listens to the channel again.

On top of IEEE 802.11p, IEEE 1609 defines an architecture and a complementary, standardized set of services and interfaces for vehicle-related wireless communication [3]. It provides foundations for a broad range of applications in the transportation environment, such as vehicle safety, automated tolling, enhanced navigation, and traffic management. The architecture of IEEE 1609 protocols is shown in Fig. 16.4.

IEEE 1609.0 describes the WAVE architecture and services necessary for multichannel DSRC/WAVE devices to communicate in a mobile vehicular environment. IEEE 1609.1 describes key components of WAVE system architecture, and defines data flows and resources. It also defines command-message formats and data-storage formats, and specifies the types of devices that may by supported by OBU. IEEE 1609.2 collects the security-processing requirements necessary for WAVE system

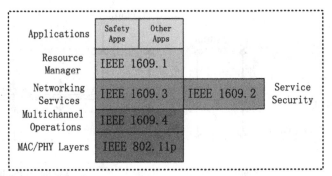

FIGURE 16.4 IEEE 1609 Standard Family

operation. IEEE 1609.3 specifies network and transport layer services, including addressing and routing, in support of secure WAVE data exchange. It also defines Wave Short Messages, providing an efficient WAVE-specific alternative to IPv6 (Internet Protocol version 6) that can be directly supported by applications [3]. IEEE 1609.4 specifies MAC sublayer functions and services for supporting multichannel wireless connectivity between WAVE devices. It controls the operation of upper-layer data transfers across multiple channels without requiring knowledge of PHY parameters, and it also describes multichannel-operation channel-routing and switching for different scenarios. IEEE 1609.11 defines the services and secure message-formats necessary for supporting secure electronic payments. IEEE 1609.12 indicates identifier values that have been allocated for use by WAVE systems.

Besides the standard protocols, researchers have also conducted a study to extend and improve the performance of MAC protocols. Based on the latest standard draft of IEEE 802.11p and IEEE 1609.4, Wang et al. [4] proposed a variable CCH interval (VCI) multichannel medium access control (MAC) scheme, which can dynamically adjust the length ratio between CCH and SCHs. The scheme also introduces a multichannel coordination mechanism to provide contention-free access of SCHs. Markov modeling is conducted to optimize the intervals based on the traffic condition. Dang et al. [5] proposed a new multichannel MAC for VANETs, named HER-MAC, which supports both TDMA and CSMA multiple-access schemes. The HER-MAC allows vehicle nodes to send safety messages without collision on the CCH, within their reserved time-slots, and to utilize the SCH resources during the control channel interval (CCHI) for the nonsafety message transmissions.

16.3.2 ROUTING PROTOCOLS

Routing protocol is the network-layer protocol to provide end-to-end message delivery service. Although many IoV applications are executed in a broadcasting way, there are still applications requiring unicast-oriented multihop communications. Unfortunately, to the best of our knowledge, there is still no specific routing protocol for IoV proposed. Therefore, routing protocols for common MANETs have to be used if unicast of messages is necessary.

Routing for MANETs has always been a hot topic, and many protocols have been proposed, including DSR and DSDV. Among others, AODV and OLSR are the most popular and widely accepted. Also, IEEE 802.11s provides a multihop forwarding mechanism for 802.11, and can also be used for message routing in unicast.

16.3.2.1 AODV

Ad hoc On-Demand Distance Vector (AODV) routing [6] is a routing protocol for mobile or other wireless ad hoc networks. It uses an on-demand approach for finding routes. The source node and the intermediate nodes store the next-hop information corresponding to each flow for data-packet transmission. The source-node floods the RouteRequest packet in the network when a route is not available for the desired destination. When an intermediate node receives a RouteRequest, it either forwards the packet or prepares a RouteReply if it has a valid route to the destination. AODV uses a destination sequence number (DestSeqNum) to determine an up-to-date path to the destination. A node updates its path information only if the DestSeqNum of the current packet received is greater than or equal to the last DestSeqNum stored at the node with smaller hop count.

16.3.2.2 OLSR

The Optimized Link State Routing Protocol (OLSR) [7] is a proactive link-state routing protocol, which uses hello and topology control (TC) messages to discover and then disseminate link-state information throughout the ad hoc network. Individual nodes use this topology information to compute next-hop destinations for all nodes in the network, using the shortest hop-forwarding paths.

The OLSR protocol uses a link-state algorithm to proactively determine the most efficient path between nodes. The key point of OLSR lies in the dynamic Multi-Point Relay (MPR) technique, which selects only a subset of neighboring nodes to relay data instead of every node acting as a relay. MPRs are elected in such a way that every node can communicate with an MPR within one hop. The localized network information is shared among MPRs to maintain network-wide routing paths. This allows every MPR to have a complete routing table while simultaneously minimizing the number of topology-control messages.

16.3.2.3 Multihop-MAC Protocol (IEEE 802.11s)

IEEE 802.11s is an IEEE 802.11 amendment for mesh networking, defining how wireless devices can interconnect to create a WLAN mesh network, which may be used for static topologies and ad hoc networks. IEEE 802.11s supports both broadcast/multicast and unicast delivery, using "radio-aware metrics over self-configuring multi-hop topologies." An 802.11s mesh-network device is labeled as Mesh Station (mesh STA). Mesh STAs form mesh links with one another, over which mesh paths can be established using a routing protocol. 802.11s defines a default mandatory routing-protocol (Hybrid Wireless Mesh Protocol, or HWMP), yet allows vendors to operate using alternate protocols. HWMP is a combination of AODV and tree-based routing.

16.3.3 BROADCASTING AND INFORMATION DISSEMINATION

Information dissemination is the transportation of information to the intended recipients while satisfying certain requirements such as delay, reliability, and so forth. These requirements vary, depending upon the information being disseminated. The main issue for information dissemination is that a simple query or on-demand methodology for disseminating information does not suit VANETs, due to their high mobility and network partitions. According to different dissemination schemes, information dissemination algorithms can be classified into three types, as follows.

16.3.3.1 V2V Based

In these algorithms, information is disseminated among vehicles via V2V connections. Yan et al. [8] focused on the problem that a sender needs to disseminate information to M recipients and collect

M receipts in an interested area consisting of k roads, which is solved by a processor scheduling scheme. In [9], the dissemination protocol is based on the probability that a vehicle will meet an event. TIGeR [10] is a traffic-aware intersection-based geographical routing protocol, where only nodes at intersections make routing decision based on vehicular traffic information of different roads and the road's angle with respect to the destination. VITP [11] is designed to provide car drivers with time-sensitive information about traffic conditions and roadside facilities.

As in other wireless networks, clustering has been used to reduce communications cost in vehicular networks. Chu et al. [12] designed a cluster based overlay solution, which creates a mobility-adaptive cluster to represent local traffic information and selects the optimal relay node of the intercluster forwarding pair to increase the efficiency. DPP [13] controls message propagation direction by using limited-range packet radios and attribute-based routing. Chen et al. [14] proposed to make use of navigation route for connected dominating set (CDS) construction. CDS is a popular approach for information dissemination in ad hoc networks. The algorithm in [14] tries to construct stable CDS so as to reduce CDS maintenance overhead and message forwarding cost.

16.3.3.2 V2R Based

In these algorithms, roadside infrastructure is involved in information dissemination. In [15], based on the orthogonality of the encoded sets of rateless codes, portions of the information can be disseminated. even if this has not yet been decoded. Kone et al. [16] used measurements of a fleet of WiFi-enabled vehicles to design an information- dissemination mechanism that scales with device density. Khabbaz [17] proposed a multiserver queuing model to accurately calculate the dynamics of vehicular networks. SADV [18] includes static nodes at intersections, to store packets and transmit them when the optimal delivery path becomes available.

16.3.3.3 DTN Based

The previous V2V or V2R algorithms usually rely on continuous network connectivity. However, high mobility of vehicles may result in frequent network partitions. Delay/Disruption Tolerant Network (DTN) is the technique to handle such a challenge, by routing packets in "store and forward" mode [19], where data is incrementally moved and stored throughout the network, in the hope that it will eventually reach its destination. The key point of DTN lies in how to maximize the probability of a message being successfully transferred.

Baccelli et al. [20] analyzed the effect of vehicle density on information propagation speed, and proved that, beneath a certain threshold, information propagates on average at vehicle speed, whereas above this threshold, information propagates dramatically faster, at a speed that increases quasi-exponentially when the vehicle density increases. Interestingly, Agarwal et al. [21] also derived both upper and lower bounds on the average message-propagation speed against traffic density, by exploiting a connection to the classical pattern-matching problem in probability theory.

16.4 APPLICATIONS

The applications of IoV are quite diverse. According to functionalities, we categorize them into three major classes. A detailed taxonomy is shown in Fig. 16.5.

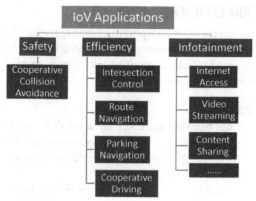

FIGURE 16.5 A Taxonomy of IoT Applications

16.4.1 DRIVING SAFETY RELATED

Driving safety related applications mainly refer to cooperative collision avoidance systems (CCAS) [22], which extend the collisions avoidance system (CAS) by sharing CAS information among neighboring vehicles, usually via V2V communication [23,24].

CAS, also known as precrash system, forward collision warning system, or collision mitigating system, uses radar or other sensors (eg, laser and camera) to detect an imminent crash, and then provides a warning to the driver or takes braking/steering action directly. CCAS adopts cooperation among vehicles to mitigate collisions among multiple vehicles, as shown in Fig. 16.6.

CarTALK 2000 [25] is a quite early work that involves CCAS. Techniques and algorithms were developed to test and assess cooperative driver-assistance applications, including CCAS function. Yang et al. [26] defined special congestion-control policies and redundant detection mechanisms for emergency warning messages, so as to achieve low delay and low communication cost. Taleb et al. [27] designed a risk-aware MAC protocol for CCAS, where the medium access delay of each vehicle is set as a function of its emergency level, and vehicles in high emergency situations can disseminate warning messages with shorter delay, so as to minimize chain collisions.

Milanés et al. [28] proposed a V2R-based vehicle control system. A fuzzy-based control algorithm is in charge of determining each vehicle's safe and comfortable distance to avoid collision. Maruoka et al. [29] focused on collision judgment. The authors proposed a judgment algorithm based on estimated relative positions and potential-collision- indicated areas, which can reduce false warnings and unnecessary warnings.

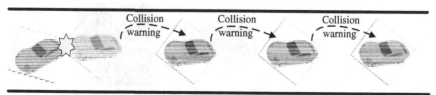

FIGURE 16.6 Cooperative Collision Avoidance System

16.4.2 TRANSPORTATION EFFICIENCY RELATED

Efficiency is one of the major concerns of transportation management. Vehicular network technology brings new possibilities of efficiency improvement. As shown in Fig. 16.6, existing transportation-efficiency-related applications can be further classified into four categories: intersection control, route navigation, parking navigation, and cooperative driving.

16.4.2.1 Intersection Control

Traffic control at intersections has been always a key issue for ITS. The key point is how to schedule traffic signals efficiently, according to traffic volume information, so as to reduce waiting time and improve fairness. There have been many algorithms or systems proposed for intelligent intersection control, which can be categorized as in Fig. 16.7.

Most existing work on intersection control is traffic-light based, and the key issue is to determine a good signal-scheduling plan. In early work, road detectors have been used to collect traffic volume information, and the traffic-signal plan constantly changes to adapt to the varying traffic conditions. Systems such as SCOOT [30] and SCATS [31] have been deployed for many years.

Traffic-light scheduling based on vehicular networks is the new stage of intelligent intersection control. Detailed vehicle information, including ID, speed, and position, are collected via V2V or V2I communication. Then, more accurate and efficient scheduling can be achieved.

V2I-based traffic-light scheduling is widely studied. In [32,33], a controller node is placed at the intersection to collect queue-length information and computer proper-cycle time of the traffic signal via the Webster formula. In addition to queue-length information, priority of vehicles is considered in [34], and a traffic signal is scheduled with quality-of-service provisioning. In some other work, signal scheduling is modeled as a combinatorial optimization problem to find an optimal scheduling plan of traffic signal. To solve such a problem, various methods such as dynamic programming (DP) [35,36], branch-and-bound [37], and linear programming [38] have been applied. Some researchers introduce intelligent algorithms to traffic-light scheduling, including fuzzy-logic-based scheduling [39], and Q-learning-based scheduling [40,41].

V2V-based adaptive traffic-light control is presented in [42]. This system reduces communication cost by clustering vehicles approaching the intersection. The density of vehicles within the cluster is computed using a clustering algorithm and sent to the traffic-signal controls to set the timing cycle.

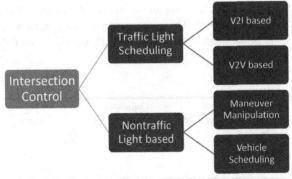

FIGURE 16.7 A Taxonomy of Intelligent Intersection Control Algorithms

There are also intersection-control approaches without using traffic lights. In maneuver- manipulation-based algorithms [28,43–45], the driving behaviors of vehicles are completely controlled by the intersection controller, which calculates the optimal trajectory for each vehicle, so that vehicles can safely pass through the intersection without colliding with each other. Since the speed and position of each vehicle needs to be accurately calculated, the optimization is very complex, especially when the number of vehicles is large.

In vehicle-scheduling algorithms, there is also no traffic light involved, but unlike maneuver-based ones, these algorithms schedule only the permissions to pass intersections rather than the driving behaviors. Dresner et al. [46,47] proposed a reservation-based intersection control system, where vehicles interact with an intersection controller through wireless communication to get reservations for passing. According to the traffic condition and current reservations, the intersection controller decides whether to accept a new reservation request or not. Wu et al. [48] adopted the distributed mutual-exclusion approach to realize vehicle scheduling without traffic lights used. Ferreira et al. [49] proposed the notion of a "virtual traffic light," where some vehicle is elected as the traffic-light node via V2V communications.

16.4.2.2 Route Navigation

Vehicular network-based navigation is studied to avoid the drawbacks of GPS-based or similar navigations. Chen et al. [50] proposed to construct a navigation route that considered real-time traffic information and fuel consumption.

Collins et al. [51] proposed a route-selection algorithm that can cope with traffic congestion by optimizing road utility. VSPN [52] is a privacy-preserving navigation scheme that utilizes speed data and road conditions collected by RSUs to guide vehicles. Leontiadis et al. [53] designed a system based on crowd-sourcing traffic information in an ad hoc manner.

16.4.2.3 Parking Navigation

Finding an available parking space in an urban environment with the help of vehicular networks is also an interesting problem. Verroios et al. [54] formulated the problem as a Time-Varying Traveling Salesman problem, and proposed an approach for computing the route that a vehicle must traverse in order to visit all parking spaces known to be available.

Lu et al. [55] designed a conditional privacy-preservation mechanism in a smart-parking scheme. In [56], atomic information, aggregated information, and an overlay grid are used to discover free parking places.

16.4.2.4 Cooperative Driving

Cooperative driving technology is used to coordinate a queue of vehicles to make them drive as one vehicle; it obviously improves the energy efficiency.

Gehring et al. [57] proposed practical results of a longitudinal control for truck platooning. Based on distance measurement between vehicles, a robust platoon controller is designed based on sliding-mode control. Seiler et al. [58] examined how the disturbance to error gain for an entire platoon scales with the number of vehicles. Cooperative driving at blind crossings is studied in [59]. A concept of safety-driving patterns is proposed to represent the collision-free movements of vehicles at crossings. In [60], a leaderless approach is proposed, based on a model of interacting agents with bidirectional and unidirectional, time-dependent communication.

16.4.3 INFOTAINMENT SERVICES

Infotainment services include mainly Internet access services and file sharing among vehicles, especially video sharing. Fig. 16.8 shows an example of video sharing.

Vehicle-to-Internet communication is a challenging task. A QoS framework to ensure data forwarding to the Internet in a gateway-free area in a highway scenario is proposed in [61]. It consists of a proxy-based Vehicle-to-Internet protocol, with a prediction-based routing algorithm and IEEE 802.11p EDCA scheme.

Video streaming over VANET has attracted more and more attention. Asefi et al. [62] introduced a quality-driven scheme for seamless delivery of video packets in urban VANET scenarios, which includes routing and mobility-management mechanisms based on Mobile IPv6. Xing et al. [63] proposed an adaptive video-streaming scheme for video- streaming services in the highway scenario. Relying on cooperative relay among vehicles, a vehicle can download video data using either a direct link or a multihop path to the RSUs. The proposed scheme can request an appropriate number of video-enhancement layers to improve video quality-of-experience.

Razzaq et al. [64] proposed a robust scheme for SVC-based streaming over an urban VANET with path diversity and network coding. The scheme calculates the quality of all candidate paths based on gray relational analysis and then assigns paths to different layers according to their importance. Nearby nodes along the transmission path may recode their received packets and store them in buffers for recovering lost packets.

Guo et al. [65] proposed a V2V live video streaming named V3, which addresses the challenges of V2V video streaming by incorporating a novel signaling mechanism to continuously trigger vehicles into video sources. It also adopts a store-carry-and-forward approach to transmit video data in partitioned network environments.

Lee et al. [66] proposed a mechanism called Cooperative Video Streaming over Vehicular Networks (CVS-VN). It adopts a new video codec called Co-SVC-MDC, which divides the multimedia stream into several descriptions. The requester can get the basic QoS for multimedia display via the requester's

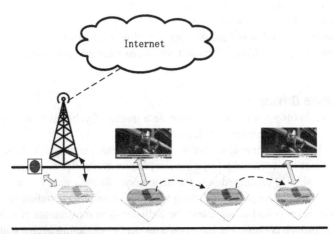

FIGURE 16.8 An Example of Video Services

3G/3.5G network channel. Other low-priority descriptions are scheduled to be transmitted via helpers' 3G/3.5G network channels.

Seferoglu et al. [67] proposed video schemes for network code selection and packet scheduling by considering the importance-deadlines of video packets, the network state, and packets received in the neighborhood. Xie et al. [68] studied the performance of video streaming under different data-forwarding and buffer-management schemes, in highway environments without frequent link disconnections and persistent network partitions.

16.5 SUMMARY AND FUTURE DIRECTIONS

IoV is an evolution of VANETs and an extension of the Internet. As an important part of IoT, IoV involves several different research fields, including wireless communication/networking, mobile computing, cloud computing, intelligent transportation, and even autopilot vehicles.

Networking technologies are the basis of IoV. There have been many efforts on the study and standardization of communication protocols for IoV, especially for the VANET part. IEEE 802.11p and its related protocol family should be the future of IoV communication protocols. On the level of routing and data dissemination, both broadcast-based paradigms and point-to-point paradigms are necessary, and they are suitable for quite different applications.

Applications are the driving power of IoV. IoV applications are quite diverse, including driving safety and efficiency service, intelligent traffic management, and informative services. Some applications, for example, traffic-light scheduling, have emerged prior to IoV, but IoV will certainly bring revolutionary changes in both technology and functionality. Other applications are totally new: for example, cooperative driving is not possible without vehicular communications. Many applications have been proposed and some have been deployed. Of course, more and more applications will emerge in the future.

Of course, IoV is still in its initial stage, and there are many technical problems to be addressed before IoV can be widely accepted and deployed. Among others, the following directions should be worthy of further study in the future.

1. *Efficient information routing and dissemination*
   Although a specialized MAC protocol family has been developed for IoV, especially VANETs, multihop communications in IoV are still a hard task. High mobility and weak connection make information forwarding and dissemination far from trivial. Researchers are putting more and more efforts toward this topic; it lags far behind MAC layer technology. More precisely, how to route messages at network level with a mechanism suitable for vehicular environments is a very interesting topic. This includes both broadcast-based information dissemination and unicast-based message delivery. Widely accepted routing or dissemination protocol does not appear yet.
2. *Communications based on Software-Defined Networking (SDN)*
   There has been some work on software-defined vehicular networks. However, it is far from enough. SDN is naturally suitable for the IoV environment, because vehicles are forwarders, and at the same time, computing nodes. Realizing an SDN paradigm is easy, but the difficulty lies in suitable link-control and allocation algorithms. Different from wired WAN environments, or even traditional ad hoc networks, vehicular links are more dynamic, so how to control and allocate

such resources is very challenging. Underlying technical issues include: vehicular-link modeling and representing, allocation of dynamically changing link-resources via network controller, forwarding-rule delivery and management, etc.

3. *Communications based on Named Data Networking (NDN)*
Similar to SDN, NDN is another promising networking technology for the future Internet. It is even more revolutionary in terms of a routing mechanism. Applications of IoV usually involve transportation information, which is naturally propagated to nonpredefined vehicles according to their content. Such a characteristic makes NDN a very suitable technology for IoV. However, NDN in IoV is not studied widely and there are many open problems to be considered. Possible directions include: transportation data-naming and organizing, design of data request and forwarding table for vehicle nodes, message caching at vehicles, application-specific NDN algorithms, etc.

4. *Generic coordination mechanisms*
IoV is network based and all applications may involve coordination among vehicles. Synchronization and agreement are used in distributed applications, such as cooperative driving and cooperative intersection-control. Current distributed coordination is usually embedded into application logic. Such design is not good in terms of protocol/algorithm design. Decoupling coordination and application, and realizing modularized design should be good choices. Therefore, generic coordination algorithms—even a middleware platform—would be very interesting.

5. *Traffic-data processing*
Besides node coordination, traffic-data processing should be another topic that may arise generic techniques or platforms in the middleware level. With more and more vehicles equipped with intelligent devices, and also more and more roadside units deployed, vehicular data will increase in an explosive way, as in other fields of IoT. On the one hand, Big Traffic Data provides more knowledge for IoV and may help improve the performance of IoV applications, or even give rise to new ones. On the other hand, traffic-data processing itself raises new challenges. Besides general Big Data techniques, IoV-specific data-processing techniques should be considered. Especially, cloud-based traffic-data processing is of special interest.

6. *New applications*
New applications of IoV are always desirable. With fast development of enabling technologies and user requirements, many new IoV applications will emerge. Although such applications are still in the categories of driving safety and efficiency, or traffic management and informative services, they may provide new service functionalities with the help of more efficient networking, cloud computing, and Big Data processing techniques. Possible new applications may include an intelligent traffic status-report service, real-time navigation service, intervehicle entertainment application, etc.

REFERENCES

[1] IEEE 802.11 wireless LAN medium access control (MAC) and physical layer (PHY) specifications. IEEE-SA; 2012. doi:10.1109/IEEESTD 2012.6178212.

[2] Part 11 wireless LAN medium access control (MAC) and physical layer (PHY) specifications amendment 6 wireless access in vehicular environments. IEEE 802.11p-2010.

[3] IEEE 1609 family of standards for wireless access in vehicular environments (WAVE). U.S. department of transportation; 2013. https://www.standards.its.dot.gov/factsheets/factsheet/80

[4] Wang Q, Leng S, Fu H, Zhang Y. An IEEE 802.11 p-based multichannel MAC scheme with channel coordination for vehicular ad hoc networks. IEEE Trans Intell Transp Syst 2012;13(2):449–58.

[5] Dang D, Dang H, Nguyen V, Htike Z, Hong C. HER-MAC: a hybrid efficient and reliable MAC for vehicular ad hoc networks. In: IEEE twenty-eighth international conference on advanced information networking and applications (AINA); 2014. p. 186–93.

[6] Perkins C, Belding-Royer E, Das S. Ad hoc On-Demand Distance Vector (AODV) Routing, IETF, RFC 3561, 2003. http://www.ietf.org/rfc/rfc3561.txt.

[7] Clausen T, Jacquet P. Optimized link state routing protocol (OLSR), IETF RFC 3626; 2003. http://www.ietf.org/rfc/rfc3626.txt

[8] Yan T, Zhang W, Wang G. DOVE: data dissemination to a desired number of receivers in VANET, vehicular technology. IEEE Trans 2014;63(4):1903–16.

[9] Cenerario N, Delot T, Ilarri S. A content-based dissemination protocol for VANETs: exploiting the encounter probability, intelligent transportation systems. IEEE Trans 2011;12(3):771–82.

[10] Tavakoli R, Nabi M. TIGeR: a traffic-aware intersection-based geographical routing protocol for urban VANETs. In: Proceedings of the IEEE seventy-seventh vehicular technology conference (VTC Spring); 2013. p. 1–5.

[11] Dikaiakos M, Florides A, Nadeem T, Iftode L. Location-aware services over vehicular ad-hoc networks using car-to-car communication, selected areas in communications. IEEE J 2007;25(8):1590–602.

[12] Chu Y, Huang N. An efficient traffic information forwarding solution for vehicle safety communications on highways, intelligent transportation systems. IEEE Trans 2012;13(2):631–43.

[13] Little T, Agarwal A. An information propagation scheme for VANETs. In: Proceedings of the intelligent transportation systems. Austria; 2005. p. 155–60.

[14] Chen Y, Wu W, Cao H. Navigation route based stable connected dominating set for vehicular ad hoc networks. Intl J Web Service Res (JWSR) 2015;12(1):12–26.

[15] Cataldi P, Tomatis A, Grilli G, Gerla MA. Novel data dissemination method for vehicular networks with rateless codes. In: Proceedings of the wireless communications and networking conference WCNC, IEEE; 2009. p. 1–6.

[16] Kone V, Zheng H, Rowstron A, O'Shea G, Zhao BY. Measurement-based design of roadside content delivery systems, mobile computing. IEEE Trans 2013;12(6):1160–73.

[17] Khabbaz M, Hasna M, Assi CM, Ghrayeb A. Modeling and analysis of an infrastructure service request queue in multichannel V2I communications. IEEE Trans Intell Transp Syst 2014;15(3):1155–67.

[18] Ding Y, Xiao L. SADV. Static-node-assisted adaptive data dissemination in vehicular networks, vehicular technology. IEEE Trans 2010;59(5):2445–55.

[19] Tornell SM, Calafate CT, Cano JC, Manzoni P. DTN protocols for vehicular networks: an application oriented overview, communications surveys & tutorials. IEEE 2015;17(2):868–87.

[20] Baccelli E, Jacquet P, Mans B, Rodolakis G. Highway vehicular delay tolerant networks: information propagation speed properties, information theory. IEEE Trans 2012;58(3):1743–56.

[21] Agarwal A, Starobinski D, Little TDC. Phase transition of message propagation speed in delay-tolerant vehicular networks. IEEE Trans Intell Transp Syst 2012;13(1):249–63.

[22] Tan H, Huang J. DGPS-based vehicle-to-vehicle cooperative collision warning: engineering feasibility viewpoints. IEEE Trans Intell Transp Syst 2006;7(4):415–28.

[23] Miller R, Huang Q. An adaptive peer-to-peer collision warning system. In: Proceedings of the vehicular technology conference. Birmingham, UK; 2002, 1. p. 317–21.

[24] Biswas S, Tatchikou R, Dion F. Vehicle-to-vehicle wireless communication protocols for enhancing highway traffic safety. Commun Mag 2006;44(1):74–82.

[25] Reichardt D, Miglietta M, Moretti L, Morsink P, Schulz W. CarTALK 2000: safe and comfortable driving based upon inter-vehicle-communication. In: Proceedings of the intelligent vehicle symposium. Versailles, France; 2002, 2: p. 545–50.

[26] Yang X, Liu J, Vaidya N, Zhao F. A vehicle-to-vehicle communication protocol for cooperative collision warning. In: Proceedings of the mobile and ubiquitous systems: networking and services. Boston, America; 2004: p. 114–23.

[27] Taleb T, Benslimane A, Ben L. Toward an effective risk-conscious and collaborative vehicular collision avoidance system. Veh Technol 2010;59(3):1474–86.

[28] Milanés V, Villagra J, Godoy J, Simo J, Perez J, Onieva E. An intelligent V2I-based traffic management system. IEEE Trans Intell Trans Syst 2012;13(1):49–58.

[29] Maruoka T, Sato Y, Nakai S, Wada T, Okada H. An extended collision judgment algorithm for vehicular collision avoidance support system (VCASS) in advanced ITS. In: Proceedings of the vehicular technology conference. Calgary, Canada; 2008. p. 1–5.

[30] Hunt PB, Robertson DI, Bretherton RD, et al. The SCOOT on-line traffic signal optimisation technique. Traffic Eng Control 1982;23(4):190–192.

[31] Sims AG, Dobinson KW. The Sydney coordinated adaptive traffic (SCAT) system philosophy and benefits. IEEE Trans Veh Technol 1980;29(2):130–7.

[32] Gradinescu V, Gorgorin C, Diaconescu R. Adaptive traffic lights using car-to-car communication. In: Proceedings of the IEEE sixty-fifth vehicular technology conference (VTC2007-Spring); 2007. p. 21–5.

[33] Prashanth LA, Bhatnagar S. Reinforcement learning with function approximation for traffic signal control. IEEE Trans Intell Transp Syst 2011;12(2):412–21.

[34] Wunderlich R, Liu C, Elhanany I, et al. A novel signal-scheduling algorithm with quality-of-service provisioning for an isolated intersection. IEEE Trans Intell Transp Syst 2008;9(3):536–47.

[35] Cai C, Wang Y, Geers G. Adaptive traffic signal control using vehicle-to-infrastructure communication: a technical note. In: Proceedings of the second international workshop on computational transportation science, ACM; 2010. p. 43–7.

[36] Priemer C, Friedrich B. A decentralized adaptive traffic signal control using V2I communication data. In: Proceedings of the twelfth international IEEE conference on intelligent transportation systems. ITSC'09; 2009. p. 1–6.

[37] Li C, Shimamoto S. An open traffic light control model for reducing vehicles emissions based on ETC vehicles. IEEE Trans Veh Technol 2012;61(1):97–110.

[38] Lin WH, Wang C. An enhanced 0–1 mixed-integer LP formulation for traffic signal control. IEEE Trans Intell Transp Syst 2004;5(4):238–45.

[39] Qiao J, Yang N, Gao J. Two-stage fuzzy logic controller for signalized intersection. Syst Man Cybern Part A: Syst Humans 2011;41(1):178–84.

[40] Abdulhai B, Pringle R, Karakoulas GJ. Reinforcement learning for true adaptive traffic signal control. J Transp Eng 2003;129(3):278–85.

[41] El-Tantawy S, Abdulhai B. An agent-based learning towards decentralized and coordinated traffic signal control. In: Proceedings of the intelligent transportation systems (ITSC). Funchal; 2010: p. 665–70.

[42] Maslekar N, Boussedjra M, Mouzna J, Labiod H. VANET based adaptive traffic signal control. In: Proceedings of the vehicular technology conference (VTC Spring). Budapest, Hungary; 2011. p. 1–5.

[43] Glaser S, Vanholme B, Mammar S, et al. Maneuver-based trajectory planning for highly autonomous vehicles on real road with traffic and driver interaction. IEEE Trans Intell Transp Syst 2010;11(3):589–606.

[44] Lee J, Park B. Development and evaluation of a cooperative vehicle intersection control algorithm under the connected vehicles environment. IEEE Trans Intell Transp Syst 2012;13(1):81–90.

[45] Milanés V, Pérez J, Onieva E, Gonzalez C. Controller for urban intersections based on wireless communications and fuzzy logic. IEEE Trans Intell Transp Syst 2010;11(1):243–8.

[46] Dresner K, Stone P. Multiagent traffic management: a reservation-based intersection control mechanism. In: Proceedings of the third international joint conference on autonomous agents and multiagent systems. New York, America; 2004. p. 530–37.

[47] Dresner K, Stone P. Multiagent traffic management: an improved intersection control mechanism. In: Proceedings of the fourth international joint conference on autonomous agents and multiagent systems. New York, America; 2005. p. 471–77.

[48] Wu W, Zhang J, Luo A, Cao J. Distributed mutual exclusion algorithms for intersection traffic control. IEEE Trans Parallel Distrib Syst 2015;26(1).

[49] Ferreira M, d'Orey PM. On the impact of virtual traffic lights on carbon emissions mitigation. IEEE Trans Intell Transp Syst 2012;13(1):284–95.

[50] Chen PY, Guo Y, Chen WT. Fuel-saving navigation system in VANETs. In: Proceedings of the vehicular technology conference. Ottawa, Canada; 2010. p. 1–5.

[51] Collins K, Muntean GM. Route-based vehicular traffic management for wireless access in vehicular environments. In: Proceedings of the vehicular technology conference. Calgary, Canada; 2008. p. 1–5.

[52] Chim T, Yiu S, Hui L, Li V. VSPN: VANET-based secure and privacy-preserving navigation. IEEE Trans Comp 2014;63(2):510–524.

[53] Leontiadis I, Marfia G, Mack D, Pau G, Mascolo C, Gerla M. On the effectiveness of an opportunistic traffic management system for vehicular networks. IEEE Trans Intell Transp Syst 2011;12(4):1537–48.

[54] Verroios V, Efstathiou V, Delis A. Reaching available public parking spaces in urban environments using ad hoc networking. In: Proceedings of the mobile data management. Lulea, Sweden; 2011, 1. p. 141–51.

[55] Lu R, Lin X, Zhu H, Shen X. SPARK: a new VANET-based smart parking scheme for large parking lots. In: Proceeding of the INFOCOM. Rio de Janeiro, Brazil; 2009. p. 1413–21.

[56] Murat C, Daniel G, Martin M. Decentralized discovery of free parking places. In: Proceedings of the third international workshop on vehicular ad hoc networks. New York, America; 2006. p. 30–9.

[57] Gehring O, Fritz H. Practical results of a longitudinal control concept for truck platooning with vehicle to vehicle communication. In: Proceedings of the intelligent transportation system. Boston, America; 1997. p. 117–22.

[58] Seiler P, Pant A, Hedrick K. Disturbance propagation in vehicle strings. Autom Control 2004;49(10):1835–42.

[59] Li L, Wang FY. Cooperative driving at blind crossings using intervehicle communication. Veh Technol 2006;55(6):1712–24.

[60] Moreau L. Leaderless coordination via bidirectional and unidirectional time-dependent communication. In: Proceedings of the decision and control. Maui, Hawaii; 2003, 3. p. 3070–5.

[61] Ksentini A, Tounsi H, Frikha M. A proxy-based framework for QoS-enabled Internet access in VANETS. In: Proceedings of the communications and networking. Tozeur , France; 2010. p. 1–8.

[62] Asefi M, Céspedes S, Shen X, Mark JW. A seamless quality-driven multi-hop data delivery scheme for video streaming in urban VANET scenarios. In: Proceedings of the communications. Kyoto, Japan; 2011. p. 1–5.

[63] Xing M, Cai L. Adaptive video streaming with inter-vehicle relay for highway VANET scenario. In: Proceedings of the communications (ICC). Ottawa, Canada; 2012. p. 5168–72.

[64] Razzaq A, Mehaoua A. Video transport over VANETs: multi-stream coding with multi-path and network coding. In: Proceedings of the local computer networks. Denver, America; 2010. p. 32–9.

[65] Guo M, Ammar MH, Zegura EW. V3: a vehicle-to-vehicle live video streaming architecture. Pervasive Mobile Comput 2005;1(4):404–24.

[66] Lee CH, Huang CM, Yang CC, Wang TH. A cooperative video streaming system over the integrated cellular and DSRC networks. In: Proceedings of the vehicular technology conference. San Francisco, America; 2011. p. 1–5.

[67] Seferoglu H, Markopoulou A. Opportunistic network coding for video streaming over wireless. In: Proceedings of the packet video. Lausanne, Switzerland; 2007. p. 191–200.

[68] Xie F, Hua KA, Wang W, Ho YH. Performance study of live video streaming over highway vehicular ad hoc networks. In: Proceedings of the vehicular technology conference. Baltimore, America; 2007. p. 2121–5.

CLOUD-BASED SMART-FACILITIES MANAGEMENT

17

S. Majumdar

Department of Systems and Computer Engineering, Carleton University, Ottawa, Canada

17.1 INTRODUCTION

The exponential growth of internet-enabled devices supported by the emerging paradigm of Internet of Things (IoT) is expected to reach 50 billion by 2020 [1]. The use of sensor-equipped smart facilities has been increasing, and is expected to become more and more prevalent as we approach the growing world of IoT that allows various sensor-based devices and systems to be monitored and/or controlled over a network. Examples of such facilities that are the ingredients of smart cities include sensor-based bridges and smart buildings, as well as industrial machines, including aerospace machinery [2]. Remote monitoring and intelligent management of these facilities can significantly reduce the maintenance cost as well as prevent failures leading to accidents that may result from the inability to detect faults in a timely manner. A great deal of research is critically needed to devise cloud-based techniques that will enable the monitoring, management, and maintenance of multiple geographically distributed remote smart-facilities.

Regardless of its exact nature, the management of a smart facility typically involves the following three steps:

1. collecting the sensor data that reflects the current state/health of the facility
2. analyzing the sensor data
3. making decisions regarding its management/maintenance.

Sensors, data repositories, data-analysis tools, and archival databases containing the previous maintenance history of a given facility, as well as computing platforms/servers that perform time-consuming data analytics on sensor data, are often scattered across a large geographical region that may span different locations on a campus, multiple sites within a city, or multiple cities in a country, for example. This chapter concerns the state of the art in smart-facility management techniques, and includes a report on existing research that is aimed at using a cloud-based solution for unifying geographically dispersed diverse resources, and making them available on demand to clients who monitor and manage their respective smart facilities.

The following section presents background material, including a discussion of a representative set of related work that addresses various issues that are important in the context of cloud-based smart-facility management. A description of a general cloud-based solution to the smart-facilities management problem is presented in Section 17.3. A layered architecture for the system, including the middleware necessary for supporting smart-facility management, is described. A discussion of generic middleware services that are needed to support the management of smart facilities is presented in Section 17.4. The two following sections focus on the management of resources. Section 17.5 discusses the management of sensor resources that are often used for monitoring various attributes of a smart facility that reflect its operational health. Applications for analyzing such sensor data are often CPU intensive. A discussion of resource management techniques on parallel systems used for performing such CPU-intensive data analytics required in the management of smart facilities is presented in Section 17.6. Sections 17.7 and 17.8 present two case-studies, one of which describes a cloud-based solution for the management of bridges, and the other focuses on a collaboration platform for performing research on smart-facilities management. Section 17.9 concludes the chapter and directions for future research are presented in Section 17.9.1.

17.2 BACKGROUND AND RELATED WORK

A smart facility is a form of a cyber-physical system that is characterized by collaborating elements controlling physical entities. Performing a detailed literature survey on cyber-physical systems is beyond the scope of this chapter. A representative set of works is included as an example of the existing work in the area. Management of cyber-physical systems has received considerable attention that is captured in [3]. The book describes a proposal from a European consortium, IMC-AESOP, to use service-oriented architectures for next-generation supervisory-control-and-data-acquisition (SCADA) ready systems. The functionalities exposed by such systems as services are proposed to be hosted on a cloud. Examples of the application of the proposed architecture for various cyber-physical systems, including the control of a manufacturing operation, are included in [3]. The challenges associated with the management of cyber-physical systems and a vision for their computer-based management is described in [4]. Systems for the management of smart homes have also been described in the literature. The work in [5] focuses on automatic sensor-control and monitoring, whereas the authors of [6] propose a futuristic cloud-based facility for monitoring multiple homes. The problems with current semimanual approaches to the maintenance of critical infrastructure, such as bridges and industrial machinery, and a proposal for cloud-based solutions, are described in [2]. Examples of available systems for smart-facility management includes a system for optimizing energy use in buildings [7] and a computerized asset-maintenance and management software [8].

Smart-facility management is a multifaceted problem. Techniques and systems from various domains that include cloud computing, senor networks deployed on a facility for monitoring its various attributes, and parallel-processing techniques for speeding up the execution of analytics programs used for analyzing sensor data, need to be integrated in order to generate an effective solution for the management of smart facilities. A discussion of each of these issues is included in this section.

The integration of sensor networks with a grid [9] or a cloud [10], referred to as a sensor grid/ cloud, enables the processing of sensor data from smart facilities on the grid/cloud. Most existing work on sensor networks has focused on a single application using all of the sensors in the Wireless Sensor Network (WSN). However, with the advent of multipurpose sensor technology that incorporates the ability to sense multiple phenomena on the same sensor node, allows a sensor node to be shared among multiple concurrent applications [11]. When the same WSN is shared among multiple applications, algorithms for resource management that include techniques for mapping application requests to sensors, along with the scheduling of application requests contending for the same sensor node, become important. However, little research seems to be available in the field of allocating and scheduling multiple applications that use a WSN. A few examples are discussed next. In [12] and [13], the authors describe an allocation technique, based on the Quality of Monitoring, for handling multiple applications in shared sensor-networks. The work described in [14] concerns techniques for scheduling requests from multiple applications, based on their deadlines. Sensor-allocation techniques that adjust the sleep/wake duty cycle of the sensors to extend the lifetime of a WSN are discussed in [15]. A more detailed literature survey on resource management techniques for shared WSNs is available from [16]. A comprehensive study on the utility of using various attributes of the WSN system, and the workload processed in devising resource management algorithms, are discussed in the context of sensor allocation in [16], and in the context of request scheduling in [17]. This research is discussed in more detail in Section 17.5.

Managing compute resources is important in order to run compute-intensive data-analytics programs that are used to analyze data collection on a smart facility. Parallel-processing frameworks such as MapReduce are often deployed for speeding up the execution of such programs. Resource management on grids and clouds is a well-researched problem. Relatively little work exists in the domain of scheduling and matchmaking MapReduce jobs with deadlines. Such deadlines are important in the context of real-time data analytics, for example. Due to space limitations, only a representative set of papers is discussed. Examples of existing work includes OpenStack, which is a collaborative open-source cloud-software project, focusing on a resource-management middleware for cloud, to make global resource-management decisions in order to achieve high-system performance [18]. A Deadline Constraint Scheduler for Hadoop, an implementation of the MapReduce framework by Apache [19] for handling jobs with deadlines, is discussed in [20], whereas a technique that focuses on the scheduling of workloads that includes both MapReduce jobs with deadlines (real-time jobs) and without deadlines (nonreal-time jobs), is discussed in [21]. In [22], the authors describe two resource-allocation policies based on the Earliest Deadline First (EDF) strategy for Hadoop. Effective resource management techniques for MapReduce jobs that are based on the theory of optimization are observed to lead to high system-performance, and are described in more detail in Section 17.6.

17.3 A CLOUD-BASED ARCHITECTURE FOR SMART-FACILITY MANAGEMENT

Fig. 17.1 displays a cloud-based smart facilities management system. The smart facility, a bridge, in the diagram is only an example and can be replaced by other smart facilities.

Although Fig. 17.1 shows multiple bridges equipped with wireless sensors, a facility-management system can be dedicated to a single facility as well. As opposed to a data-center cloud that typically handles compute and storage resources, this heterogeneous cloud unifies a diverse set of resources that may include compute and storage servers, software tools for data analysis, archival storage systems, and data bases holding various information about the facility, including its maintenance history and data repositories. The system administrator, bridge engineer, and the bridge operator are personnel that are involved in overseeing the management of the smart facility. As shown in Fig. 17.1, multiple levels of networks may be used. A backbone network typically spans multiple geographic regions, such as provinces within a country. Resources or personnel, for example, may be connected to the backbone network through their respective local access networks.

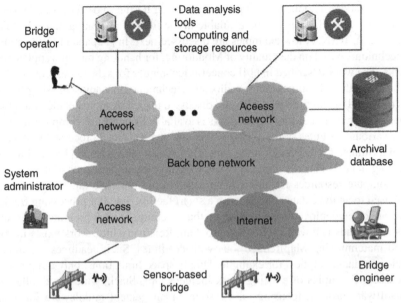

FIGURE 17.1 Cloud-Based Smart-Facility Management

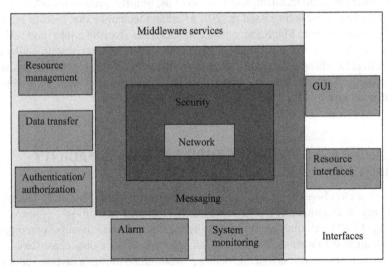

FIGURE 17.2 System Architecture

A layered architecture for the system used for managing a smart facility is presented in Fig. 17.2. The network layer provides the necessary support for communication among the various system-resources that include both hardware resources, such as computing and storage devices, as well as data-analysis software. Messages supported by the messaging layer are typically used for intercommunication among components that include these resources, as well as middleware components that are discussed in the following section. The messaging layer uses the underlying security layer to ensure that communication is performed in a secure manner. A broad range of security may be provided: from using virtual private networks to data encryption. The middleware layer and the interface set provide various services for the proper functioning of the smart facility that are discussed next.

17.4 MIDDLEWARE SERVICES

This section presents a set of core services for the cloud-based smart-facility management system. Other services in addition to the core may be deployed if warranted by the management requirements of a given facility.

Authentication and authorization service: The role of this service is to allow only valid users access to the system. Each user is typically associated with a set of operations that she or he is allowed to perform on a resource. After authentication, when a user initiates an operation on a resource, the authorization service performs the required access control and determines whether or not the user is allowed to perform the requested operation on the respective resource.

Research is underway to address the challenges of authentication and authorization on IoT-based systems. An example of such a challenge is highlighted in the literature, through an example of a hacker interfering with the operation of an insulin pump by impersonating the authorized user [23]. Techniques for addressing the authentication and authorization issues in the context of IoT are receiving a great deal of attention from researchers. Examples include techniques for efficient key establishment for an Elliptic Curve Cryptography technique, and a role-based Access Control Policy [24]. A smart card and physical unclonable functions (PUF) for authentication are considered in [25] that proposes innovative workflows of authentication protocols, and studies their behavior on an IoT testbed. Results of such research are useful in the context of incorporating the authentication and authorization service.

Data-transfer service: This service is responsible for performing the transfer of data between a source and a sink. Certain systems [26] allow two types of data-transfer operations. During *bulk data transfer*, large volumes of data may be transferred between an originating and a receiving folder. Minimization of transfer latency is often a desirable system objective, but bulk data transfers are generally performed on a best-effort basis. For real-time data transfer, a deadline may be associated with the data-transfer operation. Moreover, continuous streams of data often need to be analyzed in real time. For real-time data transfer and processing operations that are typically associated with the real-time analytics performed on sensor data generated by a smart facility, resources used in running the data-analytics application are often reserved in advance so that the real-time requirements of the system can be met.

Alarm service: This service is responsible for raising an alarm when the analysis of sensor data indicates either a fault or an exceptional situation in the system requiring further attention. The data collected by the sensors is analyzed, and an alarm condition is said to have occurred when a certain predefined system-state is attained. The service informs authorized personnel (eg, the system administrator and/or a facility operator) when such an alarm condition is reached.

Resource management service: This service is responsible for managing the various resources in the system that include compute and storage, as well as software resources such as sensor-data analysis tools. Typical resource management operations handled by this service include facilitating the discovery of a resource, or reserving a set of resources for performing a desired set of operations (jobs) on sensor data [26,27].

Multiple resources that may include compute and storage resources, for example, are often required to be reserved together for the execution of such a job. Resource management algorithms that select an appropriate resource from a set of available resources, and determine the starting time for the job execution of meeting a deadline for completion associated with the request, are important components of the resource management service. This is because performing real-time data analytics for monitoring the structural health of smart infrastructures, as well as for performing various other operations for maintaining and controlling smart facilities, often require the processing of requests with deadlines: the job associated with the request needs to be completed before the expiration of the request deadline. Resource allocation, and the scheduling of algorithms for handling an advance reservation-request associated with a deadline, are available in the grid and cloud literature [28,29] and can be adapted by the resource management service for smart facilities management [27]. If some of these requests need to be served immediately, they can still be handled by these algorithms as advance reservation-requests with zero as their earliest start-time request.

Additional issues, such as reducing the cost of operating cloud data-centers, have started receiving attention from researchers. Computational and storage resources from a data center can be used for smart facilities management. Cost of energy is a significant proportion of the operational cost for a data center. Frequency scaling of compute servers to alter the power consumption of their CPUs, and consolidating application executions on a subset of servers while switching off the others, are examples of techniques being investigated for reducing the energy consumption of servers. Auto-scaling, or increasing/decreasing the number of resources devoted to a client in response to an increase/decrease in workload, is another method of controlling operational cost. Deployment of these techniques can be beneficial in the context of large smart-facilities that require data-center resources for their control and/or maintenance.

Management of sensor resources that are shared by multiple applications often requires separate algorithms for allocation and scheduling, and is discussed in Section 17.5. Special considerations are required for managing resources that run data-analytics software on big data collected on smart facilities. Resource management algorithms for such data-analytics platforms are discussed in Section 17.6.

System-monitoring service: The objective of this service is to monitor the health of the different resources (both hardware servers and software tools). Periodic probing is often used to determine whether or not the respective resources are in running condition. Upon discovery of a failure, the system administrator is informed so that corrective action may be performed. System-monitoring tools also maintain various performance statistics, such as utilization of various resources, message transfer rates, and system throughput at various points in time. The measured metrics are then displayed by request to the system administrator.

Current research is directed toward addressing the challenges of providing a service for monitoring IoT-based systems, challenges that are rooted in the limited power and capability of flexible communication interfaces and coverage for wireless sensors [30]. Research is underway to address these challenges. Examples include an ARM9 processor-based gateway for collecting continuous, periodic, and sequential spatial telematics [30], and techniques for remote monitoring of an electric vehicle [31]. The emergence of new papers in the area demonstrates the importance of a system-monitoring service in the management of sensor-based systems such as smart facilities. A detailed survey, however, is beyond the scope of this chapter. The interested reader is referred to the list of related papers included in the two papers referred to in this paragraph.

In addition to the middleware services, interfaces that are required for the operation of the smart-facility management system are described next.

Graphical user interface (GUI): The role of the GUI is to make the various functionalities for managing smart facilities available to the person in charge of maintaining the smart facility. By activating the various buttons on the GUI, maintenance personnel can perform the desired operations on the system.

Resource interfaces: Resources such as compute and storage servers, as well as software tools, are connected to the platform for facilities management through interfaces, also known as adapters [27]. The role of the adapter is to provide a common application-programming interface that clients can implement, using diverse technologies. For example, a client running on top of a Linux operating system can invoke a software tool running on the Windows platform. Exposing resources connected to the cloud-based platform, such as Web services, is suggested in [27,32]. Any operation to be performed on the resource is performed by invoking the respective Web service (WS). Both a SOAP-based and a RESTful WS may be used. The term RESTful is often abbreviated as REST that stands for Representation State Transfer. A hybrid WS that switches between these two WS-types, based on the operation to be performed, is discussed in [32]. A hybrid WS effectively combines the lightweight feature of a RESTful WS with the support for security and atomicity that accompanies a SOAP-based WS. The authors show that a significant improvement in performance over a standard SOAP-based WS can be achieved by using a hybrid WS.

Centralized versus distributed control: Both centralized as well as distributed approaches have been used in cloud-based systems that concern smart-facility management. The control software, including the middleware services, may be run at a single node. Such a centralized approach simplifies system design and maintenance, and has been used in [26]. A distributed control that distributes the various control operations among multiple nodes is more complex, but offers the advantages of improved scalability and reliability. Such a distributed architecture, in which middleware services are spread/duplicated across multiple nodes, has been proposed for bridge management in [27].

17.5 RESOURCE MANAGEMENT TECHNIQUES FOR WIRELESS SENSOR NETWORKS

Smart facilities that include buildings, bridges, and various industrial and aerospace machinery are often based on sensor networks. Due to their ready availability and cost effectiveness, WSNs are often deployed on these types of smart facilities. Management of WSNs accessed by a single client is a well-studied problem. Although comparatively a lesser amount of work is available in the literature, WSNs serving multiple applications have also started receiving attention. These systems often deploy multifunctional sensor nodes that can sense multiple phenomena. Multiple client applications on a smart-facility management system, each using a specific type of sensor data, can access the sensor nodes that are shared among these various applications. Algorithms for resource management that need to deal with the allocation of sensors to competing applications, and the scheduling of sensor requests that queue up for the same sensor node, are important in this context. Both allocation and scheduling techniques in the case of a sensor network attached to a grid or cloud have been discussed in [17] and [16], and can be adapted to the cloud-based facility management domain. The model of a system that combines a WSN with a grid for processing the sensor data is presented in Fig. 17.3 [17]. Although

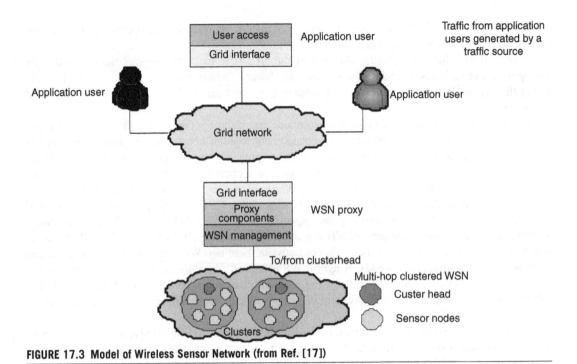

FIGURE 17.3 Model of Wireless Sensor Network (from Ref. [17])

this example is based on a grid, the same functionality can be achieved with the help of a cloud as well. Users in Fig. 17.3 send queries for getting information from the WSN via the grid network. The proxy exposes the functionality of the sensor nodes to the grid and runs the resource management algorithms. The resource management functionality of proxy node (Fig. 17.3) that performs all of these resource management decisions in [17] can be mapped to the node running the resource management service shown in Fig. 17.2, for example. Compute and storage nodes in the grid in the figure are used for running sensor-data analytics applications for the smart-facility management system. A WSN is typically organized in clusters, with a particular sensor node designated as the cluster head, handling the communication between the proxy and the other sensor nodes in the cluster (Fig. 17.3). A short discussion of both sensor allocation and sensor-request scheduling performed at the proxy is presented.

17.5.1 SENSOR ALLOCATION

Applications, which process data collected by a group of sensors, generate queries or requests for the system. These queries can be handled by multiple sensors monitoring the desired phenomena. Sensors chosen from the available set can thus serve such an application request. The allocation algorithm determines which sensors from a set of available sensors are to be used for serving the request. Allocation of sensors to applications has been discussed in the literature. Various issues, such as static versus dynamic algorithms, whether or not to use knowledge of the system, and workload characteristics in resource management giving rise to superior performance, have been investigated by researchers.

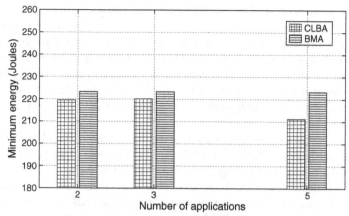

FIGURE 17.4 Performance of Static and Dynamic Allocation Algorithms (from Ref. [16])

A comparison of a number of static and dynamic allocation algorithms is presented in [16]. For a static algorithm, once the allocation is done the same sensors are always used for serving the request from a given application, whereas for a dynamic algorithm, the choice of sensors for serving a particular application request is determined after the request arrival, and can thus change during the lifetime of the system. The authors demonstrate the effectiveness of using knowledge of both application characteristics, and the knowledge of system state, in performing sensor allocation in the context of both static and dynamic algorithms. A simulation-based analysis shows the superiority of a dynamic algorithm in comparison to its static counterpart, as captured in the network lifetime for the WSN that is a measure of the time that the WSN can run without replenishing its power source. Fig. 17.4 displays a graph that shows the relationship between minimum energy and the number of applications accessing the WSN. *Minimum Energy* is the energy of a sensor node that has the lowest remaining energy among all sensor nodes at the end of the simulation period. Minimum energy is an indication of network lifetime: the higher the minimum energy, the higher is the network lifetime, and thus better is the system performance. A number of different algorithms were analyzed in [16]. Fig. 17.4 shows a performance comparison between one of the best static algorithms, called *CPU Load Balanced Allocation (CLBA)* and the best dynamic algorithm *Balanced Metric Allocation (BMA)*. Both algorithms are based on the well-known "load balancing" principle for resource management. CLBA focuses only on balancing the energy spent by the CPU component of the sensor nodes, whereas BMA aims to balance the total energy consumption that is an aggregate of the energy used by both the CPU and radio component of the sensor nodes in the WSN. The superiority of the dynamic algorithm, BMA, over the static algorithm, CLBA, displayed in Fig. 17.4, is also observed for a broad range of other system and workload parameters. The paper demonstrates the effectiveness of using system and workload characteristics in sensor allocation, and concludes that dynamic algorithms that use knowledge of both the energy-associated CPU and radio components give rise to high performance.

17.5.2 REQUEST SCHEDULING

Multiple application requests may contend for the same sensor node, and the scheduling algorithm determines the order in which these requests are to be served. Researchers have investigated the scheduling problem in the context of shared WSNs hosting multiple applications. The work presented in [17] shows that a scheduling algorithm can have a significant impact on the average request turn-around times. Using knowledge of both system and network topology information in scheduling has been observed to lead to a higher performance [17]. A number of different scheduling algorithms that use varying degrees of knowledge of system and workload parameters is investigated. The *Least Weighted Farthest Number Distance Product First (LWFNDPF)* algorithm is observed to produce the best performance for most of the configurations experimented with. In a WSN, messages associated with the sensors that are located farther away from the cluster head (Fig. 17.3) experience greater delays in comparison to sensors that are located closer to the cluster head. LWFNDPF uses a metric called *Farthest Number Distance Product (FNDP)* that is the product of the number of sensors that are farthest away from the cluster head among all the sensors used by the application, and the distance of these sensors from the cluster head. The distances of sensors are measured in the number of hops that a message needs to go through when a request travels from the cluster head to the respective sensor node. The FNDP for each application is multiplied by a weight factor that is a tuning parameter. LWFNDPF associates a higher priority for application requests with small FNDP that are expected to experience lower delays in the WSN. A detailed discussion is provided in [17].

17.6 RESOURCE MANAGEMENT TECHNIQUES FOR SUPPORTING DATA ANALYTICS

On a smart facility, analyses of sensor data, as well as archived maintenance data, are both important for its effective management. Using batch-data-analytics techniques on archived data is to be performed, for example, to determine the next maintenance cycle, whereas real-time data analytics that concerns the processing of sensor data in real time may be important for performing real-time control of the facility or for handling emergencies. MapReduce is a well-known technique [33] that is used for performing data analytics on large volumes of data that are typical of smart facilities. The basic idea behind MapReduce is briefly explained.

The input data is divided into chunks, each of which is handled by a separate *map t*ask. Multiple map tasks, each handling a specific chunk of input data, are executed concurrently on a parallel system, such as a cluster and a cloud. The outputs of the different map tasks are then combined with the help of several reduce tasks that run concurrently on the system. Although the same MapReduce architecture is used, the application logic for the map and reduce tasks can vary from one facility to another. Effective allocation of processors to tasks and task scheduling are crucial for achieving high system-performance. Resource management techniques for task allocation and scheduling for MapReduce systems that process jobs on a best-effort basis are thoroughly studied. Associating a Service Level Agreement (SLA) that includes a deadline with MapReduce jobs has recently started receiving attention [20,21,34]. The ability to associate a deadline with a job is important for performing real-time data analytics, including the real-time processing of event logs collected on the facility. Resource management is known to be a computationally hard problem. Association of a deadline, and the availability of multiple resources in a cloud, used, for example, for the deployment of the MapReduce framework that is characterized by multiple phases of operation, further complicates the problem. Innovative algorithms for resource allocation, and scheduling for handling a batch of MapReduce jobs with deadlines are described in [35]. The authors propose two different approaches, based on optimization techniques for resource

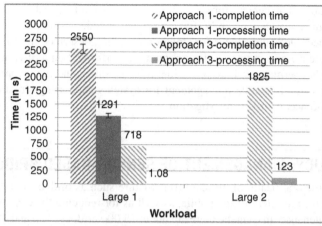

FIGURE 17.5 Performance of Different Resource Management Approaches for a System Running MapReduce Jobs (from Ref. [35])

management: Mixed Integer Linear Programming (MILP) and Constraint programming (CP). The MILP-based resource management algorithm is implemented using LINGO [36], whereas IBM ILOG CPLEX [37] is used in implementing the CP-based algorithm. The results of a simulation-based performance evaluation presented in [35] demonstrate the superiority of the CP-based technique (Fig. 17.5). The figure displays the results for two of the largest of the five workloads used in the research. Large 1 corresponds to a batch of 2 jobs, with each job having 100 map tasks and 30 reduce tasks, whereas Large 2 corresponds to a batch of 50 jobs, with each job having a number of map tasks ranging from 1 to 100, and a number of reduce tasks ranging from 1 to the number of map tasks in the respective job. Further details of the workload and system parameters are provided in [35]. The completion time for the batch, as well as the processing time for the resource management algorithm (system overhead incurred), are much lower for CP (Approach 3 in Fig. 17.5) in comparison to MILP (Approach 1 in Fig. 17.5). Note that among the two approaches, only the CP-based technique could handle the Large 2 workload. Following the success of the CP-based approach in the case of batch processing, the authors devised a CP-based technique for handling MapReduce jobs, with SLAs for clouds subjected to an open stream of arrivals of MapReduce jobs [29]. The high performance of their CP-based algorithm is reflected in the low number of jobs with missed deadlines, reported in a simulation-based investigation. Validation of the effectiveness of their algorithm on real Hadoop clusters has also been performed.

17.6.1 STREAMING DATA ANALYTICS

Batch, real-time, and streaming data-analytics are important in the context of analyzing data collected on smart facilities. As discussed earlier, batch analytics is performed on stored archival data, whereas real-time analytics is needed when an event (eg, a storm) occurs, requiring the analysis of the effect of the event on the smart facility in real time. MapReduce and MapReduce with deadlines can be used in these two situations respectively. Streaming data analytics is required when streams of sensor data need to be analyzed continuously for determining the health of the system, for example. Parallel-processing frameworks such as Storm [38] have been developed for performing streaming data-analytics. Resource management for achieving effective streaming data-analytics has started receiving attention from researchers recently. Existing work includes using parallel processing to provide Quality of Service (QoS) guarantees for stream processing, described in [39]. A reactive scaling strategy to enforce latency constraints on the computation performed on a Stream Processing Engine is presented in [40]. No permanent static provisioning is assumed, and the technique can effectively handle varying workloads. Resource management for systems supporting streaming analytics is an important problem and needs further investigation.

17.7 CASE STUDY: MANAGEMENT OF SENSOR-BASED BRIDGES

Monitoring of the structural health of critical infrastructure such as bridges and their maintenance is extremely important for the safety of the public, as well as for reducing the cost associated with their functioning and maintenance. In Canada, there are about 55,000 bridges [41], and 40% of these bridges are more than 40 years old. A 2009 report on US bridges states that a quarter of the bridges were structurally deficient or functionally obsolete [42]. Bridge maintenance is of great economic importance and concerns public safety. Billions of dollars are spent every year in Canada and the US on this critical service, as it is a key component of our transportation system and is directly tied to the safety of individuals. The existing practice in bridge engineering does not use an effective transfer of information and knowledge, nor does it encourage collaboration among the people involved: bridge engineers, researchers, and bridge owners. This fragmented approach, as well as a large number of manual steps in the maintenance process, contribute to the high cost associated with bridge maintenance.

A cloud middleware for effective management of sensor-based bridges that unifies data, computing, and storage resources, as well as data analysis tools, and automates several steps of the management process for mitigating the problems discussed in the previous paragraph, is proposed in [27]. The research was performed by Carleton University in collaboration with Cistel in Ottawa, Canada, and was supported by the Ontario Centers of Excellence. The system described in the paper focuses on the "network enabling" and management of various resources, such as sensor data repositories, computing and storage devices, databases containing historic data regarding the state and maintenance of the infrastructure, and software tools in such a way so as to allow these resources to be remotely accessed and shared through various user interfaces. The middleware thus serves as glue that unifies the geographically dispersed resources and makes them available on demand to the users of the system. It provides the connectivity and interoperability among diverse resources, and manages these resources in an effective manner. Although this work focuses on a middleware for integrating a heterogeneous set of geographically dispersed resources for improving the current practice in bridge management in a cost-effective manner, the proposed middleware is generic in nature and can be adapted to other infrastructure management problems with a modest effort. The middleware provides seamless access to multiple nodes, each of which typically runs at a specific site under the control of a Gateway Agent (GWA). Fig. 17.6 provides an implementation view of the middleware, and an indication of the respective technologies used in the system is described in [27]. The GWA provides access to the resources available at a specific site to an authenticated user who is allowed to perform the desired operation on the resource. Authentication and authorization of users are performed at a specific "master node." The security layer under the GWA is responsible for secure and authorized communication between the agent and other system components.

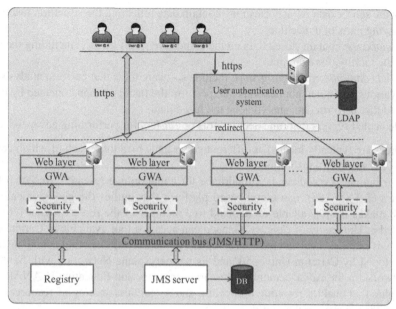

FIGURE 17.6 Middleware Architecture for Sensor-Based Bridge Management (based on Ref. [27])

Two key services are provided. A resource management service is responsible for mapping a user request to an appropriate resource that is apt for serving the request. Both on-demand (OD) and Advance Reservation (AR) requests are allowed [27]. An OD request is satisfied on a best-effort basis, whereas an AR includes an earliest start time, estimated execution time, and a deadline for request completion. In addition to resource allocation, this service is also responsible for scheduling the request on the selected resource and determining the start time for request execution. The resource registry service is used for keeping track of the resource characteristics and the method of accessing the resource. The registry is then used during the client request to resource mapping. Interoperability is provided by exposing a resource as a WS that can be accessed via an Application Programming Interface (API) associated with the resource. A detailed description of the middleware is provided in [27]. A Java Message Service (JMS) based messaging system supported by a JMS Server (Fig. 17.6) is proposed for the transfer of XML and SOAP messages. A previous version of the system had transferred requests over standard HTTP.

17.8 CASE STUDY: RESEARCH COLLABORATION PLATFORM FOR MANAGEMENT OF SMART MACHINERY

Research collaboration often involves researchers at multiple sites. Research on smart facilities management is no exception. Researchers in a collaborative team often have geographically dispersed resources that may include:

- *Sensor data repositories*: contain data generated by various sensors monitoring characteristics of smart facilities. For assessing the structural health of a sensor-based bridge, for example, such data may include vibration data as well as temperature data, whereas for smart industrial machinery the sensor data repositories may contain data reflecting the structural health of the various moving parts of a machine.

- *Archival databases*: contain stored data on the respective smart facility, including the maintenance history of the facility, for example.
- *Software tools and application programs*: include software tools that perform analysis of sensor data, and various additional applications that perform the fusion of data collected by multiple sensors, and that perform data analytics on the fused data.
- *Servers*: dedicated servers that run specific tools or clusters for performing advanced computing.

The resources are typically located at different geographic locations, each of which corresponds to the location of a researcher's institution.

Such a distribution of resources is a hindrance for collaborative research. Research Platform for Smart Facilities (RP-SMARF) is a cloud-based platform that unifies the geographically distributed resources, and makes them available on demand to a member of the research team [26]. Thus, a researcher located at University of Calgary, Canada can access a tool available at Carleton University, located thousands of miles away in Ottawa, regardless of the firewalls existing at both institutions. RP-SMARF, developed by Carleton University and its partner Solana Networks, with funding from the Canadian Network for the Advancement of Research, Industry and Education (CANARIE), provides the essential glue that enables resource unification and a seamless sharing of resources that may be scattered across the country, or the world.

The control of RP-SMARF is performed by a control server called the SMARF Control Server (SCS). Multiple resources located at different sites within an institution run behind a firewall provided by the institution. A SMARF Remote Agent (SRA) runs behind every firewall and is instrumental in the communication between SCS and the resource. The Internet Communication Engine (ICE) [43] allows a connection between SCS and an SRA running behind the respective firewall. Establishing an ICE connection between SCS and an SRA enables bidirectional communication between these two entities. The responses from a resource sent via SRA are directed to the client's browser by SCS. In a more recent release of RP-SMARF, ICE is being replaced by Websockets [44] to support the communication between SRA and SCS.

The important features of RP-SMARF include [26]:

- *Simplified usage of software tools*: RP-SMARF provides a Graphical User Interface (GUI) based process for setting up a tool that walks a user through the steps of configuring and running the respective tool on a data folder, available at any of the sites integrated by RP-SMARF. This allows a user to quickly run tools and avoid the lengthy period of time the user will otherwise need to learn to configure and use the tool.
- *Support for both batch and interactive modes*: A heterogeneous set of resources, including software tools, may be connected to RP-MARF. Some tools, including the Signal Processing Platform for Analysis of Structural Health (SPPLASH) [45], which is used for processing sensor data recorded on bridges, can operate in two modes. Multiple input data-files can be processed sequentially in the "batch" mode. In the "interactive" mode, a GUI provides interactive access to the tool, for example, for visualizing the behavior of the facility described by the dataset, specified as input for the tool. Fig. 17.7 provides an example of using SPPLASH in the interactive mode, for displaying vibrations on a bridge span that resulted from a storm, by processing the sensor data recorded during the storm. A GUI for the tool is displayed on the left, and the tool output is displayed on the right-hand side of the figure.

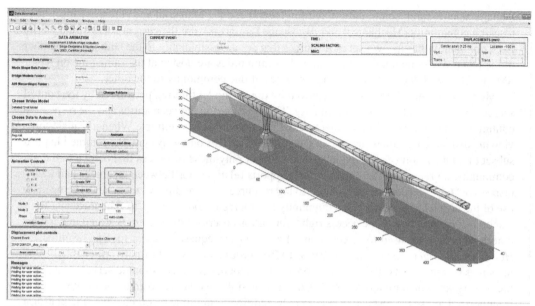

FIGURE 17.7 Screenshot of SPPLASH: Displaying Animation of Bridge Vibration Obtained from RP-SMARF (from Ref. [26])

Regardless of the tool/resource type, SRA and SCS perform the intercommunication between a tool and its user. In order to enable the two modes of tool operations described earlier, two different types of communication are supported between a client and a software tool: interactive and batch. Interactive tool invocation is supported with the help of a Virtual Network Computing (VNC) server, or the Windows Remote Desk Top Protocol (RDP) running on the remote machine hosting the tool. When a user needs to connect to the machine running the tool, the user's browser connects to a Guacamole server [46] on SCS that passes the commands for performing the desired operations on the tool to the respective SRA over the ICE link. Any request made by a second user to access the tool that is currently being used is declined.

A batch mode of tool invocation is similar to the interactive mode, except there is no Guacamole session and the user cannot directly have a remote session on the computer executing the batch commands. The input data, output folder, and the tool itself may be physically located in separate geographical locations. After the user selects the tool, the communication that occurs between the user's browser and SCS is based on REST. The tool is invoked by SRA that copies the input data to the machine running the tool, and the tool output is then copied to the output folder identified by the user. At the end of this operation, SCS informs the user that the batch invocation of the tool was successful. Similar to the interactive tools, the platform supports multiple batch tools, hence allowing heterogeneity.

- *Support for dynamic attaching and detaching of tools:* A tool owner can make a tool available temporarily to the collaborators if she or he wishes to. An "Attach" or "Detach" operation, invoked through a GUI, enables or disables the access of the tool from the platform.
- *Multitenancy*: RP-SMARF supports the coexistence of multiple research communities (collaboration teams) on the same platform. For example, two communities, the bridge-

management research community (Civil Engineers) and the industrial and aerospace machinery research community (Mechanical and Aerospace Engineers), are the current users of the platform. Each community has its own set of resources that are accessible only to the authorized members of the respective community. Although both communities are hosted at the same time on RP-SMARF, the GUI does not display the resources of one community to the other.

Multitenancy in RP-SMARF is achieved by object-model filtering performed by the control server. Every user belongs to a community. This relationship between a user and the respective community is represented in the object model through the user's settings. When a request for viewing available resources (eg, servers, data, tools) arrives on the system, the returned list is a subset of all the resources filtered in such a way that only those resources that belong to the user's community are returned. The object model supports relationships between resources and their respective "tag" objects, which are used to tag resources with additional metadata. The primary use of the tags is to specify which community a resource or tool belongs to. The metadata for a resource corresponding to the access rights for various users on the system is stored in another object. This object is used for access control when a user requests to use a specific resource.

- *Handling heterogeneous resources*: RP-SMARF unifies a diverse set of network-enabled resources that include virtual machines on a public cloud, dedicated compute servers, databases, file servers, and software tools; it makes them accessible on demand to an authenticated user who is authorized to use the respective resource. In addition to multiple resource types, the platform supports multiple interactive and batch tools that reflect its capability to handle heterogeneous resources.

  RPSMARF currently supports resources for systems running under both Linux and Windows Operating Systems (OSs). SRA requires the credentials for the machines, and logs in using SSH. Even though the OS used by the remote resources is transparent to the user, SRA must know the OS and issue suitable commands to invoke the tool requested by the user running the machine. RPSMARF uses REST for communicating between SCS and the web client. Whenever a user clicks on a button on the browser to perform any operation, the communication between SCS and the web client is enabled using REST.

- *Metadata searching:* Metadata describes the data (eg, sensor data) to be analyzed. With hundreds of data files containing sensor data collected periodically on a smart facility, an effective searching of the datasets requires using domain-specific fields to search data. For example, metadata such as wind speed and wind direction may be used to search for vibration data-files on a bridge. All of the files containing vibration data that match the specified metadata ranges provided by a researcher will be identified at the end of the search, thus avoiding a laborious manual search by the researcher through all of the files collected on the bridge. In RP-SMARF, users define metadata fields by using tools based on the Semantic Web Resource Description Framework (RDF) [47]. SPARQL queries [48] generated through a GUI are run for a set of target files identified by the researcher.

- *Elasticity:* RP-SMARF supports two types of tools: tools that can be virtualized and deployed on a cloud, and tools that run on specific servers provided by the tool owner. The first class of tools are said to be characterized by elasticity because a desired number of multiple instances can be run on the cloud.

- *Bulk data transfer:* Using the bulk data transfer service, an authorized user can transfer data from a source resource to a destination resource. RP-SMARF supports the transfer of one or multiple files from one site to another. Firewalls that may be used at both source and destination are effectively handled. This facility is used by the collaborators to exchange research data related to smart facilities. Automatic movement of files to/from a server running a tool is performed when the input and output data folders for the tool are located on different servers.

For performing a bulk data transfer, both the source and destination for the data are selected by the user. Once the service is invoked in the user's web browser, SCS receives the request via REST and forwards it to the source SRA, which has access to the source data. A command is then issued by the source SRA to transfer the data from the source data repository to SCS. SCS then contacts the destination SRA that transfers the data to the destination data-resource, and the bulk data transfer operation is completed.

• *Streaming data-transfer*: Continuous data produced by an industrial machine in a lab may need to be analyzed by a tool that is located on a different site. The streaming data-transfer service enables the transfer of data from a local or remote site to the server running the tool used for analyzing the data.

For conserving space, descriptions of other features that include tool/dataset discovery and resource reservation could not be included. The interested reader is referred to [26].

The key components of the RP-SMARF system are shown in Fig. 17.8, and a short description of these components is presented next. RP-SMARF uses an architecture based on an SCS. In addition

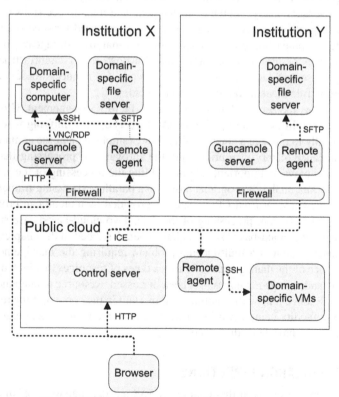

FIGURE 17.8 Key Elements of the RP-SMARF Architecture (from Ref. [26])

to executing the various services, it maintains a database of resource characteristics and their access rights. The control server (SCS) can be scaled horizontally, when required for improving availability and scalability. The control server stores all control information in an SQL database. A Python/Django framework is used to manage the objects in the database, whereas communication with objects in the Django framework is provided through REST APIs. The *client* providing a GUI through a browser is implemented in JavaScript using the AngularJS framework. The *remote agent* has a file system interface that facilitates user interaction with the system, and a job-running service used by the agent to start and stop jobs. The *Guacamole server* is a web server that facilitates interactive GUI-based access to resources through RDP for Windows-based systems, and via VNC for other systems. Further details of the system are provided in [26].

17.9 CONCLUSIONS

This section summarizes the key issues discussed and concludes the chapter. The low cost and ready availability of sensor technology is driving the incorporation of smarts in facility management. Examples of smart facilities include critical infrastructures such as sensor-based bridges and buildings, and industrial machinery, whose performance and health are monitored remotely. The basic operations that underlie the management of such smart facilities include: monitoring the state/health of the infrastructure with the help of sensors, analyzing the collected data, and making decisions on the management/maintenance of the respective facility. Various resources are required for such smart-facility management. These include compute resources for performing data analytics, storage resources for storing the sensor data, archival data for describing the maintenance history of a given infrastructure, and software tools for analyzing the sensor data. The underlying network that connects these various components also plays an important role in smart facilities management.

This chapter concerns the use of clouds in the smart-facility management. Clouds can aid in the management of smart facilities in multiple ways. A cloud is apt for unifying resources that may be dispersed geographically to manage a smart facility. For example, a database containing archived data capturing the maintenance history of a bridge and the software for processing that data may not be colocated, so the cloud plays an important role in enabling the processing of the archived data by the application software. Data-analytics programs based on a parallel-processing framework often require multiple CPUs for processing. Virtual CPU instances provided by a cloud can provide the necessary computing power for the efficient processing of the data. Two cloud-based case studies that demonstrate the effectiveness of a cloud-based solution have been described in the chapter.

Smart-facility management is a multifaceted problem requiring the management of multiple resources. The importance of the management of various types of resources that include sensor networks, as well as computing and storage resources, has been discussed. Resource management on parallel systems processing MapReduce jobs with deadlines is important in the context of the real-time processing of data collected on a facility being managed. Effective resource management algorithms that can be deployed on such systems have been discussed.

17.9.1 FUTURE RESEARCH DIRECTIONS

Most of the discussion presented in this chapter concerned the management of a single smart facility. Techniques that can handle multiple facilities warrant investigation. Such a smart-facility management system can amortize the cost of running and maintaining the management system over multiple facilities, and is likely to be attractive to an entity providing services for multiple smart buildings, or to a stakeholder owning multiple bridges, for example. Management of multiple industrial machines running in the same factory is also a good candidate for such a multifacility management system.

The capability of handling streaming data from sensors and performing streaming data-analytics on individual streams, as well as fusing data streams coming from multiple sensors, may be required in order to make decisions on the state/health of the respective facility. Incorporating such capabilities into the cloud-based smart-facility management system is important.

A number of state-of-the-art techniques for the management of WSNs, and cloud-based platforms for running data-analytics programs have been discussed. Advancing the state of the art in these areas will be highly fruitful in the management of smart facilities. Adaptation of the algorithms presented in [17] and [16] to WSNs with multiple heterogeneous clusters, comprising sensor nodes of different characteristics, is worthy of research. One of the components of the SLAs associated with MapReduce jobs is a set of estimates of task-execution times specified by the user. User estimates of task-execution times can be error prone. Enhancing the existing resource management algorithms for handling errors in user-estimated task-execution times is worthy of investigation.

ACKNOWLEDGMENTS

The author would like to thank Anshuman Biswas, Norman Lim, Navdeep Kapoor, and J. Orlando Melendez for their help in preparation of the manuscript.

REFERENCES

[1] Intel, <https://twitter.com/intelitcenter/status/601803967547465729/>; 2015.
[2] Lau DT, Liu J, Majumdar S, Nandy B, St-Hilaire M, Yang CS. A cloud-based approach for smart facilities management. In: Proceedings of the 2013 IEEE conference on prognostics and health management (PHM). Gaithersburg, USA, 2013.
[3] Colombo AW, Bangermann T, Kamouskos S, Delsing J, Stluka P, Harrison R, Jamees F, Martnez Lastra SL, editors. Industrial cloud-based cyber-physical systems, the IMC-AESOP approach. USA: Springer; 2014.
[4] Rajkumar R, Lee I, Sha L, Stankovic J. Cyber-physical systems: the next computing revolution. In: Proceedings of the ACM design automation conference. Anaheim, USA, 2010.
[5] Xianghan Z, Wenzhong G, Guolong e. Cloud-based monitoring framework for smart home. In: Proceedings of the 4th IEEE International conference on cloud computing technology and science (CloudCom). Taipei, Taiwan, 2012.
[6] Ye X, Huang J. A framework for cloud-based smart home. In: Proceedings of the 4th IEEE international conference on cloud computing technology and science (CloudCom). Athens, Greece, 2011.
[7] Arconox, smart facility management solution, <http://archonox.com/uncategorized/smartfacilitymanagementsolution/>; 2015.
[8] Manager plus, maintenance management software, <http://www.managerplus.com/?utm_medium=cpc&utm_source=google&cp1=DLeague&cp2=facilities_management&utm_term=facility%20management&match>.

[9] Tham CK, Buyya R. SensorGrid: integrating sensor networks and grid computing. CSI Commun 2005;29(1): 24–9.

[10] Alamri A, Shadab Ansari W, Mehedi Hassan M, Shamim Hossain M, Alelaiwi A, Anwar Hossain M. A survey on sensor-cloud: architecture, applications, and approaches. Intl J of Distrib Sensor Netw 2013;2013(6): 1–18.

[11] del Cid PJ, Michiels S, Joosen W, Hughes D. Middleware for resource sharing in multi-purpose wireless sensor networks. In: Proceedings of the IEEE international conference on networked embedded systems for enterprise applications (NESEA). Shuzou, China, 2010.

[12] Xu Y, Saifullah A, Chen Y, Lu C, Bhattacharya S. Near optimal multi-application allocation in shared sensor networks. In: Proceedings of the eleventh ACM international symposium on mobile ad hoc networking and computing (MobiHoc'10). Chicago, USA, 2010.

[13] Bhattacharya S, Saifullah A, Lu C, Roman GC. Multi-application deployment in shared sensor networks based on quality of monitoring. In: Proceedings of the 16th IEEE real-time and embedded technology and applications symposium (RTAS'10). Stockholm, Sweden, 2010.

[14] Lim HB, Lee D. An integrated and flexible scheduler for sensor grids. In: Proceedings of the 4th international conference on ubiquitous intelligence and computing. Hong Kong, China, 2007.

[15] Yang T, Zhang S. Dormancy scheduling algorithm based on node's self-adaptive density in WSN. In: Proceedings of the 2009 5th international joint conference on INC, IMS and IDC (NCM'09). Seoul, Korea, 2009.

[16] Kapoor NK, Majumdar S, Nandy B. Techniques for allocation of sensors in shared wireless sensor networks. J of Netw 2015;10(1):15–28.

[17] Kapoor NK, Majumdar S, Nandy B. System and application knowledge based scheduling of multiple applications in a WSN. In: Proceedings of the IEEE international conference on communications (ICC 2012)—Ad hoc, sensor and mesh networking symposium. Ottawa, Canada, 2012.

[18] Udupi Y, Dutta D. Business rules and policies driven constraints-based smart resource placement in Openstack. White Paper. Cisco.

[19] Apache software foundation, Hadoop, <http://hadoop.apache.org/>.

[20] Kc K, Anyanwu K. Scheduling Hadoop jobs to meet deadlines. In: Proceedings of the international conference on cloud computing technology and science (CloudCom). Indianapolis, USA, 2010.

[21] Dong X, Wang Y, Liao H. Scheduling mixed real-time and non-real-time applications in MapReduce environment. In: Proceedings of the international conference on parallel and distributed systems (ICPADS). Tainan, Taiwan, 2011.

[22] Verma A, Cherkasova L, Kumar VS, Campbell RH. Deadline-based workload management for MapReduce environments: pieces of the performance puzzle. In: Proceedings of the network operations and management symposium (NOMS). HI, USA, 2012.

[23] Madsen P. Authentication in the IoT—challenges and opportunities, SecureID news, <http://www.secureidnews.com/news-item/authentication-in-the-iot-challenges-and-opportunities/>.

[24] Liu J, Xiao Y, Chen CLP. Authentication and access control in the Internet of Things. In: Proceedings of the 32nd international conference on distributed computing systems workshops. Macao, China, 2012.

[25] Crossman MA, Liu H. Study of IoT with authentication testbed. In: Proceedings of the 2015 IEEE international symposium on homeland and security (HLS). Waltham, USA, 2015.

[26] McGregor A, Bennett D, Majumdar S, Nandy B, Melendez JO, St-Hilaire M, Lau DT, Liu J. A cloud-based platform for supporting research collaboration. In: Proceedings of the 8th IEEE international conference on cloud computing (CLOUD). New York, 2015.

[27] Majumdar S, Asif M, Melendez JO, Kanagasundaram R, Lau DT, Nandy B, Zaman M, Srivastava P, Goel N. Middleware architecture for sensor-based bridge infrastructure management. In: Proceedings of the 15th communications and networking symposium. Boston, USA, 2012.

[28] Buyya R, Yeo CS, Venugopal S, Broberg J, Brandic I. Cloud computing and emerging IT platforms: vision, hype, and reality for delivering computing as the 5th utility. Future Gener Comput Syst 2009;25(6):599–616.

[29] Lim N, Majumdar S, Ashwood-Smith P. Constraint programming-based resource management technique for processing MapReduce jobs with SLAs on clouds. In: Proceedings of the international conference on parallel processing (ICPP). Minneapolis, USA, 2014.

[30] Huang J-D, Hsieh HC. Design of gateway for monitoring system in IoT networks. In: Proceedings of the 2013 IEEE international conference on green computing and communications and IEEE Internet of Things and IEEE cyber, physical and social computing. Beijing, China, 2013.

[31] Jianguo X, Gang X, Mengmeng Y. Monitoring system design and implementation based on the Internet of Things. In: Proceedings of the 2013 fourth international conference on digital manufacturing and automation. Qingdao, China, 2013.

[32] Kanagasundaram R, Majumdar S, Zaman M, Srivastava P, Goel N. Exposing resources as Web services: a performance oriented approach. In: Proceedings of the 2012 international symposium on performance evaluation of computer and telecommunication systems (SPECTS'12). Genoa, Italy, 2012.

[33] Dean J, Ghemawat S. MapRedutd: simplified data processing on large clusters. In: Proceedings of the 6th symposium on operating system design and implementation. San Francisco, USA, 2004.

[34] Chang H, Kodialam M, Kompella RR, Lakshman TV, Lee M, Mukherjee S. Scheduling in MapReduce like systems for fast completion time. In: Proceedings of the IEEE, INFOCOM conference. Shanghai, China, 2011.

[35] Lim N, Majumdar S, Ashwood-Smith P. Engineering resource management middleware for optimizing the performance of clouds processing MapReduce jobs with deadlines. In: Proceedings of the 5th ACM/SPEC international conference on performance engineering (ICPE). Dublin, Ireland, 2014.

[36] LINDO systems inc, LINGO 13.0: user's guide, USA; 2011.

[37] IBM, IBM ILOG CPLEX optimization studio, <http://www-03.ibm.com/software/products/us/en/>; 2014.

[38] Apache software foundation, Apache Storm, <https://storm.apache.org/>; 2015.

[39] Lohrmann B, Warneke D, Kao O. Nephele streaming: stream processing under QoS constraints at scale. Cluster computing 2014;17(1):61–78.

[40] Lohrmann B, Janacik P, Kao O. Elastic stream processing with latency guarantees. In: Proceedings of the IEEE 35th international conference on distributed computing systems (ICDCS). Columbus, USA, 2015.

[41] Mirza S. Infrastructure durability and sustainability. In: Proceedings of the 2005 Canadian society of civil engineering annual conference. Toronto, Canada, 2005.

[42] American society for civil engineers. Engineers give U.S. infrastructure a "D", seek $2.2 trillion in stimulus: ASCE 2009 infrastructure report card. Popular Mechanics, New York, USA; 2009.

[43] Rosenberg J. Internet engineering task force (IETF) request for comments: 5245, <https://tools.ietf.org/html/rfc5245/>; 2015.

[44] Melnikov A, Fette I. Internet engineering task force (IETF), request for comments: 6455, <https://tools.ietf.org/html/rfc6455/>.

[45] Desjardins SL, Londono NA, Lau DT, Khoo H. Real-time data processing, analysis and visualization for structural monitoring of the confederation bridge. Adv in Structural Eng 2006;9(1):141–57.

[46] Jumper M. Guacamole manual, <http://guac-dev.org/doc/gug/guacamole-architecture.html/>.

[47] W3C, resource description framework, <http://www.w3.org/RDF/>; 2015.

[48] W3, SPARQL query language for RDF, <http://www.w3.org/TR/rdf-sparql-query/>.

Index

Printed in the United States
By Bookmasters